CONTENTS

Section

Key features in this edition

In addition to providing a wide ranging bank of real past exam questions, we have also included in this edition:

- An analysis of all of the recent new syllabus examination papers.

- Paper specific information.

- Our recommended approach to make your revision for this particular subject as effective as possible.

   This includes step by step guidance on how best to use our Kaplan material (Complete text, pocket notes and exam kit) at this stage in your studies.

- Enhanced tutorial answers packed with specific key answer tips, technical tutorial notes and exam technique tips from our experienced tutors.

- Complementary online resources including full tutor debriefs and question assistance to point you in the right direction when you get stuck.

June and December 2011, June and December 2012 – Real examination questions with enhanced tutorial answers

The real June 2011, December 2011, June 2012 and December 2012 exam questions with enhanced "walk through answers" and full "tutor debriefs", updated in line with legislation relevant to your exam sitting, is available on Kaplan EN-gage at:

www.EN-gage.co.uk

You will find a wealth of other resources to help you with your studies on the following sites:

www.EN-gage.co.uk

www.accaglobal.com/students/

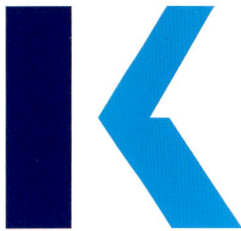

Kaplan Publishing are constantly finding new ways to make a difference to your studies and our exciting online resources really do offer something different to students looking for exam success.

This book comes with free EN-gage online resources so that you can study anytime, anywhere.

Having purchased this book, you have access to the following online study materials:

CONTENT	ACCA (including FFA,FAB,FMA)		AAT		FIA (excluding FFA,FAB,FMA)	
	Text	Kit	Text	Kit	Text	Kit
iPaper version of the book	✓	✓	✓	✓	✓	✓
Interactive electronic version of the book	✓					
Fixed tests / progress tests with instant answers	✓		✓			
Mock assessments online			✓	✓		
Material updates	✓	✓	✓	✓	✓	✓
Latest official ACCA exam questions		✓				
Extra question assistance using the signpost icon*		✓				
Timed questions with an online tutor debrief using the clock icon*		✓				
Interim assessment including questions and answers		✓			✓	
Technical articles	✓	✓			✓	✓

* Excludes F1, F2, F3, FFA, FAB, FMA

How to access your online resources

Kaplan Financial students will already have a Kaplan EN-gage account and these extra resources will be available to you online. You do not need to register again, as this process was completed when you enrolled. If you are having problems accessing online materials, please ask your course administrator.

If you are already a registered Kaplan EN-gage user go to www.EN-gage.co.uk and log in. Select the 'add a book' feature and enter the ISBN number of this book and the unique pass key at the bottom of this card. Then click 'finished' or 'add another book'. You may add as many books as you have purchased from this screen.

If you purchased through Kaplan Flexible Learning or via the Kaplan Publishing website you will automatically receive an e-mail invitation to Kaplan EN·gage online. Please register your details using this email to gain access to your content. If you do not receive the e-mail or book content, please contact Kaplan Flexible Learning.

If you are a new Kaplan EN-gage user register at www.EN-gage.co.uk and click on the link contained in the email we sent you to activate your account. Then select the 'add a book' feature, enter the ISBN number of this book and the unique pass key at the bottom of this card. Then click 'finished' or 'add another book'.

Your Code and Information

This code can only be used once for the registration of one book online. This registration and your online content will expire when the final sittings for the examinations covered by this book have taken place. Please allow one hour from the time you submit your book details for us to process your request.

Please scratch the film to access your EN-gage code.

Please be aware that this code is case-sensitive and you will need to include the dashes within the passcode, but not when entering the ISBN. For further technical support, please visit www.EN-gage.co.uk

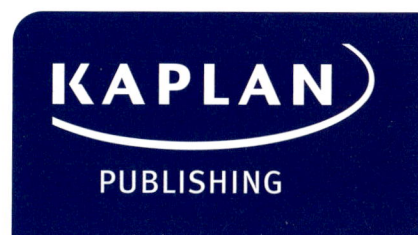

KAPLAN PUBLISHING

Paper F7 (INT & UK)

Financial Reporting

EXAM KIT

KAPLAN

PUBLISHING

British Library Cataloguing-in-Publication Data

A catalogue record for this book is available from the British Library.

Published by:

Kaplan Publishing UK

Unit 2 The Business Centre

Molly Millar's Lane

Wokingham

Berkshire

RG41 2QZ

ISBN: 978 0 85732 681 2

© Kaplan Financial Limited, 2013

Printed and bound in Great Britain

Acknowledgements

The past ACCA examination questions are the copyright of the Association of Chartered Certified Accountants. The original answers to the questions from June 1994 onwards were produced by the examiners themselves and have been adapted by Kaplan Publishing.

We are grateful to the Chartered Institute of Management Accountants and the Institute of Chartered Accountants in England and Wales for permission to reproduce past examination questions. The answers have been prepared by Kaplan Publishing.

INDEX TO QUESTIONS AND ANSWERS

INTRODUCTION

Following the update to the *Conceptual Framework for Financial Reporting*, IAS *1 Presentation of Financial Statements*, IFRS 3 *Business Combinations* and IFRS 9 *Financial Instruments* and the introduction of IFRS 10 *Consolidated Financial Statements* and IFRS 13 *Fair Value Measurement* some changes have had to be made to questions and answers in light of the recent amendments. The syllabus has also been updated for the June 2012 sitting.

Accordingly, many of the old ACCA questions within this kit have been adapted to reflect updated standards. If changed in any way from the original version, this is indicated in the end column of the index below with the mark *(A)*.

One of the fundamental alterations from 2011 is the adoption of International Financial Reporting Standards as the principal standards for the UK stream. To reflect this the UK and INT versions of the kit have been merged. Where relevant questions and answers have been appended to reflect where there is variance between the UK and INT versions, this is indicated in the end column of the index below with the mark *(UK)*.

Note that the majority of the questions within the kit are past ACCA exam questions, the more recent questions are labelled as such in the index.

The pilot paper is included at the end of the kit.

KEY TO THE INDEX

PAPER ENHANCEMENTS

We have added the following enhancements to the answers in this exam kit:

> **Key answer tips**

All answers include key answer tips to help your understanding of each question.

> **Tutorial note**

All answers include more tutorial notes to explain some of the technical points in more detail.

> **Top tutor tips**

For selected questions, we "walk through the answer" giving guidance on how to approach the questions with helpful 'tips from a top tutor', together with technical tutor notes.

These answers are indicated with the "footsteps" icon in the index.

ONLINE ENHANCEMENTS

> 🕐 *Timed question with Online tutor debrief*

For selected questions, we recommend that they are to be completed in full exam conditions (i.e. properly timed in a closed book environment).

In addition to the examiner's technical answer, enhanced with key answer tips and tutorial notes in this exam kit, online you can find an answer debrief by a top tutor that:

- works through the question in full

- points out how to approach the question

- how to ensure that the easy marks are obtained as quickly as possible, and

- emphasises how to tackle exam questions and exam technique.

These questions are indicated with the "clock" icon in the index.

> 🏁 *Online question assistance*

Have you ever looked at a question and not know where to start, or got stuck part way through?

For selected questions, we have produced "Online question assistance" offering different levels of guidance, such as:

- ensuring that you understand the question requirements fully, highlighting key terms and the meaning of the verbs used

- how to read the question proactively, with knowledge of the requirements, to identify the topic areas covered

- assessing the detail content of the question body, pointing out key information and explaining why it is important

- help in devising a plan of attack

With this assistance, you should then be able to attempt your answer confident that you know what is expected of you.

These questions are indicated with the "signpost" icon in the index.

Online question enhancements and answer debriefs will be available from Spring 2010 on Kaplan EN-gage at:

www.EN-gage.co.uk

BUSINESS COMBINATIONS

ANALYSIS OF PAST EXAM PAPERS

The table below summarises the key topics that have been tested in the new syllabus examinations to date.

Note that the references are to the number of the question in this edition of the exam kit, but the Pilot Paper is produced in its original form at the end of the kit and therefore these questions have retained their original numbering in the paper itself.

	Pilot 07	Dec 07	Jun 08	Dec 08	Jun 09	Dec 09	Jun 10	Dec 10	Jun 11	Dec 11	Jun 12
Group financial statements											
Consolidated statement of profit or loss and other comprehensive income			✓			✓			✓		
Consolidated statement of financial position	✓	✓			✓		✓			✓	✓
Consolidated I/S and SFP				✓				✓			
Associates	✓	✓	✓		✓	✓	✓			✓	✓
Non-group financial statements											
From trial balance	✓	✓		✓	✓	✓	✓	✓	✓	✓	✓
Redraft			✓								
Statement of changes in equity	✓		✓	✓				✓	✓		✓
Performance appraisal											
Ratios	✓	✓		✓				✓			
Statement of cash flows			✓							✓	
Ratios and statement of cash flows					✓	✓	✓		✓		✓
Mixed transactional											
IASB Framework	✓	✓		✓		✓			✓		✓
Accounting principles / substance		✓	✓				✓				
IAS 2			✓								
IAS 8		✓						✓			
IAS 10					✓						
IAS 11	✓								✓		
IAS 12											
IAS 16				✓	✓	✓					
IAS 17		✓									
IAS 18											
IAS 20											
IAS 23							✓				
IAS 32/IAS 39/IFRS 7/IFRS 9			✓							✓	
IAS 33						✓			✓		
IAS 36											✓
IAS 37				✓						✓	
IAS 38		✓				✓					
IAS 40											
IFRS 5								✓			
IFRS 13											

EXAM TECHNIQUE

- Use the allocated **15 minutes reading and planning time** at the beginning of the exam:
  - read the questions and examination requirements carefully, and
  - begin planning your answers.

  See the Paper Specific Information for advice on how to use this time for this paper.

- **Divide the time** you spend on questions in proportion to the marks on offer:
  - there are 1.8 minutes available per mark in the examination
  - within that, try to allow time at the end of each question to review your answer and address any obvious issues

  Whatever happens, always keep your eye on the clock and **do not over run on any part of any question!**

- Spend the last **five minutes** of the examination:
  - reading through your answers, and
  - **making any additions or corrections**.

- If you **get completely stuck** with a question:
  - leave space in your answer book, and
  - **return to it later.**

- Stick to the question and **tailor your answer** to what you are asked.
  - pay particular attention to the verbs in the question.

- If you do not understand what a question is asking, **state your assumptions**.

  Even if you do not answer in precisely the way the examiner hoped, you should be given some credit, if your assumptions are reasonable.

- You should do everything you can to make things easy for the marker.

  The marker will find it easier to identify the points you have made if your **answers are legible**.

- **Written questions**:

  Your answer should have:
  - a clear structure
  - a brief introduction, a main section and a conclusion.

  Be concise.

  It is better to write a little about a lot of different points than a great deal about one or two points.

- **Computations**:

  It is essential to include all your workings in your answers.

  Many computational questions require the use of a standard format:

  e.g. statement of profit or loss and other comprehensive income, statement of financial position and statement of cash flow.

  Be sure you know these formats thoroughly before the exam and use the layouts that you see in the answers given in this book and in model answers.

PAPER SPECIFIC INFORMATION

THE EXAM

FORMAT OF THE EXAM

Number of marks

5 compulsory questions which will be **predominantly computational**:

Question 1:	Group financial statements	25
Question 2:	Non-group financial statements	25
Question 3:	Performance appraisal	25
Question 4:	Any area of the syllabus	15
Question 5:	Any area of the syllabus	10
		100

Total time allowed: 3 hours plus 15 minutes reading and planning time.

Note that:

- Question 1 will focus on the preparation of group accounts which could include up to a five mark written element. Question 1 will always include a subsidiary company and sometimes an associate as well. You will either be required to prepare a consolidated statement of financial position a consolidated statement of profit or loss and other comprehensive income or both

- Question 2 will always require the preparation of non-group financial statements either from a trial balance or a re-draft of financial statements Knowledge for this question is required from many areas of the syllabus but common topics are depreciation, revaluations of fixed assets, substance over form and revenue recognition

- Question 3 will require the preparation of a statement of cash flow, accounting ratios or both. This question generally requires some performance appraisal and you will be assessed on your ability to interpret the underlying information from the financial statements and ratios that you have prepared.

- Questions 4 and 5 will cover the reminder of the syllabus. It is important that you are familiar with the conceptual and regulatory framework, accounting concepts and the accounting standards outline in the list of examinable documents available on the ACCA website.

PASS MARK

The pass mark for all ACCA Qualification examination papers is 50%.

READING AND PLANNING TIME

Remember that all three hour paper based examinations have an additional 15 minutes reading and planning time.

ACCA GUIDANCE

ACCA guidance on the use of this time is as follows:

This additional time is allowed at the beginning of the examination to allow candidates to read the questions and to begin planning their answers before they start to write in their answer books.

This time should be used to ensure that all the information and, in particular, the exam requirements are properly read and understood.

During this time, candidates may only annotate their question paper. They may not write anything in their answer booklets until told to do so by the invigilator.

KAPLAN GUIDANCE

As all questions are compulsory, there are no decisions to be made about choice of questions, other than in which order you would like to tackle them.

Therefore, in relation to F7, we recommend that you take the following approach with your reading and planning time:

- **Skim through the whole paper**, assessing the level of difficulty of each question.

- **Write down** on the question paper next to the mark allocation **the amount of time you should spend on each part.** Do this for each part of every question.

- **Decide the order** in which you think you will attempt each question:

    This is a personal choice and you have time on the revision phase to try out different approaches, for example, if you sit mock exams.

    A common approach is to tackle the question you think is the easiest and you are most comfortable with first.

    Others may prefer to tackle the longest questions first, or conversely leave them to the last.

    Psychologists believe that you usually perform at your best on the second and third question you attempt, once you have settled into the exam.

    It is usual however that student tackle their least favourite topic and/or the most difficult question in their opinion last.

    Whatever your approach, you must make sure that you leave enough time to attempt all questions fully and be very strict with yourself in timing each question.

- **For each question** in turn, read the requirements and then the detail of the question carefully.

  Always read the requirement first as this enables you to **focus on the detail of the question with the specific task in mind**.

  For computational questions:

  Highlight key numbers / information and key words in the question, scribble notes to yourself on the question paper to remember key points in your answer.

  Jot down proformas required if applicable.

  For written questions:

  Take notice of the format required (e.g. letter, memo, notes) and identify the recipient of the answer . You need to do this to judge the level of financial sophistication required in your answer and whether the use of a formal reply or informal bullet points would be satisfactory.

  Plan your beginning, middle and end and the key areas to be addressed and your use of titles and sub-titles to enhance your answer.

  For all questions:

  Spot the easy marks to be gained in a question and parts which can be performed independently of the rest of the question. For example laying out basic proformas correctly, answer written elements not related to the scenario etc.

  Make sure that you do these parts first when you tackle the question.

  Don't go overboard in terms of planning time on any one question – you need a good measure of the whole paper and a plan for all of the questions at the end of the 15 minutes.

  By covering all questions you can often help yourself as you may find that facts in one question may remind you of things you should put into your answer relating to a different question.

- With your plan of attack in mind, **start answering your chosen question** with your plan to hand, as soon as you are allowed to start.

🕐 **Always keep your eye on the clock and do not over run on any part of any question!**

DETAILED SYLLABUS

The detailed syllabus and study guide written by the ACCA can be found at:

www.accaglobal.com/students/

KAPLAN'S RECOMMENDED REVISION APPROACH

QUESTION PRACTICE IS THE KEY TO SUCCESS

Success in professional examinations relies upon you acquiring a firm grasp of the required knowledge at the tuition phase. In order to be able to do the questions, knowledge is essential.

However, the difference between success and failure often hinges on your exam technique on the day and making the most of the revision phase of your studies.

The **Kaplan complete text** is the starting point, designed to provide the underpinning knowledge to tackle all questions. However, in the revision phase, pouring over text books is not the answer.

Kaplan Online fixed tests help you consolidate your knowledge and understanding and are a useful tool to check whether you can remember key topic areas.

Kaplan pocket notes are designed to help you quickly revise a topic area, however you then need to practice questions. There is a need to progress to full exam standard questions as soon as possible, and to tie your exam technique and technical knowledge together.

The importance of question practice cannot be over-emphasised.

The recommended approach below is designed by expert tutors in the field, in conjunction with their knowledge of the examiner and their recent real exams.

The approach taken for the fundamental papers is to revise by topic area. However, with the professional stage papers, a multi topic approach is required to answer the scenario based questions.

You need to practice as many questions as possible in the time you have left.

OUR AIM

Our aim is to get you to the stage where you can attempt exam standard questions confidently, to time, in a closed book environment, with no supplementary help (i.e. to simulate the real examination experience).

Practising your exam technique on real past examination questions, in timed conditions, is also vitally important for you to assess your progress and identify areas of weakness that may need more attention in the final run up to the examination.

In order to achieve this we recognise that initially you may feel the need to practice some questions with open book help and exceed the required time.

The approach below shows you which questions you should use to build up to coping with exam standard question practice, and references to the sources of information available should you need to revisit a topic area in more detail.

Remember that in the real examination, all you have to do is:

- attempt all questions required by the exam

- only spend the allotted time on each question, and

- get them at least 50% right!

Try and practice this approach on every question you attempt from now to the real exam.

EXAMINER COMMENTS

We have included some of the examiners comments to the specific new syllabus examination questions in this kit for you to see the main pitfalls that students fall into with regard to technical content.

However, too many times in the general section of the report, the examiner comments that students had failed due to:

- "misallocation of time"

- "running out of time" and

- showing signs of "spending too much time on an earlier question and clearly rushing the answer to a subsequent question".

Good exam technique is vital.

THE KAPLAN PAPER F7 REVISION PLAN

Stage 1: Assess areas of strengths and weaknesses

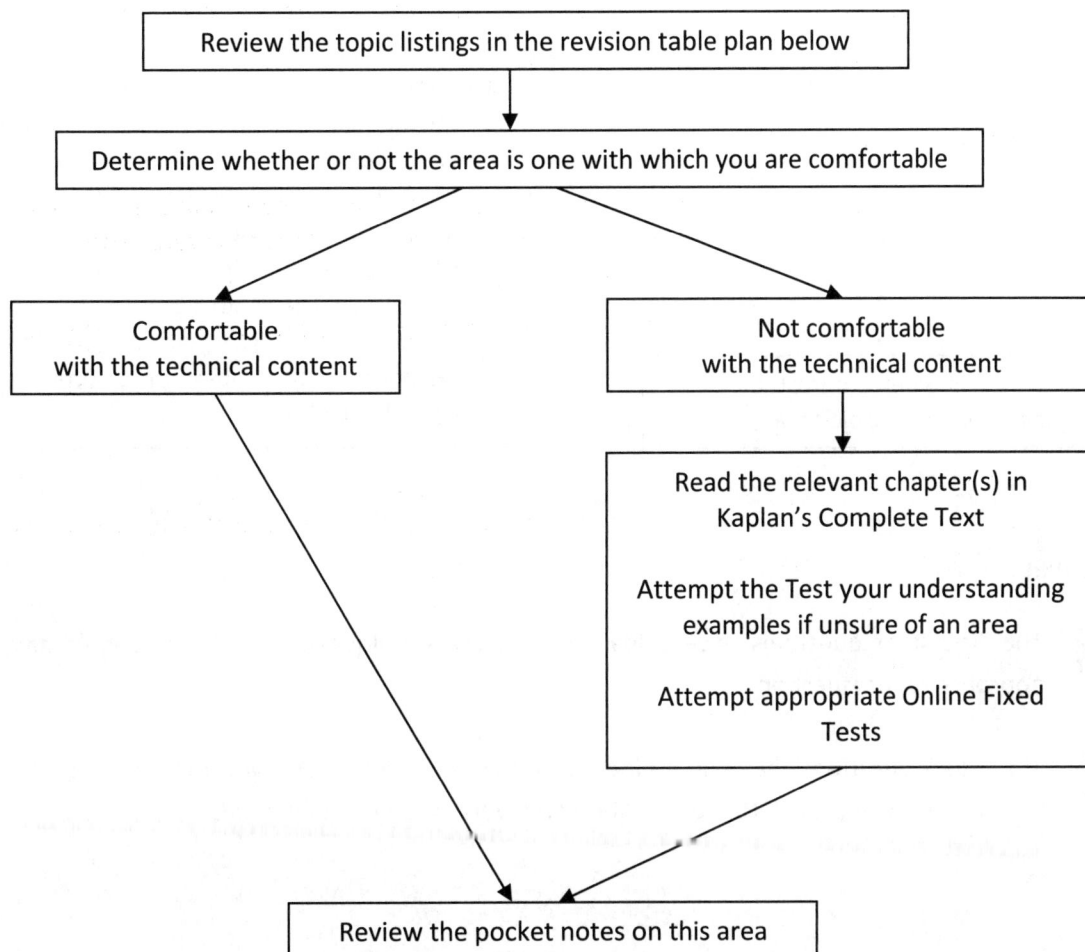

```
┌─────────────────────────────────────────────────────────┐
│  Review the topic listings in the revision table plan below │
└─────────────────────────────────────────────────────────┘
                            │
                            ▼
┌─────────────────────────────────────────────────────────┐
│ Determine whether or not the area is one with which you are comfortable │
└─────────────────────────────────────────────────────────┘
```

┌────────────────────────┐   ┌────────────────────────┐
│   Comfortable   │   │   Not comfortable   │
│ with the technical content │   │ with the technical content │
└────────────────────────┘   └────────────────────────┘
                                                │
                                                ▼
                          ┌─────────────────────────────────────┐
                          │ Read the relevant chapter(s) in   │
                          │ Kaplan's Complete Text   │
                          │   │
                          │ Attempt the Test your understanding │
                          │ examples if unsure of an area   │
                          │   │
                          │ Attempt appropriate Online Fixed   │
                          │ Tests   │
                          └─────────────────────────────────────┘

┌───┐
│   Review the pocket notes on this area   │
└───┘

Stage 2: Practice questions

Follow the order of revision of topics as recommended in the revision table plan below and attempt the questions in the order suggested.

Try to avoid referring to text books and notes and the model answer until you have completed your attempt.

Try to answer the question in the allotted time.

Review your attempt with the model answer and assess how much of the answer you achieved in the allocated exam time.

Fill in the self-assessment box below and decide on your best course of action.

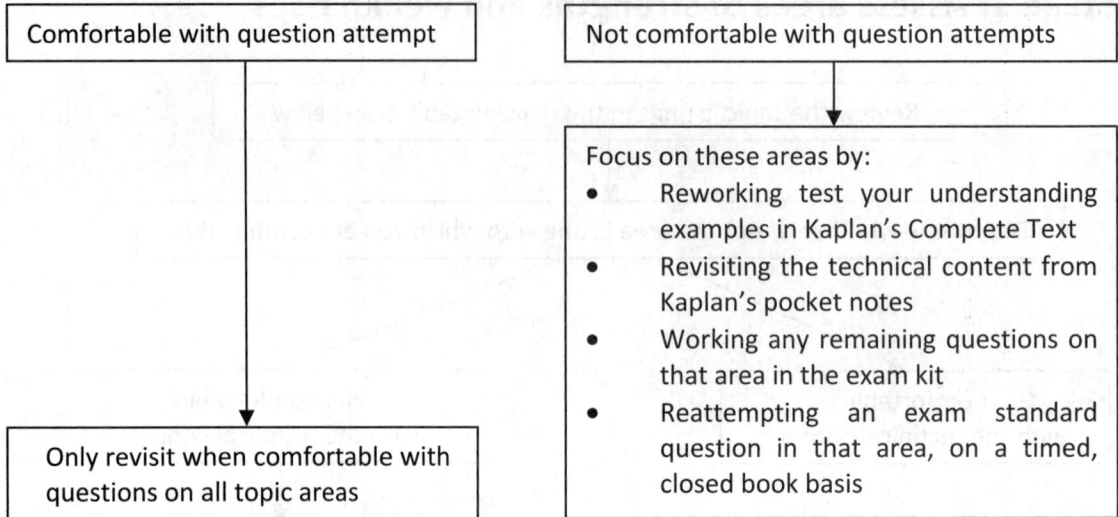

Comfortable with question attempt	Not comfortable with question attempts

Focus on these areas by:
- Reworking test your understanding examples in Kaplan's Complete Text
- Revisiting the technical content from Kaplan's pocket notes
- Working any remaining questions on that area in the exam kit
- Reattempting an exam standard question in that area, on a timed, closed book basis

Only revisit when comfortable with questions on all topic areas

Note that :

The "footsteps questions" give guidance on exam techniques and how you should have approached the question.

The "clock questions" have an online debrief where a tutor talks you through the exam technique and approach to that question and works the question in full.

Stage 3: Final pre-exam revision

We recommend that you **attempt at least one three hour mock examination** containing a set of previously unseen exam standard questions.

It is important that you get a feel for the breadth of coverage of a real exam without advanced knowledge of the topic areas covered – just as you will expect to see on the real exam day.

Ideally this mock should be sat in timed, closed book, real exam conditions and could be:

- a mock examination offered by your tuition provider, and/or
- the pilot paper in the back of this exam kit, and/or
- the last real examination paper (available shortly afterwards on Kaplan EN-gage with "enhanced walk through answers" and a full "tutor debrief").

KAPLAN'S DETAILED REVISION PLAN

Topic	Complete Text Chapter	Pocket note Chapter	Questions to attempt	Tutor guidance	Date attempted	Self assessment
Consolidated statement of financial position	2 / 4	2 / 4	49 50 55	Practice the Kaplan 5 working approach. Ensure you get the easy marks available in the question from adding the parent and subsidiary assets and liabilities together.		
Consolidated statement of profit or loss and other comprehensive income	3 / 4	3 / 4	51 54	Watch the dates carefully – is there a mid-year acquisition? If so you have to time apportion the subsidiary company results when adding the parent and subsidiary together.		
Consolidated statement of profit or loss and other comprehensive income and statement of financial position			46 52	Set up your proformas first and get the easy marks by adding the parent and subsidiary results together – then complete the 5 standard statement of financial position workings before moving on to complete the statement of profit or loss and other comprehensive income.		

Topic	Complete Text Chapter	Pocket note Chapter	Questions to attempt	Tutor guidance	Date attempted	Self assessment
Accounting standards:						
IAS 16	8	8	14 / 26	Be clear on initial recognition rules, subsequent measurement and component depreciation.		
IAS 23	8	8	31	Ensure you know the definition of borrowing costs at the 3 recognition and 2 derecognition criteria.		
IAS 36	10	10	15 / 18 (part b)	Learn the impairment test proforma and the cash generating unit write down rules.		
IAS 17	12	12	8 / 17 (part b)	Be sure you can identify the differences between an operating and a finance lease.		
IAS 37	16	16	1 (part c (i)) / 25	For IAS 37 the recognition rules are very clear – learn the 3 recognition rules.		
IAS 10	16	16	21 (part b) / 27	Learn the differences between adjusting and non-adjusting events.		
IAS 2 / IAS 11	14	14	16 / 18 (part d)	The measurement of inventory is key and plenty of practice on construction contracts is recommended.		

Topic	Complete Text Chapter	Pocket note Chapter	Questions to attempt	Tutor guidance	Date attempted	Self assessment
IAS 32/39/IFRS 7/IFRS 9	15	15	1 (part c (iii)) 18 (part a) 20	Amortised cost is the core area of financial liabilities here. Make sure you can deal with loans issued at a discount & redeemed at a premium. You will also need an awareness of the categories of financial asset in accordance with IFRS 9 and the accounting treatment for them.		
IAS 18	13	13	3	Learn the rules associated with revenue recognition for the sale of goods and provision of services and the specific exam scenario treatment such as sale and repurchase agreements and agency sales.		
IAS 8	7	7	6	Learn the recognition criteria for the 3 areas.		
IAS 12	17	17	17 (part a)	Learn the definition of a temporary difference and practice its application.		
IAS 33	18	18	43 30	Learn the formula and apply to share issues.		
Substance over form	13	13	2 9	This subject regularly features at qn 2 and sometimes as a qn 4 or 5 in its own right. Learn the definition and the 4 specific areas.		

Topic	Complete Text Chapter	Pocket note Chapter	Questions to attempt	Tutor guidance	Date attempted	Self assessment
Non-group financial statements	6	6	32 33 37 38	You have to learn the accounting standards examinable first and then apply your knowledge to these recommended questions.		
Cash flow statements	20	20	63 64 69 70	A popular exam topic on a primary accounting statement. Learn the proforma. Start with question 63 and 64 which are basic warm up questions. Questions 69/70 require the preparation of cash flow and some ratio analysis which is a common style at question 3 in the exam.		
Ratio interpretation	19	19	56 65	Learn the ratio calculations and practice identifying where you pull the information for the formula out of the financial statements.		

Note that not all of the questions are referred to in the programme above. We have recommended an approach to build up from the basic to exam standard questions.

The remaining questions are available in the kit for extra practice for those who require more questions on some areas.

Technical update

IFRS 9 FINANCIAL INSTRUMENTS

IFRS 9 was issued in November 2010 is an examinable document for 2013-14 examinations.

Initially, IFRS 9 dealt only with financial assets The intention is that IFRS 9 will be updated and extended to deal with all recognition and measurement issues, and that IAS 39 will be replaced. As IFRS 9 is extended, the equivalent provisions from IAS 39 will cease to be effective. In this regard, on 28 October 2010, the IASB extended the provision of IFRS 9 to now include financial liabilities.

Classification of financial assets:

The four previous classifications of financial assets have been withdrawn. IFRS 9 now has only three classifications of financial assets, with increased emphasis upon fair value measurement, as follows:

1   Financial assets at fair value through profit or loss

This is the normal presumption of how financial assets should be accounted for, unless they are designated upon initial recognition to be one of the other two possible classifications. It would appear that there is likely to be increased emphasis upon fair value accounting as a result of this change in emphasis.

As under IAS 39 previously, this will include any financial assets held for trading purposes and the accounting treatment effectively incorporates an annual impairment review.

2   Financial assets at fair value through other comprehensive income (FVTOCI)

Financial assets can be designated to be measured at FVTOCI and it can apply only to equity instruments. Any increases or decreases in fair value upon remeasurement, including impairment losses, are taken to equity. There is no recycling of amounts previously taken to equity upon disposal. Any impairment losses remain within equity and are not recycled to profit or loss for the year.

3   Financial assets at amortised cost

Financial assets can be designated to be measured at amortised cost upon initial recognition. For this to happen, two tests must be passed:

- The business model test – what is the underlying business purpose for having the financial asset? Is it to take advantage of movements in fair value, or to collect in the cash flows associated with the asset? In the former case, the test is fail, whereas in the latter case, the test is passed.

- The contractual cash flows characteristics test – do the cash flows associated with the financial asset consist *solely* of repayments of interest and capital? If the answer is yes, the test is passed; if no, the test is failed.

Where either or both tests are failed, the financial asset must be measured at fair value through profit or loss. This would apply to the holder of convertible debt, as the cashflows are affected by the fact that, upon maturity date, there is a choice to be made between taking cash or converting the convertible debt into equity shares.

Note that, even when both tests have been passed, the financial asset can still be measured at fair value through profit or loss, rather than having it designated to be measured at amortised cost.

This reporting standard is effective for accounting periods commencing on or after 1 January 2015.

IAS 1 PRESENTATION OF FINANCIAL STATEMENTS (AMENDED)

IAS 1 was amended in June 2011. As a result of the amendment the term income statement is to be replaced with statement of profit or loss and the term statement of comprehensive income is to be replaced with statement of profit or loss and other comprehensive income. The exam kit has been updated to reflect these name changes.

Section 1

PRACTICE QUESTIONS

A CONCEPTUAL FRAMEWORK FOR FINANCIAL REPORTING

1   IASB FRAMEWORK   *Walk in the footsteps of a top tutor*

(a)   The IASB's *Conceptual Framework for Financial Reporting* sets out the concepts that underlie the preparation and presentation of financial statements that external users are likely to rely on when making economic decisions about an enterprise.

Required:

Explain the purpose and authoritative status of the Framework.   **(5 marks)**

(b)   Of particular importance within the Framework are the definitions and recognition criteria for assets and liabilities.

Required:

Define assets and liabilities and explain the important aspects of their definitions. Explain why these definitions are of particular importance to the preparation of an entity's statement of financial position and statement of profit or loss.

(8 marks)

(c)   Peterlee is preparing its financial statements for the year ended 31 March 20X6. The following items have been brought to your attention:

(i)   Peterlee acquired the entire share capital of Trantor during the year. The acquisition was achieved through a share exchange. The terms of the exchange were based on the relative values of the two companies obtained by capitalising the companies' estimated future cash flows. When the fair value of Trantor's identifiable net assets was deducted from the value of the company as a whole, its goodwill was calculated at $2.5 million. A similar exercise valued the goodwill of Peterlee at $4 million. The directors wish to incorporate both the goodwill values in the companies' consolidated financial statements.   **(4 marks)**

(ii)   During the year Peterlee acquired an iron ore mine at a cost of $6 million. In addition, when all the ore has been extracted (estimated in 10 years time) the company will face estimated costs for landscaping the area affected by the mining that have a present value of $2 million. These costs would still have to be incurred even if no further ore was extracted. The directors have proposed that an accrual of $200,000 per year for the next ten years should be made for the landscaping.   **(4 marks)**

(iii)   On 1 April 20X5 Peterlee issued an 8% $5 million convertible loan at par. The loan is convertible in three years time to ordinary shares or redeemable at par in cash. The directors decided to issue a convertible loan because a non-convertible loan would have required an interest rate of 10%. The directors intend to show the loan at $5 million under non-current liabilities. The following discount rates are available:

	8%	10%
Year 1	0.93	0.91
Year 2	0.86	0.83
Year 3	0.79	0.75

(4 marks)

Required:

Describe (and quantify where possible) how Peterlee should treat the items in (i) to (iii) in its financial statements for the year ended 31 March 20X6 commenting on the directors' views where appropriate. (The mark allocation is shown against each of the three items above.)

(Total: 25 marks)

2   ANGELINO

(a)   Recording the substance of transactions, rather than their legal form, is an important principle in financial accounting. Abuse of this principle can lead to profit manipulation, non-recognition of assets and substantial debt not being recorded on the statement of financial position.

Required:

Describe how the use of off balance sheet financing (off statement of financial position) can mislead users of financial statements.

Note: **Your answer should refer to specific user groups and include examples where recording the legal form of transactions may mislead them.**   **(9 marks)**

(b)   Angelino has entered into the following transactions during the year ended 30 September 20X6:

(i)   In September 20X6 Angelino sold (factored) some of its trade receivables to Omar, a finance house. On selected account balances Omar paid Angelino 80% of their book value. The agreement was that Omar would administer the collection of the amounts receivable and remit a residual amount to Angelino depending upon how quickly individual customers paid. Any balance uncollected by Omar after six months will be refunded to Omar by Angelino.
(5 marks)

(ii)   On 1 October 20X5 Angelino owned a freehold building that had a carrying amount of $7.5 million and had an estimated remaining life of 20 years. On this date it sold the building to Finaid for a price of $12 million and entered into an agreement with Finaid to rent back the building for an annual rental of $1.3 million for a period of five years. The auditors of Angelino have commented that in their opinion the building had a market value of only $10 million at the date of its sale and to rent an equivalent building under similar terms to the agreement between Angelino and Finaid would only cost $800,000 per annum. Assume any finance costs are 10% per annum. **(6 marks)**

(iii)   Angelino is a motor car dealer selling vehicles to the public. Most of its new vehicles are supplied on consignment by two manufacturers, Monza and Capri, who trade on different terms.

Monza supplies cars on terms that allow Angelino to display the vehicles for a period of three months from the date of delivery or when Angelino sells the cars on to a retail customer if this is less than three months. Within this period Angelino can return the cars to Monza or can be asked by Monza to transfer the cars to another dealership (both at no cost to Angelino). Angelino pays the manufacturer's list price at the end of the three month period (or at the date of sale if sooner). In recent years Angelino has returned several cars to Monza that were not selling very well and has also been required to transfer cars to other dealerships at Monza's request.

Capri's terms of supply are that Angelino pays 10% of the manufacturer's price at the date of delivery and 1% of the outstanding balance per month as a display charge. After six months (or sooner if Angelino chooses), Angelino must pay the balance of the purchase price or return the cars to Capri. If the cars are returned to the manufacturer, Angelino has to pay for the transportation costs and forfeits the 10% deposit. Because of this Angelino has only returned vehicles to Capri once in the last three years.   **(5 marks)**

Required:

Describe how the above transactions and events should be treated in the financial statements of Angelino for the year ended 30 September 20X6. Your answer should explain, where relevant, the difference between the legal form of the transactions and their substance.

Note: **The mark allocation is shown against each of the three transactions above.**

(Total: 25 marks)

3   REVENUE RECOGNITION

Revenue recognition is the process by which companies decide when and how much income should be recognized in profit or loss. It is a topical area of great debate in the accounting profession. The IASB looks at revenue recognition from conceptual and substance points of view. There are occasions where a more traditional approach to revenue recognition does not entirely conform to the IASB guidance; indeed neither do some International Accounting Standards.

Required:

(a)   **Explain the implications that the IASB's Conceptual *Framework for Financial Reporting* and the application of substance over form have on the recognition of income in profit or loss. Give examples of how this may conflict with traditional practice and some accounting standards.**   **(6 marks)**

(b)   Derringdo sells goods supplied by Gungho. The goods are classed as A grade (perfect quality) or B grade, having slight faults. Derringdo sells the A grade goods acting as an agent for Gungho at a fixed price calculated to yield a gross profit margin of 50%. Derringdo receives a commission of 12.5% of the sales it achieves for these goods. The arrangement for B grade goods is that they are sold by Gungho to Derringdo and Derringdo sells them at a gross profit margin of 25%. The following information has been obtained from Derringdo's financial records:

	$000
Inventory held on premises 1 April 20X2	
– A grade	2,400
– B grade	1,000
Goods from Gungho plc year to 31 March 20X3	
– A grade	18,000
– B grade	8,800
Inventory held on premises 31 March 20X3	
– A grade	2,000
– B grade	1,250

Required:

Prepare the statement of profit or loss extracts for Derringdo for the year to 31 March 20X3 reflecting the above information.   **(5 marks)**

(c)   Derringdo acquired an item of plant at a gross cost of $800,000 on 1 October 20X2. The plant has an estimated life of 10 years with a residual value equal to 15% of its gross cost. Derringdo uses straight-line depreciation on a time apportioned basis. The company received a government grant of 30% of its cost price at the time of its purchase. The terms of the grant are that if the company retains the asset for four years or more, then no repayment liability will be incurred. If the plant is sold within four years a repayment on a sliding scale would be applicable. The repayment is 75% if sold within the first year of purchase and this amount decreases by 25% per annum. Derringdo has no intention to sell the plant within the first four years. Derringdo's accounting policy for capital based government grants is to treat them as deferred credits and release them to profit or loss over the life of the asset to which they relate.

Required:

(i)   **Discuss whether the company's policy for the treatment of government grants meets the definition of a liability in the IASB's *Framework*.**   **(3 marks)**

(ii)   **Prepare extracts of Derringdo's financial statements for the year to 31 March 20X3 in respect of the plant and the related grant:**

   –   **applying the company's policy;**

   –   **in compliance with the definition of a liability in the *Framework*.**

   Your answer should consider whether the sliding scale repayment should be used in determining the deferred credit for the grant.   **(6 marks)**

(d)   Derringdo sells carpets from several retail outlets. In previous years the company has undertaken responsibility for fitting the carpets in customers' premises. Customers pay for the carpets at the time they are ordered. The average length of time from a customer ordering a carpet to its fitting is 14 days. In previous years, Derringdo had not recognized a sale in profit or loss until the carpet had been successfully fitted as the rectification costs of any fitting error would be expensive. From 1 April 20X2 Derringdo changed its method of trading by sub-contracting the fitting to approved contractors. Under this policy the sub-contractors are paid by Derringdo and they (the sub-contractors) are liable for any errors made in the fitting. Because of this Derringdo is proposing to recognize sales when customers order and pay for the goods, rather than when they have been fitted. Details of the relevant sales figures are:

	$000
Sales made in retail outlets for the year to 31 March 20X3	23,000
Sales value of carpets fitted in the 14 days to 14 April 20X2	1,200
Sales value of carpets fitted in the 14 days to 14 April 20X3	1,600

Note: The sales value of carpets fitted in the 14 days to 14 April 20X2 are not included in the annual sales figure of $23 million, but those for the 14 days to 14 April 20X3 are included.

Required:

Discuss whether the above represents a change of accounting policy, and, based on your discussion, calculate the amount that you would include in revenue for carpets in the year to 31 March 20X3. **(5 marks)**

(Total: 25 marks)

4   HISTORIC COST

Over the years there have been many attempts by national and international standard setters to find an accepted method of dealing with the reporting of the effects of price changes.

There have been two main methods put forward by various accounting standard bodies for reporting the effects of price changes. One method is based on the movements in general price inflation and is referred to as a General (or Current) Purchasing Power Approach, the other method is based on specific price changes of goods and assets and is generally referred to as a Current Cost Approach. Some bodies have also suggested an approach which combines features of each method.

Required:

(i)   **Explain the limitations of (pure) historic cost accounts when used as a basis for assessing the performance of an enterprise. You should give an example of how each of three different user groups may be misled by such information.** **(8 marks)**

(ii)   **Describe the advantages and criticisms of General Purchasing Power and Current Cost Accounting.** **(7 marks)**

(Total: 15 marks)

5   FINANCIAL STATEMENTS 👣 *Walk in the footsteps of a top tutor*

(a)   The IASB's Framework *Conceptual Framework for Financial Reporting* requires financial statements to be prepared on the basis that they comply with certain accounting concepts, underlying assumptions and (qualitative) characteristics. Five of these are:

Matching/accruals

Substance over form

Prudence

Comparability

Materiality

Required:

Briefly explain the meaning of each of the above concepts/assumptions.   (5 marks)

(b)   For most entities, applying the appropriate concepts/assumptions in accounting for inventories is an important element in preparing their financial statements.

Required:

Illustrate with examples how each of the concepts/assumptions in (a) may be applied to accounting for inventory.   (10 marks)

(Total: 15 marks)

6   EMERALD 👣 *Walk in the footsteps of a top tutor*

Product development costs are a material cost for many companies. They are either written off as an expense or capitalised as an asset.

Required:

(a)   **Discuss the conceptual issues involved and the definition of an asset that may be applied in determining whether development expenditure should be treated as an expense or an asset.   (4 marks)**

(b)   Emerald has had a policy of writing off development expenditure to the statement of profit or loss as it was incurred. In preparing its financial statements for the year ended 30 September 2007 it has become aware that, under IFRS rules, qualifying development expenditure should be treated as an intangible asset. Below is the qualifying development expenditure for Emerald:

	$000
Year ended 30 September 2004	300
Year ended 30 September 2005	240
Year ended 30 September 2006	800
Year ended 30 September 2007	400

All capitalised development expenditure is deemed to have a four year life. Assume amortisation commences at the beginning of the accounting period following capitalisation. Emerald had no development expenditure before that for the year ended 30 September 2004.

Required:

Treating the above as the correction of an error in applying an accounting policy, calculate the amounts which should appear in the statement of profit or loss and statement of financial position (including comparative figures), and statement of changes in equity of Emerald in respect of the development expenditure for the year ended 30 September 2007.

Note: Ignore taxation.   **(6 marks)**

                                                                          (Total: 10 marks)

7   LMN

(a)   The IASB's *Conceptual Framework for Financial Reporting* has a section on recognition in financial statements.

Required:

Explain the *Framework*'s recognition criteria in general and in particular how assets, liabilities, income and expenses are to be recognized in financial statements.   **(5 marks)**

(b)   LMN trades in motor vehicles, which are manufactured and supplied by their manufacturer, IJK. Trading between the two entities is subject to a contractual agreement, the principal terms of which are as follows:

- LMN is entitled to hold on its premises at any one time up to 80 vehicles supplied by IJK. LMN is free to specify the ranges and models of vehicle supplied to it. IJK retains legal title to the vehicles until such time as they are sold to a third party by LMN.

- While the vehicles remain on its premises, LMN is required to insure them against loss or damage.

- The price at which vehicles are supplied is determined at the time of delivery; it is not subject to any subsequent alteration.

- When LMN sells a vehicle to a third party, it is required to inform IJK within three working days. IJK submits an invoice to LMN at the originally agreed price; the invoice is payable by LMN within 30 days.

- LMN is entitled to use any of the vehicles supplied to it for demonstration purposes and road testing. However, if more than a specified number of kilometres are driven in a vehicle, LMN is required to pay IJK a rental charge.

- LMN has the right to return any vehicle to IJK at any time without incurring a penalty, except for any rental charge incurred in respect of excess kilometres driven.

Required:

Discuss the economic substance of the contractual arrangement between the two entities in respect of the recognition of inventory and of sales.   **(10 marks)**

                                                                          (Total: 15 marks)

8   FINO   *Walk in the footsteps of a top tutor*

(a)   An important requirement of the IASB's *Conceptual Framework for Financial Reporting* is that an entity's financial statements should represent faithfully the transactions and events that it has undertaken.

Required:

Explain what is meant by faithful representation according to the IASB's Conceptual Framework for Financial Reporting.   **(5 marks)**

(b)   On 1 April 2007, Fino increased the operating capacity of its plant. Due to a lack of liquid funds it was unable to buy the required plant which had a cost of $350,000. On the recommendation of the finance director, Fino entered into an agreement to lease the plant from the manufacturer. The lease required four annual payments in advance of $100,000 each commencing on 1 April 2007. The plant would have a useful life of four years and would be scrapped at the end of this period. The finance director, believing the lease to be an operating lease, commented that the agreement would improve the company's return on capital employed (compared to outright purchase of the plant).

Required:

(i)   **Discuss the validity of the finance director's comment and describe how IAS 17 Leases ensures that leases such as the above are faithfully represented in an entity's financial statements.**   **(4 marks)**

(ii)   **Prepare extracts of Fino's statement of profit or loss and statement of financial position for the year ended 30 September 2007 in respect of the rental agreement assuming:**

(1)   **It is an operating lease**   **(2 marks)**

(2)   **It is a finance lease (use an implicit interest rate of 10% per annum).**   **(4 marks)**

(Total: 15 marks)

UK SYLLABUS FOCUS ONLY

A UK element to this question could ask you to:

"SSAP 21 Leases outlines the recognition criteria for a lease to be categorised as a finance lease.

Under SSAP 21 what is considered to be the primary factor when determining whether a lease is a finance or an operating lease?"

---

9   WARDLE

(a)   An important aspect of the International Accounting Standards Board's *Conceptual Framework for Financial Reporting* is that transactions should be recorded on the basis of their substance over their form.

Required:

Explain why it is important that financial statements should reflect the substance of the underlying transactions and describe the features that may indicate that the substance of a transaction may be different from its legal form.   (5 marks)

(b)   Wardle's activities include the production of maturing products which take a long time before they are ready to retail. Details of one such product are that on 1 April 2009 it had a cost of $5 million and a fair value of $7 million. The product would not be ready for retail sale until 31 March 2012.

On 1 April 2009 Wardle entered into an agreement to sell the product to Easyfinance for $6 million. The agreement gave Wardle the right to repurchase the product at any time up to 31 March 2012 at a fixed price of $7,986,000, at which date Wardle expected the product to retail for $10 million. The compound interest Wardle would have to pay on a three-year loan of $6 million would be:

	$
Year 1	600,000
Year 2	660,000
Year 3	726,000

This interest is equivalent to the return required by Easyfinance.

Required:

Assuming the above figures prove to be accurate, prepare extracts from the statement of profit or loss of Wardle for the three years to 31 March 2012 in respect of the above transaction:

(i)   Reflecting the legal form of the transaction;   (2 marks)

(ii)   Reflecting the substance of the transaction.   (3 marks)

Note: **Statement of financial position extracts are NOT required.**

(c)   **Comment on the effect the two treatments have on the statement of profit or loss and the statements of financial position and how this may affect an assessment of Wardle's performance.   (5 marks)**

(Total: 15 marks)

A REGULATORY FRAMEWORK FOR FINANCIAL REPORTING

10   IFRS FOUNDATION

Historically financial reporting throughout the world has differed widely. The International Financial Reporting Standards Foundation (IFRS Foundation) is committed to developing, in the public interest, a single set of high quality, understandable and enforceable global accounting standards that require transparent and comparable information in general purpose financial statements. The various pronouncements of the IFRS Foundation are sometimes collectively referred to as International Financial Reporting Standards (IFRS) GAAP.

Required:

(a)   **Explain why a regulatory framework is necessary.**   **(2 marks)**

(b)   **Describe the functions of the various internal bodies of the IFRS Foundation, and how the IFRS Foundation interrelates with other national standard setters.**

(8 marks)

(c)   **Describe the IFRS Foundation's standard setting process including how standards are produced, enforced and occasionally supplemented.**   **(10 marks)**

(d)   **Comment on whether you feel the move to date towards global accounting standards has been successful.**   **(5 marks)**

(Total: 25 marks)

11   CONCEPTUAL FRAMEWORK

In 1989 the forerunner to the current IASB, the IASC, issued its *Conceptual Framework for Financial Reporting.* This document is part of the overall conceptual framework within which the current IASB works.

Required:

(a)   **Describe what is meant by a conceptual framework.**   **(3 marks)**

(b)   **Explain the main reasons for having a conceptual framework**   **(8 marks)**

(c)   **Explain the purpose of the Conceptual Framework for Financial Reporting. (8 marks)**

(d)   **Discuss the extent to which IFRS are relevant to not-for-profit entities.**   **(6 marks)**

(Total: 25 marks)

12 USERS AND QUALITIES

The *Conceptual Framework for Financial Reporting* indicates the overall purpose of financial statements and considers the various users of these financial statements. It also gives much detail about the qualitative characteristics of financial statements which make them useful.

Required:

(a) Explain the overall objective of financial statements. **(2 marks)**

(b) Discuss the information needs of the different types of users of financial statements considered in the *Framework*. **(8 marks)**

(c) Discuss the qualitative characteristics which make information useful to users of the financial statements. **(12 marks)**

(d) Explain why in practice a balance is often required between the various characteristics. **(3 marks)**

(Total: 25 marks)

13 FINANCIAL PERFORMANCE & OCI

The International Accounting Standards Board (IASB) has recently completed a joint project with the Financial Accounting Standards Board (FASB) in the USA on the topic reporting financial performance, with particular focus on reporting of other comprehensive income (OCI). This process was completed with the publication of *Presentation of Items of Other Comprehensive Income – Amendments to IAS 1* in June 2011.

Required:

Explain the requirements introduced by the amendments made to IAS 1 and evaluate the extent to which they may improve the quality of information included within annual financial reports.

(10 marks)

FINANCIAL STATEMENTS

14 ELITE LEISURE AND ADVENT

(a) Elite Leisure is a private limited liability company that operates a single cruise ship. The ship was acquired on 1 October 19W5. Details of the cost of the ship's components and their estimated useful lives are:

Component	Original cost ($ million)	Depreciation basis
Ship's fabric (hull, decks etc)	300	25 years straight-line
Cabins and entertainment area fittings	150	12 years straight-line
Propulsion system	100	useful life of 40,000 hours

At 30 September 20X3 no further capital expenditure had been incurred on the ship.

In the year ended 30 September 20X3 the ship had experienced a high level of engine trouble which had cost the company considerable lost revenue and compensation costs. The measured expired life of the propulsion system at 30 September 20X3 was 30,000 hours. Due to the unreliability of the engines, a decision was taken in early October 20X3 to replace the whole of the propulsion system at a cost of $140 million. The expected life of the new propulsion system was 50,000 hours and in the year ended 30 September 20X4 the ship had used its engines for 5,000 hours.

At the same time as the propulsion system replacement, the company took the opportunity to do a limited upgrade to the cabin and entertainment facilities at a cost of $60 million and repaint the ship's fabric at a cost of $20 million. After the upgrade of the cabin and entertainment area fittings it was estimated that their remaining life was five years (from the date of the upgrade). For the purpose of calculating depreciation, all the work on the ship can be assumed to have been completed on 1 October 20X3. All residual values can be taken as nil.

Required:

Calculate the carrying amount of Elite Leisure's cruise ship at 30 September 20X3 and prepare extracts in respect of it from Elite Leisure's statement of profit or loss for the year ended 30 September 20X4 and its statement of financial position at that date. Your answer should explain the treatment of each item. **(12 marks)**

(b) Advent is a publicly listed company.

Details of Advent's non-current assets at 1 October 20X3 were:

	Land and buildings $m	Plant $m	Telecommunications licence $m	Total $m
Cost/valuation	280	150	300	730
Accumulated depreciation/amortization	(40)	(105)	(30)	(175)
Carrying value	240	45	270	555

The following information is relevant:

(i) The land and building were revalued on 1 October 19W8 with $80 million attributable to the land and $200 million to the building. At that date the estimated remaining life of the building was 25 years. A further revaluation was not needed until 1 October 20X3 when the land and building were valued at $85 million and $180 million respectively. The remaining estimated life of the building at this date was 20 years.

(ii) Plant is depreciated at 20% per annum on cost with time apportionment where appropriate. On 1 April 20X4 new plant costing $45 million was acquired. In addition, this plant cost $5 million to install and commission. No plant is more than four years old.

(iii) The telecommunications licence was bought from the government on 1 October 20X2 and has a 10 year life. It is amortized on a straight line basis. In September 20X4, a review of the sales of the products related to the licence showed them to be very disappointing. As a result of this review the estimated recoverable amount of the licence at 30 September 20X4 was estimated at only $100 million.

There were no disposals of non-current assets during the year to 30 September 20X4.

Required:

(i) **Prepare statement of financial position extracts of Advent's non-current assets as at 30 September 20X4 (including comparative figures), together with any disclosures required (other than those of the accounting policies) under current International Financial Reporting Standards.** **(9 marks)**

(ii) **Explain the usefulness of the above disclosures to the users of the financial statements.** **(4 marks)**

(Total: 25 marks)

15 WILDERNESS GROUP

(a) The main objective of IAS 36 *Impairment of Assets* is to prescribe the procedures that should ensure that an entity's assets are included in its statement of financial position at no more than their recoverable amounts. Where an asset is carried at an amount in excess of its recoverable amount, it is said to be impaired and IAS 36 requires an impairment loss to be recognized.

Required:

(i) **Define an impairment loss explaining the relevance of fair value less costs to sell and value in use; and state how frequently assets should be tested for impairment;** **(6 marks)**

Note: **Your answer should NOT describe the possible indicators of an impairment.**

(ii) **Explain how an impairment loss is accounted for after it has been calculated.** **(5 marks)**

(b) The assistant financial controller of the Wilderness group, a public listed company, has identified the matters below which she believes may indicate an impairment to one or more assets:

(i) Wilderness owns and operates an item of plant that cost $640,000 and had accumulated depreciation of $400,000 at 1 October 20X4. It is being depreciated at $12\frac{1}{2}\%$ per annum on cost. On 1 April 20X5 (exactly half way through the year) the plant was damaged when a factory vehicle collided into it. Due to the unavailability of replacement parts, it is not possible to repair the plant, but it still operates, albeit at a reduced capacity. Also it is expected that as a result of the damage the remaining life of the plant from the date of the damage will be only two years. Based on its reduced capacity, the estimated present value of the plant in use is $150,000. The plant has a current disposal value of $20,000 (which will be nil in two years' time), but Wilderness has been offered a trade-in value of $180,000 against a replacement machine which has a cost of $1 million (there would be no disposal costs for the replaced plant).

Wilderness is reluctant to replace the plant as it is worried about the long-term demand for the product produced by the plant. The trade-in value is only available if the plant is replaced.

Required:

Prepare extracts from the statement of financial position and statement of profit or loss of Wilderness in respect of the plant for the year ended 30 September 20X5. Your answer should explain how you arrived at your figures. **(7 marks)**

(ii) On 1 April 20X4 Wilderness acquired 100% of the share capital of Mossel, whose only activity is the extraction and sale of spa water. Mossel had been profitable since its acquisition, but bad publicity resulting from several consumers becoming ill due to a contamination of the spa water supply in April 20X5 has led to unexpected losses in the last six months. The carrying amounts of Mossel's assets at 30 September 20X5 are:

	$000
Brand (Quencher – see below)	7,000
Land containing spa	12,000
Purifying and bottling plant	8,000
Inventories	5,000
	———
	32,000
	———

The source of the contamination was found and it has now ceased.

The company originally sold the bottled water under the brand name of 'Quencher', but because of the contamination it has rebranded its bottled water as 'Phoenix'. After a large advertising campaign, sales are now starting to recover and are approaching previous levels. The value of the brand in the statement of financial position is the depreciated amount of the original brand name of 'Quencher'.

The directors have acknowledged that $1.5 million will have to be spent in the first three months of the next accounting period to upgrade the purifying and bottling plant.

Inventories contain some old 'Quencher' bottled water at a cost of $2 million; the remaining inventories are labelled with the new brand 'Phoenix'. Samples of all the bottled water have been tested by the health authority and have been passed as fit to sell. The old bottled water will have to be relabelled at a cost of $250,000, but is then expected to be sold at the normal selling price of (normal) cost plus 50%.

Based on the estimated future cash flows, the directors have estimated that the value in use of Mossel at 30 September 20X5, calculated according to the guidance in IAS 36, is $20 million. There is no reliable estimate of the fair value less costs to sell of Mossel.

Required:

Calculate the amounts at which the assets of Mossel should appear in the consolidated statement of financial position of Wilderness at 30 September 20X5. Your answer should explain how you arrived at your figures. **(7 marks)**

(Total: 25 marks)

16 LINNET

(a) (i) Linnet is a large public listed company involved in the construction industry. Accounting standards normally require construction contracts to be accounted for using the percentage (stage) of completion basis. However under certain circumstances they should be accounted for using the completed contracts basis.

Required:

Discuss the principles that underlie each of the two methods and describe the circumstances in which their use is appropriate. **(6 marks)**

(ii) Linnet is part way through a contract to build a new football stadium at a contracted price of $300 million. Details of the progress of this contract at 1 April 20X3 are shown below:

	$ million
Cumulative revenue invoiced	150
Cumulative cost of sales to date	112
Profit to date	38

The following information has been extracted from the accounting records at 31 March 20X4:

	$ million
Total progress payment received for work certified at 29 Feb 20X4	180
Total costs incurred to date (excluding rectification costs below)	195
Rectification costs	17

Linnet has received progress payments of 90% of the work certified at 29 February 20X4. Linnet's surveyor has estimated the sales value of the further work completed during March 20X4 was $20 million.

At 31 March 20X4 the estimated remaining costs to complete the contract were $45 million.

The rectification costs are the costs incurred in widening access roads to the stadium. This was the result of an error by Linnet's architect when he made his initial drawings.

Linnet calculates the percentage of completion of its contracts as the proportion of sales value earned to date compared to the contract price.

All estimates can be taken as being reliable.

Required:

Prepare extracts of the financial statements for Linnet for the above contract for the year to 31 March 20X4. **(11 marks)**

(b) Linnet also manufactures and sells high quality printing paper. The auditor has drawn the company's attention to the sale of some packs of paper on 20 April 20X4 at a price of $45 each. These items were included in closing inventory on 31 March 20X4 at their manufactured cost of $48 each. Further investigations revealed that during the inventory count on 31 March 20X4 a quantity of packs of A3-size paper had been damaged by a water leak. The following week the company removed the damage by cutting the paper down to A4 size (A4 size is smaller than A3). The paper was then repackaged and put back into inventory. The cost of cutting and repackaging was $4 per pack. The normal selling price of the paper is $75 per pack for the A3 and $50 per pack for the A4, however on 12 April 20X4 the company reduced the selling prices of all its paper by 10% in response to similar price cuts by its competitors.

Securiprint, one of the customers that bought some of the 'damaged' paper, had used it to print some share certificates for a customer. Securiprint informed Linnet that these share certificates had been returned by the customer because they contained marks that were not part of the design. Securiprint believes the marks were part of a manufacturing flaw on the part of Linnet and is seeking compensation.

Required:

Discuss the impact the above information may have on the draft financial statements of Linnet for the year to 31 March 20X4. **(8 marks)**

(Total: 25 marks)

17 BOWTOCK

(a) (i) IAS 12 Income Taxes details the requirements relating to the accounting treatment of deferred tax.

Required:

Explain why it is considered necessary to provide for deferred tax and briefly outline the principles of accounting for deferred tax contained in IAS 12 *Income Taxes*. **(5 marks)**

UK SYLLABUS FOCUS ONLY

A UK element to this question could ask you to:

"How do revaluations impact the deferred tax balance and how can long-term deferred tax balances be accounted for under FRS 19 *Deferred Tax*?"

(ii) Bowtock purchased an item of plant for $2,000,000 on 1 October 20X0. It had an estimated life of eight years and an estimated residual value of $400,000. The plant is depreciated on a straight-line basis. The tax authorities do not allow depreciation as a deductible expense. Instead a tax expense of 40% of the cost of this type of asset can be claimed against income tax in the year of purchase and 20% per annum (on a reducing balance basis) of its tax base thereafter. The rate of income tax can be taken as 25%.

Required:

In respect of the above item of plant, calculate the deferred tax charge/credit in Bowtock's statement of profit or loss for the year to 30 September 20X3 and the deferred tax balance in the statement of financial position at that date. **(6 marks)**

Note: **Work to the nearest $000.**

(b) Bowtock has leased an item of plant under the following terms:

Commencement of the lease was 1 January 20X2

Term of lease five years

Annual payments in advance $12,000

Cash price and fair value of the asset – $52,000 at 1 January 20X2

Implicit interest rate within the lease (as supplied by the lessor) 8% per annum (to be apportioned on a time basis where relevant).

The company's depreciation policy for this type of plant is 20% per annum on cost (apportioned on a time basis where relevant).

Required:

Prepare extracts of the statement of profit or loss and statement of financial position for Bowtock for the year to 30 September 20X3 for the above lease.

(5 marks)

(c) (i) Explain why events occurring after the reporting date may be relevant to the financial statements of the previous period. **(4 marks)**

(ii) At 30 September 20X3 Bowtock had included in its draft statement of financial position inventory of $250,000 valued at cost. Up to 5 November 20X3, Bowtock had sold $100,000 of this inventory for $150,000. On this date new government legislation (enacted after the year end) came into force which meant that the unsold inventory could no longer be marketed and was worthless.

Bowtock is part way through the construction of a housing development. It has prepared its financial statements to 30 September 20X3 in accordance with IAS 11 *Construction Contracts* and included a proportionate amount of the total estimated profit on this contract. The same legislation referred to above (in force from 5 November 20X3) now requires modifications to the way the houses within this development have to be built. The cost of these modifications will be $500,000 and will reduce the estimated total profit on the contract by that amount, although the contract is still expected to be profitable.

Required:

Assuming the amounts are material, state how the information above should be reflected in the financial statements of Bowtock for the year ended 30 September 20X3.

(5 marks)

(Total: 25 marks)

18   MULTIPLEX

The following transactions and events have arisen during the preparation of the draft financial statements of Multiplex for the year to 31 March 20X0:

(a)   On 1 April 19W9 Multiplex issued $80 million 8% convertible loan stock at par. The stock is convertible into equity shares, or redeemable at par, on 31 March 20X4, at the option of the stockholders. The terms of conversion are that each $100 of loan stock will be convertible into 50 equity shares of Multiplex. A finance consultant has advised that if the option to convert to equity had not been included in the terms of the issue, then a coupon (interest) rate of 12% would have been required to attract subscribers for the stock. Interest is paid in arrears on 31 March each year.

The value of $1 receivable at the end of each year at a discount rate of 12% are:

Year	$
1	0.89
2	0.80
3	0.71
4	0.64
5	0.57

Required:

Calculate the statement of profit or loss finance charge for the year to 31 March 20X0 and the statement of financial position extracts at 31 March 20X0 in respect of the issue of the convertible loan stock.   **(5 marks)**

(b)   On 1 January 20X0 Multiplex acquired the whole of Steamdays, a company that operates a scenic railway along the coast of a popular tourist area. The summarized statement of financial position at fair values of Steamdays on 1 January 20X0, reflecting the terms of the acquisition was:

	$000
Goodwill	200
Operating licence	1,200
Property – train stations and land	300
Rail track and coaches	300
Two steam engines	1,000
	———
Purchase consideration	3,000
	———

The operating licence is for ten years. It was renewed on 1 January 20X0 by the transport authority and is stated at the cost of its renewal. The carrying values of the property and rail track and coaches are based on their value in use. The engines are valued at their net selling prices.

On 1 February 20X0 the boiler of one of the steam engines exploded, completely destroying the whole engine. Fortunately no one was injured, but the engine was beyond repair. Due to its age a replacement could not be obtained. Because of the reduced passenger capacity the estimated value in use of the whole of the business after the accident was assessed at $2 million.

Passenger numbers after the accident were below expectations even after allowing for the reduced capacity. A market research report concluded that tourists were not using the railway because of their fear of a similar accident occurring to the remaining engine. In the light of this the value in use of the business was re-assessed on 31 March 20X0 at $1.8 million. On this date Multiplex received an offer of $900,000 in respect of the operating licence (it is transferable). The realizable value of the other net assets has not changed significantly.

Required:

Calculate the carrying value of the assets of Steamdays (in Multiplex's consolidated statement of financial position) at 1 February 20X0 and 31 March 20X0 after recognising the impairment losses. **(6 marks)**

(c) On 1 January 20X0 the Board of Multiplex approved a resolution to close the whole of its loss-making engineering operation. A binding agreement to dispose of the assets was signed shortly afterwards. The sale will be completed on 10 June 20X0 at an agreed value of $30 million. The costs of the closure are estimated at:

  – $2 million for redundancy/retrenchment

  – $3 million in penalty costs for non-completion of contracted orders

  – $1.5 million for associated professional costs

  – losses on the sale of the net assets and liabilities, whose book value at 31 March 20X0 was $66 million and $20 million respectively

  – operating losses for the period from 1 April 20X0 to the date of sale are estimated at $4.5 million.

Multiplex accounts for its various operations on a divisional basis.

Required:

Advise the directors on the correct treatment of the closure of the engineering division. **(5 marks)**

(d) Multiplex is in the intermediate stage of a construction contract for the building of a new privately owned road bridge over a river estuary. The original details of the contract are:

Approximate duration of contract:	3 years
Date of commencement:	1 October 19W8
Total contract price:	$40 million
Estimated total cost:	$28 million

An independent surveyor certified the value of the work in progress as follows:
– on 31 March 19W9	$12 million
– on 31 March 20X0	$30 million (including the $12 million in 19W9)
Total costs incurred at:	
– 31 March 19W9	$9 million
– 31 March 20X0	$28.5 million (including the $9 million in 19W9)

Progress billings at 31 March 20X0 were $25 million

On 1 April 19W9 Multiplex agreed to a contract variation that would involve an additional fee of $5 million with associated additional estimated costs of $2 million.

The costs incurred during the year to 31 March 20X0 include $2.5 million relating to the replacement of some bolts which had been made from material that had been incorrectly specified by the firm of civil engineers who were contracted by Multiplex to design the bridge. These costs were not included in the original estimates, but Multiplex is hopeful that they can be recovered from the firm of civil engineers. The advice to Multiplex from its lawyers is that there is about a 60% chance of success.

Multiplex calculates profit on construction contracts using the percentage of completion method. The percentage of completion of the contract is based on the value of the work certified to date compared to the total contract price.

Required:

Prepare the statement of profit or loss and statement of financial position extracts in respect of the contract for the year to 31 March 20X0 only. **(9 marks)**

(Total: 25 marks)

19 TORRENT

(a) Torrent is a large publicly listed company whose main activity involves construction contracts. Details of three of its contracts for the year ended 31 March 20X6 are:

Contract	Alpha	Beta	Ceta
Date commenced	1 April 20X4	1 October 20X5	1 October 20X5
Estimated duration	3 years	18 months	2 years
	$m	$m	$m
Fixed contract price	20	6	12
Estimated costs at start of contract	15	7.5 (note (iii))	10
Costs to date:			
at 31 March 20X5	5	Nil	Nil
at 31 March 20X6	12.5 (note (ii))	2	4
Estimated costs at 31 March 20X6 to complete	3.5	5.5 (note (iii))	6
Progress payments received at 31 March 20X5 (note (i))	5.4	Nil	Nil
Progress payments received at 31 March 20X6 (note (i))	12.6	1.8	Nil

Notes

(i) The company's normal policy for determining the percentage completion of contracts is based on the value of work invoiced to date compared to the contract price. Progress payments received represent 90% of the work invoiced. However, no progress payments will be invoiced or received from contract Ceta until it is completed, so the percentage completion of this contract is to be based on the cost to date compared to the estimated total contract costs.

(ii) The cost to date of $12.5 million at 31 March 20X6 for contract Alpha includes $1 million relating to unplanned rectification costs incurred during the current year (ended 31 March 20X6) due to subsidence occurring on site.

(iii) Since negotiating the price of contract Beta, Torrent has discovered the land that it purchased for the project is contaminated by toxic pollutants. The estimated cost at the start of the contract and the estimated costs to complete the contract include the unexpected costs of decontaminating the site before construction could commence.

Required:

Prepare extracts of the statement of profit or loss and statement of financial position for Torrent in respect of the above construction contracts for the year ended 31 March 20X6 **(12 marks)**

(b) (i) The issued share capital of Savoir, a publicly listed company, at 31 March 20X3 was $10 million. Its shares are denominated at 25 cents each. Savoir's profits attributable to its ordinary shareholders for the year ended 31 March 20X3 were also $10 million, giving an earnings per share of 25 cents.

Year ended 31 March 20X4

On 1 July 20X3 Savoir issued eight million ordinary shares at full market value. On 1 January 20X4 a bonus issue of one new ordinary share for every four ordinary shares held was made. Profits attributable to ordinary shareholders for the year ended 31 March 20X4 were $13,800,000.

Year ended 31 March 20X5

On 1 October 20X4 Savoir made a rights issue of shares of two new ordinary shares at a price of $1.00 each for every five ordinary shares held. The offer was fully subscribed. The market price of Savoir's ordinary shares immediately prior to the offer was $2.40 each. Profits attributable to ordinary shareholders for the year ended 31 March 20X5 were $19,500,000.

Required:

Calculate Savoir's earnings per share for the years ended 31 March 20X4 and 20X5 including comparative figures. **(9 marks)**

(ii) On 1 April 20X5 Savoir issued $20 million 8% convertible loan stock at par. The terms of conversion (on 1 April 20X8) are that for every $100 of loan stock, 50 ordinary shares will be issued at the option of loan stockholders. Alternatively the loan stock will be redeemed at par for cash. Also on 1 April 20X5 the directors of Savoir were awarded share options on 12 million ordinary shares exercisable from 1 April 20X8 at $1.50 per share. The average market value of Savoir's ordinary shares for the year ended 31 March 20X6 was $2.50 each. The income tax rate is 25%. Profits attributable to ordinary shareholders for the year ended 31 March 20X6 were $25,200,000. The share options have been correctly recorded in the statement of profit or loss.

Required:

Calculate Savoir's basic and diluted earnings per share for the years ended 31 March 20X6 (comparative figures are NOT required).

You may assume that both the convertible loan stock and the directors' options are dilutive. **(4 marks)**

(Total: 25 marks)

20 PINGWAY   *Walk in the footsteps of a top tutor*

Pingway issued a $10 million 3% convertible loan note at par on 1 April 2007 with interest payable annually in arrears. Three years later, on 31 March 2010, the loan note is convertible into equity shares on the basis of $100 of loan note for 25 equity shares or it may be redeemed at par in cash at the option of the loan note holder. One of the company's financial assistants observed that the use of a convertible loan note was preferable to a non-convertible loan note as the latter would have required an interest rate of 8% in order to make it attractive to investors. The assistant has also commented that the use of a convertible loan note will improve the profit as a result of lower interest costs and, as it is likely that the loan note holders will choose the equity option, the loan note can be classified as equity which will improve the company's high gearing position.

The present value of $1 receivable at the end of the year, based on discount rates of 3% and 8% can be taken as:

	3%	8%
	$	$
End of year 1	0.97	0.93
2	0.94	0.86
3	0.92	0.79

Required:

Comment on the financial assistant's observations and show how the convertible loan note should be accounted for in Pingway's statement of profit or loss and other comprehensive income for the year ended 31 March 2008 and statement of financial position as at that date. **(10 marks)**

21 ERRSEA

(a) The following is an extract of Errsea's balances of property, plant and equipment and related government grants at 1 April 2006.

	Cost	Accumulated depreciation	Carrying amount
	$000	$000	$000
Property, plant and equipment	240	180	60
Non-current liabilities			
Government grants			30
Current liabilities			
Government grants			10

Details including purchases and disposals of plant and related government grants during the year are:

(i) Included in the above figures is an item of plant that was disposed of on 1 April 2006 for $12,000 which had cost $90,000 on 1 April 2003. The plant was being depreciated on a straight-line basis over four years assuming a residual value of $10,000. A government grant was received on its purchase and was being recognised in the statement of profit or loss in equal amounts over four years. In accordance with the terms of the grant, Errsea repaid $3,000 of the grant on the disposal of the related plant.

(ii)   An item of plant was acquired on 1 July 2006 with the following costs:

	$
Base cost	192,000
Modifications specified by Errsea	12,000
Transport and installation	6,000

The plant qualified for a government grant of 25% of the base cost of the plant, but it had not been received by 31 March 2007. The plant is to be depreciated on a straight-line basis over three years with a nil estimated residual value.

(iii)   All other plant is depreciated by 15% per annum on cost.

(iv) $11,000 of the $30,000 non-current liability for government grants at 1 April 2006 should be reclassified as a current liability as at 31 March 2007.

(v)   Depreciation is calculated on a time apportioned basis.

Required:

Prepare extracts of Errsea's statement of profit or loss and statement of financial position in respect of the property, plant and equipment and government grants for the year ended 31 March 2007.

Note: **Disclosure notes are not required.**   **(10 marks)**

(b)   In the post statement of financial position period, prior to authorising for issue the financial statements of Tentacle for the year ended 31 March 2007, the following material information has arisen.

(i)   The notification of the bankruptcy of a customer. The balance of the trade receivable due from the customer at 31 March 2007 was $23,000 and at the date of the notification it was $25,000. No payment is expected from the bankruptcy proceedings.   **(3 marks)**

(ii)   Sales of some items of product W32 were made at a price of $5.40 each in April and May 2007. Sales staff receive a commission of 15% of the sales price on this product. At 31 March 2007 Tentacle had 12,000 units of product W32 in inventory included at cost of $6 each.   **(4 marks)**

(iii)   Tentacle is being sued by an employee who lost a limb in an accident while at work on 15 March 2007. The company is contesting the claim as the employee was not following the safety procedures that he had been instructed to use. Accordingly the financial statements include a note of a contingent liability of $500,000 for personal injury damages. In a recently decided case where a similar injury was sustained, a settlement figure of $750,000 was awarded by the court. Although the injury was similar, the circumstances of the accident in the decided case are different from those of Tentacle's case.   **(4 marks)**

(iv) Tentacle is involved in the construction of a residential apartment building. It is being accounted for using the percentage of completion basis in IAS 11 *Construction contracts*. The recognised profit at 31 March 2007 was $1.2 million based on costs to date of $3 million as a percentage of the total estimated costs of $6 million. Early in May 2007 Tentacle was informed that due to very recent industry shortages, building materials will cost $1.5 million more than the estimate of total cost used in the calculation of the percentage of completion. Tentacle cannot pass on any additional costs to the customer.

(4 marks)

Required:

State and quantify how items (i) to (iv) above should be treated when finalising the financial statements of Tentacle for the year ended 31 March 2007.

Note: **The mark allocation is shown against each of the four items above.**

(Total: 25 marks)

22 TUNSHILL

(a) IAS *8 Accounting Policies, Changes in Accounting Estimates and Errors* contains guidance on the use of accounting policies and accounting estimates.

Required:

Explain the basis on which the management of an entity must select its accounting policies and distinguish, with an example, between changes in accounting policies and changes in accounting estimates. **(5 marks)**

(b) The directors of Tunshill are disappointed by the draft profit for the year ended 30 September 2010. The company's assistant accountant has suggested two areas where she believes the reported profit may be improved:

(i) A major item of plant that cost $20 million to purchase and install on 1 October 2007 is being depreciated on a straight-line basis over a five-year period (assuming no residual value). The plant is wearing well and at the beginning of the current year (1 October 2009) the production manager believed that the plant was likely to last eight years in total (i.e. from the date of its purchase). The assistant accountant has calculated that, based on an eight-year life (and no residual value) the accumulated depreciation of the plant at 30 September 2010 would be $7.5 million ($20 million/8 years × 3). In the financial statements for the year ended 30 September 2009, the accumulated depreciation was $8 million ($20 million/5 years × 2). Therefore, by adopting an eight-year life, Tunshill can avoid a depreciation charge in the current year and instead credit $0.5 million ($8 million – $7.5 million) to the statement of profit or loss in the current year to improve the reported profit. **(5 marks)**

(ii) Most of Tunshill's competitors value their inventory using the average cost (AVCO) basis, whereas Tunshill uses the first in first out (FIFO) basis. The value of Tunshill's inventory at 30 September 2010 (on the FIFO basis) is $20 million, however on the AVCO basis it would be valued at $18 million. By adopting the same method (AVCO) as its competitors, the assistant accountant says the company would improve its profit for the year ended 30 September 2010 by $2 million. Tunshill's inventory at 30 September 2009 was reported as $15 million, however on the AVCO basis it would have been reported as $13.4 million. **(5 marks)**

Required:

Comment on the acceptability of the assistant accountant's suggestions and quantify how they would affect the financial statements if they were implemented under IFRS. Ignore taxation.

Note: the mark allocation is shown against each of the two items above.

(Total: 15 marks)

23 MANCO

Manco has been experiencing substantial losses at its furniture making operation which is treated as a separate operating segment. The company's year-end is 30 September. At a meeting on 1 July 2010 the directors decided to close down the furniture making operation on 31 January 2011 and then dispose of its non-current assets on a piecemeal basis. Affected employees and customers were informed of the decision and a press announcement was made immediately after the meeting. The directors have obtained the following information in relation to the closure of the operation:

(i) On 1 July 2010, the factory had a carrying amount of $3.6 million and is expected to be sold for net proceeds of $5 million. On the same date the plant had a carrying amount of $2.8 million, but it is anticipated that it will only realise net proceeds of $500,000.

(ii) Of the employees affected by the closure, the majority will be made redundant at cost of $750,000, the remainder will be retrained at a cost of $200,000 and given work in one of the company's other operations.

(iii) Trading losses from 1 July to 30 September 2010 are expected to be $600,000 and from this date to the closure on 31 January 2011 a further $1 million of trading losses are expected.

Required:

Explain how the decision to close the furniture making operation should be treated in Manco's financial statements for the years ending 30 September 2010 and 2011. Your answer should quantify the amounts involved.

(10 marks)

24   SITUATIONS

You have been asked to advise on a number of accounting problems which are each given separately below.

(a)   XY recently acquired a new subsidiary, AB. Upon undertaking the fair value exercise in respect of AB the following issues arose:

   (i)   At the date of acquisition a customer had brought a legal action against AB. The outcome of the case was uncertain at the date of acquisition, but it was considered possible that AB would be found liable to pay compensation to the customer. The individual financial statements of AB drawn up at the date of acquisition did not include any amount payable in respect of the legal case.

   (ii)   The group will need to spend approximately $100 million in order to integrate the new subsidiary into the existing operation.

   Explain how each of the above issues will affect the net assets of AB to be included in the initial calculation of goodwill on consolidation.   **(3 marks)**

(b)   B issued new interest-bearing borrowings to finance a construction project on the following terms:

   •   The new borrowings had a nominal value of $50 million.

   •   The borrowings carried an annual interest rate of 4%.

   •   The costs of issuing the borrowings totalled $600,000. This comprised under-writing fees relating to the issue of $500,000 and fees of $100,000 payable for general advice on which of a number of sources of finance should be pursued.

   •   The borrowings were theoretically repayable at $60 million after five years. However, the borrowings contained an option to convert into ordinary shares after five years as an alternative to repayment. At the date of issue, the directors of B were reasonably certain that the investors would choose the conversion option.

   Calculate the total financing cost relating to these borrowings.   **(3 marks)**

(c)   At its year end, 31 March 20X5, entity JBK held 60,000 shares in a listed entity, X. The shares were purchased on 11 February 20X5 at a price of 85¢ per share. The market value of the shares on 31 March 20X5 was 87.5¢. It is expected that the shares will be sold shortly after he year-end (held-for-trading).

   Explain how this investment would be treated both at initial acquisition of the investment and when subsequently remeasured on 31 March 20X5.   **(3 marks)**

(d)   PQR holds several investments in subsidiaries. In December 20X5, it acquired 100% of the ordinary share capital of STU. PQR intends to exclude STU from consolidation in its group financial statements for the year ended 28 February 20X6, on the grounds that it does not intend to retain the investment in the longer term.

   Explain, with reference to the relevant International Financial Reporting Standard, the conditions relating to exclusion of this type of investment from consolidation.

   (3 marks)

(e)   On 1 January 20X6, EFG issued 10,000 5% convertible bonds at their par value of $50 each. The bonds will be redeemed on 1 January 2011. Each bond is convertible at the option of the holder at any time during the five-year period. Interest on the bond will be paid annually in arrears.

The prevailing market interest rate for similar debt without conversion options at the date of issue was 6%.

Explain how this financial instrument should be recognized in the financial statements of EFG at the date of issue and calculate any relevant amounts.

Discount factor at 6% for year 5 is 0.747 and the cumulative discount factor for years 1 to 5 is 4.212. **(3 marks)**

(Total: 15 marks)

25   PROMOIL   *Walk in the footsteps of a top tutor*

(a)   The definition of a liability forms an important element of the International Accounting Standards Board's *Conceptual Framework for Financial Reporting* which, in turn, forms the basis for IAS 37 *Provisions, Contingent Liabilities and Contingent Assets*.

Required:

Define a liability and describe the circumstances under which provisions should be recognised. Give two examples of how the definition of liabilities enhances the faithful representation of financial statements. **(5 marks)**

(b)   On 1 October 2007, Promoil acquired a newly constructed oil platform at a cost of $30 million together with the right to extract oil from an offshore oilfield under a government licence. The terms of the licence are that Promoil will have to remove the platform (which will then have no value) and restore the sea bed to an environmentally satisfactory condition in 10 years' time when the oil reserves have been exhausted. The estimated cost of this on 30 September 2017 will be $15 million. The present value of $1 receivable in 10 years at the appropriate discount rate for Promoil of 8% is $0.46.

Required:

(i)   **Explain and quantify how the oil platform should be treated in the financial statements of Promoil for the year ended 30 September 2008;** **(7 marks)**

(ii)   **Describe how your answer to (b)(i) would change if the government licence did not require an environmental cleanup.** **(3 marks)**

(Total: 15 marks)

26   DEARING   *Walk in the footsteps of a top tutor*

On 1 October 2005 Dearing acquired a machine under the following terms:

	Hours	$
Manufacturer's base price		1,050,000
Trade discount (applying to base price only)		20%
Early settlement discount taken (on the payable amount of the base cost only)		5%
Freight charges		30,000
Electrical installation cost		28,000
Staff training in use of machine		40,000
Pre-production testing		22,000
Purchase of a three-year maintenance contract		60,000
Estimated residual value		20,000
Estimated life in machine hours	6,000	
Hours used – year ended 30 September 2006	1,200	
– year ended 30 September 2007	1,800	
– year ended 30 September 2008 (see below)	850	

On 1 October 2007 Dearing decided to upgrade the machine by adding new components at a cost of $200,000. This upgrade led to a reduction in the production time per unit of the goods being manufactured using the machine. The upgrade also increased the estimated remaining life of the machine at 1 October 2007 to 4,500 machine hours and its estimated residual value was revised to $40,000.

Required:

Prepare extracts from the statement of profit or loss and statement of financial position for the above machine for each of the three years to 30 September 2008.   (10 marks)

Online question assistance

---

27   WAXWORK

(a)   The objective of IAS 10 *Events after the Reporting Period is* to prescribe the treatment of events that occur after an entity's reporting period has ended.

Required:

Define the period to which IAS 10 relates and distinguish between adjusting and non-adjusting events.   (5 marks)

(b)   Waxwork's current year end is 31 March 2009. Its financial statements were authorised for issue by its directors on 6 May 2009 and the AGM (annual general meeting) will be held on 3 June 2009. The following matters have been brought to your attention:

   (i)   On 12 April 2009 a fire completely destroyed the company's largest warehouse and the inventory it contained. The carrying amounts of the warehouse and the inventory were $10 million and $6 million respectively. It appears that the company has not updated the value of its insurance cover and only expects to be able to recover a maximum of $9 million from its insurers. Waxwork's trading operations have been severely disrupted since the fire and it expects large trading losses for some time to come.   **(4 marks)**

(ii)   A single class of inventory held at another warehouse was valued at its cost of $460,000 at 31 March 2009. In April 2009 70% of this inventory was sold for $280,000 on which Waxworks' sales staff earned a commission of 15% of the selling price.   **(3 marks)**

(iii)   On 18 May 2009 the government announced tax changes which have the effect of increasing Waxwork's deferred tax liability by $650,000 as at 31 March 2009.   **(3 marks)**

Required:

Explain the required treatment of the items (i) to (iii) by Waxwork in its financial statements for the year ended 31 March 2009. *Note:* **Assume all items are material and are independent of each other.**   **(10 marks as indicated)**

(Total: 15 marks)

28   FLIGHTLINE

> **Timed question with Online tutor debrief**

Flightline is an airline which treats its aircraft as complex non-current assets. The cost and other details of one of its aircraft are:

	$000	**Estimated life**
Exterior structure – purchase date 1 April 1995	120,000	20 years
Interior cabin fittings – replaced 1 April 2005	25,000	5 years
Engines (2 at $9 million each) – replaced 1 April 2005		
No residual values are attributed to any of the component parts.	18,000	36,000 flying hours

At 1 April 2008 the aircraft log showed it had flown 10,800 hours since 1 April 2005. In the year ended 31 March 2009, the aircraft flew for 1,200 hours for the six months to 30 September 2008 and a further 1,000 hours in the six months to 31 March 2009.

On 1 October 2008 the aircraft suffered a 'bird strike' accident which damaged one of the engines beyond repair. This was replaced by a new engine with a life of 36,000 hours at cost of $10.8 million. The other engine was also damaged, but was repaired at a cost of $3 million; however, its remaining estimated life was shortened to 15,000 hours. The accident also caused cosmetic damage to the exterior of the aircraft which required repainting at a cost of $2 million. As the aircraft was out of service for some weeks due to the accident, Flightline took the opportunity to upgrade its cabin facilities at a cost of $4.5 million. This did not increase the estimated remaining life of the cabin fittings, but the improved facilities enabled Flightline to substantially increase the air fares on this aircraft

Required:

Calculate the charges to the statement of profit or loss in respect of the aircraft for the year ended 31 March 2009 and its carrying amount in the statement of financial position as at that date. *Note:* **The post accident changes are deemed effective from 1 October 2008.**

(10 marks)

Calculate your allowed time, allocate the time to the separate parts

---

29 DARBY

(a) An assistant of yours has been criticised over a piece of assessed work that he produced for his study course for giving the definition of a non-current asset as 'a physical asset of substantial cost, owned by the company, which will last longer than one year'.

Required:

Provide an explanation to your assistant of the weaknesses in his definition of non-current assets when compared to the International Accounting Standards Board's (IASB) view of assets. **(4 marks)**

(b) The same assistant has encountered the following matters during the preparation of the draft financial statements of Darby for the year ending 30 September 2009. He has given an explanation of his treatment of them.

(i) Darby spent $200,000 sending its staff on training courses during the year. This has already led to an improvement in the company's efficiency and resulted in cost savings. The organiser of the course has stated that the benefits from the training should last for a minimum of four years. The assistant has therefore treated the cost of the training as an intangible asset and charged six months' amortisation based on the average date during the year on which the training courses were completed. **(3 marks)**

(ii) During the year the company started research work with a view to the eventual development of a new processor chip. By 30 September 2009 it had spent $1.6 million on this project. Darby has a past history of being particularly successful in bringing similar projects to a profitable conclusion. As a consequence the assistant has treated the expenditure to date on this project as an asset in the statement of financial position.

Darby was also commissioned by a customer to research and, if feasible, produce a computer system to install in motor vehicles that can automatically stop the vehicle if it is about to be involved in a collision. At 30 September 2009, Darby had spent $2.4 million on this project, but at this date it was uncertain as to whether the project would be successful. As a consequence the assistant has treated the $2.4 million as an expense in the statement of profit or loss. **(4 marks)**

(iii) Darby signed a contract (for an initial three years) in August 2009 with a company called Media Today to install a satellite dish and cabling system to a newly built group of residential apartments. Media Today will provide telephone and television services to the residents of the apartments via the satellite system and pay Darby $50,000 per annum commencing in December 2009. Work on the installation commenced on 1 September 2009 and the expenditure to 30 September 2009 was $58,000. The installation is expected to be completed by 31 October 2009. Previous experience with similar contracts indicates that Darby will make a total profit of $40,000 over the three years on this initial contract. The assistant correctly recorded the costs to 30 September 2009 of $58,000 as a non-current asset, but then wrote this amount down to $40,000 (the expected total profit) because he believed the asset to be impaired.

The contract is not a finance lease. Ignore discounting. **(4 marks)**

Required:

For each of the above items (i) to (iii) comment on the assistant's treatment of them in the financial statements for the year ended 30 September 2009 and advise him how they should be treated under International Financial Reporting Standards.

Note: **The mark allocation is shown against each of the three items above.**

(Total: 15 marks)

30 BARSTEAD *Walk in the footsteps of a top tutor*

(a) The following figures have been calculated from the financial statements (including comparatives) of Barstead for the year ended 30 September 2009:

Increase in profit after taxation	80%
Increase in (basic) earnings per share	5%
Increase in diluted earnings per share	2%

Required:

Explain why the three measures of earnings (profit) growth for the same company over the same period can give apparently differing impressions. **(4 marks)**

(b) The profit after tax for Barstead for the year ended 30 September 2009 was $15 million. At 1 October 2008 the company had in issue 36 million equity shares and a $10 million 8% convertible loan note. The loan note will mature in 2010 and will be redeemed at par or converted to equity shares on the basis of 25 shares for each $100 of loan note at the loan-note holders' option. On 1 January 2009 Barstead made a fully subscribed rights issue of one new share for every four shares held at a price of $2.80 each. The market price of the equity shares of Barstead immediately before the issue was $3.80. The earnings per share (EPS) reported for the year ended 30 September 2008 was 35 cents.

Barstead's income tax rate is 25%.

Required:

Calculate the (basic) EPS figure for Barstead (including comparatives) and the diluted EPS (comparatives not required) that would be disclosed for the year ended 30 September 2009. **(6 marks)**

(Total: 10 marks)

31 APEX *Walk in the footsteps of a top tutor*

(a) Apex is a publicly listed supermarket chain. During the current year it started the building of a new store. The directors are aware that in accordance with IAS 23 Borrowing costs certain borrowing costs have to be capitalised.

Required:

Explain the circumstances when, and the amount at which, borrowing costs should be capitalised in accordance with IAS 23. **(5 marks)**

(b) Details relating to construction of Apex's new store:

Apex issued a $10 million unsecured loan with a coupon (nominal) interest rate of 6% on 1 April 2009. The loan is redeemable at a premium which means the loan has an effective finance cost of 7.5% per annum. The loan was specifically issued to finance the building of the new store which meets the definition of a qualifying asset in IAS 23. Construction of the store commenced on 1 May 2009 and it was completed and ready for use on 28 February 2010, but did not open for trading until 1 April 2010. During the year trading at Apex's other stores was below expectations so Apex suspended the construction of the new store for a two-month period during July and August 2009. The proceeds of the loan were temporarily invested for the month of April 2009 and earned interest of $40,000.

Required:

Calculate the net borrowing cost that should be capitalised as part of the cost of the new store and the finance cost that should be reported in the statement of profit or loss for the year ended 31 March 2010. **(5 marks)**

(Total: 10 marks)

UK SYLLABUS FOCUS ONLY

A UK element to this question could ask you to:

"Outline the difference between accounting for borrowing costs under UK GAAP and IFRS".

---

32   WELLMAY

The summarised draft financial statements of Wellmay are shown below.

Statement of profit or loss year ended 31 March 2007

	$000
Revenue (note (i))	4,200
Cost of sales (note (ii))	(2,700)
Gross profit	1,500
Operating expenses	(470)
Investment property rental income	20
Finance costs	(55)
Profit before tax	995
Income tax	(360)
Profit for the period	635

Statement of financial position as at 31 March 2007

	$000	$000
Assets		
Non-current assets		
Property, plant and equipment (note (iii))		4,200
Investment property (note (iii))		400
		4,600
Current assets		1,400
Total assets		6,000
Equity and liabilities		
Equity		
Equity shares of 50 cents each (note (vii))		1,200
Reserves:		
Revaluation reserve	350	
Retained earnings (note (iv))	2,850	3,200
		4,400
Non-current liabilities		
8% Convertible loan note (2010) (note (v))	600	
Deferred tax (note (vi))	180	780
Current liabilities		820
Total equity and liabilities		6,000

The following information is relevant to the draft financial statements:

(i)   Revenue includes $500,000 for the sale on 1 April 2006 of maturing goods to Westwood. The goods had a cost of $200,000 at the date of sale. Wellmay can repurchase the goods on 31 March 2008 for $605,000 (based on achieving a lender's return of 10% per annum) at which time the goods are estimated to have a value of $750,000.

(ii)   Past experience shows that in the post reporting period the company often receives unrecorded invoices for materials relating to the previous year. As a result of this an accrued charge of $75,000 for contingent costs has been included in cost of sales and as a current liability.

(iii) **Non-current assets**

Wellmay owns two properties. One is a factory (with office accommodation) used by Wellmay as a production facility and the other is an investment property that is leased to a third party under an operating lease. Wellmay revalues all its properties to current value at the end of each year and uses the fair value model in IAS 40 Investment property. Relevant details of the fair values of the properties are:

	Factory	Investment property
	$000	$000
Valuation 31 March 2006	1,200	400
Valuation 31 March 2007	1,350	375

The valuations at 31 March 2007 have not yet been incorporated into the financial statements. Factory depreciation for the year ended 31 March 2007 of $40,000 was charged to cost of sales. As the factory includes some office accommodation, 20% of this depreciation should have been charged to operating expenses.

(iv)   The balance of retained earnings is made up of:

	$000
Balance b/f 1 April 2006	2,615
Profit for the period	635
Dividends paid during year ended 31 March 2007	(400)
	2,850

(v)   **8% Convertible loan note (2010)**

On 1 April 2006 an 8% convertible loan note with a nominal value of $600,000 was issued at par. It is redeemable on 31 March 2010 at par or it may be converted into equity shares of Wellmay on the basis of 100 new shares for each $200 of loan note. An equivalent loan note without the conversion option would have carried an interest rate of 10%. Interest of $48,000 has been paid on the loan and charged as a finance cost.

The present value of $1 receivable at the end of each year, based on discount rates of 8% and 10% are:

	8%	10%
End of year 1	0.93	0.91
2	0.86	0.83
3	0.79	0.75
4	0.73	0.68

(vi) The carrying amounts of Wellmay's net assets at 31 March 2007 are $600,000 higher than their tax base. The rate of taxation is 35%. The income tax charge of $360,000 does not include the adjustment required to the deferred tax provision which should be charged in full to the statement of profit or loss.

(vii) Bonus/scrip issue: On 15 March 2007, Wellmay made a bonus issue from retained earnings of one share for every four held. The issue has not been recorded in the draft financial statements.

Required:

Redraft the financial statements of Wellmay, including a statement of changes in equity, for the year ended 31 March 2007 reflecting the adjustments required by notes (i) to (vii) above.

Note: **Calculations should be made to the nearest $000.**

(25 marks)

33 LLAMA

The following trial balance relates to Llama, a listed company, at 30 September 2007:

	$000	$000
Land and buildings – at valuation 1 October 2006 (note (i))	130,000	
Plant – at cost (note (i))	128,000	
Accumulated depreciation of plant at 1 October 2006		32,000
Investments – at fair value through profit and loss (note (i))	26,500	
Investment income		2,200
Cost of sales (note (i))	89,200	
Distribution costs	11,000	
Administrative expenses	12,500	
Loan interest paid	800	
Inventory at 30 September 2007	37,900	
Income tax (note (ii))		400
Trade receivables	35,100	
Revenue		180,400
Equity shares of 50 cents each fully paid		60,000
Retained earnings at 1 October 2006		25,500
2% loan note 2009 (note (iii))		80,000
Trade payables		34,700
Revaluation reserve (arising from land and buildings)		14,000
Deferred tax		11,200
Suspense account (note (iv))		24,000
Bank		6,600
	471,000	471,000

The following notes are relevant:

(i) Llama has a policy of revaluing its land and buildings at each year end. The valuation in the trial balance includes a land element of $30 million. The estimated remaining life of the buildings at that date (1 October 2006) was 20 years. On 30 September 2007, a professional valuer valued the buildings at $92 million with no change in the value of the land. Depreciation of buildings is charged 60% to cost of sales and 20% each to distribution costs and administrative expenses.

During the year Llama manufactured an item of plant that it is using as part of its own operating capacity. The details of its cost, which is included in cost of sales in the trial balance, are:

	$000
Materials cost	6,000
Direct labour cost	4,000
Machine time cost	8,000
Directly attributable overheads	6,000

The manufacture of the plant was completed on 31 March 2007 and the plant was brought into immediate use, but its cost has not yet been capitalised.

All plant is depreciated at 12.5% per annum (time apportioned where relevant) using the reducing balance method and charged to cost of sales. No non-current assets were sold during the year.

The fair value of the investments held at fair value through profit and loss at 30 September 2007 was $27.1 million.

(ii) The balance of income tax in the trial balance represents the under/over provision of the previous year's estimate. The estimated income tax liability for the year ended 30 September 2007 is $18.7 million. At 30 September 2007 there were $40 million of taxable temporary differences. The income tax rate is 25%. *Note:* You may assume that the movement in deferred tax should be taken to the statement of profit or loss.

(iii) The 2% loan note was issued on 1 April 2007 under terms that provide for a large premium on redemption in 2009. The finance department has calculated that the effect of this is that the loan note has an effective interest rate of 6% per annum.

(iv) The suspense account contains the corresponding credit entry for the proceeds of a rights issue of shares made on 1 July 2007. The terms of the issue were one share for every four held at 80 cents per share. Llama's share price immediately before the issue was $1. The issue was fully subscribed.

Required:

Prepare for Llama:

(a)   A statement of profit or loss and other comprehensive income for the year ended 30 September 2007.   **(9 marks)**

(b)   A statement of financial position as at 30 September 2007.   **(13 marks)**

(c)   A calculation of the earnings per share for the year ended 30 September 2007.

        Note: **A statement of changes in equity is not required.**   **(3 marks)**

                                                                              (Total: 25 marks)

UK SYLLABUS FOCUS ONLY

A UK element to part (c) could instead ask you to:

"Identify and outline the circumstances in which a single entity is required to prepare and present statutory financial statements.

---

34   DEXON

Below is the summarised draft statement of financial position of Dexon, a publicly listed company, as at 31 March 2008.

	$000	$000	$000
Assets			
Non-current assets			
Property at valuation (land $20,000; buildings $165,000 (note (ii))			185,000
Plant (note (ii))			180,500
Investments at fair value through profit and loss at 1 April 2007 (note (iii))			12,500
			378,000
Current assets			
Inventory		84,000	
Trade receivables (note (iv))		52,200	
Bank		3,800	140,000
Total assets			518,000

Equity and liabilities
Equity

Ordinary shares of $1 each			250,000
Share premium		40,000	
Revaluation reserve		18,000	
Retained earnings – at 1 April 2007	12,300		
– for the year ended 31 March 2008	96,700	109,000	167,000
			417,000
Non-current liabilities			
Deferred tax – at 1 April 2007 (note (v))			19,200
Current liabilities			81,800
Total equity and liabilities			518,000

The following information is relevant:

(i)   Dexon's statement of profit or loss includes $8 million of revenue for credit sales made on a 'sale or return' basis. At 31 March 2008, customers who had not paid for the goods, had the right to return $2.6 million of them. Dexon applied a mark up on cost of 30% on all these sales. In the past, Dexon's customers have sometimes returned goods under this type of agreement.

(ii)   The non-current assets have not been depreciated for the year ended 31 March 2008.

        Dexon has a policy of revaluing its land and buildings at the end of each accounting year. The values in the above statement of financial position are as at 1 April 2007 when the buildings had a remaining life of fifteen years. A qualified surveyor has valued the land and buildings at 31 March 2008 at $180 million.

        Plant is depreciated at 20% on the reducing balance basis.

(iii)   The investments at fair value through profit and loss are held in a fund whose value changes directly in proportion to a specified market index. At 1 April 2007 the relevant index was 1,200 and at 31 March 2008 it was 1,296.

(iv)   In late March 2008 the directors of Dexon discovered a material fraud perpetrated by the company's credit controller that had been continuing for some time. Investigations revealed that a total of $4 million of the trade receivables as shown in the statement of financial position at 31 March 2008 had in fact been paid and the money had been stolen by the credit controller. An analysis revealed that $1.5 million had been stolen in the year to 31 March 2007 with the rest being stolen in the current year. Dexon is not insured for this loss and it cannot be recovered from the credit controller, nor is it deductible for tax purposes.

(v)   During the year the company's taxable temporary differences increased by $10 million of which $6 million related to the revaluation of the property. The deferred tax relating to the remainder of the increase in the temporary differences should be taken to the statement of profit or loss. The applicable income tax rate is 20%.

(vi)   The above figures do not include the estimated provision for income tax on the profit for the year ended 31 March 2008. After allowing for any adjustments required in items (i) to (iv), the directors have estimated the provision at $11.4 million (this is in addition to the deferred tax effects of item (v)).

(vii) On 1 September 2007 there was a fully subscribed rights issue of one new share for every four held at a price of $1.20 each. The proceeds of the issue have been received and the issue of the shares has been correctly accounted for in the above statement of financial position.

(viii) In May 2007 a dividend of 4 cents per share was paid. In November 2007 (after the rights issue in item (vii) above) a further dividend of 3 cents per share was paid. Both dividends have been correctly accounted for in the above statement of financial position.

Required:

Taking into account any adjustments required by items (i) to (viii) above:

(a) **Prepare a statement showing the recalculation of Dexon's profit for the year ended 31 March 2008.** **(8 marks)**

(b) **Prepare the statement of changes in equity of Dexon for the year ended 31 March 2008.** **(8 marks)**

(c) **Redraft the statement of financial position of Dexon as at 31 March 2008. (9 marks)**

Note: **Notes to the financial statements are NOT required.**

(Total: 25 marks)

35 TOURMALET

The following extracted balances relate to Tourmalet at 30 September 20X3:

	$000	$000
Ordinary shares of 20 cents each		50,000
Retained earnings at 1 October 20X2		61,800
Revaluation reserve at 1 October 20X2		18,500
6% Redeemable preference shares 20X5 (redeemable 20X8)		30,000
Trade payables		35,300
Tax		2,100
Land and buildings – at valuation (note (iii))	150,000	
Plant and equipment – cost (note (v))	98,600	
Investment property – valuation at 1 October 20X2 (note (iv))	10,000	
Depreciation 1 October 20X2 – land and buildings		9,000
Depreciation 1 October 20X2 – plant and equipment		24,600
Trade receivables	31,200	
Inventory – 1 October 20X2	26,550	
Bank	3,700	
Revenue (note (i))		313,000
Investment income (from properties)		1,200
Purchases	158,450	
Finance lease rental	14,000	
Distribution expenses	26,400	
Administration expenses	23,200	
Interim preference dividend	900	
Ordinary dividend paid	2,500	
	545,500	545,500

The following notes are relevant:

(i) Revenue includes $50 million for an item of plant sold at fair value on 1 October 20X2. The plant had a book value of $40 million at the date of its sale, which was charged to cost of sales. On the same date, Tourmalet entered into an agreement to lease back the plant for the next five years (being the estimated remaining life of the plant) at a cost of $14 million per annum payable annually in arrears. An arrangement of this type is deemed to have a financing cost of 12% per annum. No depreciation has been charged on the item of plant in the current year.

(ii) The inventory at 30 September 20X3 was valued at cost of $28.5 million. This includes $4.5 million of slow moving goods. Tourmalet is trying to sell these to another retailer but has not been successful in obtaining a reasonable offer. The best price it has been offered is $2 million.

(iii) On 1 October 19W9 Tourmalet had its land and buildings revalued by a firm of surveyors at $150 million, with $30 million of this attributed to the land. At that date the remaining life of the building was estimated to be 40 years. These figures were incorporated into the company's books. There has been no significant change in property values since the revaluation. $500,000 of the revaluation reserve will be realized in the current year as a result of the depreciation of the buildings.

(iv) Details of the investment property are:

Value – 1 October 20X2 $10 million

Value – 30 September 20X3 $9.8 million

The company adopts the fair value method in IAS 40 *Investment Property* of valuing its investment property.

(v) Plant and equipment (other than that referred to in note (i) above) is depreciated at 20% per annum on the reducing balance basis. All depreciation is to be charged to cost of sales.

(vi) The above balances contain the results of Tourmalet's car retailing operations which ceased on 31 December 20X2 due to mounting losses. The results of the car retailing operation, which is to be treated as a discontinued operation, for the year to 30 September 20X3 are:

	$000
Sales	15,200
Cost of sales	16,000
Operating expenses	3,200

The operating expenses are included in administration expenses in the trial balance.

Tourmalet is still paying rentals for the lease of its car showrooms. The rentals are included in operating expenses. Tourmalet is hoping to use the premises as an expansion of its administration offices. This is dependent on obtaining planning permission from the local authority for the change of use, however this is very difficult to obtain. Failing this, the best option would be early termination of the lease which will cost $1.5 million in penalties. This amount has not been provided for.

(vii) The balance on the taxation account in the trial balance is the result of the settlement of the previous year's tax charge. The directors have estimated the provision for income tax for the year to 30 September 20X3 at $9.2 million.

Required:

(a)   Comment on the substance of the sale of the plant and the directors' treatment of it.   **(5 marks)**

(b)   Prepare the statement of profit or loss and other comprehensive income **(17 marks)**

(c)   Prepare a statement of changes in equity for Tourmalet for the year to 30 September 20X3 in accordance with current International Accounting Standards.   **(3 marks)**

Note: **A statement of financial position is NOT required. Disclosure notes are NOT required.**

(Total: 25 marks)

36   HARRINGTON

Reproduced below are the draft financial statements of Harrington, a public company, for the year to 31 March 20X5:

Statement of profit or loss – Year to 31 March 20X5

	$000
Revenue (note (i))	13,700
Cost of sales (note (ii))	(9,200)
Gross profit	4,500
Operating expenses	(2,400)
Loan note interest paid (refer to statement of financial position)	(25)
Profit before tax	2,075
Income tax expense (note (vi))	(55)
Profit for the period	2,020

Statement of financial position as at 31 March 20X5

	$000	$000
Property, plant and equipment (note (iii))		6,270
Investments (note (iv))		1,200
		7,470
Current assets		
Inventory	1,750	
Trade receivables	2,450	
Bank	350	4,550
Total assets		12,020
Equity and liabilities:		
Ordinary shares of 25c each (note (v))		2,000
Reserves:		
Share premium		600
Retained earnings – 1 April 20X4	2,990	
– Year to 31 March 20X5	2,020	
– dividends paid	(500)	4,510
		7,110
Non-current liabilities		
10% loan note (issued 20X2)	500	
Deferred tax (note (vi))	280	780
Current liabilities		
Trade payables		4,130
		12,020

The company policy for ALL depreciation is that it is charged to cost of sales and a full year's charge is made in the year of acquisition or completion and none in the year of disposal.

The following matters are relevant:

(i)   Included in revenue is $300,000 being the sale proceeds of an item of plant that was sold in January 20X5. The plant had originally cost $900,000 and had been depreciated by $630,000 at the date of its sale. Other than recording the proceeds in sales and cash, no other accounting entries for the disposal of the plant have been made. All plant is depreciated at 25% per annum on the reducing balance basis.

(ii) On 31 December 20X4 the company completed the construction of a new warehouse. The construction was achieved using the company's own resources as follows:

	$000
Purchased materials	150
Direct labour	800
Supervision	65
Design and planning costs	20

Included in the above figures are $10,000 for materials and $25,000 for labour costs that were effectively lost due to the foundations being too close to a neighbouring property. All the above costs are included in cost of sales. The building was brought into immediate use on completion and has an estimated life of 20 years (straight-line depreciation).

(iii) Details of the other property, plant and equipment at 31 March 20X5 are:

	$000	$000
Land at cost		1,000
Buildings at cost	4,000	
Less accumulated depreciation at 31 March 20X4	(800)	3,200
Plant at cost	5,200	
Less accumulated depreciation at 31 March 20X4	(3,130)	2,070
		6,270

At the beginning of the current year (1 April 20X4), Harrington had an open market basis valuation of its properties (excluding the warehouse in note (ii) above). Land was valued at $1.2 million and the property at $4.8 million. The directors wish these values to be incorporated into the financial statements. The properties had an estimated remaining life of 20 years at the date of the valuation (straight-line depreciation is used). Harrington makes a transfer to realized profits in respect of the excess depreciation on revalued assets.

Note: Depreciation for the year to 31 March 20X5 has not yet been accounted for in the draft financial statements.

(iv) The investments are in quoted companies that are carried at their stock market values and are classified as at fair value through profit or loss. The value shown in the statement of financial position is that at 31 March 20X4 and during the year to 31 March 20X5 the investments have risen in value by an average of 10%. Harrington has not reflected this increase in its financial statements.

(v) On 1 October 20X4 there had been a fully subscribed rights issue of 1 for 4 at 60c. This has been recorded in the above statement of financial position.

(vi) Income tax on the profits for the year to 31 March 20X5 is estimated at $260,000. The figure in the statement of profit or loss is the underprovision for income tax for the year to 31 March 20X4. The carrying value of Harrington's net assets is $1.4 million more than their tax base at 31 March 20X5. The income tax rate is 25%.

Required:

(a) Prepare a restated statement of profit or loss and other comprehensive income for the year to 31 March 20X5 reflecting the information in notes (i) to (vi) above.

(9 marks)

(b) Prepare a statement of changes in equity for the year to 31 March 20X5.   (6 marks)

(c) Prepare a restated statement of financial position at 31 March 20X5 reflecting the information in notes (i) to (vi) above.   (10 marks)

(Total: 25 marks)

37   TINTAGEL   *Online question assistance*

Reproduced below is the draft statement of financial position of Tintagel as at 31 March 20X4.

	$000	$000
Non-current assets (note (i))		
Freehold property		126,000
Plant		110,000
Investment property at 1 April 20X3 (note (ii))		15,000
		251,000
Current assets		
Inventory (note (iii))	60,400	
Trade receivables and prepayments	31,200	
Bank	13,800	105,400
Total assets		356,400
Equity and liabilities		
Ordinary shares of 25c each		150,000
Reserves:		
Share premium	10,000	
Retained earnings – 1 April 20X3	52,500	
Retained earnings – Year to 31 March 20X4	47,500	110,000
		260,000

	$000	$000
Non-current liabilities		
Deferred tax – at 1 April 20X3 (note (v))	.	18,700
Current liabilities		
Trade payables (note (iii))	47,400	
Provision for plant overhaul (note (iv))	12,000	
Taxation	4,200	
	———	63,600
Suspense account (note (vi))		14,100
		———
Total equity and liabilities		356,400
		———

Notes

(i) The statement of profit or loss has been charged with $3.2 million being the first of four equal annual rental payments for an item of excavating plant. This first payment was made on 1 April 20X3. Tintagel has been advised that this is a finance lease with an implicit interest rate of 10% per annum. The plant had a fair value of $11.2 million at the inception of the lease.

   None of the non-current assets have been depreciated for the current year. The freehold property should be depreciated at 2% on its cost of $130 million, the leased plant is depreciated at 25% per annum on a straight-line basis and the non-leased plant is depreciated at 20% on the reducing balance basis.

(ii) Tintagel adopts the fair value model for its investment property. Its value at 31 March 20X4 has been assessed by a qualified surveyor at $12.4 million.

(iii) During an inventory count on 31 March 20X4 items that had cost $6 million were identified as being either damaged or slow moving. It is estimated that they will only realize $4 million in total, on which sales commission of 10% will be payable. An invoice for materials delivered on 12 March 20X4 for $500,000 has been discovered. It has not been recorded in Tintagel's bookkeeping system, although the materials were included in the inventory count.

(iv) Tintagel operates some heavy excavating plant which requires a major overhaul every three years. The overhaul is estimated to cost $18 million and is due to be carried out in April 20X5. The provision of $12 million represents two annual amounts of $6 million made in the years to 31 March 20X3 and 20X4.

(v) The deferred tax provision required at 31 March 20X4 has been calculated at $22.5 million.

(vi) The suspense account contains the credit entry relating to the issue on 1 October 20X3 of a $15 million 8% loan note. It was issued at a discount of 5% and incurred direct issue costs of $150,000. It is redeemable after four years at a premium of 10%. Interest is payable six months in arrears. The first payment of interest has not been accrued and is due on 1 April 20X4. The effective interest rate on the loan note is 6% per half year.

Required:

(a) Commencing with the retained earnings figures in the above statement of financial position ($52.5 million and $47.5 million), prepare a schedule of adjustments required to these figures taking into account any adjustments required by notes (i) to (vi) above. **(11 marks)**

(b) Redraft the statement of financial position of Tintagel as at 31 March 20X4 taking into account the adjustments required in notes (i) to (vi) above. **(14 marks)**

(Total: 25 marks)

Online question assistance

38 CAVERN

The following trial balance relates to Cavern as at 30 September 2010:

	$000	$000
Equity shares of 20 cents each (note (i))		50,000
8% loan note (note (ii))		30,600
Retained earnings – 30 September 2009		15,100
Revaluation reserve		7,000
Share premium		11,000
Land and buildings at valuation – 30 September 2009:		
Land ($7 million) and building ($36 million) (note (iii))	43,000	
Plant and equipment at cost (note (iii))	67,400	
Accumulated depreciation plant and equipment – 30 September 2009		13,400
Equity investments (note (iv))	15,800	
Inventory at 30 September 2010	19,800	
Trade receivables	29,000	
Bank		4,600
Deferred tax (note (v))		4,000
Trade payables		21,700
Revenue		182,500
Cost of sales	128,500	
Administrative expenses (note (i))	25,000	
Distribution costs	8,500	
Loan note interest paid	2,400	
Bank interest	300	
Investment income		700
Current tax (note (v))	900	
	340,600	340,600

The following notes are relevant:

(i)   Cavern has accounted for a fully subscribed rights issue of equity shares made on 1 April 2010 of one new share for every four in issue at 42 cents each. The company paid ordinary dividends of 3 cents per share on 30 November 2009 and 5 cents per share on 31 May 2010. The dividend payments are included in administrative expenses in the trial balance.

(ii)   The 8% loan note was issued on 1 October 2008 at its nominal (face) value of $30 million. The loan note will be redeemed on 30 September 2012 at a premium which gives the loan note an effective finance cost of 10% per annum.

(iii)   Non-current assets:

Cavern revalues its land and building at the end of each accounting year. At 30 September 2010 the relevant value to be incorporated into the financial statements is $41.8 million. The building's remaining life at the beginning of the current year (1 October 2009) was 18 years. Cavern does not make an annual transfer from the revaluation reserve to retained earnings in respect of the realisation of the revaluation surplus. Ignore deferred tax on the revaluation surplus.

Plant and equipment includes an item of plant bought for $10 million on 1 October 2009 that will have a 10-year life (using straight-line depreciation with no residual value). Production using this plant involves toxic chemicals which will cause decontamination costs to be incurred at the end of its life. The present value of these costs using a discount rate of 10% at 1 October 2009 was $4 million. Cavern has not provided any amount for this future decontamination cost. All other plant and equipment is depreciated at 12.5% per annum using the reducing balance method.

No depreciation has yet been charged on any non-current asset for the year ended 30 September 2010. All depreciation is charged to cost of sales.

(iv)   The equity investments had a fair value of $13.5 million on 30 September 2010. There were no acquisitions or disposals of these investments during the year ended 30 September 2010. The equity investments are recorded as fair value through profit or loss in accordance with IFRS 9 *Financial Instruments*.

(v)   A provision for income tax for the year ended 30 September 2010 of $5.6 million is required. The balance on current tax represents the under/over provision of the tax liability for the year ended 30 September 2009. At 30 September 2010 the tax base of Cavern's net assets was $15 million less than their carrying amounts. The movement on deferred tax should be taken to the statement of profit or loss. The income tax rate of Cavern is 25%.

Required:

(a)   Prepare the statement of profit or loss for Cavern for the year ended 30 September 2010.   (11 marks)

(b)   Prepare the statement of changes in equity for Cavern for the year ended 30 September 2010.   (5 marks)

**(c)   Prepare the statement of financial position of Cavern as at 30 September 2010.
                                                                                                        (9 marks)**

Notes to the financial statements are not required.

(Total: 25 marks)

39 CANDEL 🔲 *Walk in the footsteps of a top tutor*

The following trial balance relates to Candel at 30 September 2008:

	$000	$000
Leasehold property – at valuation 1 October 2007 (note (i))	50,000	
Plant and equipment – at cost (note (i))	76,600	
Plant and equipment – accumulated depreciation at 1 October 2007		24,600
Capitalised development expenditure – at 1 October 2007 (note (ii))	20,000	
Development expenditure – accumulated amortisation at 1 October 2007		6,000
Closing inventory at 30 September 2008	20,000	
Trade receivables	43,100	
Bank		1,300
Trade payables and provisions (note (iii))		23,800
Revenue (note (i))		300,000
Cost of sales	204,000	
Distribution costs	14,500	
Administrative expenses (note (iii))	22,200	
Preference dividend paid	800	
Interest on bank borrowings	200	
Equity dividend paid	6,000	
Research and development costs (note (ii))	8,600	
Equity shares of 25 cents each		50,000
8% redeemable preference shares of $1 each (note (iv))		20,000
Retained earnings at 1 October 2007		24,500
Deferred tax (note (v))		5,800
Leasehold property revaluation reserve		10,000
	466,000	466,000

The following notes are relevant:

(i) **Non-current assets – tangible:**

The leasehold property had a remaining life of 20 years at 1 October 2007. The company's policy is to revalue its property at each year end and at 30 September 2008 it was valued at $43 million. Ignore deferred tax on the revaluation.

On 1 October 2007 an item of plant was disposed of for $2.5 million cash. The proceeds have been treated as sales revenue by Candel. The plant is still included in the above trial balance figures at its cost of $8 million and accumulated depreciation of $4 million (to the date of disposal).

All plant is depreciated at 20% per annum using the reducing balance method.

Depreciation and amortisation of all non-current assets is charged to cost of sales.

(ii)   **Non-current assets – intangible:**

In addition to the capitalised development expenditure (of $20 million), further research and development costs were incurred on a new project which commenced on 1 October 2007. The research stage of the new project lasted until 31 December 2007 and incurred $1.4 million of costs. From that date the project incurred development costs of $800,000 per month. On 1 April 2008 the directors became confident that the project would be successful and yield a profit well in excess of its costs. The project is still in development at 30 September 2008.

Capitalised development expenditure is amortised at 20% per annum using the straight-line method. All expensed research and development is charged to cost of sales.

(iii)   Candel is being sued by a customer for $2 million for breach of contract over a cancelled order. Candel has obtained legal opinion that there is a 20% chance that Candel will lose the case. Accordingly Candel has provided $400,000 ($2 million × 20%) included in administrative expenses in respect of the claim. The unrecoverable legal costs of defending the action are estimated at $100,000. These have not been provided for as the legal action will not go to court until next year.

(iv)   The preference shares were issued on 1 April 2008 at par. They are redeemable at a large premium which gives them an effective finance cost of 12% per annum.

(v)   The directors have estimated the provision for income tax for the year ended 30 September 2008 at $11.4 million. The required deferred tax provision at 30 September 2008 is $6 million.

Required:

(a)   **Prepare the statement of profit or loss and other comprehensive income for the year ended 30 September 2008.**   **(12 marks)**

(b)   Prepare the statement of changes in equity for the year ended 30 September 2008.
                                                                                         (3 marks)

(c)   **Prepare the statement of financial position as at 30 September 2008.**   **(10 marks)**

Note: Notes to the financial statements are not required.

                                                                              (Total: 25 marks)

UK SYLLABUS FOCUS ONLY

A UK element to part (b) could instead ask you to:

"Explain the treatment of revaluation losses under UK GAAP and state how the treatment of development costs might differ to the international treatment".

---

40 PRICEWELL

Timed question with Online tutor debrief

The following trial balance relates to Pricewell at 31 March 2009:

	$000	$000
Leasehold property – at valuation 31 March 2008 (note (i))	25,200	
Plant and equipment (owned) – at cost (note (i))	46,800	
Plant and equipment (leased) – at cost (note (i))	20,000	
Accumulated depreciation at 31 March 2008		12,800
Owned plant and equipment		
Leased plant and equipment		5,000
Finance lease payment (paid on 31 March 2009) (note (i))	6,000	
Obligations under finance lease at 1 April 2008 (note (i))		15,600
Construction contract (note (ii))	14,300	
Inventory at 31 March 2009	28,200	
Trade receivables	33,100	
Bank	5,500	
Trade payables		33,400
Revenue (note (iii))		310,000
Cost of sales (note (iii))	234,500	
Distribution costs	19,500	
Administrative expenses	27,500	
Preference dividend paid (note (iv))	2,400	
Equity dividend paid	8,000	
Equity shares of 50 cents each		40,000
6% redeemable preference shares at 31 March 2008 (note (iv))		41,600
Retained earnings at 31 March 2008		4,900
Current tax (note (v))	700	
Deferred tax (note (v))		8,400
	471,700	471,700

The following notes are relevant:

(i) *Non-current assets:*

The 15 year leasehold property was acquired on 1 April 2007 at cost $30 million. The company policy is to revalue the property at market value at each year end. The valuation in the trial balance of $25.2 million as at 31 March 2008 led to an impairment charge of $2.8 million which was reported in the statement of profit or loss and other comprehensive income of the previous year (i.e. year ended 31 March 2008). At 31 March 2009 the property was valued at $24.9 million.

Owned plant is depreciated at 25% per annum using the reducing balance method.

The leased plant was acquired on 1 April 2007. The rentals are $6 million per annum for four years payable in arrears on 31 March each year. The interest rate implicit in the lease is 8% per annum. Leased plant is depreciated at 25% per annum using the straight-line method.

No depreciation has yet been charged on any non-current assets for the year ended 31 March 2009. All depreciation is charged to cost of sales.

(ii) On 1 October 2008 Pricewell entered into a contract to construct a bridge over a river. The agreed price of the bridge is $50 million and construction was expected to be completed on 30 September 2010. The $14.3 million in the trial balance is:

	$000
Materials, labour and overheads	12,000
Specialist plant acquired 1 October 2008	8,000
Payment from customer	(5,700)
	14,300

The sales value of the work done at 31 March 2009 has been agreed at $22 million and the estimated cost to complete (excluding plant depreciation) is $10 million. The specialist plant will have no residual value at the end of the contract and should be depreciated on a monthly basis. Pricewell recognises profits on uncompleted contracts on the percentage of completion basis as determined by the agreed work to date compared to the total contract price.

(iii) Pricewell's revenue includes $8 million for goods it sold acting as an agent for Trilby. Pricewell earned a commission of 20% on these sales and remitted the difference of $6.4 million (included in cost of sales) to Trilby.

(iv) The 6% preference shares were issued on 1 April 2007 at par for $40 million. They have an effective finance cost of 10% per annum due to a premium payable on their redemption.

(v) The directors have estimated the provision for income tax for the year ended 31 March 2009 at $4.5 million. The required deferred tax provision at 31 March 2009 is $5.6 million; all adjustments to deferred tax should be taken to the statement of profit or loss and other comprehensive income. The balance of current tax in the trial balance represents the under/over provision of the income tax liability for the year ended 31 March 2008.

Required:

(a) **Prepare the statement of profit or loss and other comprehensive income for the year ended 31 March 2009.** **(12 marks)**

(b) **Prepare the statement of financial position as at 31 March 2009.** **(13 marks)**

Note: **A statement of changes in equity and notes to the financial statements are not required.**

(Total: 25 marks)

Calculate your allowed time, allocate the time to the separate parts

---

UK SYLLABUS FOCUS ONLY

A UK element to this question could ask you to:

"Show how the amounts due from/to customers would be disclosed in the statement of financial position in accordance with SSAP 9 Stocks and long-term contracts."

---

41 SANDOWN

The following trial balance relates to Sandown at 30 September 2009:

	$000	$000
Revenue (note (i))		380,000
Cost of sales	246,800	
Distribution costs	17,400	
Administrative expenses (note (ii))	50,500	
Loan interest paid (note (iii))	1,000	
Investment income		1,300
Current tax (note (v))	2,100	
Freehold property – at cost 1 October 2000 (note (vi))	63,000	
Plant and equipment – at cost (note (vi))	42,200	
Brand – at cost 1 October 2005 (note (vi))	30,000	
Accumulated depreciation – 1 October 2008 – building		8,000
– plant and equipment		19,700
Accumulated amortisation – 1 October 2008 – brand		9,000
Investment property (note (iv))	26,500	
Inventory at 30 September 2009	38,000	
Trade receivables	44,500	
Bank	8,000	
Trade payables		42,900
Equity shares of 20 cents each		50,000
Equity option		2,000
5% convertible loan note 2012 (note (iii))		18,440
Retained earnings at 1 October 2008		33,260
Deferred tax (note (v))		5,400
	———	———
	570,000	570,000
	———	———

The following notes are relevant:

(i)   Sandown's revenue includes $16 million for goods sold to Pending on 1 October 2008. The terms of the sale are that Sandown will incur ongoing service and support costs of $1.2 million per annum for three years after the sale. Sandown normally makes a gross profit of 40% on such servicing and support work. Ignore the time value of money.

(ii)   Administrative expenses include an equity dividend of 4.8 cents per share paid during the year.

(iii) The 5% convertible loan note was issued for proceeds of $20 million on 1 October 2007. It has an effective interest rate of 8% due to the value of its conversion option.

(iv)   The investment property is considered to have a fair value of $29 million at 30 September 2009. Sandown uses the fair value model allowed in IAS 40 to account for investment property.

(v)   The balance on current tax represents the under/over provision of the tax liability for the year ended 30 September 2008. The directors have estimated the provision for income tax for the year ended 30 September 2009 at $16.2 million. At 30 September 2009 the carrying amounts of Sandown's net assets were $13 million in excess of their tax base. The income tax rate of Sandown is 30%.

(vi) Non-current assets:

The freehold property has a land element of $13 million. The building element is being depreciated on a straight-line basis.

Plant and equipment is depreciated at 40% per annum using the reducing balance method.

Sandown's brand in the trial balance relates to a product line that received bad publicity during the year which led to falling sales revenues. An impairment review was conducted on 1 April 2009 which concluded that, based on estimated future sales, the brand had a value in use of $12 million and a remaining life of only three years. However, on the same date as the impairment review, Sandown received an offer to purchase the brand for $15 million. Prior to the impairment review, it was being depreciated using the straight-line method over a 10-year life.

No depreciation/amortisation has yet been charged on any non-current asset for the year ended 30 September 2009. Depreciation, amortisation and impairment charges are all charged to cost of sales.

Required:

(a)   **Prepare the statement of profit or loss for Sandown for the year ended 30 September 2009.**   **(13 marks)**

(b)   **Prepare the statement of financial position of Sandown as at 30 September 2009.**   **(12 marks)**

Notes to the financial statements are not required.

A statement of changes in equity is not required.

(Total: 25 marks)

42   DUNE

The following trial balance relates to Dune at 31 March 2010:

	$000	$000
Equity shares of $1 each		60,000
5% loan note (note (i))		20,000
Retained earnings at 1 April 2009		38,400
Leasehold (15 years) property – at cost (note (ii))	45,000	
Plant and equipment – at cost (note (ii))	67,500	
Accumulated depreciation – 1 April 2009 – leasehold property		6,000
– plant and equipment		23,500
Investments at fair value through profit or loss (note (iii))	26,500	
Inventory at 31 March 2010	48,000	
Trade receivables	40,700	
Bank		4,500
Deferred tax (note (v))		6,000
Trade payables		52,000
Revenue (note (iv))		400,000
Cost of sales	294,000	
Construction contract (note (vi))	20,000	
Distribution costs	26,400	
Administrative expenses (note (i))	34,200	
Dividend paid	10,000	
Loan note interest paid (six months)	500	
Bank interest	200	
Investment income		1,200
Current tax (note (v))		1,400
	613,000	613,000

The following notes are relevant:

(i)   The 5% loan note was issued on 1 April 2009 at its nominal (face) value of $20 million. The direct costs of the issue were $500,000 and these have been charged to administrative expenses. The loan note will be redeemed on 31 March 2012 at a substantial premium. The effective finance cost of the loan note is 10% per annum.

(ii)   Non-current assets:

In order to fund a new project, on 1 October 2009 the company decided to sell its leasehold property. From that date it commenced a short-term rental of an equivalent property. The leasehold property is being marketed by a property agent at a price of $40 million, which was considered a reasonably achievable price at that date. The expected costs to sell have been agreed at $500,000. Recent market transactions suggest that actual selling prices achieved for this type of property in the current market conditions are 15% less than the value at which they are marketed. At 31 March 2010 the property had not been sold.

Plant and equipment is depreciated at 15% per annum using the reducing balance method.

No depreciation/amortisation has yet been charged on any non-current asset for the year ended 31 March 2010. Depreciation, amortisation and impairment charges are all charged to cost of sales.

(iii)   The investments at fair value through profit or loss had a fair value of $28 million on 31 March 2010. There were no purchases or disposals of any of these investments during the year.

(iv)   It has been discovered that goods with a cost of $6 million, which had been correctly included in the count of the inventory at 31 March 2010, had been invoiced in April 2010 to customers at a gross profit of 25% on sales, but included in the revenue (and receivables) of the year ended 31 March 2010.

(v)   A provision for income tax for the year ended 31 March 2010 of $12 million is required. The balance on current tax represents the under/over provision of the tax liability for the year ended 31 March 2009. At 31 March 2010 the tax base of Dune's net assets was $14 million less than their carrying amounts. The income tax rate of Dune is 30%.

(vi)   The details of the construction contract are:

	Costs to 31 March 2010	Further costs to complete
	$000	$000
Materials	5,000	8,000
Labour and other direct costs	3,000	7,000
	8,000	15,000
Plant acquired at cost	12,000	
Per trial balance	20,000	

The contract commenced on 1 October 2009 and is scheduled to take 18 months to complete. The agreed contract price is fixed at $40 million. Specialised plant was purchased at the start of the contract for $12 million. It is expected to have a residual value of $3 million at the end of the contract and should be depreciated using the straight-line method on a monthly basis. An independent surveyor has assessed that the contract is 30% complete at 31 March 2010. The customer has not been invoiced for any progress payments. The outcome of the contract is deemed to be reasonably certain as at the year end.

Required:

(a)   Prepare the statement of profit or loss for Dune for the year ended 31 March 2010.

(13 marks)

(b)   Prepare the statement of financial position for Dune as at 31 March 2010.

(12 marks)

Notes to the financial statements are not required. A statement of changes in equity is not required.

(Total: 25 marks)

UK SYLLABUS FOCUS ONLY

A UK element to this question could ask you to:

"Outline how the held for sale asset and the construction contract would be accounted for under UK GAAP".

---

43   JKL

JKL is a listed entity preparing financial statements to 31 August. At 1 September 20X3, JKL had 6,000,000 50¢ shares in issue. On 1 February 20X4, the entity made a rights issue of 1 for 4 at 125¢ per share; the issue was successful and all rights were taken up. The market price of one share immediately prior to the issue was 145¢ per share. Profit after tax for the year ended 31 August 20X4 were $2,763,000.

Several years ago, JKL issued a convertible loan of $2,000,000. The loan carries an effective interest rate of 7% and its terms of conversion (which are at the option of the stockholder) are as follows:

For each $100 of loan stock:

Conversion at 31 August 20X8   105 shares

Conversion at 31 August 20X9   103 shares

JKL is subject to an income tax rate of 32%.

Required:

(a)   Calculate basic earnings per share and diluted earnings per share for the year ended 31 August 20X4.   **(7 marks)**

(b)   The IASB's *Conceptual Framework for Financial Reporting* states that the objective of financial statements is to provide information that is:

'useful to a wide range of users in making economic decisions'.

Explain to a holder of ordinary shares in JKL both the usefulness and limitations of the diluted earnings per share figure.   **(3 marks)**

(Total: 10 marks)

BUSINESS COMBINATIONS

44   HIGHMOOR   *Walk in the footsteps of a top tutor*

Highmoor, a public listed company, acquired 80% of Slowmoor's ordinary shares on 1 October 20X2. Highmoor paid an immediate $1.50 per share in cash and agreed to pay a further $0.60 per share in two years' time if Slowmoor made a profit within two years of its acquisition. Highmoor has not yet recorded the contingent consideration. The fair value of contingent consideration is to be measured as the present value of the future cash flow. Highmoor's cost of capital is 10% per annum.

The statements of financial position of the two companies at 30 September 20X3 are shown below:

	Highmoor		Slowmoor	
	$ million	$ million	$ million	$ million
Property, plant and equipment		585		172
Investments (note (ii))		225		13
Software (note (iii))		nil		40
		810		225
Current assets				
Inventory	85		42	
Trade receivables	95		36	
Tax asset	nil		80	
Bank	20	200	nil	158
Total assets		1,010		383
Equity and liabilities				
Equity:				
Ordinary shares of $1 each		400		100
Retained earnings – 1 October 20X2	230		150	
– profit/loss for year	100	330	(35)	115
		730		215
Non-current liabilities				
12% loan note	nil		35	
16% Inter-company loan (note (ii))	nil	nil	45	80
Current liabilities				
Trade payables	210		71	
Taxation	70		nil	
Overdraft	nil	280	17	88
Total equity and liabilities		1,010		383

The following information is relevant:

(i) At the date of acquisition the fair values of Slowmoor's net assets approximated to their book values.

(ii) Included in Highmoor's investments is a loan of $50 million made to Slowmoor on 1 April 20X3. On 28 September 20X3, Slowmoor paid $9 million to Highmoor. This represented interest of $4 million for the year and the balance was a capital repayment. Highmoor had not received nor accounted for the payment, but it had accrued for the loan interest receivable as part of its accounts receivable figure. There are no other intra group balances.

(iii) The software was developed by Highmoor during 20X2 at a total cost of $30 million. It was sold to Slowmoor for $50 million immediately after its acquisition. The software had an estimated life of five years and is being amortized by Slowmoor on a straight-line basis.

(iv) Highmoor's policy is to value the non-controlling interest using the proportionate share of the subsidiary's identifiable net assets.

Note: Work to the nearest $ million.

Required:

(a) Prepare the consolidated statement of financial position of Highmoor as at 30 September 20X3, explaining your treatment of the contingent consideration.

(20 marks)

(b) Describe the circumstances in which the consideration for an acquisition may be less than the share of the assets acquired. Your answer should refer to the particular issues of the above acquisition.

(5 marks)

(Total: 25 marks)

UK SYLLABUS FOCUS ONLY

A UK element to part (b) could instead ask you to:

"How will the negative goodwill be accounted for under UK GAAP, in accordance with FRS 10 *Goodwill and Intangible Assets?*"

---

45   HIGHVELDT   *Walk in the footsteps of a top tutor*

Highveldt, a public listed company, acquired 75% of Samson's ordinary shares on 1 April 20X4. Highveldt paid an immediate $3.50 per share in cash and agreed to pay a further amount of $108 million on 1 April 20X5. Highveldt's cost of capital is 8% per annum. Highveldt has only recorded the cash consideration of $3.50 per share.

The summarized statements of financial position of the two companies at 31 March 20X5 are shown below:

	Highveldt		Samson	
	$ million	$ million	$ million	$ million
Property, plant and equipment (note (i))		420		320
Development costs (note (iv))		Nil		40
Investments (note (ii))		300		20
		720		380
Current assets		133		91
Total assets		853		471
Equity and liabilities:				
Ordinary shares of $1 each		270		80
Reserves:				
Share premium		80		40
Revaluation reserve		45		Nil
Retained earnings – 1 April 20X4	160		134	
– year to 31 March 20X5	190	350	76	210
		745		330
Non-current liabilities				
10% intercompany loan (note (ii))		Nil		60
Current liabilities		108		81
Total equity and liabilities		853		471

The following information is relevant:

(i) Highveldt has a policy of revaluing land and buildings to fair value. At the date of acquisition Samson's land and buildings had a fair value $20 million higher than their book value and at 31 March 20X5 this had increased by a further $4 million (ignore any additional depreciation).

(ii) Included in Highveldt's investments is a loan of $60 million made to Samson at the date of acquisition. Interest is payable annually in arrears. Samson paid the interest due for the year on 31 March 20X5, but Highveldt did not receive this until after the year end. Highveldt has not accounted for the accrued interest from Samson.

(iii) Samson had established a line of products under the brand name of Titanware. Acting on behalf of Highveldt, a firm of specialists, had valued the brand name at a value of $40 million with an estimated life of 10 years as at 1 April 20X4. The brand is not included in Samson's statement of financial position.

(iv) Samson's development project was completed on 30 September 20X4 at a cost of $50 million. $10 million of this had been amortized by 31 March 20X5. Development costs capitalized by Samson at the date of acquisition were $18 million. Highveldt's directors are of the opinion that Samson's development costs do not meet the criteria in IAS 38 Intangible Assets for recognition as an asset.

(v) Samson sold goods to Highveldt during the year at a profit of $6 million, one-third of these goods were still in the inventory of Highveldt at 31 March 20X5.

(vi) Highveldt's policy is to value non-controlling interests using the fair value at the date of acquisition. At this date the fair value of the non-controlling interests was $83 million.

At an impairment test at 31 March 20X5 indicated that it should be written down by $20 million. No other assets were impaired.

Required:

(a) **Calculate the following figures as they would appear in the consolidated statement of financial position of Highveldt at 31 March 20X5:**

    (i) **goodwill;**   **(8 marks)**

    (ii) **non-controlling interest;**   **(4 marks)**

    (iii) **the following consolidated reserves:**

        share premium, revaluation reserve and retained earnings.   **(8 marks)**

    Note: **Show your workings.**

(b) **Explain why consolidated financial statements are useful to the users of financial statements (as opposed to just the parent company's separate (entity) financial statements).**   **(5 marks)**

                                                  (Total: 25 marks)

46 PREMIER ⬛ *Walk in the footsteps of a top tutor*

On 1 June 2010, Premier acquired 80% of the equity share capital of Sanford. The consideration consisted of two elements: a share exchange of three shares in Premier for every five acquired shares in Sanford and the issue of a $100 6% loan note for every 500 shares acquired in Sanford. The share issue has not yet been recorded by Premier, but the issue of the loan notes has been recorded. At the date of acquisition shares in Premier had a market value of $5 each and the shares of Sanford had a stock market price of $3·50 each. Below are the summarised draft financial statements of both companies.

Statements of comprehensive income for the year ended 30 September 2010

	Premier	Sanford
	$000	$000
Revenue	92,500	45,000
Cost of sales	(70,500)	(36,000)
Gross profit	22,000	9,000
Distribution costs	(2,500)	(1,200)
Administrative expenses	(5,500)	(2,400)
Finance costs	(100)	nil
Profit before tax	13,900	5,400
Income tax expense	(3,900)	(1,500)
Profit for the year	10,000	3,900
Other comprehensive income:		
Gain on revaluation of land (note (i))	500	nil
Total comprehensive income	10,500	3,900

Statements of financial position as at 30 September 2010

	Premier	Sanford
Assets		
Non-current assets		
Property, plant and equipment	25,500	13,900
Investments	1,800	nil
	27,300	13,900
Current assets	12,500	2,400
Total assets	39,800	16,300

Equity and liabilities		
Equity		
Equity shares of $1 each	12,000	5,000
Land revaluation reserve – 30 September 2010 (note (i))	2,000	nil
Other equity reserve – 30 September 2009 (note (iv))	500	nil
Retained earnings	12,300	4,500
	26,800	9,500
Non-current liabilities		
6% loan notes	3,000	nil
Current liabilities	10,000	6,800
Total equity and liabilities	39,800	16,300

The following information is relevant:

(i)   At the date of acquisition, the fair values of Sanford's assets were equal to their carrying amounts with the exception of its property. This had a fair value of $1.2 million **below** its carrying amount. This would lead to a reduction of the depreciation charge (in cost of sales) of $50,000 in the post-acquisition period. Sanford has not incorporated this value change into its entity financial statements.

Premier's group policy is to revalue all properties to current value at each year end. On 30 September 2010, the value of Sanford's property was unchanged from its value at acquisition, but the land element of Premier's property had increased in value by $500,000 as shown in other comprehensive income.

(ii)   Sales from Sanford to Premier throughout the year ended 30 September 2010 had consistently been $1 million per month. Sanford made a mark-up on cost of 25% on these sales. Premier had $2 million (at cost to Premier) of inventory that had been supplied in the post-acquisition period by Sanford as at 30 September 2010.

(iii)   Premier had a trade payable balance owing to Sanford of $350,000 as at 30 September 2010. This agreed with the corresponding receivable in Sanford's books.

(iv)   Premier's investments include an investment in shares which at the date of acquisition were classified as fair value through other comprehensive income (FVTOCI). The investments have increased in value by $300,000 during the year. The other equity reserve relates to these investments and is based on their value as at 30 September 2009. There were no acquisitions or disposals of any of these investments during the year ended 30 September 2010.

(v)   Premier's policy is to value the non-controlling interest at fair value at the date of acquisition. For this purpose Sanford's share price at that date can be deemed to be representative of the fair value of the shares held by the non-controlling interest.

(vi)   There has been no impairment of consolidated goodwill.

Required:

(a)   **Prepare the consolidated statement of profit or loss and other comprehensive income for Premier for the year ended 30 September 2010.**   **(9 marks)**

(b)   **Prepare the consolidated statement of financial position for Premier as at 30 September 2010.**   **(16 marks)**

(Total: 25 marks)

47 HAPSBURG   *Walk in the footsteps of a top tutor*

(a) Hapsburg, a public listed company, acquired the following investments:

– On 1 April 20X3, 24 million shares in Sundial. This was by way of an immediate share exchange of two shares in Hapsburg for every three shares in Sundial plus a cash payment of $1 per Sundial share payable on 1 April 20X6. The market price of Hapsburg's shares on 1 April 20X3 was $2 each and the market price of Sundial's shares was $1.50 each.

– On 1 October 20X3, 6 million shares in Aspen paying an immediate $2.50 in cash for each share.

Based on Hapsburg's cost of capital (taken as 10% per annum), $1 receivable in three years' time can be taken to have a present value of $0.75.

Hapsburg has not yet recorded the acquisition of Sundial but it has recorded the investment in Aspen. The summarized statements of financial position at 31 March 20X4 are:

	Hapsburg		Sundial		Aspen	
	$000	$000	$000	$000	$000	$000
Non-current assets						
Property, plant and equipment		41,000		34,800		37,700
Investments		15,000		3,000		nil
		————		————		————
		56,000		37,800		37,700
Current assets						
Inventory	9,900		4,800		7,900	
Trade and other receivables	13,600		8,600		14,400	
Cash	1,200	24,700	3,800	17,200	nil	22,300
		————		————		————
Total assets		**80,700**		**55,000**		**60,000**
		————		————		————
Equity and liabilities						
Capital and reserves						
Ordinary shares $1 each		20,000		30,000		20,000
Reserves:						
Share premium	8,000		2,000		nil	
Retained earnings	10,600	18,600	8,500	10,500	8,000	8,000
		————		————		————
		38,600		40,500		28,000
Non-current liabilities						
10% loan note		16,000		4,200		12,000
Current liabilities						
Trade and other payables	16,500		6,900		13,600	
Bank overdraft	nil		Nil		4,500	
Taxation	9,600	26,100	3,400	10,300	1,900	20,000
		————		————		————
Total equity and liabilities		**80,700**		**55,000**		**60,000**

The following information is relevant:

(i)   Below is a summary of the results of a fair value exercise for Sundial carried out at the date of acquisition:

Asset	Carrying value at acquisition	Fair value at acquisition	Notes
	$000	$000	
Plant	10,000	15,000	remaining life at acquisition four years
Investments	3,000	4,500	no change in value since acquisition

The book values of the net assets of Aspen at the date of acquisition approximated to their fair values.

(ii)   The profits of Sundial and Aspen for the year to 31 March 20X4, as reported in their entity financial statements, were $4.5 million and $6 million respectively. No dividends have been paid by any of the companies during the year. All profits are deemed to accrue evenly throughout the year.

(iii)   In January 20X4 Aspen sold goods to Hapsburg at a selling price of $4 million. These goods had cost Aspen $2.4 million. Hapsburg had $2.5 million (at cost to Hapsburg) of these goods still in inventory at 31 March 20X4.

(iii)   All depreciation is charged on a straight-line basis.

(iv)   Hapsburg's policy is to value the non-controlling interest at fair value at the date of acquisition. For this purpose, the share price of Sundial should be used.

(v)   Impairment tests on 31 March 20X4 concluded that consolidated goodwill of Sundial should be written down by $3.5 million and that the investment in Aspen was now worth $15 million.

Required:

Prepare the consolidated statement of financial position of Hapsburg as at 31 March 20X4.   **(20 marks)**

(b)   Some commentators have criticized the use of equity accounting on the basis that it can be used as a form of off statement of financial position financing.

Required:

Explain the reasoning behind the use of equity accounting and discuss the above comment.   **(5 marks)**

(Total: 25 marks)

Online question assistance

48 HOSTERLING *Walk in the footsteps of a top tutor*

Hosterling purchased the following equity investments:

On 1 October 20X5: 80% of the issued share capital of Sunlee. The acquisition was through a share exchange of three shares in Hosterling for every five shares in Sunlee. The market price of Hosterling's shares at 1 October 20X5 was $5 per share.

On 1 July 20X6: 6 million shares in Amber paying $3 per share in cash and issuing to Amber's shareholders 6% (actual and effective rate) loan notes on the basis of $100 loan note for every 100 shares acquired.

The summarized statements of profit or loss for the three companies for the year ended 30 September 20X6 are:

	Hosterling	Sunlee	Amber
	$000	$000	$000
Revenue	105,000	62,000	50,000
Cost of sales	(68,000)	(36,500)	(61,000)
Gross profit/(loss)	37,000	25,500	(11,000)
Other income (note (i))	400	nil	nil
Distribution costs	(4,000)	(2,000)	(4,500)
Administrative expenses	(7,500)	(7,000)	(8,500)
Finance costs	(1,200)	(900)	nil
Profit/(loss) before tax	24,700	15,600	(24,000)
Income tax (expense)/credit	(8,700)	(2,600)	4,000
Profit/(loss) for the period	16,000	13,000	(20,000)

The following information is relevant:

(i)   The other income is a dividend received from Sunlee on 31 March 20X6.

(ii)   The details of Sunlee's and Amber's share capital and reserves at 1 October 20X5 were:

	Sunlee	Amber
	$000	$000
Equity shares of $1 each	20,000	15,000
Retained earnings	18,000	35,000

(iii)   A fair value exercise was carried out at the date of acquisition of Sunlee with the following results:

	Carrying amount	Fair value	Remaining life (straight line)
	$000	$000	
Intellectual property	18,000	22,000	still in development
Land	17,000	20,000	not applicable
Plant	30,000	35,000	five years

The fair values have not been reflected in Sunlee's financial statements.

Plant depreciation is included in cost of sales.

No fair value adjustments were required on the acquisition of the shares in Amber.

(iv)   In the year ended 30 September 20X6 Hosterling sold goods to Sunlee at a selling price of $18 million. Hosterling made a profit of cost plus 25% on these sales. $7.5 million (at cost to Sunlee) of these goods were still in the inventories of Sunlee at 30 September 20X6.

(v)   Hosterling's policy is to value the non-controlling interest using the proportionate share of the subsidiary's identifiable net assets.

Impairment tests for both Sunlee and Amber were conducted on 30 September 20X6. They concluded that the goodwill of Sunlee should be written down by $2 million and, due to its losses since acquisition, the investment in Amber was worth $21.5 million.

(vi)   All trading profits and losses are deemed to accrue evenly throughout the year.

Required:

(a)   **Calculate the goodwill arising on the acquisition of Sunlee at 1 October 20X5.**

(5 marks)

(b)   **Calculate the carrying amount of the investment in Amber at 30 September 20X6 under the equity method prior to the impairment test.**   **(4 marks)**

(c)   **Prepare the consolidated statement of profit or loss for the Hosterling Group for the year ended 30 September 20X6.**   **(16 marks)**

(Total: 25 marks)

49 PARENTIS *Walk in the footsteps of a top tutor*

Parentis, a public listed company, acquired 600 million equity shares in Offspring on 1 April 2006. The purchase consideration was made up of:

- a share exchange of one share in Parentis for two shares in Offspring

- the issue of $100 10% loan note for every 500 shares acquired; and

- a deferred cash payment of 11 cents per share acquired payable on 1 April 2007.

Parentis has only recorded the issue of the loan notes. The value of each Parentis share at the date of acquisition was 75 cents and Parentis has a cost of capital of 10% per annum.

The statement of financial positions of the two companies at 31 March 2007 are shown below:

	Parentis		Offspring	
	$ million	$ million	$ million	$ million
Assets				
Property, plant and equipment (note (i))		640		340
Investments		120		Nil
Intellectual property (note (ii))		Nil		30
		———		———
		760		370
Current assets				
Inventory (note (iii))	76		22	
Trade receivables (note (iii))	84		44	
Bank	Nil	160	4	70
	———	———	———	———
Total assets		920		440
		———		———
Equity and liabilities				
Equity shares of 25 cents each		300		200
Retained earnings				
– 1 April 2006	210		120	
– year ended 31 March 2007	90	300	20	140
	———	———	———	———
		600		340
Non-current liabilities				
10% loan notes		120		20
Current liabilities				
Trade payables (note (iii))	130		57	
Current tax payable	45		23	
Overdraft	25	200	Nil	80
	———	———	———	———
Total equity and liabilities		920		440
		———		———

The following information is relevant:

(i)   At the date of acquisition the fair values of Offspring's net assets were approximately equal to their carrying amounts with the exception of its properties. These properties had a fair value of $40 million in excess of their carrying amounts which would create additional depreciation of $2 million in the post acquisition period to 31 March 2007. The fair values have not been reflected in Offspring's statement of financial position.

(ii)   The intellectual property is a system of encryption designed for internet use. Offspring has been advised that government legislation (passed since acquisition) has now made this type of encryption illegal. Offspring will receive $10 million in compensation from the government.

(iii)   Offspring sold Parentis goods for $15 million in the post acquisition period. $5 million of these goods are included in the inventory of Parentis at 31 March 2007. The profit made by Offspring on these sales was $6 million. Offspring's trade payable account (in the records of Parentis) of $7 million does not agree with Parentis's trade receivable account (in the records of Offspring) due to cash in transit of $4 million paid by Parentis.

(iv)   Due to the impact of the above legislation, Parentis has concluded that the consolidated goodwill has been impaired by $40 million.

(v)   Parentis's policy is to value the non controlling interests using the fair value of the subsidiary's identifiable net assets. The fair value of the non-controlling interests at the date of acquisition is $125 million.

Required:

Prepare the consolidated statement of financial position of Parentis as at 31 March 2007.

(Total: 25 marks)

UK SYLLABUS FOCUS ONLY

A UK element to part (b) could instead ask you to:

"How will the goodwill on acquisition be accounted for under UK GAAP, in accordance with FRS 10 *Goodwill and Intangible Assets*?"

---

50   PLATEAU   *Walk in the footsteps of a top tutor*

On 1 October 2006 Plateau acquired the following non-current investments:

–   3 million equity shares in Savannah by an exchange of one share in Plateau for every two shares in Savannah plus $1.25 per acquired Savannah share in cash. The market price of each Plateau share at the date of acquisition was $6 and the market price of each Savannah share at the date of acquisition was $3.25.

–   30% of the equity shares of Axle at a cost of $7.50 per share in cash.

Only the cash consideration of the above investments has been recorded by Plateau. In addition $500,000 of professional costs relating to the acquisition of Savannah are also included in the cost of the investment.

The summarised draft statement of financial positions of the three companies at 30 September 2007 are:

	Plateau $000	Savannah $000	Axle $000
Assets			
Non-current assets			
Property, plant and equipment	18,400	10,400	18,000
Investments in Savannah and Axle	13,250	Nil	Nil
Fair value through profit or loss investments	6,500	Nil	Nil
	38,150	10,400	18,000
Current assets			
Inventory	6,900	6,200	3,600
Trade receivables	3,200	1,500	2,400
Total assets	48,250	18,100	24,000
Equity and liabilities			
Equity shares of $1 each	10,000	4,000	4,000
Retained earnings – at 30 September 2006	16,000	6,500	11,000
– for year ended 30 September 2007	9,250	2,400	5,000
	35,250	12,900	20,000
Non-current liabilities			
7% Loan notes	5,000	1,000	1,000
Current liabilities	8,000	4,200	3,000
Total equity and liabilities	48,250	18,100	24,000

The following information is relevant:

(i) At the date of acquisition the fair values of Savannah's assets were equal to their carrying amounts with the exception of Savannah's land which had a fair value of $500,000 below its carrying amount; it was written down by this amount shortly after acquisition and has not changed in value since then.

(ii) On 1 October 2006, Plateau sold an item of plant to Savannah at its agreed fair value of $2.5 million. Its carrying amount prior to the sale was $2 million. The estimated remaining life of the plant at the date of sale was five years (straight-line depreciation).

(iii) During the year ended 30 September 2007 Savannah sold goods to Plateau for $2.7 million. Savannah had marked up these goods by 50% on cost. Plateau had a third of the goods still in its inventory at 30 September 2007. There were no intra-group payables/receivables at 30 September 2007.

(iv) Plateau has a policy of valuing non-controlling interests at fair value at the date of acquisition. For this purpose the share price of Savannah at this date should be used. Impairment tests on 30 September 2007 concluded that neither consolidated goodwill or the value of the investment in Axle have been impaired.

(v) The fair value through profit or loss investments are included in Plateau's statement of financial position (above) at their fair value on 1 October 2006, but they have a fair value of $9 million at 30 September 2007

(vi) No dividends were paid during the year by any of the companies.

Required:

(a) Prepare the consolidated statement of financial position for Plateau as at 30 September 2007. **(20 marks)**

(b) A financial assistant has observed that the fair value exercise means that a subsidiary's net assets are included at acquisition at their fair (current) values in the consolidated statement of financial position. The assistant believes that it is inconsistent to aggregate the subsidiary's net assets with those of the parent because most of the parent's assets are carried at historical cost.

Required:

Comment on the assistant's observation and explain why the net assets of acquired subsidiaries are consolidated at acquisition at their fair values. **(5 marks)**

(Total: 25 marks)

UK SYLLABUS FOCUS ONLY

A UK element to part (b) could instead ask you to:

"Outline the difference between the accounting treatment for minority interests and acquisition costs if the statement of financial position were prepared under UK GAAP".

---

51 PATRONIC *Walk in the footsteps of a top tutor*

On 1 August 2007 Patronic purchased 18 million of a total of 24 million equity shares in Sardonic. The acquisition was through a share exchange of two shares in Patronic for every three shares in Sardonic. Both companies have shares with a par value of $1 each. The market price of Patronic's shares at 1 August 2007 was $5.75 per share. Patronic will also pay in cash on 31 July 2009 (two years after acquisition) $2.42 per acquired share of Sardonic. Patronic's cost of capital is 10% per annum. The reserves of Sardonic on 1 April 2007 were $69 million.

Patronic has held an investment of 30% of the equity shares in Acerbic for many years.

The summarised statement of profit or loss for the three companies for the year ended 31 March 2008 are:

	Patronic $000	Sardonic $000	Acerbic $000
Revenue	150,000	78,000	80,000
Cost of sales	(94,000)	(51,000)	(60,000)
Gross profit	56,000	27,000	20,000
Distribution costs	(7,400)	(3,000)	(3,500)
Administrative expenses	(12,500)	(6,000)	(6,500)
Finance costs (note (ii))	(2,000)	(900)	Nil
Profit before tax	34,100	17,100	10,000
Income tax expense	(10,400)	(3,600)	(4,000)
Profit for the period	23,700	13,500	6,000

The following information is relevant:

(i)   The fair values of the net assets of Sardonic at the date of acquisition were equal to their carrying amounts with the exception of property and plant. Property and plant had fair values of $4.1 million and $2.4 million respectively in excess of their carrying amounts. The increase in the fair value of the property would create additional depreciation of $200,000 in the consolidated financial statements in the post acquisition period to 31 March 2008 and the plant had a remaining life of four years (straight-line depreciation) at the date of acquisition of Sardonic. All depreciation is treated as part of cost of sales.

The fair values have not been reflected in Sardonic's financial statements.

No fair value adjustments were required on the acquisition of Acerbic.

(ii)   The finance costs of Patronic do not include the finance cost on the deferred consideration.

(iii)   Prior to its acquisition, Sardonic had been a good customer of Patronic. In the year to 31 March 2008, Patronic sold goods at a selling price of $1.25 million per month to Sardonic both before and after its acquisition. Patronic made a profit of 20% on the cost of these sales. At 31 March 2008 Sardonic still held inventory of $3 million (at cost to Sardonic) of goods purchased in the post acquisition period from Patronic.

(iv)   Patronic has a policy of valuing non-controlling interests using the fair value at the date of acquisition, which was $30.5 million. An impairment test on the goodwill of Sardonic conducted on 31 March 2008 concluded that it should be written down by $2 million. The value of the investment in Acerbic was not impaired.

(v)   All items in the above statement of profit or loss's are deemed to accrue evenly over the year.

(vi)   Ignore deferred tax.

Required:

(a)   Calculate the goodwill arising on the acquisition of Sardonic at 1 August 2007.

(6 marks)

(b)   Prepare the consolidated statement of profit or loss for the Patronic Group for the year ended 31 March 2008.

Note: Assume that the investment in Acerbic has been accounted for using the equity method since its acquisition.   (15 marks)

(c)   At 31 March 2008 the other equity shares (70%) in Acerbic were owned by many separate investors. Shortly after this date Spekulate (a company unrelated to Patronic) accumulated a 60% interest in Acerbic by buying shares from the other shareholders. In May 2008 a meeting of the board of directors of Acerbic was held at which Patronic lost its seat on Acerbic's board.

Required:

Explain, with reasons, the accounting treatment Patronic should adopt for its investment in Acerbic when it prepares its financial statements for the year ending 31 March 2009.   (4 marks)

(Total: 25 marks)

52   PEDANTIC   *Walk in the footsteps of a top tutor*

On 1 April 2008, Pedantic acquired 60% of the equity share capital of Sophistic in a share exchange of two shares in Pedantic for three shares in Sophistic. The issue of shares has not yet been recorded by Pedantic. At the date of acquisition shares in Pedantic had a market value of $6 each. Below are the summarised draft financial statements of both companies.

Statement of profit or loss for the year ended 30 September 2008

	Pedantic $000	Sophistic $000
Revenue	85,000	42,000
Cost of sales	(63,000)	(32,000)
Gross profit	22,000	10,000
Distribution costs	(2,000)	(2,000)
Administrative expenses	(6,000)	(3,200)
Finance costs	(300)	(400)
Profit before tax	13,700	4,400
Income tax expense	(4,700)	(1,400)
Profit for the year	9,000	3,000

Statements of financial position as at 30 September 2008

Assets		
Non-current assets		
Property, plant and equipment	40,600	12,600
Current assets	16,000	6,600
Total assets	56,600	19,200
Equity and liabilities		
Equity shares of $1 each	10,000	4,000
Retained earnings	35,400	6,500
		45,400
	10,500	
Non-current liabilities		
10% loan notes	3,000	4,000
Current liabilities	8,200	4,700
Total equity and liabilities	56,600	19,200

The following information is relevant:

(i)   At the date of acquisition, the fair values of Sophistic's assets were equal to their carrying amounts with the exception of an item of plant, which had a fair value of $2 million in excess of its carrying amount. It had a remaining life of five years at that date [straight-line depreciation is used]. Sophistic has not adjusted the carrying amount of its plant as a result of the fair value exercise.

(ii) Sales from Sophistic to Pedantic in the post acquisition period were $8 million. Sophistic made a mark up on cost of 40% on these sales. Pedantic had sold $5.2 million (at cost to Pedantic) of these goods by 30 September 2008.

(iii) Other than where indicated, statement of profit or loss items are deemed to accrue evenly on a time basis.

(iv) Sophistic's trade receivables at 30 September 2008 include $600,000 due from Pedantic which did not agree with Pedantic's corresponding trade payable. This was due to cash in transit of $200,000 from Pedantic to Sophistic. Both companies have positive bank balances.

(v) Pedantic has a policy of accounting for any non-controlling interest at fair value. The fair value of the non-controlling interest at the acquisition date was $5.9 million. Consolidated goodwill was not impaired at 30 September 2008.

Required:

(a) **Prepare the consolidated statement of profit or loss for Pedantic for the year ended 30 September 2008.** **(9 marks)**

(b) **Prepare the consolidated statement of financial position for Pedantic as at 30 September 2008.** **(16 marks)**

(Total: 25 marks)

53 **PACEMAKER** *Walk in the footsteps of a top tutor*

Timed question with Online tutor debrief

Below are the summarised statements of financial position for three companies as at 31 March 2009:

	Pacemaker		Syclop		Vardine	
	$ million	$ million	$ million	$ million	$ million	$ million
Assets						
Non-current assets						
Property, plant and equipment		520		280		240
Investments		345		40		nil
		———		———		———
		865		320		240
Current assets						
Inventory	142		160		120	
Trade receivables	95		88		50	
Cash and bank	8	245	22	270	10	180
	———	———	———	———	———	———
Total assets		1,110		590		420
		———		———		———

Equity and liabilities					
Equity shares of $1 each		500		145	100
Share premium	100		Nil		nil
Retained earnings	130	230	260	260	240	240
		730		405	340
Non-current liabilities					
10% loan notes		180		20	nil
Current liabilities		200		165	80
Total equity and liabilities		1,110		590	420

Notes

Pacemaker is a public listed company that acquired the following investments:

(i)   *Investment in Syclop*

On 1 April 2007 Pacemaker acquired 116 million shares in Syclop for an immediate cash payment of $210 million and issued at par one 10% $100 loan note for every 200 shares acquired. Syclop's retained earnings at the date of acquisition were $120 million.

(ii)   *Investment in Vardine*

On 1 October 2008 Pacemaker acquired 30 million shares in Vardine in exchange for 75 million of its own shares. The stock market value of Pacemaker's shares at the date of this share exchange was $1.60 each. Pacemaker has not yet recorded the investment in Vardine.

(iii)   Pacemaker's other investments, and those of Syclop, are fair value through profit or loss investments which are carried at their fair values as at 31 March 2008. The fair value of these investments at 31 March 2009 is $82 million and $37 million respectively.

Other relevant information:

(iv)   Pacemaker's policy is to value non-controlling interests at their fair values. The directors of Pacemaker assessed the fair value of the non-controlling interest in Syclop at the date of acquisition to be $65 million.

There has been no impairment to goodwill or the value of the investment in Vardine.

(v)   At the date of acquisition of Syclop owned a recently built property that was carried at its (depreciated) construction cost of $62 million. The fair value of this property at the date of acquisition was $82 million and it had an estimated remaining life of 20 years.

For many years Syclop has been selling some of its products under the brand name of 'Kyklop'. At the date of acquisition the directors of Pacemaker valued this brand at $25 million with a remaining life of 10 years. The brand is not included in Syclop's statement of financial position.

The fair value of all other identifiable assets and liabilities of Syclop were equal to their carrying values at the date of its acquisition.

(vi) The inventory of Syclop at 31 March 2009 includes goods supplied by Pacemaker for $56 million (at selling price from Pacemaker). Pacemaker adds a mark-up of 40% on cost when selling goods to Syclop. There are no intra-group receivables or payables at 31 March 2009.

(vii) Vardine's profit is subject to seasonal variation. Its profit for the year ended 31 March 2009 was $100 million. $20 million of this profit was made from 1 April 2008 to 30 September 2008.

(viii) None of the companies have paid any dividends for many years.

Required:

Prepare the consolidated statement of financial position of Pacemaker as at 31 March 2009.

(25 marks)

Calculate your allowed time, allocate the time to the separate parts

---

54 PANDAR *Walk in the footsteps of a top tutor*

On 1 April 2009 Pandar purchased 80% of the equity shares in Salva. The acquisition was through a share exchange of three shares in Pandar for every five shares in Salva. The market prices of Pandar's and Salva's shares at 1 April 2009 were $6 per share and $3.20 respectively.

On the same date Pandar acquired 40% of the equity shares in Ambra paying $2 per share.

The summarised statement of profit or loss for the three companies for the year ended 30 September 2009 are:

	Pandar $000	Salva $000	Ambra $000
Revenue	210,000	150,000	50,000
Cost of sales	(126,000)	(100,000)	(40,000)
Gross profit	84,000	50,000	10,000
Distribution costs	(11,200)	(7,000)	(5,000)
Administrative expenses	(18,300)	(9,000)	(11,000)
Investment income (interest and dividends)	9,500		
Finance costs	(1,800)	(3,000)	Nil
Profit (loss) before tax	62,200	31,000	(6,000)
Income tax (expense) relief	(15,000)	(10,000)	1,000
Profit (loss) for the year	47,200	21,000	(5,000)

The following information for the equity of the companies at 30 September 2009 is available:

Equity shares of $1 each	200,000	120,000	40,000
Share premium	300,000	Nil	Nil
Retained earnings 1 October 2008	40,000	152,000	15,000
Profit (loss) for the year ended 30 September 2009	47,200	21,000	(5,000)
Dividends paid (26 September 2009)	Nil	(8,000)	Nil

The following information is relevant:

(i)   The fair values of the net assets of Salva at the date of acquisition were equal to their carrying amounts with the exception of an item of plant which had a carrying amount of $12 million and a fair value of $17 million. This plant had a remaining life of five years (straight-line depreciation) at the date of acquisition of Salva. All depreciation is charged to cost of sales.

In addition Salva owns the registration of a popular internet domain name. The registration, which had a negligible cost, has a five year remaining life (at the date of acquisition); however, it is renewable indefinitely at a nominal cost. At the date of acquisition the domain name was valued by a specialist company at $20 million.

The fair values of the plant and the domain name have not been reflected in Salva's financial statements.

No fair value adjustments were required on the acquisition of the investment in Ambra.

(ii)   Immediately after its acquisition of Salva, Pandar invested $50 million in an 8% loan note from Salva. All interest accruing to 30 September 2009 had been accounted for by both companies. Salva also has other loans in issue at 30 September 2009.

(iii)   Pandar has credited the whole of the dividend it received from Salva to investment income.

(iv)   After the acquisition, Pandar sold goods to Salva for $15 million on which Pandar made a gross profit of 20%. Salva had one third of these goods still in its inventory at 30 September 2009. There are no intra-group current account balances at 30 September 2009.

(v)   The non-controlling interest in Salva is to be valued at its (full) fair value at the date of acquisition. For this purpose Salva's share price at that date can be taken to be indicative of the fair value of the shareholding of the non-controlling interest.

(vi)   The goodwill of Salva has not suffered any impairment; however, due to its losses, the value of Pandar's investment in Ambra has been impaired by $3 million at 30 September 2009.

(vii)   All items in the above statement of profit or loss are deemed to accrue evenly over the year unless otherwise indicated.

Required:

(a)   **(i)**   **Calculate the goodwill arising on the acquisition of Salva at 1 April 2009;**

(6 marks)

(ii)   **Calculate the carrying amount of the investment in Ambra to be included within the consolidated statement of financial position as at 30 September 2009.**   **(3 marks)**

(b)   **Prepare the consolidated statement of profit or loss for the Pandar Group for the year ended 30 September 2009.**   **(16 marks)**

(Total: 25 marks)

55 PICANT 🐾 *Walk in the footsteps of a top tutor*

On 1 April 2009 Picant acquired 75% of Sander's equity shares in a share exchange of three shares in Picant for every two shares in Sander. The market prices of Picant's and Sander's shares at the date of acquisition were $3.20 and $4.50 respectively.

In addition to this Picant agreed to pay a further amount on 1 April 2010 that was contingent upon the post-acquisition performance of Sander. At the date of acquisition Picant assessed the fair value of this contingent consideration at $4.2 million, but by 31 March 2010 it was clear that the actual amount to be paid would be only $2.7 million (ignore discounting). Picant has recorded the share exchange and provided for the initial estimate of $4.2 million for the contingent consideration.

On 1 October 2009 Picant also acquired 40% of the equity shares of Adler paying $4 in cash per acquired share and issuing at par one $100 7% loan note for every 50 shares acquired in Adler. This consideration has also been recorded by Picant.

Picant has no other investments.

The summarised statements of financial position of the three companies at 31 March 2010 are:

	Picant	Sander	Adler
Assets	$000	$000	$000
Non-current assets			
Property, plant and equipment	37,500	24,500	21,000
Investments	45,000	nil	nil
	82,500	24,500	21,000
Current assets			
Inventory	10,000	9,000	5,000
Trade receivables	6,500	1,500	3,000
Total assets	99,000	35,000	29,000
Equity			
Equity shares of $1 each	25,000	8,000	5,000
Share premium	19,800	nil	nil
Retained earnings – at 1 April 2009	16,200	16,500	15,000
– for the year ended 31 March 2010	11,000	1,000	6,000
	72,000	25,500	26,000
Non-current liabilities			
7% loan notes	14,500	2,000	nil
Current liabilities			
Contingent consideration	4,200	nil	nil
Other current liabilities	8,300	7,500	3,000
Total equity and liabilities	99,000	35,000	29,000

The following information is relevant:

(i) At the date of acquisition the fair values of Sander's property, plant and equipment was equal to its carrying amount with the exception of Sander's factory which had a fair value of $2 million above its carrying amount. Sander has not adjusted the carrying amount of the factory as a result of the fair value exercise. This requires additional annual depreciation of $100,000 in the consolidated financial statements in the post-acquisition period.

Also at the date of acquisition, Sander had an intangible asset of $500,000 for software in its statement of financial position. Picant's directors believed the software to have no recoverable value at the date of acquisition and Sander wrote it off shortly after its acquisition.

(ii) At 31 March 2010 Picant's current account with Sander was $3.4 million (debit). This did not agree with the equivalent balance in Sander's books due to some goods-in-transit invoiced at $1.8 million that were sent by Picant on 28 March 2010, but had not been received by Sander until after the year end. Picant sold all these goods at cost plus 50%.

(iii) Picant's policy is to value the non-controlling interest at fair value at the date of acquisition. For this purpose Sander's share price at that date can be deemed to be representative of the fair value of the shares held by the non-controlling interest.

(iv) Impairment tests were carried out on 31 March 2010 which concluded that the value of the investment in Adler was not impaired but, due to poor trading performance, consolidated goodwill was impaired by $3.8 million.

(v) Assume all profits accrue evenly through the year.

Required:

(a) Prepare the consolidated statement of financial position for Picant as at 31 March 2010.

(21 marks)

(b) Picant has been approached by a potential new customer, Trilby, to supply it with a substantial quantity of goods on three months credit terms. Picant is concerned at the risk that such a large order represents in the current difficult economic climate, especially as Picant's normal credit terms are only one month's credit. To support its application for credit, Trilby has sent Picant a copy of Tradhat's most recent audited consolidated financial statements. Trilby is a wholly-owned subsidiary within the Tradhat group. Tradhat's consolidated financial statements show a strong statement of financial position including healthy liquidity ratios.

Required:

Comment on the importance that Picant should attach to Tradhat's consolidated financial statements when deciding on whether to grant credit terms to Trilby.

(4 marks)

(Total: 25 marks)

UK SYLLABUS FOCUS ONLY

A UK element to part (b) could instead ask you to:

"Outline the difference between the accounting for the contingent consideration under UK GAAP and IFRS".

ANALYSING AND INTERPRETING FINANCIAL STATEMENTS

56   HARDY   *Walk in the footsteps of a top tutor*

Hardy is a public listed manufacturing company. Its summarised financial statements for the year ended 30 September 2010 (and 2009 comparatives are:

Statements of profit or loss for the year ended 30 September:

	2010	2009
	$000	$000
Revenue	29,500	36,000
Cost of sales	(25,500)	(26,000)
Gross profit	4,000	10,000
Distribution costs	(1,050)	(800)
Administrative expenses	(4,900)	(3,900)
Investment income	50	200
Finance costs	(600)	(500)
Profit (loss) before taxation	(2,500)	5,000
Income tax (expense) relief	400	(1,500)
Profit (loss) for the year	(2,100)	3,500

Statements of financial position as at 30 September:

	2010		2009	
	$000	$000	$000	$000
Assets				
Non-current assets				
Property, plant and equipment		17,600		24,500
Investments at fair value through profit or loss		2,400		4,000
		20,000		28,500
Current assets				
Inventory and work-in-progress	2,200		1,900	
Trade receivables	2,200		2,800	
Tax asset	600		nil	
Bank	1,200	6,200	100	4,800
Total assets		26,200		33,300

Equity and liabilities				
Equity				
Equity shares of $1 each		13,000		12,000
Share premium		1,000		nil
Revaluation reserve		nil		4,500
Retained earnings		3,600		6,500
		17,600		23,000
Non-current liabilities				
Bank loan		4,000		5,000
Deferred tax		1,200		700
Current liabilities				
Trade payables	3,400		2,800	
Current tax payable	nil	3,400	1,800	4,600
Total equity and liabilities		26,200		33,300

The following information has been obtained from the Chairman's Statement and the notes to the financial statements:

'Market conditions during the year ended 30 September 2010 proved very challenging due largely to difficulties in the global economy as a result of a sharp recession which has led to steep falls in share prices and property values. Hardy has not been immune from these effects and our properties have suffered impairment losses of $6 million in the year.'

The excess of these losses over previous surpluses has led to a charge to cost of sales of $1·5 million in addition to the normal depreciation charge.

'Our portfolio of investments at fair value through profit or loss has been 'marked to market' (fair valued) resulting in a loss of $1·6 million (included in administrative expenses).'

There were no additions to or disposals of non-current assets during the year.

'In response to the downturn the company has unfortunately had to make a number of employees redundant incurring severance costs of $1·3 million (included in cost of sales) and undertaken cost savings in advertising and other administrative expenses.'

'The difficulty in the credit markets has meant that the finance cost of our variable rate bank loan has increased from 4·5% to 8%. In order to help cash flows, the company made a rights issue during the year and reduced the dividend per share by 50%.'

'Despite the above events and associated costs, the Board believes the company's underlying performance has been quite resilient in these difficult times.'

Required:

Analyse and discuss the financial performance and position of Hardy as portrayed by the above financial statements and the additional information provided.

Your analysis should be supported by profitability, liquidity and gearing and other appropriate ratios (up to 10 marks available).

(25 marks)

57   RYTETREND

Rytetrend is a retailer of electrical goods. Extracts from the company's financial statements are set out below:

Statement of profit or loss

	20X3		20X2	
for the year ended 31 March:	$000	$000	$000	$000
Revenue		31,800		23,500
Cost of sales		(22,500)		(16,000)
		────		────
Gross profit		9,300		7,500
Other operating expenses		(5,440)		(4,600)
		────		────
Operating profit		3,860		2,900
Interest payable – loan notes	(260)		(500)	
overdraft	(200)	(460)	nil	(500)
	────		────	
Profit before taxation		3,400		2,400
Taxation		(1,000)		(800)
		────		────
Profit for the year		2,400		1,600
		────		────

Extract from statement of changes in equity

Retained earnings – brought forward	5,880	4,680
Profit for the year	2,400	1,600
Dividends	(600)	(400)
	────	────
Retained earnings – carried forward	7,680	5,880
	────	────

Statements of financial position as at 31 March:

	20X3		20X2	
	$000	$000	$000	$000
Non-current assets (note (i))		24,500		17,300
Current assets				
Inventory	2,650		3,270	
Receivables	1,100		1,950	
Bank	nil		400	
	────	3,750	────	5,620
		────		────
Total assets		28,250		22,920
		────		────

Equity and liabilities

Ordinary capital ($1 shares)	11,500	10,000
Share premium	1,500	nil
Retained earnings	7,680	5,880
	20,680	15,880

Non-current liabilities

10% loan notes	nil	4,000
6% loan notes	2,000	nil

Current liabilities

Bank overdraft	1,050		nil	
Trade payables	3,300		2,260	
Taxation	720		630	
Warranty provision (note (ii))	500	5,570	150	3,040
Total equity and liabilities		28,250		22,920

Notes

(i)   The details of the non-current assets are:

	Cost	Accumulated depreciation	Carrying value
	$000	$000	$000
At 31 March 20X2	27,500	10,200	17,300
At 31 March 20X3	37,250	12,750	24,500

During the year there was a major refurbishment of display equipment. Old equipment that had cost $6 million in September 19W8 was replaced with new equipment at a gross cost of $8 million. The equipment manufacturer had allowed Rytetrend a trade in allowance of $500,000 on the old display equipment. In addition to this Rytetrend used its own staff to install the new equipment. The value of staff time spent on the installation has been costed at $300,000, but this has not been included in the cost of the asset. All staff costs have been included in operating expenses. All display equipment held at the end of the financial year is depreciated at 20% on its cost. No equipment is more than five years old.

(ii)   Operating expenses contain a charge of $580,000 for the cost of warranties on the goods sold by Rytetrend. The company makes a warranty provision when it sells its products and cash payments for warranty claims are deducted from the provision as they are settled.

Required:

(a)   **Prepare a statement of cash flows for Rytetrend for the year ended 31 March 20X3.**

(12 marks)

(b)   **Write a report briefly analysing the operating performance and financial position of Rytetrend for the years ended 31 March 20X2 and 20X3.**   **(13 marks)**

Your report should be supported by appropriate ratios.

(Total: 25 marks)

58   BIGWOOD

Bigwood, a public company, is a high street retailer that sells clothing and food. The managing director is very disappointed with the current year's results. The company expanded its operations and commissioned a famous designer to restyle its clothing products. This has led to increased sales in both retail lines, yet overall profits are down.

Details of the financial statements for the two years to 30 September 20X4 are shown below.

Statements of profit or loss:

		Year to 30 September 20X4		Year to 30 September 20X3	
		$000	$000	$000	$000
Revenue	– clothing	16,000		15,600	
	– food	7,000	23,000	4,000	19,600
Cost of sales	– clothing	14,500		12,700	
	– food	4,750	(19,250)	3,000	(15,700)
Gross profit			3,750		3,900
Other operating expenses			(2,750)		(1,900)
Operating profit			1,000		2,000
Interest expense			(300)		(80)
Profit before tax			700		1,920
Income tax expense			(250)		(520)
Profit for period			450		1,400

Movement on retained earnings:

	Year to 30 September 20X4	Year to 30 September 20X3
	$000	$000
Retained earnings b/f	1,900	1,100
Profit for the period	450	1,400
Dividends paid	(600)	(600)
Retained earnings c/f	1,750	1,900

Statements of financial position as at:

	Year to 30 September 20X4		Year to 30 September 20X3	
	$000	$000	$000	$000
Property, plant and equipment at cost		17,000		9,500
Accumulated depreciation		(5,000)		(3,000)
		12,000		6,500
Current Assets				
Inventory – clothing	2,700		1,360	
– food	200		140	
Trade receivables	100		50	
Bank	Nil	3,000	450	2,000
Total assets		15,000		8,500
Equity and liabilities				
Issued ordinary capital ($1 shares)		5,000		3,000
Share premium		1,000		Nil
Retained earnings		1,750		1,900
		7,750		4,900
Non-current liabilities				
Long-term loans		3,000		1,000
Current liabilities				
Bank overdraft	930		Nil	
Trade payables	3,100		2,150	
Current tax payable	220	4,250	450	2,600
		15,000		8,500

Note: The directors have signalled their intention to maintain annual dividends at $600,000 for the foreseeable future.

The following information is relevant:

(i)   The increase in property, plant and equipment was due to the acquisition of five new stores and the refurbishment of some existing stores during the year. The carrying value of fixtures scrapped at the refurbished stores was $1.2 million; they had originally cost $3 million. Bigwood received no scrap proceeds from the fixtures, but did incur costs of $50,000 to remove and dispose of them. The losses on the refurbishment have been charged to operating expenses. Depreciation is charged to cost of sales apportioned in relation to floor area (see overleaf).

(ii)   The floor sales areas (in square metres) were:

	30 September 20X4	30 September 20X3
Clothing	48,000	35,000
Food	6,000	5,000
	54,000	40,000

(iii)   The share price of Bigwood averaged $6.00 during the year to 30 September 20X3, but was only $3.00 at 30 September 20X4.

(iv)   The following ratios have been calculated:

	20X4	20X3
Return on capital employed	9.3%	33.9%
Net asset turnover	2.1 times	3.3 times
Gross profit margin		
– clothing	9.4%	18.6%
– food	32.1%	25%
Net profit (after tax) margin	2.0%	7.1%
Current ratio	0.71:1	0.77:1
Inventory holding period		
– clothing	68 days	39 days
– food	15 days	17 days
Accounts payable period	59 days	50 days
Gearing	28%	17%
Interest cover	3.3 times	25 times

Required:

(a)   Prepare, using the indirect method, a statement of cash flows for Bigwood for the year to 30 September 20X4.   **(12 marks)**

(b)   Write a report analysing the financial performance and financial position of Bigwood for the two years ended 30 September 20X4.   **(13 marks)**

Your report should utilize the above ratios and the information in your statement of cash flows. It should refer to the relative performance of the clothing and food sales and be supported by any further ratios you consider appropriate.

(Total: 25 marks)

59 MINSTER *Online question assistance*

Minster is a publicly listed company. Details of its financial statements for the year ended 30 September 20X6, together with a comparative statement of financial position, are:

Statement of financial position at	30 September 20X6		30 September 20X5	
	$000	$000	$000	$000
Non-current assets (note (i))				
Property, plant and equipment		1,280		940
Software		135		Nil
Investments at fair value through profit and loss		150		125
		1,565		1,065
Current assets				
Inventories	480		510	
Trade receivables	270		380	
Amounts due from construction contracts	80		55	
Bank	Nil	830	35	980
Total assets		2,395		2,045
Equity and liabilities				
Equity shares of 25 cents each		500		300
Reserves				
Share premium (note (ii))	150		85	
Revaluation reserve	60		25	
Retained earnings	950	1,160	965	1,075
		1,660		1,375
Non-current liabilities				
9% loan note	120		Nil	
Environmental provision	162		Nil	
Deferred tax	18	30	25	25
Current liabilities				
Trade payables	350		555	
Bank overdraft	25		40	
Current tax payable	60	435	50	645
Total equity and liabilities		2,395		2,045

Statement of profit or loss for the year ended 30 September 20X6

Revenue	1,397
Cost of sales	(1,110)
	———
Gross profit	287
Operating expenses	(125)
	———
	162
Finance costs (note (i))	(40)
Investment income and gain on investments	20
	———
Profit before tax	142
Income tax expense	(57)
	———
Profit for the year	85
	———

The following supporting information is available:

(i)   Included in property, plant and equipment is a coal mine and related plant that Minster purchased on 1 October 20X5. Legislation requires that in ten years' time (the estimated life of the mine) Minster will have to landscape the area affected by the mining. The future cost of this has been estimated and discounted at a rate of 8% to a present value of $150,000. This cost has been included in the carrying amount of the mine and, together with the unwinding of the discount, has also been treated as a provision. The unwinding of the discount is included within finance costs in the statement of profit or loss.

Other land was revalued (upward) by $35,000 during the year.

Depreciation of property, plant and equipment for the year was $255,000.

There were no disposals of property, plant and equipment during the year.

The software was purchased on 1 April 20X6 for $180,000.

The market value of the investments had increased during the year by $15,000. There have been no sales of these investments during the year.

(ii)   On 1 April 20X6 there was a bonus (scrip) issue of equity shares of one for every four held utilising the share premium reserve. A further cash share issue was made on 1 June 20X6. No shares were redeemed during the year.

(iii)   A dividend of 5 cents per share was paid on 1 July 20X6.

Required:

(a)   **Prepare a statement of cash flows for Minster for the year to 30 September 20X6 in accordance with IAS 7 *Statements of cash flows*.**   **(15 marks)**

(b)   **Comment on the financial performance and position of Minster as revealed by the above financial statements and your statement of cash flows.**   **(10 marks)**

(Total: 25 marks)

Online question assistance

60 PENDANT

Pendant is a small family owned business. A client of yours has been asked to provide credit for Pendant. The client has provided you with the statements of financial position and some supporting information for Pendant for the years to 31 March 20X0 and 20X1. The client wants an opinion on Pendant's financial position.

Pendant – Statement of financial position

	31 March 20X1		31 March 20X0	
	$000	$000	$000	$000
Non-current assets				
Property, plant and equipment		1,290		1,120
Software (in development)		300		100
		–––––		–––––
		1,590		1,220
Current assets				
Inventory	490		540	
Trade receivables	787		584	
Investments – Government securities	30		180	
Bank	nil	1,307	125	1,429
	–––––		–––––	
Total assets		2,897		2,649
		–––––		–––––
Equity and liabilities				
Equity shares of $1 each		500		400
Reserves				
Share premium	150		80	
Retained earnings	1,084	1,234	1,092	1,172
	–––––		–––––	
Equity		1,734		1,572
Non-current liabilities				
Finance lease obligations	290		60	
Deferred tax	12	302	172	232
	–––––		–––––	
Current liabilities				
Trade payables	663		602	
Bank overdraft	45		nil	
Taxation	83		213	
Finance lease obligations	70	861	30	845
	–––––		–––––	
Total equity and liabilities		2,897		2,649
		–––––		–––––

The following supporting information is available:

(i)   Details relating to the non-current assets are (in $000s):

	31 March 20X1			31 March 20X0		
	Cost	Depreciation	NBV	Cost	Depreciation	NBV
Freehold land and buildings	nil	nil	nil	700	120	580
Leasehold land and buildings	500	20	480	nil	nil	nil
Purchased plant	550	250	300	620	200	420
Plant on finance lease	650	140	510	150	30	120
			1,290			1,120

On 1 April 20X0 Pendant sold its freehold property for $800,000. Pendant then acquired another property on a 25-year lease at a capital cost of $500,000.

The total amount of payments made in the year to 31 March 20X1 in respect of finance leases was $265,000, of which $35,000 was for interest. Interest costs of the bank overdraft were $10,000.

During the same period 'purchased' plant which had originally cost $200,000 was sold for $75,000 giving a profit of $18,000.

(ii)   The total tax charge (including deferred tax) in the statement of profit or loss for the year to 31 March 20X1 was $31,000.

(iii)   During the year some Government securities, which are shown at cost in the statement of financial position, were sold at a profit of $27,000. This profit was credited to the statement of profit or loss, as was $15,000 of income received from the securities. No other Government securities were traded during the year.

(iv)   Pendant paid an interim dividend during the year to 31 March 20X1 of $150,000.

Required:

(a)   As far as the information permits, prepare a statement of cash flows for Pendant for the year to 31 March 20X1 in accordance with IAS 7 *Statements of cash flows*.

(20 marks)

(b)   Identify the important areas that you would draw your client's attention to based on the information in the question and the statement of cash flows prepared in (a). You are not required to calculate ratios. **(5 marks)**

(Total: 25 marks)

61 CHARMER

The summarised financial statements of Charmer for the year to 30 September 20X1, together with a comparative statement of financial position, are:

Statement of profit or loss	$000
Revenue	7,482
Cost of sales	(4,284)
Gross profit	3,198
Operating expenses	(1,479)
Interest payable	(260)
Investment income	120
Profit before tax	1,579
Income tax	(520)
Profit for the period	1,059

Statement of financial position as at:

	30 September 20X1			30 September 20X0		
	$000	$000	$000	$000	$000	$000
Assets	Cost/valuation	Depreciation	NBV	Cost/valuation	Depreciation	NBV
Non-current assets						
Property, plant and equipment	3,568	1,224	2,344	3,020	1,112	1,908
Investment			690			nil
			3,034			1,908
Current assets						
Inventory		1,046			785	
Accounts receivable		935			824	
Short term treasury bills		120			50	
Bank		nil	2,101		122	1,781
Total assets			5,135			3,689
Total equity and liabilities						
Equity:						
Ordinary shares of $1 each			1,400			1,000
Reserves:						
Share premium		460			160	
Revaluation		190			40	
Retained earnings						
b/f	92			47		
Net profit for period	1,059			65		
Dividends	(180)			(20)		
Retained earnings c/f		971	1,621		92	292
			3,021			1,292

Non-current liabilities					
Deferred tax	439			400	
Government grants	275			200	
10% Convertible loan stock	nil	714		400	1,000
	___			___	
Current liabilities					
Trade accounts payable	644			760	
Accrued interest	40			25	
Provision for negligence claim	nil			120	
Provision for income tax	480			367	
Government grants	100			125	
Overdraft	136	1,400		Nil	1,397
	___			___	
Total equity and liabilities		5,135			3,689
		___			___

The following information is relevant:

(i) **Non-current assets**

Property, plant and equipment is analysed as follows:

	30 September 20X1			30 September 20X0		
	Cost/ valuation	Depreciation	NBV	Cost/ valuation	Depreciation	NBV
	$000	$000	$000	$000	$000	$000
Land and Buildings	2,000	760	1,240	1,800	680	1,120
Plant	1,568	464	1,104	1,220	432	788
	___	___	___	___	___	___
	3,568	1,224	2,344	3,020	1,112	1,908
	___	___	___	___	___	___

On 1 October 20X0 Charmer recorded an increase in the value of its land of $150,000.

During the year an item of plant that had cost $500,000 and had accumulated depreciation of $244,000 was sold at a loss (included in cost of sales) of $86,000 on its carrying value.

(ii) **Government grant**

A credit of $125,000 for the current year's amortization of government grants has been included in cost of sales.

(iii) **Share capital and loan stocks**

The increase in the share capital during the year was due to the following events:

(1) On 1 January 20X1 there was a bonus issue (out of the share premium account) of one bonus share for every 10 shares held.

(2) On 1 April 20X1 the 10% convertible loan stock holders exercised their right to convert to ordinary shares. The terms of conversion were 25 ordinary shares of $1 each for each $100 of 10% convertible loan stock.

and

(3) The remaining increase in the ordinary shares was due to a stock market placement of shares for cash on 12 August 20X1.

(iv) **Provision for negligence claim**

In June 20X1 Charmer made an out of court settlement of a negligence claim brought about by a former employee. The dispute had been in progress for two years and Charmer had made provisions for the potential liability in each of the two previous years. The unprovided amount of the claim at the time of settlement was $30,000 and this was charged to operating expenses.

Required:

Prepare a statement of cash flows for Charmer for the year to 30 September 20X1 in accordance with IAS 7 *Statements of Cash flows*. **(25 marks)**

62 CASINO

(a) Casino is a publicly listed company. Details of its statements of financial position as at 31 March 20X5 and 20X4 are shown below together with other relevant information:

Statement of financial position as at	31 March 20X5		31 March 20X4	
Non-current assets (note (i))	$m	$m	$m	$m
Property, plant and equipment		880		760
Intangible assets		400		510
		1,280		1,270
Current assets				
Inventory	350		420	
Trade receivables	808		372	
Interest receivable	5		3	
Short term deposits	32		120	
Bank	15	1,210	75	990
Total assets		2,490		2,260
Share capital and reserves				
Ordinary shares of $1 each		300		200
Reserves				
Share premium	60		nil	
Revaluation reserve	112		45	
Retained earnings	1,098	1,270	1,165	1,210
		1,570		1,410
Non-current liabilities				
12% loan note	nil		150	
8% variable rate loan note	160		nil	
Deferred tax	90	250	75	225
Current liabilities				
Trade payables	530		515	
Bank overdraft	125		nil	
Taxation	15		110	
		670		625
Total equity and liabilities		2,490		2,260

The following supporting information is available:

(i)   Details relating to the non-current assets are:

Property, plant and equipment at:

| | 31 March 20X5 | | | 31 March 20X4 | | |
	Cost/ Valuation	Depreciation	Carrying value	Cost/ Valuation	Depreciation	Carrying value
	$m	$m	$m	$m	$m	$m
Land and buildings	600	12	588	500	80	420
Plant	440	148	292	445	105	340
			880			760

Casino revalued the carrying value of its land and buildings by an increase of $70 million on 1 April 20X4. On 31 March 20X5 Casino transferred $3 million from the revaluation reserve to retained earnings representing the realization of the revaluation reserve due to the depreciation of buildings.

During the year Casino acquired new plant at a cost of $60 million and sold some old plant for $15 million at a loss of $12 million.

There were no acquisitions or disposals of intangible assets.

(ii)   The following extract is from the draft statement of profit or loss for the year to 31 March 20X5:

	$m	$m
Operating loss		(32)
Interest receivable		12
Finance costs		(24)
Loss before tax		(44)
Income tax repayment claim	14	
Deferred tax charge	(15)	(1)
Loss for the period		(45)
The finance costs are made up of:		
Interest expenses		(18)
Penalty cost for early redemption of fixed rate loan		(6)
		(24)

(iii)   The short-term deposits meet the definition of cash equivalents.

(iv)   Dividends of $25 million were paid during the year.

Required:

As far as the information permits, prepare a statement of cash flows for Casino for the year to 31 March 20X5 in accordance with IAS 7 *Statements of cash flows*.

(20 marks)

(b) In recent years many analysts have commented on a growing disillusionment with the usefulness and reliability of the information contained in some companies' statements of profit or loss and other comprehensive income.

Required:

Discuss the extent to which a company's statement of cash flows may be more useful and reliable than its statement of profit or loss and other comprehensive income. (5 marks)

(Total: 25 marks)

63 TABBA *Walk in the footsteps of a top tutor*

The following draft financial statements relate to Tabba, a private company.

Statements of financial position as at:	30 September 20X5		30 September 20X4	
	$000	$000	$000	$000
Tangible non-current assets (note (ii))		10,600		15,800
Current assets				
Inventories	2,550		1,850	
Trade receivables	3,100		2,600	
Insurance claim (note (iii))	1,500		1,200	
Cash and bank	850	8,000	Nil	5,650
Total assets		18,600		21,450
Equity and liabilities				
Share capital ($1 each)		6,000		6,000
Reserves:				
Revaluation (note (ii))	nil		1,600	
Retained earnings	2,550	2,550	850	2,450
		8,550		8,450
Non-current liabilities				
Finance lease obligations (note (ii))	2,000		1,700	
6% loan notes	800		Nil	
10% loan notes	nil		4,000	
Deferred tax	200		500	
Government grants (note (ii))	1,400	4,400	900	7,100
Current liabilities				
Bank overdraft	nil		550	
Trade payables	4,050		2,950	
Government grants (note (ii))	600		400	
Finance lease obligations (note (ii))	900		800	
Current tax payable	100	5,650	1,200	5,900
Total equity and liabilities		18,600		21,450

The following information is relevant:

(i)   Statement of profit or loss extract for the year ended 30 September 20X5:

	$000
Operating profit before interest and tax	270
Interest expense	(260)
Interest receivable	40
Profit before tax	50
Net tax credit	50
Profit for the period	100

Note: The interest expense includes finance lease interest.

(ii)   The details of the tangible non-current assets are:

	Cost	Accumulated depreciation	Carrying value
	$000	$000	$000
At 30 September 20X4	20,200	4,400	15,800
At 30 September 20X5	16,000	5,400	10,600

During the year Tabba sold its factory for its fair value $12 million and agreed to rent it back, under an operating lease, for a period of five years at $1 million per annum. At the date of sale it had a carrying value of $7.4 million based on a previous revaluation of $8.6 million less depreciation of $1.2 million since the revaluation. The profit on the sale of the factory has been included in operating profit. The surplus on the revaluation reserve related entirely to the factory. No other disposals of non-current assets were made during the year.

Plant acquired under finance leases during the year was $1.5 million. Other purchases of plant during the year qualified for government grants of $950,000 received in the year.

Amortization of government grants has been credited to cost of sales.

(iii)   The insurance claim relates to flood damage to the company's inventories which occurred in September 20X4. The original estimate has been revised during the year after negotiations with the insurance company. The claim is expected to be settled in the near future.

Required:

(a)   **Prepare a statement of cash flows using the indirect method for Tabba in accordance with IAS 7 *Statements of cash flows* for the year ended 30 September 20X5.**   **(17 marks)**

(b)   **Using the information in the question and your statement of cash flows, comment on the change in the financial position of Tabba during the year ended 30 September 20X5.**   **(8 marks)**

Note: You are not required to calculate any ratios.   **(Total: 25 marks)**

64 PINTO *Walk in the footsteps of a top tutor*

Pinto is a publicly listed company. The following financial statements of Pinto are available:

Statement of profit or loss and other comprehensive income for the year ended 31 March 2008

	$000
Revenue	5,740
Cost of sales	(4,840)
Gross profit	900
Income from and gains on investment property	60
Distribution costs	(120)
Administrative expenses (note (ii))	(350)
Finance costs	(50)
Profit before tax	440
Income tax expense	(160)
Profit for the year	280
Other comprehensive income	
Gains on property revaluation	100
Total comprehensive income	380

Statements of financial position as at	31 March 2008		31 March 2007	
	$000	$000	$000	$000
Assets				
Non-current assets (note (i))				
Property, plant and equipment		2,880		1,860
Investment property		420		400
		3,300		2,260
Current assets				
Inventory	1,210		810	
Trade receivables	480		540	
Income tax asset	nil		50	
Bank	10	1,700	nil	1,400
Total assets		5,000		3,660
Equity and liabilities				
Equity shares of 20 cents each (note (iii))		1,000		600
Share premium	600		nil	
Revaluation reserve	150		50	
Retained earnings	1,440	2,190	1,310	1,360
		3,190		1,960

Non-current liabilities				
6% loan notes (note (ii))	nil		400	
Deferred tax	50	50	30	430
		———		———
Current liabilities				
Trade payables	1,410		1,050	
Bank overdraft	nil		120	
Warranty provision (note (iv))	200		100	
Current tax payable	150	1,760	nil	1,270
		———		———
Total equity and liabilities		5,000		3,660
		———		———

The following supporting information is available:

(i) An item of plant with a carrying amount of $240,000 was sold at a loss of $90,000 during the year. Depreciation of $280,000 was charged (to cost of sales) for property, plant and equipment in the year ended 31 March 2008.

Pinto uses the fair value model in IAS 40 *Investment Property*. There were no purchases or sales of investment property during the year.

(ii) The 6% loan notes were redeemed early incurring a penalty payment of $20 thousand which has been charged as an administrative expense in the statement of profit or loss and other comprehensive income.

(iii) There was an issue of shares for cash on 1 October 2007. There were no bonus issues of shares during the year.

(iv) Pinto gives a 12 month warranty on some of the products it sells. The amounts shown in current liabilities as warranty provision are an accurate assessment, based on past experience, of the amount of claims likely to be made in respect of warranties outstanding at each year end. Warranty costs are included in cost of sales.

(v) A dividend of 3 cents per share was paid on 1 January 2008.

Required:

(a) **Prepare a statement of cash flows for Pinto for the year to 31 March 2008 in accordance with IAS 7 *Statement of cash flows*.** **(15 marks)**

(b) **Comment on the cash flow management of Pinto as revealed by the statement of cash flows and the information provided by the above financial statements.**

Note: **Ratio analysis is not required, and will not be awarded any marks. (10 marks)**

(Total: 25 marks)

65   HARBIN 👣 *Walk in the footsteps of a top tutor*

Shown below are the recently issued (summarised) financial statements of Harbin, a listed company, for the year ended 30 September 2007, together with comparatives for 2006 and extracts from the Chief Executive's report that accompanied their issue.

Statements of profit or loss

	2007	2006
	$000	$000
Revenue	250,000	180,000
Cost of sales	(200,000)	(150,000)
Gross profit	50,000	30,000
Operating expenses	(26,000)	(22,000)
Finance costs	(8,000)	(Nil)
Profit before tax	16,000	8,000
Income tax expense (at 25%)	(4,000)	(2,000)
Profit for the period	12,000	6,000

Statement of financial position

	2007	2006
	$000	$000
Non-current assets		
Property, plant and equipment	210,000	90,000
Goodwill	10,000	Nil
	220,000	90,000
Current assets		
Inventory	25,000	15,000
Trade receivables	13,000	8,000
Bank	nil	14,000
	38,000	37,000
Total assets	258,000	127,000
Equity and liabilities		
Equity shares of $1 each	100,000	100,000
Retained earnings	14,000	12,000
	114,000	112,000

Non-current liabilities		
8% loan notes	100,000	Nil
Current liabilities		
Bank overdraft	17,000	Nil
Trade payables	23,000	13,000
Current tax payable	4,000	2,000
	44,000	15,000
Total equity and liabilities	258,000	127,000

Extracts from the Chief Executive's report:

'Highlights of Harbin's performance for the year ended 30 September 2007:

- an increase in sales revenue of 39%
- gross profit margin up from 16.7% to 20%
- a doubling of the profit for the period.

In response to the improved position the Board paid a dividend of 10 cents per share in September 2007 an increase of 25% on the previous year.'

You have also been provided with the following further information.

On 1 October 2006 Harbin purchased the whole of the net assets of Fatima (previously a privately owned entity) for $100 million. The contribution of the purchase to Harbin's results for the year ended 30 September 2007 was:

	$000
Revenue	70,000
Cost of sales	(40,000)
Gross profit	30,000
Operating expenses	(8,000)
Profit before tax	22,000

There were no disposals of non-current assets during the year.

The following ratios have been calculated for Harbin for the year ended 30 September 2006:

Return on year-end capital employed	7.1%
(profit before interest and tax over total assets less current liabilities)	
Net asset (equal to capital employed) turnover	1.6
Net profit (before tax) margin	4.4%
Current ratio	2.5
Closing inventory holding period (in days)	37
Trade receivables' collection period (in days)	16
Trade payables' payment period (based on cost of sales) (in days)	32
Gearing (debt over debt plus equity)	Nil

Required:

(a)   Calculate ratios for Harbin for the year ended 30 September 2007 equivalent to those calculated for the year ended 30 September 2006 (showing your workings).

(8 marks)

(b)   Assess the financial performance and position of Harbin for the year ended 30 September 2007 compared to the previous year. Your answer should refer to the information in the Chief Executive's report and the impact of the purchase of the net assets of Fatima.

(17 marks)

(Total: 25 marks)

66   GREENWOOD

Greenwood is a public listed company. During the year ended 31 March 2007 the directors decided to cease operations of one of its activities and put the assets of the operation up for sale (the discontinued activity has no associated liabilities). The directors have been advised that the cessation qualifies as a discontinued operation and has been accounted for accordingly.

Extracts from Greenwood's financial statements are set out below.

Note: The statement of profit or loss figures down to the profit for the period from continuing operations are those of the continuing operations only.

Statement of profit or loss for the year ended 31 March

	2007	2006
	$000	$000
Revenue	27,500	21,200
Cost of sales	(19,500)	(15,000)
Gross profit	8,000	6,200
Operating expenses	(2,900)	(2,450)
	5,100	3,750
Finance costs	(600)	(250)
Profit before taxation	4,500	3,500
Income tax expense	(1,000)	(800)
Profit for the period from continuing operations	3,500	2,700
Profit/(Loss) from discontinued operations	(1,500)	320
Profit for the period	2,000	3,020

Analysis of discontinued operations

Revenue	7,500	9,000
Cost of sales	(8,500)	(8,000)
Gross profit/(loss)	(1,000)	1,000
Operating expenses	(400)	(550)
Profit/(loss) before tax	(1,400)	450
Tax (expense)/relief	300	(130)
	(1,100)	320
Loss on measurement to fair value of disposal group	(500)	–
Tax relief on disposal group	100	–
Profit/(Loss) from discontinued operations	(1,500)	320

Statement of financial positions as at 31 March

	2007		2006	
	$000	$000	$000	$000
Non-current assets		17,500		17,600
Current assets				
Inventory	1,500		1,350	
Trade receivables	2,000		2,300	
Bank	Nil		50	
Assets held for sale (at fair value)	6,000	9,500	Nil	3,700
Total assets		27,000		21,300
Equity and liabilities				
Equity shares of $1 each		10,000		10,000
Retained earnings		4,500		2,500
		14,500		12,500
Non-current liabilities				
5% loan notes		8,000		5,000
Current liabilities				
Bank overdraft	1,150		Nil	
Trade payables	2,400		2,800	
Current tax payable	950	4,500	1,000	3,800
Total equity and liabilities		27,000		21,300

Note: The carrying amount of the assets of the discontinued operation at 31 March 2006 was $6.3 million.

Required:

(a) Analyse the financial performance and position of Greenwood for the two years ended 31 March 2007.

Note: Your analysis should be supported by appropriate ratios and refer to the effects of the discontinued operation. **(22 marks)**

(b) Discuss the limitations that are inherent when using financial statements to analyse performance. **(3 marks)**

(Total: 25 marks)

67   VICTULAR   *Walk in the footsteps of a top tutor*

Victular is a public company that would like to acquire (100% of) a suitable private company. It has obtained the following draft financial statements for two companies, Grappa and Merlot. They operate in the same industry and their managements have indicated that they would be receptive to a takeover.

Statements of profit or loss for the year ended 30 September 2008

	$000	Grappa $000	$000	Merlot $000
Revenue		12,000		20,500
Cost of sales		(10,500)		(18,000)
Gross profit		1,500		2,500
Operating expenses		(240)		(500)
Finance costs – loan		(210)		(300)
– overdraft		Nil		(10)
– lease		Nil		(290)
Profit before tax		1,050		1,400
Income tax expense		(150)		(400)
Profit for the year		900		1,000
Note: Dividends paid during the year		250		700

Statements of financial position as at 30 September 2008

Assets

Non-current assets

Freehold factory (note (i))		4,400		Nil
Owned plant (note (ii))		5,000		2,200
Leased plant (note (ii))		Nil		5,300
		9,400		7,500
Current assets				
Inventory	2,000		3,600	
Trade receivables	2,400		3,700	
Bank	600	5,000	Nil	7,300
Total assets		14,400		14,800
Equity and liabilities				
Equity shares of $1 each		2,000		2,000
Property revaluation reserve	900		Nil	
Retained earnings	2,600	3,500	800	800
		5,500		2,800
Non-current liabilities				
Finance lease obligations (note (iii))	Nil		3,200	
7% loan notes	3,000		Nil	
10% loan notes	Nil		3,000	
Deferred tax	600		100	
Government grants	1,200	4,800	Nil	6,300
Current liabilities				
Bank overdraft	Nil		1,200	
Trade payables	3,100		3,800	
Government grants	400		Nil	
Finance lease obligations (note (iii))	Nil		500	
Taxation	600	4,100	200	5,700
Total equity and liabilities		14,400		14,800

Notes

(i)   Both companies operate from similar premises.

(ii)   Additional details of the two companies' plant are:

	Grappa	Merlot
	$000	$000
Owned plant – cost	8,000	10,000
Leased plant – original fair value	Nil	7,500

There were no disposals of plant during the year by either company.

(iii)   The interest rate implicit within Merlot's finance leases is 7.5% per annum. For the purpose of calculating ROCE and gearing, **all** finance lease obligations are treated as long-term interest bearing borrowings.

(iv)   The following ratios have been calculated for Grappa and can be taken to be correct:

Return on year end capital employed (ROCE)	14.8%
(capital employed taken as shareholders' funds plus long-term interest bearing borrowings – see note (iii) above)	
Pre-tax return on equity (ROE)	19.1%
Net asset (total assets less current liabilities) turnover	1.2 times
Gross profit margin	12.5%
Operating profit margin	10.5%
Current ratio	1.2:1
Closing inventory holding period	70 days
Trade receivables' collection period	73 days
Trade payables' payment period (using cost of sales)	100 days
Gearing (see note (iii) above)	35.3%
Interest cover	6 times
Dividend cover	3.6 times

Required:

(a)   **Calculate for Merlot the ratios equivalent to all those given for Grappa above.**

(8 marks)

(b)   **Assess the relative performance and financial position of Grappa and Merlot for the year ended 30 September 2008 to inform the directors of Victular in their acquisition decision.**   **(12 marks)**

(c)   **Explain the limitations of ratio analysis and any further information that may be useful to the directors of Victular when making an acquisition decision.**   **(5 marks)**

(Total: 25 marks)

68 COALTOWN Walk in the footsteps of a top tutor

 Timed question with Online tutor debrief

Coaltown is a wholesaler and retailer of office furniture. Extracts from the company's financial statements are set out below:

Statement of profit or loss and other comprehensive income for the year ended:

	31 March 2009		31 March 2008	
	$000	$000	$000	$000
Revenue – cash	12,800		26,500	
– credit	53,000	65,800	28,500	55,000
Cost of sales		(43,800)		(33,000)
Gross profit		22,000		22,000
Operating expenses		(11,200)		(6,920)
Finance costs – loan notes	(380)		(180)	
– overdraft	(220)	(600)	nil	(180)
Profit before tax		10,200		14,900
Income tax expense		(3,200)		(4,400)
Profit for period		7,000		10,500
Other comprehensive income				
Gain on property revaluation		5,000		1,200
Total comprehensive income for the year		12,000		11,700

Statement of changes in equity for the year ended 31 March 2009:

	$000	$000	$000	$000	$000
	Equity shares	Share premium	Revaluation reserve	Retained earnings	Total
Balances b/f	8,000	500	2,500	15,800	26,800
Share issue	8,600	4,300			12,900
Comprehensive income			5,000	7,000	12,000
Dividends paid				(4,000)	(4,000)
Balances c/f	16,600	4,800	7,500	18,800	47,700

Statements of financial position as at 31 March:

	2009		2008	
	$000	$000	$000	$000
Assets				
Non-current assets (see note)				
Cost		93,500		80,000
Accumulated depreciation		(43,000)		(48,000)
		50,500		32,000
Current assets				
Inventory	5,200		4,400	
Trade receivables	7,800		2,800	
Bank	nil	13,000	700	7,900
Total assets		63,500		39,900
Equity and liabilities				
Equity shares of $1 each		16,600		8,000
Share premium		4,800		500
Revaluation reserve		7,500		2,500
Retained earnings		18,800		15,800
		47,700		26,800
Non-current liabilities		4,000		3,000
10% loan notes				
Current liabilities	3,600		nil	
Bank overdraft				
Trade payables	4,200		4,500	
Taxation	3,000		5,300	
Warranty provision	1,000	11,800	300	10,100
Total equity and liabilities		63,500		39,900

***Note:* Non-current assets**

During the year the company redesigned its display areas in all of its outlets. The previous displays had cost $10 million and had been written down by $9 million. There was an unexpected cost of $500,000 for the removal and disposal of the old display areas. Also during the year the company revalued the carrying amount of its property upwards by $5 million, the accumulated depreciation on these properties of $2 million was reset to zero.

All depreciation is charged to operating expenses.

Required:

(a) Prepare a statement of cash flows for Coaltown for the year ended 31 March 2009 in accordance with IAS 7 *Statement of Cash Flows* by the indirect method.

(15 marks)

(b) The directors of Coaltown are concerned at the deterioration in its bank balance and are surprised that the amount of gross profit has not increased for the year ended 31 March 2009. At the beginning of the current accounting period (i.e. on 1 April 2008), the company changed to importing its purchases from a foreign supplier because the trade prices quoted by the new supplier were consistently 10% below those of its previous supplier. However, the new supplier offered a shorter period of credit than the previous supplier (all purchases are on credit). In order to encourage higher sales, Coaltown increased its credit period to its customers, and some of the cost savings (on trade purchases) were passed on to customers by reducing selling prices on both cash and credit sales by 5% across all products.

Required:

(i) Calculate the gross profit margin that you would have expected Coaltown to achieve for the year ended 31 March 2009 based on the selling and purchase price changes described by the directors; **(2 marks)**

(ii) Comment on the directors' surprise at the unchanged gross profit and suggest what other factors may have affected gross profit for the year ended 31 March 2009; **(4 marks)**

(iii) Applying the trade receivables and payables credit periods for the year ended 31 March 2008 to the credit sales and purchases of the year ended 31 March 2009, calculate the effect this would have had on the company's bank balance at 31 March 2009 assuming sales and purchases would have remained unchanged. **(4 marks)**

Note: The inventory at 31 March 2008 was unchanged from that at 31 March 2007; assume 365 trading days.

(Total: 25 marks)

Calculate your allowed time, allocate the time to the separate parts

---

69 CROSSWIRE *Walk in the footsteps of a top tutor*

(a) The following information relates to Crosswire a publicly listed company.

Summarised statements of financial position as at:

	30 September 2009		30 September 2008	
	$000	$000	$000	$000
Assets				
Non-current assets				
Property, plant and equipment (note (i))		32,500		13,100
Development costs (note (ii))		1,000		2,500
		33,500		15,600
Current assets		8,200		6,800
Total assets		41,700		22,400
Equity and liabilities				
Equity				
Equity shares of $1 each		5,000		4,000
Share premium	6,000		2,000	
Other equity reserve	500		500	
Revaluation reserve	2,000		Nil	
Retained earnings	5,700	14,200	3,200	5,700
		19,200		9,700
Non-current liabilities				
10% convertible loan notes (note (iii))	1,000		5,000	
Environmental provision	3,300		Nil	
Finance lease obligations	5,040		Nil	
Deferred tax	3,360	12,700	1,200	6,200
Current liabilities				
Finance lease obligations	1,760		Nil	
Trade payables	8,040	9,800	6,500	6,500
Total equity and liabilities		41,700		22,400

Information from the statement of profit or loss for the year ended:

	30 September 2009	30 September 2008
	$000	$000
Revenue	52,000	42,000
Finance costs (note (iv))	1,050	500
Income tax expense	1,000	800
Profit for the year (after tax)	4,000	3,000

The following information is available:

(i) During the year to 30 September 2009, Crosswire embarked on a replacement and expansion programme for its non-current assets. The details of this programme are:

On 1 October 2008 Crosswire acquired a platinum mine at a cost of $5 million. A condition of mining the platinum is a requirement to landscape the mining site at the end of its estimated life of ten years. The present value of this cost at the date of the purchase was calculated at $3 million (in addition to the purchase price of the mine of $5 million).

Also on 1 October 2008 Crosswire revalued its freehold land for the first time. The credit in the revaluation reserve is the net amount of the revaluation after a transfer to deferred tax on the gain. The tax rate applicable to Crosswire for deferred tax is 20% per annum.

On 1 April 2009 Crosswire took out a finance lease for some new plant. The fair value of the plant was $10 million. The lease agreement provided for an initial payment on 1 April 2009 of $2.4 million followed by eight six-monthly payments of $1.2 million commencing 30 September 2009.

Plant disposed of during the year had a carrying amount of $500,000 and was sold for $1.2 million. The remaining movement on the property, plant and equipment, after charging depreciation of $3 million, was the cost of replacing plant.

(ii) From 1 October 2008 to 31 March 2009 a further $500,000 was spent completing the development project at which date marketing and production started. The sales of the new product proved disappointing and on 30 September 2009 the development costs were written down to $1 million via an impairment charge.

(iii) During the year ended 30 September 2009, $4 million of the 10% convertible loan notes matured. The loan note holders had the option of redemption at par in cash or to exchange them for equity shares on the basis of 20 new shares for each $100 of loan notes. 75% of the loan-note holders chose the equity option. Ignore any effect of this on the other equity reserve.

All the above items have been treated correctly according to International Financial Reporting Standards.

(iv) The finance costs are made up of:

For year ended:	30 September 2009 $000	30 September 2008 $000
Finance lease charges	400	Nil
Unwinding of environmental provision	300	Nil
Loan-note interest	350	500
	1,050	500

Required:

(i) Prepare a statement of the movements in the carrying amount of Crosswire's non-current assets for the year ended 30 September 2009; **(9 marks)**

(ii) Calculate the amounts that would appear under the headings of 'cash flows from investing activities' and 'cash flows from financing activities' in the statement of cash flows for Crosswire for the year ended 30 September 2009.

Note: Crosswire includes finance costs paid as a financing activity. **(8 marks)**

(b) A substantial shareholder has written to the directors of Crosswire expressing particular concern over the deterioration of the company's return on capital employed (ROCE)

Required:

Calculate Crosswire's ROCE for the two years ended 30 September 2008 and 2009 and comment on the apparent cause of its deterioration.

Note: ROCE should be taken as profit before interest on long-term borrowings and tax as a percentage of equity plus loan notes and finance lease obligations (at the year end). **(8 marks)**

(Total: 25 marks)

70 DELTOID *Walk in the footsteps of a top tutor*

(a) The following information relates to the draft financial statements of Deltoid.

Summarised statements of financial position as at:

	31 March 2010		31 March 2009	
	$000	$000	$000	$000
Assets				
Non-current assets				
Property, plant and equipment (note (i))		19,000		25,500
Current assets				
Inventory		12,500		4,600
Trade receivables		4,500		2,000
Tax refund due		500		nil
Bank		nil		1,500
Total assets		36,500		33,600
Equity and liabilities				
Equity				
Equity shares of $1 each (note (ii))		10,000		8,000
Share premium (note (ii))	3,200		4,000	
Retained earnings	4,500	7,700	6,300	10,300
		17,700		18,300

PAPER F7 (INT & UK) : FINANCIAL REPORTING

Non-current liabilities				
10% loan note (note (iii))	nil		5,000	
Finance lease obligations	4,800		2,000	
Deferred tax	1,200	6,000	800	7,800

Current liabilities				
10% loan note (note (iii))	5,000		nil	
Tax	nil		2,500	
Bank overdraft	1,400		nil	
Finance lease obligations	1,700		800	
Trade payables	4,700	12,800	4,200	7,500

Total equity and liabilities		36,500		33,600

Summarised statement of profit or loss for the years ended:

	31 March 2010	31 March 2009
	$000	$000
Revenue	55,000	40,000
Cost of sales	(43,800)	(25,000)
Gross profit	11,200	15,000
Operating expenses	(12,000)	(6,000)
Finance costs (note (iv))	(1,000)	(600)
Profit (loss) before tax	(1,800)	8,400
Income tax relief (expense)	700	(2,800)
Profit (loss) for the year	(1,100)	5,600

The following additional information is available:

(i)   Property, plant and equipment is made up of:

As at:	31 March 2010	31 March 2009
	$000	$000
Leasehold property	nil	8,800
Owned plant	12,500	14,200
Leased plant	6,500	2,500
	19,000	25,500

During the year Deltoid sold its leasehold property for $8·5 million and entered into an arrangement to rent it back from the purchaser. There were no additions to or disposals of owned plant during the year. The depreciation charges (to cost of sales) for the year ended 31 March 2010 were:

	$000
Leasehold property	200
Owned plant	1,700
Leased plant	1,800
	3,700

KAPLAN PUBLISHING

(ii) On 1 July 2009 there was a bonus issue of shares from share premium of one new share for every 10 held. On 1 October 2009 there was a fully subscribed cash issue of shares at par.

(iii) The 10% loan note is due for repayment on 30 June 2010. Deltoid is in negotiations with the loan provider to refinance the same amount for another five years.

(iv) The finance costs are made up of:

For year ended:	31 March 2010	31 March 2009
	$000	$000
Finance lease charges	300	100
Overdraft interest	200	nil
Loan note interest	500	500
	1,000	600

Required:

(i) **Prepare a statement of cash flows for Deltoid for the year ended 31 March 2010 in accordance with IAS 7 *Statement of cash flows*, using the indirect method;**   **(12 marks)**

(ii) **Based on the information available, advise the loan provider on the matters you would take into consideration when deciding whether to grant Deltoid a renewal of its maturing loan note.**   **(8 marks)**

(b) On a separate matter, you have been asked to advise on an application for a loan to build an extension to a sports club which is a not-for-profit organisation. You have been provided with the audited financial statements of the sports club for the last four years.

Required:

Identify and explain the ratios that you would calculate to assist in determining whether you would advise that the loan should be granted.   **(5 marks)**

(Total: 25 marks)

UK SYLLABUS FOCUS ONLY

A UK element to this question could ask you to:

"Describe the differences in format under a UK presentation of a cash flow as required by FRS 1".

Section 2

ANSWERS TO PRACTICE QUESTIONS

A CONCEPTUAL FRAMEWORK FOR FINANCIAL REPORTING

1   IASB FRAMEWORK *Walk in the footsteps of a top tutor*

> **Key answer tips**
>
> Parts (a) and (b) are very straightforward if you have done your work properly. The three adjustments required in part (c) focus on controversial areas. Remember that with compound financial instruments such as a convertible loan, the liability amount is calculated by discounting the cash flows at the rate applicable to a non-convertible loan; this rate will be higher than the rate on the convertible, because it does not include the 'equity sweetener'. The highlighted words are key phrases that markers are looking for.

(a)   The purpose of the Framework is to assist the various bodies and users that may be interested in the financial statements of an entity. It is there to assist the IASB itself, other standard setters, preparers, auditors and users of financial statements and any other party interested in the work of the IASB. More specifically:

–   to assist the Board in the development of new and the review of existing standards. It is also believed that the Framework will assist in promoting harmonization of the preparation of financial statements and also reduce the number of alternative accounting treatments permitted by IFRSs

–   national standard setters that have expressed a desire for local standards to be compliant with IFRS will be assisted by the Framework

–   the Framework will help preparers to apply IFRS more effectively if they understand the concepts underlying the Standards; additionally the Framework should help in dealing with new or emerging issues which are, as yet, not covered by an IFRS

–   the above is also true of the work of the auditor; in particular the Framework can assist the auditor in determining whether the financial statements conform to IFRS

–   users should be assisted by the Framework in interpreting the performance of entities that have complied with IFRS.

It is important to realize that the Framework is not itself an accounting standard and thus cannot override a requirement of a specific standard. Indeed, the Board recognizes that there may be (rare) occasions where a particular IFRS is in conflict with the Framework; in these cases the requirements of the standard should prevail. The Board believes that such conflicts will diminish over time as the development of new and (revised) existing standards will be guided by the Framework and the Framework itself is being revised based on the experience of working with it.

(b)   **Definition of assets:**

The IASB's Framework defines assets as 'a resource controlled by an entity as a result of past events and from which future economic benefits are expected to flow to the entity'. The first part of the definition puts the emphasis on control rather than ownership. This is done so that the statement of financial position reflects the substance of transactions rather than their legal form. This means that assets that are not legally owned by an entity, but over which the entity has the rights that are normally conveyed by ownership, are recognized as assets of the entity. Common examples of this would be finance leased assets and other contractual rights such as aircraft landing rights. An important aspect of control of assets is that it allows the entity to restrict the access of others to them. The reference to past events prevents assets that may arise in future from being recognized early.

Definition of liabilities:

The IASB's Framework defines liabilities as 'a present obligation of the entity arising from past events, the settlement of which is expected to result in an outflow from the entity of resources embodying economic benefits'. Many aspects of this definition are complementary (as a mirror image) to the definition of assets, however the IASB stresses that the essential characteristic of a liability is that the entity has a present obligation. Such obligations are usually legally enforceable (by a binding contract or by statute), but obligations also arise where there is an expectation (by a third party) of an entity assuming responsibility for costs where there is no legal requirement to do so. Such obligations are referred to as constructive (by IAS 37 *Provisions, contingent liabilities and contingent assets*). An example of this would be repairing or replacing faulty goods (beyond any warranty period) or incurring environmental costs (e.g. landscaping the site of a previous quarry) where there is no legal obligation to do so. Where entities do incur constructive obligations it is usually to maintain the goodwill and reputation of the entity. One area of difficulty is where entities cannot be sure whether an obligation exists or not; it may depend upon a future uncertain event. These are more generally known as contingent liabilities.

Importance of the definitions of assets and liabilities:

The definitions of assets and liabilities are fundamental to the Framework. Apart from forming the obvious basis for the preparation of a statement of financial position, they are also the two elements of financial statements that are used to derive the equity interest (ownership) which is the residue of assets less liabilities. Assets and liabilities also have a part to play in determining performance, when income (which includes gains) and expenses (which include losses) should be recognized. Income is recognized (in the statement of comprehensive income) when there is an increase in future economic benefits relating to increases in assets or decreases in liabilities, provided they can be measured reliably (complete, neutral and free from error). Expenses are the opposite of this. Changes in assets and liabilities arising from contributions from, and distributions to, the owners are excluded from the definitions of income and expenses.

Currently there is a great deal of concern over 'off balance sheet finance'. This is an aspect of what is commonly referred to as creative accounting. Many recent company failure scandals have been in part due to companies having often massive liabilities that have not been included on the statement of financial position. Robust definitions, based on substance, of assets and liabilities in particular should ensure that only real assets are included on the statement of financial position and all liabilities are also included. In contradiction to the above point, there have also been occasions where companies have included liabilities on their statements of financial position where they do not meet the definition of liabilities in the Framework. Common examples of this are general provisions and accounting for future costs and losses (usually as part of the acquisition of a subsidiary). Companies have used these general provisions to smooth profits, i.e. creating a provision when the company has a good year (in terms of profit) and releasing them to boost profits in a bad year. Providing for future costs and losses during an acquisition may effectively allow them to bypass the statement of profit or loss as they would become part of the goodwill figure.

(c) (i) Whilst it is acceptable to value the goodwill of $2.5 million of Trantor (the subsidiary) on the basis described in the question and include it in the consolidated statement of financial position, the same treatment cannot be afforded to Peterlee's own goodwill. The calculation may indeed give a realistic value of $4 million for Peterlee's goodwill, and there may be no difference in nature between the goodwill of the two companies, but it must be realized that the goodwill of Peterlee is internal goodwill and IFRSs prohibit such goodwill appearing in the financial statements. The main basis of this conclusion is one of reliable measurement. The value of acquired (purchased) goodwill can be evidenced by the method described in the question (there are also other acceptable methods), but this method of valuation is not acceptable as a basis for recognising internal goodwill.

(ii) Accruing for future costs such as this landscaping on an annual basis may seem appropriate and was previously common practice. However, it is no longer possible to account for this type of future cost in this manner, so the directors' suggestion is unacceptable. IAS 37 *Provisions, contingent liabilities and contingent assets* requires such costs to be accounted for in full as soon as they become unavoidable. The standard says that the estimate of the future cost should be discounted to a present value (as in this example at $2 million). The accounting treatment is rather controversial; the cost should be included in the statement of financial position as a provision (a credit entry/balance), but the debit is to the cost of the asset to give an initial carrying amount of $8 million. This has the effect of 'grossing up' the statement of financial position by including the landscaping costs as both an asset and a liability. As the asset is depreciated on a systematic basis ($800,000 per annum assuming straight-line depreciation), the landscaping costs are charged to the statement of comprehensive income over the life of the asset. As the discount is 'unwound' (and charged as a finance cost) this is added to the statement of financial position provision such that, at the date when the liability is due to be settled, the provision is equal to the amount due (assuming estimates prove to be accurate).

(iii) The directors' suggestion that the convertible loan should be recorded as a liability of the full $5 million is incorrect. The reason why a similar loan without the option to convert to equity shares (such that it must be redeemed by cash only) carries a higher interest rate is because of the value of the equity option that is contained within the issue proceeds of the $5 million. If the company performs well over the period of the loan, the value of its equity shares should rise and thus it would (probably) be beneficial for the loan note holders to opt for the equity share alternative. IAS 32 and IFRS 9 dealing with financial instruments require the value of the option is to be treated as equity rather than debt. The calculation of value of the equity is as follows:

	$000
Year 1 400 × 0.91	364
Year 2 400 × 0.83	332
Year 3 (5,000 + 400) × 0.75	4,050
Present value of the cash flows at 10% = initial liability	4,746
Proceeds of issue	5,000
Equity (β)	254
The 20X6 finance charge in the statement of comprehensive income is 10% × 4,746	475
The end-20X6 liability is 4,746 + 475 − interest paid (8% × 5,000)	4,821

2 ANGELINO

> **Key answer tips**
>
> Part (a) is a fairly standard discussion but in part (b) you must apply your knowledge to receivables factoring, sale and leaseback and consignment inventory. These are likely to be popular areas of the syllabus with the examiner.

(a)   Most forms of off balance sheet financing (off statement of financial position) have the effect of what is, in substance, debt finance either not appearing on the statement of financial position at all or being netted off against related assets such that it is not classified as debt. Common examples would be structuring a lease such that it fell to be treated as an operating lease when it has the characteristics of a finance lease, complex financial instruments classified as equity when they may have, at least in part, the substance of debt and 'controlled' entities having large borrowings (used to benefit the group as a whole), that are not consolidated because the financial structure avoids the entities meeting the definition of a subsidiary.

The main problem of off balance sheet finance is that it results in financial statements that do not faithfully represent the transactions and events that have taken place. Faithful representation is one of the fundamental qualitative characteristics of useful information (as described in the *Conceptual Framework*). Financial statements that do not faithfully represent that which they purport to, lack reliability. A lack of reliability may mean that any decisions made on the basis of the information contained in financial statements are likely to be incorrect or, at best, suboptimal.

The level of debt on a statement of financial position is a direct contributor to the calculation of an entity's statement of financial position gearing, which is considered as one of the most important financial ratios. It should be understood that, to a point, the use of debt financing is perfectly acceptable. Where statement of financial position gearing is considered low, borrowing is relatively inexpensive, often tax efficient and can lead to higher returns to shareholders. However, when the level of borrowings becomes high, it increases risk in many ways. Off balance sheet financing may lead to a breach of loan covenants (a serious situation) if such debt were to be recognized on the statement of financial position in accordance with its substance.

High gearing is a particular issue to equity investors. Equity (ordinary shares) is sometimes described as residual return capital. This description identifies the dangers (to owners) when an entity has high gearing. The dividend that the equity shareholders might expect is often based on the level of reported profits. The finance cost of debt acts as a reduction of the profits available for dividends. As the level of debt increases, higher interest rates are also usually payable to reflect the additional risk borne by the lender, thus the higher the debt the greater the finance charges and the lower the profit. Many off balance sheet finance schemes also disguise or hide the true finance cost which makes it difficult for equity investors to assess the amount of profits that will be needed to finance the debt and consequently how much profit will be available to equity investors. Furthermore, if the market believes or suspects an entity is involved in 'creative accounting' (and off balance sheet finance is a common example of this) it may adversely affect the entity's share price.

An entity's level of gearing will also influence any decision to provide further debt finance (loans) to the entity. Lenders will consider the nature and value of the assets that an entity owns which may be provided as security for the borrowings. The presence of existing debt will generally increase the risk of default of interest and capital repayments (on further borrowings) and existing lenders may have a prior charge on assets available as security. In simple terms if an entity has high borrowings, additional borrowing is more risky and consequently more expensive. A prospective lender to an entity that already has high borrowings, but which do not appear on the statement of financial position is likely to make the wrong decision. If the correct level of borrowings were apparent, either the lender would not make the loan at all (too high a lending risk) or, if it did make the loan, it would be on substantially different terms (e.g. charge a higher interest rate) so as to reflect the real risk of the loan.

Some forms of off balance sheet financing may specifically mislead suppliers that offer credit. It is a natural precaution that a prospective supplier will consider the statement of financial position strength and liquidity ratios of the prospective customer. The existence of consignment inventories may be particularly relevant to trade suppliers. Sometimes consignment inventories and their related current liabilities are not recorded on the statement of financial position as the wording of the purchase agreement may be such that the legal ownership of the goods remains with the supplier until specified events occur (often the onward sale of the goods). This means that other suppliers cannot accurately assess an entity's true level of trade payables and consequently the average payment period to suppliers, both of which are important determinants in deciding whether to grant credit.

(b)   (i)   Factoring is a common method of entities releasing the liquidity of their trade receivables. The accounting issue that needs to be decided is whether the trade receivables have been sold, or whether the income from the finance house for their 'sale' should be treated as a short term loan. The main substance issue with this type of transaction is to identify which party bears the risks (i.e. of slow and non-payment by the customer) relating to the asset. If the risk lies with the finance house (Omar), the trade receivables should be removed from the statement of financial position (derecognized in accordance with IFRS 9). In this case it is clear that Angelino still bears the risk relating to slow and non-payment. The residual payment by Omar depends on how quickly the receivables are collected; the longer it takes, the less the residual payment (this imputes a finance cost). Any balance uncollected by Omar after six months will be refunded by Angelino which reflects the non-payment risk.

Thus the correct accounting treatment for this transaction is that the cash received from Omar (80% of the selected receivables) should be treated as a current liability (a short term loan) and the difference between the gross trade receivables and the amount ultimately received from Omar (plus any amounts directly from the credit customers themselves) should be recognized in profit or loss. The classification of the amount recognized is likely to be a mixture of administrative expenses (for Omar collecting receivables), finance expenses (reflecting the time taken to collect the receivables) and the impairment of trade receivables (bad debts).

(ii) This is an example of a sale and leaseback of a property. Such transactions are part of normal commercial activity, often being used as a way to improve cash flow and liquidity. However, if an asset is sold at an amount that is different to its fair value there is likely to be an underlying reason for this. In this case it appears (based on the opinion of the auditor) that Finaid has paid Angelino $2 million more than the building is worth. No (unconnected) company would do this knowingly without there being some form of 'compensating' transaction. This sale is 'linked' to the five year rental agreement. The question indicates the rent too is not at a fair value, being $500,000 per annum ($1,300,000 − $800,000) above what a commercial rent for a similar building would be.

It now becomes clear that the excess purchase consideration of $2 million is an 'in substance' loan (rather than sales proceeds − the legal form) which is being repaid through the excess ($500,000 per annum) of the rentals. Although this is a sale and leaseback transaction, as the building is freehold and has an estimated remaining life (20 years) that is much longer than the five year leaseback period, the lease is not a finance lease and the building should be treated as sold and thus derecognized.

The correct treatment for this item is that the sale of the building should be recorded at its fair value of $10 million, thus the profit on disposal would be $2.5 million ($10 million − $7.5 million). The 'excess' of $2 million ($12 million − $10 million) should be treated as a loan (non-current liability). The rental payment of $1.3 million should be split into three elements; $800,000 building rental cost, $200,000 finance cost (10% of $2 million) and the remaining $300,000 is a capital repayment of the loan.

(iii) The treatment of consignment inventory depends on the substance of the arrangements between the manufacturer and the dealer (Angelino). The main issue is to determine if and at what point in time the cars are 'sold'. The substance is determined by analysing which parties bear the risks (e.g. slow moving/obsolete inventories, finance costs) and receive the benefits (e.g. use of inventories, potential for higher sales, protection from price increases) associated with the transaction.

Supplies from Monza

Angelino has, and has actually exercised, the right to return the cars without penalty (or been required by Monza to transfer them to another dealer), which would indicate that it has not 'bought' the cars. There are no finance costs incurred by Angelino, however Angelino would suffer from any price increases that occurred during the three month holding/display period. These factors seem to indicate that the substance of this arrangement is the same as its legal form i.e. Monza should include the cars in its statement of financial position as inventory and therefore Angelino will not record a purchase transaction until it becomes obliged to pay for the cars (three months after delivery or until sold to customers if sooner).

Supplies from Capri

Although this arrangement seems similar to the above, there are several important differences. Angelino is bearing the finance costs of 1% per month (calling it a display charge is a distraction). The option to return the cars should be ignored because it is not likely to be exercised due to commercial penalties (payment of transport costs and loss of deposit). Finally the purchase price is fixed at the date of delivery rather than at the end of six months. These factors strongly indicate that Angelino bears the risks and rewards associated with ownership and should recognize the inventory and the associated liability in its financial statements at the date of delivery.

3 REVENUE RECOGNITION

Key answer tips

The introductory paragraph is there to set the scene and to lead you in the general direction that the Examiner intends you to go. Therefore in part (a) it is not enough to discuss general examples of the differences between substance and form without relating this to revenue recognition issues.

Be prepared to consider other issues in the rest of your answer, for example part (c) tests your knowledge of IASs 20 and 37 and part (d) also tests your knowledge of IAS 8.

(a) The *Framework* advocates that revenue recognition issues are resolved within the definition of assets (gains) and liabilities (losses). Gains include all forms of income and revenue as well as gains on non-revenue items. Gains and losses are defined as increases or decreases in net assets other than those resulting from transactions with owners. Thus in its *Framework*, the IASB takes a statement of financial position approach to defining revenue. In effect a recognisable increase in an asset results in a gain. The more traditional view, which is largely the basis used in IAS 18 *Revenue*, is that (net) revenue recognition is part of a transactions based accruals or matching process with the statement of financial position recording any residual assets or liabilities such as receivables and payables. The issue of revenue recognition arises out of the need to report company performance for specific periods. The *Framework* identifies three stages in the recognition of assets (and liabilities):

• initial recognition, when an item first meets the definition of an asset;

- subsequent remeasurement, which may involve changing the value (with a corresponding effect on income) of a recognized item; and

- possible derecognition, where an item no longer meets the definition of an asset.

For many simple transactions both the *Framework's* approach and the traditional approach (IAS 18) will result in the same profit (net income). If an item of inventory is bought for $100 and sold for $150, net assets have increased by $50 and the increase would be reported as a profit. The same figure would be reported under the traditional transactions based reporting (sales of $150 less cost of sales of $100). However, in more complex areas the two approaches can produce different results.

An example of this would be deferred income. If a company received a fee for a 12 month tuition course in advance, IAS 18 would treat this as deferred income (on the statement of financial position) and release it to income as the tuition is provided and matched with the cost of providing the tuition. Thus the profit would be spread (accrued) over the period of the course. If an asset/liability approach were taken, then the only liability the company would have after the receipt of the fee would be for the cost of providing the course. If only this liability is recognized in the statement of financial position, the whole of the profit on the course would be recognized on receipt of the income. This is not a prudent approach and has led to criticism of the *Framework* for this very reason. Arguably the treatment of government grants under IAS 20 (as deferred income) does not comply with the Framework as deferred income does not meet the definition of a liability.

Other standards that may be in conflict with the Framework are the use of the accretion approach in IAS 11 *Construction Contracts* and a deferred tax liability in IAS 12 *Income Taxes* may not fully meet the *Framework's* definition of a liability.

The principle of substance over form should also be applied to revenue recognition. An example of where this can impact on reporting practice is on sale and repurchase agreements. Companies sometimes 'sell' assets to another company with the right to buy them back on predetermined terms that will almost certainly mean that they will be repurchased in the future. In substance this type of arrangement is a secured loan and the 'sale' should not be treated as revenue. A less controversial area of the application of substance in relation to revenue recognition is with agency sales. IAS 18 says, where a company sells goods acting as an agent, those sales should not be treated as sales of the agent, instead only the commission from the sales is income of the agent. Recently several internet companies have been accused of boosting their revenue figures by treating agency sales as their own.

(b) Sales made by Derringdo of goods from Gungho must be treated under two separate categories. Sales of the A grade goods are made by Derringdo acting as an agent of Gungho. For these sales Derringdo must only record in revenue the amount of commission (12.5%) it is entitled to under the sales agreement. There may also be a receivable or payable for Gungho in the statement of financial position. Sales of the B grade goods are made by Derringdo acting as a principal, not an agent. Thus they will be included in revenue with their cost included in cost of sales.

	$000
Revenue (4,600 (W1) + 11,400 (W2))	16,000
Cost of sales (W2)	(8,550)
Gross profit	7,450

Workings: (all figures in $000)	*A grade*
(W1) **Opening inventory**	2,400
Transfers/purchases	18,000
	20,400
Closing inventory	(2,000)
Cost of sales	18,400
Selling price (to give 50% gross profit)	36,800
Gross profit	18,400
Commission (12.5% × 36,800)	4,600

	B grade
(W2) **Opening inventory**	1,000
Transfers/purchases	8,800
	9,800
Closing inventory	(1,250)
Cost of sales	8,550
Selling price (8,550 × 4 /3 see below)	11,400

A gross profit margin of 25% is equivalent to a mark up on cost of $^1/_3$. Thus if cost of sales is multiplied by $^4/_3$ this will give the relevant selling price.

(c) (i) The IASB's *Framework* defines liabilities as obligations to transfer economic benefits as a result of past transactions. Such transfers of economic benefits are to third parties and normally as cash payments. Traditionally and in compliance with IAS 20, capital based government grants are treated as deferred credits and spread over the life of the related assets. This is the application of the matching concept. A strict interpretation of the *Framework* would not normally allow deferred credits to be treated as liabilities as there is usually no obligation to transfer economic benefits. In this particular example the only liability that may occur in respect of the grant would be if Derringdo were to sell the related asset within four years of its purchase. A possible argument would be that the grant should be treated as a reducing liability (in relation to a potential repayment) over the four-year claw back period. On closer consideration this would not be appropriate. The repayment would only occur if the asset were sold, thus it is potentially a contingent liability. As

Derringdo has no intention to sell the asset there is no reason to believe that the repayment will occur, thus it is not a reportable contingent liability. The implication of this is that the company's policy for the government grant does not comply with the definition of a liability in the *Framework*. Applying the guidance in the *Framework* would require the whole of the grant to be included in income as it is 'earned' i.e. in the year of receipt.

(ii) **Treatment under the company's policy**

Statement of comprehensive income extract year to 31 March 20X3

	$
Depreciation – plant ((800,000 – 120,000 estimated residual value)/10 years × $^6/_{12}$)	Dr 34,000
Government grant ((800,000 × 30%)/10 years × $^6/_{12}$)	Cr 12,000

Statement of financial position extracts as at 31 March 20X3 $

Non-current assets:
	$
Plant at cost	800,000
Accumulated depreciation	(34,000)
	766,000

Current liabilities:
Government grant (240,000/10 years)	24,000

Non-current liabilities:
Government grant (240,000 – 12,000 – 24,000)	204,000

Treatment under the *Framework*

Statement of comprehensive income extract year to 31 March 20X3 $

Depreciation – plant ((800,000 – 120,000 estimated residual value) /10 years × $^6/_{12}$)	Dr 34,000
Government grant (whole amount)	Cr 240,000

Statement of financial position extracts as at 31 March 20X3 $

Non-current assets:
	$
Plant at cost	800,000
Accumulated depreciation	(34,000)
	766,000

(d) On first impression, it appears that the company has changed its accounting policy from recognising carpet sales at the point of fitting to recognising them at the point when they are ordered and paid for. If this were the case then the new accounting policy should be applied as if it had always been in place and the revenue recognized in the year to 31 March 20X3 would be $23 million. Without the change in policy, sales would have been $22.6 million (23m + 1.2m – 1.6m). Sales made from the retail premises during the current year, but not yet fitted ($1.6 million) will not be recognized until the following period. A corresponding adjustment is made recognising the equivalent figure ($1.2 million) from the previous year. The difference between the $23 million and $22.6 million would be a prior period adjustment (less the cost of sales relating to this amount). This analysis assumes that the figures are material.

Despite first impressions, the above is not a change of accounting policy. This is because a change of accounting policy only occurs where the same circumstances are treated differently. In this case there are different circumstances. Derringdo has changed its method of trading; it is no longer responsible for any errors that may occur during the fitting of the carpets. An accounting policy that is applied to circumstances that differ from previous circumstances is not a change of accounting policy. Thus the amount to be recognized in revenue for the year to 31 March 20X3 would be $24.2 million (23m + 1.2m). Whilst this appears to boost the current year's income it would be mitigated by the payments to the sub-contractors for the carpet fitting.

4   HISTORIC COST

Key answer tips

(a)   Describe the effect of price inflation on the statement of financial position and the statement of comprehensive income. Move on to describe the limitations of the use of HCA as a means of assessing a business's performance. Do not forget to describe how three different users may be misled by such information.

(b)   GPP •   *advantages:* transaction based, objective, verifiable, adjusted by government inflation index.

•   understood by shareholders.

•   *disadvantages:* statistical; relevance of government index depends on company's activities; misleading for highly geared companies.

CCA •   *advantages:* corrects most limitations of HCA; reflects current values; more relevant to calculations of dividends, wage claims.

•   *disadvantages:* difficulty in setting values; methods of determining values; effect on share prices.

(a)   The main drawback of the use of historic cost accounts for assessing the performance of a business is that they do not take into account the current values of assets and, to a lesser extent, liabilities. This can become a serious problem and give misleading information when either specific or general price inflation rates are considered to be high. The effect is that many of the values of the assets in the statement of financial position are understated, and, partly because of related depreciation, profits tend to be overstated. More detailed criticisms of historic cost accounts during a period of rising prices are:

Effects on the statement of financial position

(i)   Most non-current assets can be considerably understated in terms of their current worth. The most affected assets tend to be land and buildings, investments and some plant.

(ii)   In general net current assets tend not to be affected by inflation mainly because they are monetary in nature. The possible exception is trading inventories.

(iii) Liabilities tend to be ignored when current values are discussed. This may be an error because, for example, a long term loan carrying a fixed rate of interest, may have a current value that is considerably different to when it was taken out (ignoring the possibility of any repayments). This is because current interest rates may have changed (often as a reaction to levels of inflation) since the loan was originally taken out.

(iv)   The statement of financial position equation dictates that if the net assets are understated, then so too are equity.

Effects on the statement of comprehensive income

Many costs tend to be understated in terms of their current value. Where this occurs it means the profit is overstated in as much as the use of lower costs leads to a higher profit. Many commentators argue that pure historical cost profits are made up of a current operating profit (see below) plus inflationary gains relating to the:

- costs of goods sold (both purchased and manufactured). This can be mitigated, but not completely removed, by the use of LIFO, however this is not common practice in many countries and is now prohibited by IAS 2 *Inventories*

- depreciation charges for non-current assets. In historic cost accounts these are based on historical values rather than current values, and therefore understate the values of the assets that have been used (consumed) during the period

- some methods of accounting for inflation include monetary working capital and/or 'gearing' adjustments to historical cost profits. These are intended to reflect the inflation effects of holding net monetary working capital and debt.

The above combined effects lead to the following criticisms and limitations of the use of historic cost accounts to assess a business's performance:

Lack of comparability

It may be invalid to compare the results of two companies. One company may have assets that are relatively old (and of lower cost) whereas another company may have similar, but more recently purchased (and of higher cost) assets. In effect such companies would have a similar operating capacity, but it would be recorded at different values. This situation can also be found within a single company that has operating divisions with similar characteristics to the above scenario. Management may assess their relative performance using historical costs (which would be an invalid basis) to make decisions relating to future investment or even closure.

There is also a lack of comparability between a company's current year's results and those of previous years i.e. trend analysis may be distorted.

Conceptual inconsistency

Accounting theorists sometimes argue that historic cost accounts are not internally consistent because they are in fact 'mixed value' accounts. This means that some historical costs are at current values, whereas other historical costs are at out-of-date values. Thus current values, of say revenue, are being matched with out-of-date values such as depreciation relating to older assets.

Many important ratios which are calculated as a basis for interpreting and assessing company performance can be distorted by inflation. Important examples are: return on capital employed, profit margins, many asset turnover ratios, gearing levels and earnings per share.

The misleading effects of the above on different users

Investors may find it difficult to compare the results of different companies as a basis for investment decisions. A shareholder may be tempted to accept a low bid for his/her shares if weight is given to the asset backing, based on book values, of the shares. Dividends may seem low in relation to reported profits, this may be because management is recommending dividends based on a current operating profit.

Employees may make high wage demands based on reported profit rather than current operating profits.

Governments generally tax reported profits which means companies pay tax on higher, inflation boosted, profits.

(b) The advantages and criticisms of General (Current) Purchasing Power and Current Cost Accounting are set out below:

General (Current) Purchasing Power Accounts

It is claimed that GPP accounts retain many of the advantages of historic cost accounts and overcome some of their deficiencies. Like historic cost accounts GPP accounts are transaction based, and are therefore objective and verifiable. This is because they are a restatement of historic cost accounts (which possess the above qualities) adjusted for the movement in an inflation index, usually published by the government.

Because the statement of comprehensive income and the statement of financial position are adjusted for price movements over time, GPP accounts are said to be comparable between companies and over time. This overcomes many of the difficulties of historic cost accounts.

If the index used to adjust the historic cost accounts is a consumer based index (as it usually is), then they are more appropriate to shareholders because this index is well understood by them and more appropriate to their spending patterns. The figure for equity is said to be a measure of the spending power (or consumption) that is being forgone in making (or holding) the investment in the company, and can be judged in those terms.

Opponents or critics of GPP accounting argue that many of the claimed advantages may not be true. GPP accounts suffer from some practical as well as theoretical problems:

(i) GPP values are not real values, current or otherwise; they are the result of statistical calculations. For many companies the GPP values of their non-current assets will only be similar to their real (current) values if the movement of the specific price indexes relating to those assets is similar to that of the General Price Index. An extreme case of this problem would occur where there was general (retail) price inflation, but the company trades in an activity where the prices of the goods they manufacture and supply are falling. Hi-fi, video and computer equipment may be examples of this. Average measures of inflation, particularly if they are measures of consumer inflation, are not usually appropriate to account for specific price inflation experienced by companies, which differs from company to company.

(ii)   Most items in the statement of comprehensive income are adjusted by the average inflation factor for the period. During periods of inflation this is greater than one and can give the general effect of increased profits. Although this effect is mitigated by higher depreciation charges, GPP profits for profitable companies can be higher than their historic cost profits. A major criticism of historic cost accounts is that they overstate operating profits, GPP accounts can worsen this problem rather than solve it. Highly geared companies tend to show even greater GPP profits (due to gains on net monetary liabilities), and such companies are more vulnerable when inflation is high. This is because interest rates are often increased by Governments in an attempt to control inflation. This has a detrimental effect on companies with high variable rate borrowings.

Current Cost Accounting

Current cost accounting principles, from a conceptual point of view, are more soundly based and therefore more difficult to criticize than GPP accounts. They correct most of the limitations of historic cost accounts that are due to increased price levels. They reflect the current values of a company's specific assets although this is not necessarily the current cost of those assets. The reported current operating profit is considered to be more relevant to many decisions such as dividend distribution, employee wage claims and even as a basis for taxation.

The problems of CCA lie in their preparation and understanding. In practical terms it can be very difficult to determine the current value of assets, and many alternative forms of current value exist e.g. replacement cost, realisable value and value in use. Methods of determining current costs include the use of manufacturers' price lists for plant and inventory, professional revaluation of assets e.g. land and buildings and the use of specific price indexes published by government agencies. Whatever method is used it is often subjective and sometimes complex. This makes the cost of the preparation and audit of current cost accounts expensive.

An interesting point arising from the past use of CCA in some countries is that when current cost results of companies were published there was no significant differential change in share prices relating to the current cost information. The Efficient Market Hypothesis would suggest that if CCA provided 'new' information then market prices would react. An interpretation of the above observation is that the information revealed by CCA was already 'known' by the market makers and imputed into share prices. Thus many feel that the expense of producing CCA gives no benefit to users. This perhaps explains why historic cost accounts are still dominant in financial reporting.

5   FINANCIAL STATEMENTS *Walk in the footsteps of a top tutor*

Key answer tips

Part (a) was extremely straightforward requiring the definitions of assumed knowledge accounting concepts. To score full marks here a candidate would need to support their definitions with an example. Part (b) required candidates to relate the accounting concepts specifically to inventory, again an example would be required to add depth to your answer – simply restating what has already been written in part (a) would not score any marks. The highlighted words are key phrases that markers are looking for.

(a)   The accruals basis requires transactions (or events) to be recognised when they occur (rather than on a cash flow basis). Revenue is recognised when it is earned (rather than when it is received) and expenses are recognised when they are incurred (i.e. when the entity has received the benefit from them), rather than when they are paid.

Recording the substance of transactions (and other events) requires them to be treated in accordance with economic reality or their commercial intent rather than in accordance with the way they may be legally constructed. This is an important element of faithful representation, one of the fundamental characteristics from the IASB Framework.

Prudence is used where there are elements of uncertainty surrounding transactions or events. Prudence requires the exercise of a degree of caution when making judgements or estimates under conditions of uncertainty. Thus when estimating the expected life of a newly acquired asset, if we have past experience of the use of similar assets and they had had lives of (say) between five and eight years, it would be prudent to use an estimated life of five years for the new asset.

Comparability is essential when assessing the performance of an entity by using its financial statements and is an enhancing characteristic from the IASB's framework. Assessing the performance of an entity over time (trend analysis) requires that the financial statements used have been prepared on a comparable (consistent) basis. Generally this can be interpreted as using consistent accounting policies (unless a change is required to show a fairer presentation). A similar principle is relevant to comparing one entity with another; however it is more difficult to achieve consistent accounting policies across entities.

Information is material if its omission or misstatement could influence (economic) decisions of users based on the reported financial statements. Clearly an important aspect of materiality is the (monetary) size of a transaction, but in addition the nature of the item can also determine that it is material. For example the monetary results of a new activity may be small, but reporting them could be material to any assessment of what it may achieve in the future. Materiality is considered to be a threshold quality, meaning that information should only be reported if it is considered material. Too much detailed (and implicitly immaterial) reporting of (small) items may confuse or distract users.

(b)   Accounting for inventory, by adjusting purchases for opening and closing inventories is a classic example of the application of the accruals principle whereby revenues earned are matched with costs incurred. Closing inventory is by definition an example of goods that have been purchased, but not yet consumed. In other words the entity has not yet had the 'benefit' (i.e. the sales revenue they will generate) from the closing inventory; therefore the cost of the closing inventory should not be charged to the current year's statement of comprehensive income.

Consignment inventory is where goods are supplied (usually by a manufacturer) to a retailer under terms which mean the legal title to the goods remains with the supplier until a specified event (say payment in three months time). Once the goods have been transferred to the retailer, normally the risks and rewards relating to those goods then lie with the retailer. Where this is the case then (in substance) the consignment inventory meets the definition of an asset and the goods should appear as such (inventory) on the retailer's statement of financial position (along with the associated liability to pay for them) rather than on the statement of financial position of the manufacturer.

At the year end, the value of an entity's closing inventory is, by its nature, uncertain. In the next accounting period it may be sold at a profit or a loss. Accounting standards require inventory to be valued at the lower of cost and net realisable value. This is the application of prudence. If the inventory is expected to sell at a profit, the profit is deferred (by valuing inventory at cost) until it is actually sold. However, if the goods are expected to sell for a (net) loss, then that loss must be recognised immediately by valuing the inventory at its net realisable value.

There are many acceptable ways of valuing inventory (e.g. average cost or FIFO). In order to meet the requirement of comparability, an entity should decide on the most appropriate valuation method for its inventory and then be consistent in the use of that method. Any change in the method of valuing (or accounting for) inventory would break the principle of comparability.

For most businesses inventories are a material item. An error (omission or misstatement) in the value or treatment of inventory has the potential to affect decisions users may make in relation to financial statements. Therefore (correctly) accounting for inventory is a material event. Conversely there are occasions where on the grounds of immateriality certain 'inventories' are not (strictly) accounted for correctly. For example, at the year end a company may have an unused supply of stationery. Technically this is inventory, but in most cases companies would charge this 'inventory' of stationery to the statement of comprehensive income of the year in which it was purchased rather than show it as an asset.

Note: Other suitable examples would be acceptable.

Examiner's comments

Part (a) asked candidates to explain the meaning of five common accounting concepts/assumptions followed by a section requiring candidates to illustrate how these could be applied to a specific item, namely inventory. The first part of this question really bordered on the level of the lower paper F3 Financial Accounting. Not surprisingly many candidates did very well on this section, but there were a significant number of candidates that showed a very poor and deeply worrying lack of knowledge of basic concepts. There was also evidence of further poor examination; the question asked candidates to explain the concepts whereas many answer gave unsupported examples of the concepts. For example an answer that says providing for bad debts is an example of prudence is quite true, but it is not an explanation of prudence. Other weak answers said things like income and expenditure should be matched or accountants use substance over form; again these are not explanations of the concepts. A few candidates got carried away with this section not realising that there was only 1 mark for each explanation.

Part (b), requiring the application of the concepts to inventory, was very mixed. Well-prepared candidates often gained full marks and weaker candidates scored very little. Many markers reported that candidates were repeating their answers to part (a) and made no attempt to relate the concepts to inventory. Some candidates related the concepts to other accounting items, for example leasing was often cited as an example of substance over form; it is, but this is nothing to with inventory.

Other candidates wrote all they knew about the rules for inventory without relating it to which concepts the rules were applying. Neither of the above examples would gain any marks because they are not answering the question asked.

A few candidates seemed to think it was an auditing paper and described the audit work they would do in relation to inventory.

ACCA marking scheme		Marks
(a)	explanations 1 mark each	5
(b)	examples 2 marks each	10
Total		15

6 EMERALD 👣 *Walk in the footsteps of a top tutor*

🔑

Key answer tips

Part (a) requires the conceptual issues of whether development expenditure should be treated as an expense or an asset to be discussed. Be careful not to simply recite the criteria for R&D as this will limit the marks you can achieve to one! Part (b) requires application of IAS 8 & IAS 38 to be applied – both of which are assumed knowledge standards. The highlighted words are key phrases that markers are looking for.

(a)   The Framework defines an asset as a resource controlled by an entity as a result of past transactions or events from which future economic benefits (normally net cash inflows) are expected to flow to the entity. However assets can only be recognised (on the statement of financial position) when those expected benefits are probable and can be measured reliably. The Framework recognises that there is a close relationship between incurring expenditure and generating assets, but they do not necessarily coincide. Development expenditure, perhaps more than any other form of expenditure, is a classic example of the relationship between expenditure and creating an asset. Clearly entities commit to expenditure on both research and development in the hope that it will lead to a profitable product, process or service, but at the time that the expenditure is being incurred, entities cannot be certain (or it may not even be probable) that the project will be successful. Relating this to accounting concepts would mean that if there is doubt that a project will be successful the application of prudence would dictate that the expenditure is charged (expensed) to the statement of comprehensive income. At the stage where management becomes confident that the project will be successful, it meets the definition of an asset and the accruals/matching concept would mean that it should be capitalised (treated as an asset) and amortised over the period of the expected benefits. Accounting Standards (IAS 38 *Intangible Assets*) interpret this as writing off all research expenditure and only capitalising development costs from the point in time where they meet strict conditions which effectively mean the expenditure meets the definition of an asset.

(b)

	30 September 2007 $000		30 September 2006 $000	
Emerald Statement of comprehensive income				
Amortisation of development Expenditure	335	(w (ii))	135	(w (i))
Statement of financial position				
Development expenditure	1,195	(w (iv))	1,130	(w (iii))
Statement of changes in equity				
Prior period adjustment (credit required to restate retained earnings at 1 October 2005				
(cumulative carrying amount at 2005 of 300 + 165)			465	

Workings

(All figures in $000. **Note:** References to 2004, 2005 etc should be taken as for the year ended 30 September 2004 and 2005 etc.)

Year	2004	2005		2006		Cumulative 2006		2007		Cumulative 2007
Expenditure	300	240		800		1,340		400		1,740
	—	—		—		—		—		—
Amortisation (25%)	Nil	(75)		(75)		(150)		(75)		(225)
	Nil	Nil		(60)		(60)		(60)		(120)
	Nil	Nil		Nil		Nil		(200)		(200)
	—	—		—		—		—		—
Total amortisation	Nil	(75)	(w (i))	(135)		(210)	(w (ii))	(335)		(545)
	—	—		—		—		—		—
Carrying amount	300	165		665	(w (iii))	1,130		65	(w (iv))	1,195
	—	—		—		—		—		—

Examiner's comments

This question required candidates to apply the definition of an asset to the issue of research and development expenditure, followed by a calculation of the effect of changing from writing off development costs to capitalising them.

This was often the last question attempted and answers were generally quite poor.

In **part (a)** many candidates recited the definition of an asset then listed the criteria to be applied to determine whether development expenditure should be written off or deferred as two quite separate and unrelated issues. In other words, they did not attempt to apply the definition of an asset to the point at issue.

Some candidates who attempted **part (b)** assumed that amortisation commenced in the year of capitalisation rather than in the year following. Generally candidates found the approach to this question difficult, the answers were often confused and very rarely mentioned the prior period adjustment.

ACCA marking scheme		
		Marks
(a)	One mark per valid point to maximum	4
(b)	Statement of comprehensive income amortisation	1½
	Cost in statement of financial positions	1
	Accumulated amortization	1½
	Prior year adjustment in changes in equity	2
		—
		6
		—
Total		10
		—

7   LMN

(a)   (i)   Recognition is the depiction of an element of the financial statements in words and by a monetary amount and the inclusion of that amount in the financial statement totals.

The general recognition criteria in the *Framework* are that an item should be recognized in the financial statements if:

- It meets one of the definitions of an element of the financial statements

- There is sufficient evidence that the change in assets or liabilities inherent in the item has occurred (including, where appropriate, evidence that a future inflow or outflow of benefit will occur).

For example, a contract is an enforceable, but as yet unperformed, promise given to or by an external party to transfer assets and/or liabilities in the future.

These only provide sufficient evidence where there is a 'firm commitment', i.e. the contract can be enforced (either commercially or legally and practically) by an external party (usually another party to the contract).

The item can be measured at a monetary amount with sufficient reliability.

For many items an estimate will be necessary. The use of reasonable estimates is a normal part of the preparation of financial statements. Provided the estimate is reasonably reliable and prudent it should be recognized.

A good example of the above is in the recognition of attributable profit on construction contracts. Provided a reasonable estimate can be made of the degree of completion and the gain, and the gain is prudently estimated, then profit is recognized.

Recognition is triggered where a past event indicates that there has been a measurable change in the assets or liabilities of the entity.

Derecognition is appropriate where a past event has eliminated a previously recognized asset or liability or where evidence is no longer sufficiently strong to support continued recognition.

An asset will only be recognized if it gives rights or other access to future economic benefits controlled by an entity as a result of past transactions or events, and it can be measured with sufficient reliability

A liability will only be recognized if there is an obligation to transfer economic benefits as a result of past transactions or events, and it can be measured with sufficient reliability.

Income is recognized in the statement of comprehensive income when an increase in future economic benefits arises from an increase in an asset (or a reduction in a liability), and it can be measured reliably.

Evidence is needed to ascertain whether the gain has been 'earned', i.e. an increase in equity interest/net assets had occurred before the end of the reporting period. Income reflected in the statement of comprehensive income is seen as particularly important since the statement of comprehensive income is used as a primary measure of performance. Hence a gain included here must be earned and realized.

Realization is concerned with restricting recognition to those items whose existence and amount is particularly well evidenced. This will usually mean that conversion into cash or cash equivalents has occurred or is reasonably assured.

If a gain fails to meet the tests of being earned and realized, it may still meet the general recognition criteria. In this case, such a gain should be recognized in other comprehensive income, e.g. unrealized holding gain on the revaluation of a property held for consumption in the business (rather than for its investment potential).

Expenses are recognized in the statement of comprehensive income when a decrease in future economic benefits arises from a decrease in an asset or an increase in a liability, and it can be measured reliably.

Evidence is needed to ascertain whether a decrease in equity /net assets had occurred before the end of the reporting period. Where a loss is not to be recognized, i.e. the expenditure is carried forward to the next period as an asset under the matching concept, sufficient evidence must exist.

(b) The key issue here is whether the motor vehicles are actually assets of LMN in substance, or whether IJK continues to hold them. The fact that IJK continues to have legal title to the vehicles may be irrelevant.

Revenue from the sale of goods should be recognized when the seller transfers the significant risks and rewards of ownership to the buyer. The vehicles have been sold to LMN if the significant risks and rewards of ownership have also been transferred.

LMN appears to bear some of the risks of ownership:

- It is required to incur the costs of insuring the vehicles against loss or damage.

- Because the price of the vehicles is fixed at the time of their delivery, it bears the risk of loss if the price is reduced between the date of delivery and the date of sale.

However, LMN does not appear to bear the risk of loss due to obsolescence, because it can return the vehicles to IJK without incurring a penalty. In addition, LMN does not have to pay for the vehicles until they are sold to a third party.

LMN has some of the benefits of ownership:

- It can hold whichever ranges and models it wishes, subject to an upper limit of 80 vehicles.

- The price of the vehicles is fixed at the time of delivery, so LMN is protected from price rises between the date of delivery and the date of sale to a third party.

- It can use any of the vehicles for demonstration purposes or road testing.

However, LMN does have to pay a rental charge to IJK if it drives the vehicles for more than a specified number of kilometres. This suggests that LMN does not have all the benefits of ownership.

From the analysis above it is not clear which of the parties has the significant risks and rewards of ownership. It may be necessary to look at what actually happens in practice. For example, how often are vehicles actually returned to IJK? If the answer is 'never', this suggests that the vehicles are assets of LMN. However, on the basis of the information above, IJK appears to have the more significant risks and rewards, including the risk of obsolescence and the risk of slow payment, as it does not receive payment until the vehicles are sold to a third party.

This suggests that IJK should recognize the unsold vehicles as inventory and should not recognize revenue until the goods are sold to a third party.

8 FINO 👣 *Walk in the footsteps of a top tutor*

> 🔑
>
> **Key answer tips**
>
> Part (a) simply requires the discussion of faithful representation – to add depth to your answer make sure you include examples. Part (b) required you to criticise the finance director's current accounting treatment/demonstrate how IAS 17 enables a faithful representation and to show how the lease would be accounted for both as an operating and a finance lease. The highlighted words are key phrases that markers are looking for.

(a) **Faithful representation**

The Framework states that in order to be useful, information must faithfully representation the information that it intends to purport. The Framework describes faithful representation as where the financial statements (or other information) have the characteristic that they faithfully represent the transactions and other events that have occurred. If information is to represent faithfully the transactions and other events that it purports to represent, they must be accounted for and presented in accordance with their substance and economic reality and not merely their legal form. Thus a statement of financial position should faithfully represent transactions that result in assets, liabilities and equity of an entity. Some would refer to this as showing a true and fair view. An essential element of faithful representation is the application of the concept of substance over form. There are many examples where recording the legal form of a transaction does not convey its real substance or commercial reality. For example an entity may sell some inventory to a finance house and later buy it back at a price based on the original selling price plus a finance cost. Such a transaction is really a secured loan attracting interest costs. To portray it as a sale and subsequent repurchase of inventory would not be a faithful representation of the transaction. The 'sale' would probably create a 'profit', there would be no finance cost in the statement of comprehensive income and the statement of financial position would not show the asset of inventory or the liability to the finance house – all of which would not be representative of the economic reality. A further example is that an entity may issue loan notes that are (optionally) convertible to equity. In the past, sometimes management has argued that as they expect the loan note holders to take the equity option, the loan notes should be treated as equity (which of course would flatter the entity's gearing). In some cases transactions similar to the above, particularly off balance sheet finance schemes, have been deliberately entered into to manipulate the statement of financial position and statement of comprehensive income (so called creative accounting). Ratios such as return on capital employed (ROCE), asset turnover, interest cover and gearing are often used to assess the performance of an entity. If these ratios were calculated from financial statements that have been manipulated, they would be distorted (usually favourably) from the underlying substance. Clearly users cannot rely on such financial statements or any ratios calculated from them.

(b) (i) The finance director's comment that the ROCE would improve, based on the agreement being classified as an operating lease is correct (but see below). Over the life of the lease the reported profit is not affected by the lease being designated as an operating or finance lease, but the statement of financial position is. This is because the depreciation and finance costs charged on a finance lease would equal (over the full life of the lease) what would be charged as lease rentals if it were classed as an operating lease instead. However, classed as an operating lease, there would not be a leased asset or lease obligation recorded in the statement of financial position; whereas there would be if it were a finance lease or an outright purchase. Thus capital employed under an operating lease would be lower leading to a higher (more favourable) ROCE. IAS 17 *Leases* defines a finance lease as one which transfers to the lessee substantially all the risks and rewards incidental to ownership (an application of the principle of substance over form). In this case, as the asset will be used by Fino for four years (its entire useful life) and then be scrapped, it is almost certain to require classification as a finance lease. Thus the finance director's comments are unlikely to be valid.

Fino

(ii) (1) **Operating lease**

	$
Statement of comprehensive income cost of sales (machine rental) (100,000 × 6/12)	50,000
Statement of financial position	
Current assets	
Prepayment (100,000 × 6/12)	50,000

(2) **Finance lease**

Statement of comprehensive income

– cost of sales (depreciation) (350,000/4 × 6/12)	43,750
– finance costs (see working)	12,500

Statement of financial position

Non-current assets

Leased plant at cost	350,000
Depreciation (from above)	(43,750)
	306,250

Non-current liabilities

Lease obligation (250,000 – 75,000)	175,000

Current liabilities

Accrued interest (see working)	12,500
Lease obligation (100,000 – 25,000 see below)	75,000
	87,500

Working:

Cost	350,000
Deposit	(100,000)
	250,000
Interest to 30 September 2007 (6 months at 10%)	12,500
Total obligation at 30 September 2007	262,500

The payment of $100,000 on 1 April 2008 will contain $25,000 of interest ($250,000 × 10%) and a capital repayment of $75,000.

UK SYLLABUS FOCUS ONLY

SSAP 21 states that the transfer of risks and rewards of ownership can be presumed, if, at the inception of the lease the present value of the minimum lease payments (normally 90% or more) amounts to substantially all of the fair value of the leased asset. There is a rebuttable presumption that if:

• The present value reaches the 90% level, the lease is a finance lease

• The present value does not reach 90% the lease is an operating lease.

In the case of Fino the present value of the minimum lease payments amounts to $316,977 and therefore represents 90.5% of the fair value of the asset ($316,977/$350,000). In this instance, the lease is considered to be a finance lease.

Examiner's comments

Part (a) Answers to this question were very mixed and covered the whole range of marks. Good answers to part (a) recognised the important issues; however weaker candidates could not adequately identify that faithful representation necessitated reflecting the commercial substance of transactions rather than their legal form. Many answers dealt with all the qualitative characteristics of financial information. These seemed more a regurgitation of what had been taught/learned rather than answering the question asked.

Part (b)(i) required candidates to assess the differential effect of treating a lease as an operating lease compared to a finance lease and relating this to the director's comments in relation to ROCE.

There were a number of good answers to this section, most recognising that the lease was in fact a finance lease along with the effect that this would have on the financial statements and the ROCE. Weaker answers spent too much time defining a finance lease (this was not required) and not addressing the issue of the effect on ROCE. In a few very poor answers the point was missed altogether with candidates discussing leasing as a means of purchasing assets when cash was unavailable.

ACCA marking scheme				
				Marks
(a)		One mark per valid point to maximum		5
(b)	(i)	One mark per valid point to maximum		4
	(ii)	(1)	Operating lease	
			– statement of comprehensive income charge	1
			– prepayment	1
		(2)	Finance lease	
			– statement of comprehensive income: depreciation and finance costs	1
			– sfp:	
			non-current asset	1
			non-current liabilities	1
			current liabilities interest and capital	1
				6
Total				15

9   WARDLE

(a)   For financial statements to be of value to their users they must possess certain characteristics; faithful representation is one such important characteristic. For financial statements to achieve a faithful representation, transactions must be accounted for and presented in accordance with their substance and economic reality where this differs from their legal form. For example, if an entity 'sold' an asset to a third party, but continued to enjoy the future benefits embodied in that asset, then this transaction would not be represented faithfully by recording it as a sale (in all probability this would be a financing transaction).

The features that may indicate that the substance of a transaction is different from its legal form are:

- where the control of an asset differs from the ownership of the asset

- where assets are 'sold' at prices that are greater or less than their fair values

- the use of options as part of an agreement

- where there are a series of 'linked' transactions.

(b)   It should be noted that none of the above necessarily mean there is a difference between substance and legal form.

Extracts from the statement of comprehensive incomes

(i)   **reflecting the legal form:**

Year ended:	31 March 2010	31 March 2011	31 March 2012	Total
	$000	$000	$000	$000
Revenue	6,000	nil	10,000	16,000
Cost of sales	(5,000)	nil	(7,986)	(12,986)
Gross profit	1,000	nil	2,014	3,014
Finance costs	nil	nil	nil	nil
Net profit	1,000	nil	2,014	3,014

(ii)   **reflecting the substance:**

Year ended:	31 March 2010	31 March 2011	31 March 2012	Total
	$000	$000	$000	$000
Revenue	nil	nil	10,000	10,000
Cost of sales	(nil)	nil	(5,000)	(5,000)
Gross profit	nil	nil	5,000	5,000
Finance costs	(600)	(660)	(726)	(1,986)
Net profit	(600)	(660)	4,274	3,014

(c) It can be seen from the above that the two treatments have no effect on the total net profit reported in the statement of comprehensive incomes, however, the profit is reported in different periods and the classification of costs is different. In effect the legal form creates some element of profit smoothing and completely hides the financing cost. Although not shown, the effect on the statements of financial position is that recording the legal form of the transaction does not show the inventory, nor does it show the in-substance loan. Thus recording the legal form would be an example of off balance sheet (statement of financial position) financing. The effect on an assessment of Wardle using ratio analysis may be that recording the legal form rather than the substance of the transaction would be that interest cover and inventory turnover would be higher and gearing lower. All of which may be considered as reporting a more favourable performance.

ACCA marking scheme		
		Marks
(a)	1 mark per valid point	5
(b)	(i) and (ii) – 1 mark per reported profit figure	5
(c)	1 mark per valid point	5
Total		15

A REGULATORY FRAMEWORK FOR FINANCIAL REPORTING

10 IFRS FOUNDATION

Key answer tips

Parts (a) and (b) are standard bookwork. Make sure that you answer all of the requirements that are listed. Part (c) invites you to give your opinion. Don't be dogmatic, but state both successes and failures in the move towards convergence.

Note: The International Accounting Standards Board (IASB) has decided that its standards will be called International Financial Reporting Standards (IFRSs), and that this term should be taken to encompass both Standards and Interpretations issued by the IASB (IFRS and IFRS IC), and the International Accounting Standards (IASs) issued by its predecessor standard setter, the IASC Board. References in this answer to IFRS should be taken to have the same meaning as that used by the IASB.

(a) Regulation of accounting information is aimed at ensuring that users of financial statements receive a minimum amount of information that will enable them to make meaningful decisions regarding their interest in a reporting entity. A regulatory framework is required to ensure that relevant and reliable financial reporting is achieved to meet the needs of shareholders and other users. Accounting standards alone would not be a complete regulatory framework. In order to fully regulate the preparation of financial statements and the obligations of companies and directors, legal and market regulations are also required.

(b) In recognition of the increasing importance of international accounting standards, in 1999 the Board of the IASB recommended and subsequently adopted a new constitution and structure. A new supervisory body, The International Financial Reporting Standards Foundation (IFRS Foundation) (previously known as the International Accounting Standards Committee Foundation - IASCF), was incorporated in the USA in February 2001 as an independent not-for-profit organization. Its constitution was further revised in 2005 and then again in March 2010. It is governed by 22 IFRS Foundation Trustees who must have an understanding of international issues relevant to accounting standards for use in the world's capital markets. The main objectives of the IFRS Foundation are:

- to develop a single set of global accounting standards that require high quality, transparent and comparable information in financial statements to help users in making economic decisions;

- to promote the use and rigorous application of these standards; and

- to bring about convergence of national accounting standards and international accounting standards.

The subsidiary bodies of the IFRS Foundation are the International Accounting Standards Board (IASB) (based in London, UK), the IFRS Advisory Council (IFRS AC) and the IFRS Interpretations Committee (IFRS IC).

The International Accounting Standards Board. The result of a restructuring process saw the IASB assume the responsibility for setting accounting standards from its predecessor body, the International Accounting Standards Committee. The Trustees of the IFRS Foundation appoint the members of all of the above bodies. They also set the agenda of, and raise finance for, the IASB; however the IASB has sole responsibility for setting accounting standards, International Financial Reporting Standards (IFRSs), following rigorous and open due process.

The IFRS Advisory Council provides a forum for experts from different countries and different business sectors with an interest in international financial reporting to offer advice when drawing up new standards. Its main objectives are to give advice to the Trustees and IASB on agenda decisions and work priorities and on the major standard-setting projects.

The **IFRS Interpretations Committee** has taken over the work of the previous Standing Interpretations Committee. It is really a compliance body whose role is to provide rapid guidance on the application and interpretation of international accounting standards where contentious or divergent interpretations have arisen. It operates an open due process in accordance with its approved procedures. Its pronouncements (interpretations – SICs and IFRICs) are important because financial statements cannot be described as complying with IFRSs unless they also comply with the interpretations.

Other bodies

The prominence of the IASB has been enhanced even further by its relationship with the **International Organization of Securities Commissions (IOSCO)**. IOSCO is an influential organization of the world's security commissions (stock exchanges). In 1995 the IFRS Foundation agreed to develop a core set of standards which, when endorsed by IOSCO, would be used as an acceptable basis for cross-border listings. In May 2000 this was achieved. Thus it can be said that international accounting standards may be the first tentative steps towards global accounting harmonization. As part of its harmonization process the European Union requires listed companies in all member states to prepare their consolidated financial statements using IFRSs from 2005.

National standard setters such as the UK's Accounting Standards Board and the USA's Financial Accounting Standards Board have a role to play in the formulation of international accounting standards. Seven of the leading national standard setters work closely with the IASB. The IASB see this as a 'partnership' between IASB and these national bodies as they work together to achieve the convergence of accounting standards worldwide. Often the IASB will ask members of national standard setting bodies to work on particular projects in which those countries have greater experience or expertise. Many countries that are committed to closer integration with IFRSs will publish domestic standards equivalent (sometimes identical) to IFRSs on a concurrent timetable.

(c) **The International Accounting Standard Setting Process**

As referred to above the IASB is ultimately responsible for setting international accounting standards. The Board (advised by the IFRS AC) identifies a subject and appoints an Advisory Committee to advise on the issues relevant to the given topic. Depending on the complexity and importance of the subject matter the IASB may develop and publish Discussion Documents for public comment. Following the receipt and review of comments the IASB then develops and publishes an Exposure Draft for public comment. The usual comment period for both of these is ninety days. Finally, and again after a review of any further comments, an International Financial Reporting Standard (IFRS) is issued. The IASB also publishes a Basis for Conclusions which explains how it reached its conclusions and gives information to help users to apply the Standard in practice. In addition to the above the IASB will sometimes conduct public hearings where proposed standards are openly discussed and occasionally field tests are conducted to ensure that proposals are practical and workable around the world.

The authority of international accounting standards is a rather difficult area. The IASB has no power to enforce international accounting standards within those countries/ enterprises that choose to adopt them. This means that the enforcement of international accounting standards is in the hands of the regulatory systems of the individual adopting countries. There is no doubt the regulatory systems in different parts of the world differ from each other considerably in their effectiveness. For example in the UK the Financial Reporting Review Panel (FRRP) is a body that investigates departures from the UK's regulatory system (which now includes the use of international accounting standards for listed companies). The FRRP has wide and effective powers of enforcement, but not all countries have equivalent bodies, thus it can be argued that international accounting standards are not enforced in a consistent manner throughout the world.

Complementary to international accounting standards, there also exist international auditing standards and part of the rigour and transparency that the use of international accounting standards brings is due to the fact that those companies adopting international accounting standards should also be audited in accordance with international auditing standards. This auditing aspect is part of IOSCO's requirements for financial statements to be used for cross-border listing purposes.

Where it becomes apparent (often through press reports) that there is widespread inconsistency in the interpretation of an international accounting standard, or where it is perceived that a standard is not clear enough in a particular area, the IFRS IC may act to remedy/clarify the position thus supplementing the body of international standards. However where it becomes apparent (perhaps through a modified audit report) that a company has departed from IFRSs there is little that the IASB can do directly to enforce them.

(d) **The success of the process**

Any measure of success is really a matter of opinion. There is no doubt that the growing acceptance of IFRSs through IOSCO's endorsement, the European Union requirement for their use by listed companies and the ever increasing number of countries that are either adopting international accounting standards outright or basing their domestic standards very closely on IFRSs is a measure of the success of the IASB. Equally there is widespread recognition that in recent years the quality of international accounting standards has improved enormously due to the improvements project and subsequent continuing improvements.

However the IASB is not without criticism. Some countries that have developed sophisticated regulatory systems feel that IFRSs are not as rigorous as the local standards and this may give cross-border listing companies an advantage over domestic companies. Some requirements of international accounting standards are regarded as quite controversial, e.g. deferred tax (part of IAS 12), financial instruments and derivatives (IAS 32, IFRS 7 and IFRS 9) and accounting for retirement benefits (IAS 19). Many IFRSs are complex and the benefits of applying them to smaller enterprises may outweigh the costs. Also some securities exchanges that are part of IOSCO require non-domestic companies that are listing by filing financial statements prepared under IFRSs to produce a reconciliation to local GAAP. This involves reconciling the IFRS statement of comprehensive income and statement of financial position assets, liabilities and equity, to what they would be if local GAAP had been used. The USA is an important example of this requirement. Critics argue that this requirement of the Securities Exchange Commission (SEC) negates many of the benefits of being able to use a single set of financial statements to list on different security exchanges. This is because to produce reconciliation to local GAAP is almost as much work and expense as preparing financial statements in the local GAAP which was usually the previous requirement.

However in recent years the IASB and the FASB in the US have formed an agreement known as the Memorandum of Understanding whereby they will jointly progress the process of harmonization of IFRS and US GAAP. This has led to a number of joint projects in process such as the development of a new conceptual framework, a project on business combinations and one of fair values in financial statements.

Despite these criticisms there is no doubt that the work of IASB has already led, and in the future will lead, to further improvement in financial reporting throughout the world.

11 CONCEPTUAL FRAMEWORK

> ### Key answer tips
>
> Parts (a), (b) and (c) are standard bookwork from the Framework but it is essential background knowledge. Part (d) introduces not-for-profit entities which are a new element of the F7 syllabus.

(a) A conceptual framework could be defined as a coherent system of interrelated objectives and fundamental principles. It is a framework which prescribes the nature, function and limits of financial accounting and financial statements. In the US there is a more specific definition which is that it is 'a constitution, a coherent system of interrelated objectives and fundamentals that can lead to consistent standards and that prescribes the nature, function and limits of financial accounting and financial statements'.

(b) There are a variety of arguments for having a conceptual framework. Firstly it enables accounting standards and GAAP to be developed in accordance with agreed principles and underlying assumptions and concepts. It therefore avoids 'fire fighting', whereby accounting standards are developed in a piecemeal way in response to specific problems or abuses. Such an approach can lead to inconsistencies between different accounting standards and also between accounting standards and relevant local legislation.

The lack of a conceptual framework may mean that certain critical issues are not addressed.

For example, until the *Conceptual Framework for Financial Reporting* was published there was no definition of basic terms such as 'asset' or 'liability' in any accounting standard which is obviously fundamental to a consistent treatment of accounting transactions and events.

In a world where transactions have become more complex and businesses more sophisticated an overall conceptual framework can help preparers of financial statements and their auditors deal with complex transactions and particularly those which are not the subject of an accounting standard.

The alternative to a principles based conceptual framework as we have under the IASB is a rules based framework which some would argue is what is seen in the US. However it can be argued that a principles based framework means that accounting standards based upon such principles are harder to circumvent. It also means that the standard setting process is less likely to be influenced by those with vested interests such as large companies or particular business sectors.

(c) The *Conceptual Framework for Financial Reporting* was originally developed by the IASC (now the IASB) in 1989. It sets out concepts underlying the preparation and presentation of financial statements. However it is not an accounting standard and nothing in the Framework overrides a specific accounting standard.

The stated purpose of the *Framework* is to:

- assist the IASB in the development of future accounting standards and in its review of existing International Accounting Standards

- assist the IASB by providing a basis for reducing the number of alternative accounting treatments permitted by International Accounting Standards

- assist national standard-setting bodies in developing national standards

- assist preparers of financial statements in applying International Accounting Standards

- and in dealing with topics that do not form the subject of an International Accounting Standard

- assist auditors in forming an opinion about whether financial statements conform with International Accounting Standards

- assist users of financial statements in interpreting the information contained in financial statements prepared in conformity with International Accounting Standards

- provide those who are interested in the work of the IASB with information about its approach to the formulation of International Accounting Standards.

(d) The main aim of not-for-profit entities is to provide value for money rather than making a profit. Value for money is achieved by a combination of effectiveness, efficiency and economy.

Effectiveness means achieving the objectives (usually non-monetary) of the organization. The objectives of not-for-profit and public sector entities will differ depending upon the type of entity. For example a school may have the objectives of teaching a certain number of children and achieving certain academic standards. A hospital may have the objectives of treating out-patients within a particular time scale or minimising the number of empty beds. Effectiveness is therefore measured by identifiable measures of achievement in reaching those goals or objectives.

Efficiency means using the resources available well. It is effectively the quantity of output obtained for a given measure of input. Efficiency means getting more out of fewer inputs and thereby reducing the cost of output. In a school it might be measured by the pupil to teacher ratio and in a hospital by the number of patients seen by a consultant during a surgery.

Economy means keeping the cost of input resources as low as possible. This is achieved by paying less for the inputs that are required to meet the objectives or provide the service. In a school giving more teaching time to classroom assistants rather than higher paid teachers would be a form of economy or in a hospital scheduling duties to a nurse rather than a doctor.

In general accounting standards are designed to measure financial performance accurately and consistently, to report the financial position accurately and consistently and to account for the stewardship of the directors of the resources and assets.

Not-for-profit and public sector organizations do not aim to achieve a profit but will have to account for their income and costs. Such entities will have to account for their effectiveness, economy and efficiency even if they do not have to produce financial statements for the public (although in many cases may do so).

Therefore some measurement accounting standards will be relevant such as those relating to inventory, non-current assets, leasing etc. However others relating purely to reporting such as earnings per share will not be so relevant.

12   USERS AND QUALITIES

> **Key answer tips**
>
> All of the topics covered in this question are essential background knowledge which you may have to use or apply in other questions.

(a)   The objective of financial statements is to provide information about the financial position, performance and changes in financial position of an enterprise that is useful to a wide range of users in making economic decisions. Financial statements also show the results of the stewardship of management, that is the accountability of management for the resources entrusted to it.

(b)   Financial statements meet the common needs of most users. However, financial statements do not provide all the information that users may need to make economic decisions, since they largely portray the financial effects of past events and do not necessarily provide non-financial information.

Arguably the most important group of users are investors or shareholders who are the providers of risk capital.

They are interested in information that is useful in taking decisions about their investment or potential investment in the entity. As a result, they are concerned with the risk inherent in, and return provided by, their investments. They need information on the entity's financial performance and financial position that helps them to assess its cash generation abilities and its financial adaptability.

Other users of financial statements, and their information needs, include the following:

- Lenders who will be interested in information that enables them to determine whether their loans will be repaid, and whether the interest attaching to them will be paid, when due. Potential lenders are interested in information that helps them to decide whether to lend to the entity and on what terms.

- Suppliers and other trade payables who will be interested in information that enables them to decide whether to sell to the entity and to assess the likelihood that amounts owing to them will be paid when due.

- Employees who will be interested in information about the stability and profitability of their employer and their long-term employment prospects. They will also be interested in information that helps them to assess the ability of their employer to provide remuneration, employment opportunities and retirement benefits.

- Customers will be interested in information about the entity's continued existence. This is especially so when they are dependent on the entity for example if product warranties are involved or if specialized replacement parts may be needed.

- Governments and their agencies will be interested in the allocation of resources and, therefore, the activities of entities. They also require information in order to regulate the activities of entities, assess taxation and provide a basis for national statistics.

- The public will be interested in information about the trends and recent developments in the entity's prosperity and the range of its activities. For example, an entity may make a substantial contribution to a local economy by providing employment and using local suppliers.

(c) Qualitative characteristics are the attributes that make information provided in financial statements useful to others. The *Framework* identifies two primary qualitative characteristics – relevance (which is subject to a threshold quality of materiality) and faithful representation. There are also four enhancing characteristics – comparability, verifiability, timeliness and understand ability.

Primary characteristics:

Information has the quality of **relevance** when it influences the economic decisions of users by helping them evaluate past, present or future events or by confirming, or correcting, their past evaluations. Information about financial position and past performance is frequently used as the basis for predicting future financial position and performance and other matters in which users are directly interested, such as dividend and wage payments. To have predictive value, information need not be in the form of an explicit forecast.

The ability to make predictions from financial statements is enhanced, however, by the manner in which information concerning past transactions and events is displayed. For example, the predictive value of the statement of comprehensive income is enhanced if unusual, abnormal and infrequent items of income or expense are separately disclosed.

The predictive and confirmatory roles of information are interrelated. For example, information about the current level and structure of asset holdings has value to users when they endeavour to predict the ability of the enterprise to take advantage of opportunities and its ability to react to adverse situations.

There are several monetary attributes that could be used in financial statements, e.g. historical cost, current cost or net realisable value. The choice of attribute to be reported should be based on its relevance to the economic decisions of users.

To be a perfectly **Faithful representation** financial information would possess the characteristics of completeness, neutrality and be error free.

If information is to represent faithfully the transactions and other events that it purports to represent, they must be accounted for and presented in accordance with their substance and economic reality and not merely their legal form. Information must also be neutral to be reliable, that is, free from bias. Financial statements are not neutral if, by the selection or presentation of information, they influence the making of a decision or judgement in order to achieve a predetermined result or outcome.

Information must be complete and free from error within the bounds of materiality. A material error or an omission can cause the financial statements to be false or misleading and thus unreliable and deficient in terms of their relevance.

Uncertainty surrounds many of the events and circumstances that are reported on in financial statements. It is dealt with in those statements by disclosing the nature and extent of the uncertainty involved and by exercising prudence. Prudence means exercising a degree of caution in making judgements about estimates required under conditions of uncertainty, such that gains and assets are not overstated and losses and liabilities are not understated. The existence of assets and gains requires more confirmatory evidence and greater reliability of measurement than are required for liabilities and losses.

It is not necessary to exercise prudence where there is no uncertainty. Nor is it appropriate to use prudence as a reason for, for example, creating hidden reserves or excessive provisions, deliberately understating assets or gains, or deliberately overstating liabilities or losses. That would mean that the financial statements are not neutral and, therefore, are not reliable.

Enhancing Characteristics:

Comparability is also a required attribute of financial information. Users must be able to compare the financial statements of an entity over time to identify trends in its financial position and performance and also be able to compare the financial statements of different entities to evaluate their relative financial performance and financial position.

For this to be the case there must be consistency of accounting treatment and adequate disclosure. An important implication of comparability is that users are informed of the accounting policies employed in preparation of the financial statements, any changes in those policies and the effects of such changes. Compliance with accounting standards, including the disclosure of the accounting policies used by the enterprise, helps to achieve comparability.

Because users wish to compare the financial position, performance and changes in financial position of an enterprise over time, it is important that the financial statements show corresponding information for the preceding periods.

Verifiability is a sub characteristic helping to enhance the relevance and faithful representation of transactions. Verification can be direct or indirect. Direct verification means verifying an amount or other representation through direct observation i.e. counting cash. Indirect verification means checking the inputs to a model, formula or other technique and recalculating the outputs using the same methodology i.e. recalculating inventory amounts using the same cost flow assumption such as first in, first out method.

Timeliness means having information available to decision makers in time to be capable of influencing their decisions. Generally, the older the information is the less useful it becomes.

Finally information must be understandable. **Understandability** depends on the way in which information is presented and the capabilities of users. It is assumed that users have a reasonable knowledge of business and economic activities and are willing to study the information provided with reasonable diligence.

For information to be understandable users need to be able to perceive its significance however information that is relevant and is faithfully represented should not be excluded from the financial statements simply because it is difficult for some users to understand.

(d) In practice, a balancing, or trade-off, between qualitative characteristics is often necessary. Generally the aim is to achieve an appropriate balance among the characteristics in order to meet the objective of financial statements.

Relevance and faithful representation

Where there is a conflict between qualitative characteristics, the aim is to achieve an appropriate balance among them in order to meet the objectives of financial statements. The relative importance of different characteristics is a matter of professional judgement.

Conflicts may arise over timeliness. A delay in providing information can make it out of date and less relevant, but reporting on transactions and other events before all the uncertainties are resolved may mean information is not faithfully represented.

Neutrality and prudence

Neutrality involves freedom from bias. Prudence is potentially biased because it seeks to ensure that gains or assets are not overstated and losses or liabilities are not understated in conditions of uncertainty. It is necessary to find a balance that ensures that deliberate understatement of assets or gains and overstatement of liabilities or losses does not occur.

Cost and benefit

It is also important to balance the benefit and the cost of providing information and this is a pervasive constraint rather than a qualitative characteristic. The benefits derived from information should exceed the cost of providing it.

13   FINANCIAL PERFORMANCE & OCI

The amendments to IAS 1 do not specify which items should be presented as part of other comprehensive income (OCI), or require that any new or additional items are presented in this way. This will be determined by the requirements of individual reporting standards which specify that particular items must be accounted for in this way. One example is IFRS 9, Financial Instruments, which permits changes in fair value of some financial asset equity instruments to be taken to OCI in the year, provided appropriate designation has been made upon initial recognition. This may change as existing reporting standards are either revised or withdrawn and replaced by new reporting standards which may require reporting of items in OCI, rather than profit or loss for the year.

Instead, the amendments focus upon how items of OCI should be presented in the annual financial statements. One issue considered was whether there should be one combined statement of total comprehensive income for the year, or whether separate statements should be permitted for profit or loss for the year, and items of OCI. The arguments in favour of having a single statement of total comprehensive income include:

•   a lack of consistency and comparability in reported information where a choice of presentation method is permitted.

•   many recently issued new or revised reporting standards have narrowed down or eliminated choice of accounting treatment together with associated presentation and disclosures in order to reduce complexity in financial reporting. One example of this is recently revised IAS 19 Employee Benefits (not examinable in F7), which now requires remeasurement gains and losses to be accounted for as part of other comprehensive income. Previously, there were three permitted accounting treatments for such gains and losses. Having one specified accounting treatment would follow the lead given by those recently issued or revised reporting standards to reduce complexity in financial reporting.

- It would confirm the importance of items of OCI in reporting overall financial performance and position of an entity. If two separate statements were permitted, it would be possible for items of OCI to be de-emphasised or relegated in importance in comparison with other elements of reporting financial performance and position.

The amendments have retained the right of entities to choose whether or not to report items of OCI as part of a single statement of total performance, or to have separate statements for profit or loss and OCI respectively. However, to ensure that items of OCI are not de-emphasised in any way, when separate statements are prepared:

- the statement of OCI must immediately follow the statement of profit or loss, and ensure that there is no confusion between which items have been classified to profit or loss and which items have been classified to OCI.

- the statement of OCI must be given equal prominence with the statement of profit or loss for the year.

- a second issue considered was whether to present items of OCI net of tax, or to show them before related tax, with one tax adjustment for all items of reported OCI. Arguably, presentation of amounts of OCI before their tax effects could be useful and relevant information to users of financial statements. This is a continuation of the existing requirements, which ensure that entities disclose the tax effects of all items of comprehensive income, but permits some flexibility in how it is reported.

A third issue considered was whether items of OCI should be classified or grouped together based upon specified criteria. This could be useful if the criteria applied was regarded as logical, appropriate and reportable by those who applied any such criteria, and also by those who used that information.

This has the danger of being regarded as arbitrary classification or grouping of information, which may undermine consistency and comparability of financial reporting information. However, if done on a basis which is generally regarded as being relevant to users of financial statements, such grouping or classification of information could be helpful.

The amendments to IAS 1 require that items of OCI are grouped together, based upon whether or not they may be reclassified (recycled) to profit or loss in a subsequent accounting period. Based upon this classification, items which may be recycled to profit or loss in a subsequent accounting period include:

- foreign exchange gains and losses arising on translation of financial statements of a foreign operation per IAS 21. This will normally arise upon disposal of a foreign subsidiary, with the net cumulative foreign exchange gain or loss being included as part of the reported profit or loss on disposal (not examinable in F7);

- Cash flow hedging arrangements per IAS 39 (not examinable in F7).

Items which will not be subject to reclassification (recycling) to profit or loss in a subsequent accounting period include:

- Revaluation of property, plant and equipment per IAS 16 and revaluation of intangible assets per IAS 38;

- Financial assets measured at fair value through other comprehensive income per IFRS 9.

FINANCIAL STATEMENTS

14   ELITE LEISURE AND ADVENT

> **Key answer tips**
>
> Both parts of this question are fairly straightforward non-current asset questions.

(a)   The cruise ship is an example of what can be called a complex asset. This is a single asset that should be treated as if it was a collection of separate assets, each of which may require a different depreciation method/life. In this case the question identifies three components to the cruise ship.

The carrying amount of the asset at 30 September 20X3 (eight years after acquisition) would be:

Component	Cost $m	Depreciation $m		Carrying value $m
Ship's fabric	300	96	(300/25 × 8)	204
Cabins and entertainment area	150	100	(150/12 × 8)	50
Fittings				
Propulsion system	100	75	(100/40,000 × 30,000)	25
	550	271		279

Ship's fabric

This is the most straightforward component. It is being depreciated over a 25 year life and depreciation of $12 million (300/25 years) would be required in the year ended 30 September 20X4. The repainting of the ship's fabric does not meet the recognition criteria of an asset and should be treated as repairs and maintenance.

Cabins and entertainment area and fittings

During the year these have had a limited upgrade at a cost of $60 million. This has extended the remaining useful life from four to five years. The costs of the upgrade meet the criteria for recognition as an asset. The original fittings have not been replaced thus the additional $60 million would be added to the cost of the fittings and the new carrying amount of $110 million will be depreciated over the remaining life of five years to give a charge for the year of $22 million.

Propulsion system

This has been replaced by a new system so the carrying value of the system ($25 million) must be written off and depreciation of the new system for the year ended 30 September 20X5 (based on use) would be $14 million (140 million/50,000 × 5,000).

Elite Leisure – statement of comprehensive income extract – year ended 30 September 20X4:

		$m
Depreciation	– ship's fabric	12
	– cabin and entertainment fittings	22
	– propulsion system	14
Disposal loss	– propulsion system	25
Repainting ship's fabric		20
		93

Elite Leisure – statement of financial position extract – as at 30 September 20X4

Non-current assets

Cruise ship (see working)   406

Workings (in $ million):

Component	Cost $m	Depreciation $m		Carrying value $m
Ship's fabric	300	108	(300/25 × 9)	192
Cabins and entertainment area fittings	210	122	(100 + 22)	88
Propulsion system	140	14		126
	650	244		406

(b) (i) **Non-current assets**

	30 September 20X4 $million	30 September 20X3 $million
Property, plant and equipment (note 1)	316	285
Intangible assets (note 2)	100	270

Note 1 Property, plant and equipment	Land and buildings $million	Plant $million	Total $million
Cost or valuation:			
At 1 October 20X3	280	150	430
Additions		50	50
Revaluation (see tutorial note)	(15)	Nil	(15)
At 30 September 20X4	265	200	465
Accumulated depreciation:			
At 1 October 20X3	40	105	145
Charge for year (see tutorial note)	9	35	44
Revaluation (see tutorial note)	(40)	Nil	(40)
At 30 September 20X4	9	140	149
Carrying value 30 September 20X4	256	60	316

The land and buildings were revalued on an existing use basis on 1 October 20X3. They are being depreciated on a straight-line basis over a 25 year life. Plant is depreciated at 20% per annum on cost.

Tutorial note

These amounts can be calculated as:

	Land $million	Buildings $million
Cost	80	200
Depreciation (5/25)	Nil	(40)
Carrying value at 30.9.X3	80	160
Revaluation surplus	5	20
Revalued amount at 1.10.X3	85	180

The $40 million buildings depreciation accumulated at 30.9.X3 must be written back. As the total revaluation surplus is only $25 million, the $15 million difference must write down the valuation amount, to $265 million (85 + 180).

Deprecation on the buildings in 20X4 is $9 million (180/20 remaining useful life).

	$million
Plant depreciation	
Re b/f: 150 × 20%	30
Re acquisition: 50 × 20% × ½	5
	35

Note 2 Intangible assets:

	Telecomm-unication licence $million	Total $million
Cost at 1 October 20X3	300	300
And at 30 September 20X4	300	300
Accumulated amortization		
1 October 20X3	30	30
Amortization charge for year	30	30
Impairment charge for year (bal fig)	140	140
At 30 September 20X4	200	200
Carrying value 30 September 20X4	100	100

After the impairment charge the licence will be amortized over its remaining life of eight years on a straight-line basis.

(ii) The usefulness of the above disclosures is:

– users can determine which type of non-current assets a business owns. There is a great deal of difference between owning say land and buildings compared with intangibles. The above figures give an illustration of this; the property has increased in value whereas the licence has fallen dramatically. Another factor relevant to this distinction is that it is usually easier to raise finance using property as security, whereas it can be difficult to raise finance on intangibles due to the volatility of their values.

– it is useful to know whether non-current assets are carried at historical cost or at revalued amount. If a company is using historical cost, it may be that statement of financial position values are seriously understated with a consequential effect on depreciation charges.

– information on accumulated depreciation gives a broad indication of the age of the relevant assets. In the case of Advent above, other than the plant acquired during the year, plant is almost fully depreciated. The implication of this, assuming the depreciation policy is appropriate, is that further acquisitions will be required in the near future. This in turn has future cash flow implications.

- it can also be noted that no disposals of plant have occurred, thus the acquisition of plant represents an increase in capacity. This may be an indication of growth.

- the disclosure of the impairment charge as part of the accumulated depreciation disclosures is self-evident. Users can determine that the acquisition of the licence appears to have been a financial disaster. Where a non-current asset is carried at historical cost, as in this case, the impairment is included as part of the depreciation rather than as a write down (revaluation) of the cost of the asset.

15 WILDERNESS GROUP

Key answer tips

In part (a), remember to discuss cash generating units as well as individual assets. Part (b) (i) requires application of this knowledge but part (ii) also requires you to consider IAS 38 and brands.

(a) (i) An impairment loss arises where the carrying amount of an asset is higher than its recoverable amount. The recoverable amount of an asset is defined in IAS 36 *Impairment of assets* as the higher of its fair value less costs to sell and its value in use (fair value less cost to sell was previously referred to as net selling price). Thus an impairment loss is simply the difference between the carrying amount of an asset and the higher of its fair value less costs to sell and its value in use.

Fair value:

The fair value could be based on the amount of a binding sale agreement or the market price where there is an active market. However many (used) assets do not have active markets and in these circumstances the fair value is based on a 'best estimate' approach to an arm's length transaction. It would not normally be based on the value of a forced sale. In each case the costs to sell would be the incremental costs directly attributable to the disposal of the asset.

Value in use:

The value in use of an asset is the estimated future net cash flows expected to be derived from the asset discounted to a present value. The estimates should allow for variations in the amount, timing and inherent risk of the cash flows. A major problem with this approach in practice is that most assets do not produce independent cash flows i.e. they usually produce cash flows in conjunction with other assets. For this reason IAS 36 introduces the concept of a cash-generating unit (CGU) which is the smallest identifiable group of assets, which may include goodwill, that generates (largely) independent cash flows.

Frequency of testing for impairment:

Goodwill and any intangible asset that is deemed to have an indefinite useful life should be tested for impairment at least annually, as too should any intangible asset that has not yet been brought into use. In addition, at each reporting period end an entity must consider if there has been any indication that other assets may have become impaired and, if so, an impairment test should be done. If there are no indications of impairment, testing is not required.

(ii) Once an impairment loss for an individual asset has been identified and calculated it is applied to reduce the carrying amount of the asset, which will then be the base for future depreciation charges. The impairment loss should be recognized in profit or loss. However, if the asset has previously been revalued upwards, the impairment loss should first be set against any revaluation surplus. The application of impairment losses to a CGU is more complex. They should first be applied to eliminate any goodwill and then to the other assets on a pro rata basis to their carrying amounts. However, an entity should not reduce the carrying amount of an asset (other than goodwill) to below the higher of its fair value less costs to sell and its value in use if these are determinable.

(b) (i) The plant had a carrying amount of $240,000 on 1 October 20X4. The accident that may have caused an impairment occurred on 1 April 20X5 and an impairment test would be done at this date. The depreciation on the plant from 1 October 20X4 to 1 April 20X5 would be $40,000 (640,000 × $12\frac{1}{2}$% × 6/12) giving a carrying amount of $200,000 at the date of impairment. An impairment test requires the plant's carrying amount to be compared with its recoverable amount. The recoverable amount of the plant is the higher of its value in use of $150,000 or its fair value less costs to sell. If Wilderness trades in the plant it would receive $180,000 by way of a part exchange, but this is conditional on buying new plant which Wilderness is reluctant to do. A more realistic amount of the fair value of the plant is its current disposal value of only $20,000. Thus the recoverable amount would be its value in use of $150,000 giving an impairment loss of $50,000 ($200,000 − $150,000). The remaining effect on income would be that a depreciation charge for the last six months of the year would be required. As the damage has reduced the remaining life to only two years (from the date of the impairment) the remaining depreciation would be $37,500 ($150,000/ 2 years × 6/12).

Thus extracts from the financial statements for the year ended 30 September 20X5 would be:

Statement of financial position	$
Non-current assets	
Plant (150,000 − 37,500)	112,500
Statement of comprehensive income	
Plant depreciation (40,000 + 37,500)	77,500
Plant impairment loss	50,000

(ii) There are a number of issues relating to the carrying amount of the assets of Mossel that have to be considered. It appears the value of the brand is based on the original purchase of the 'Quencher' brand. The company no longer uses this brand name; it has been renamed 'Phoenix'. Thus it would appear the purchased brand of 'Quencher' is now worthless. Mossel cannot transfer the value of the old brand to the new brand, because this would be the recognition of an internally developed intangible asset and the brand of 'Phoenix' does not appear to meet the recognition criteria in IAS 38. Thus prior to the allocation of the impairment loss the value of the brand should be written off as it no longer exists.

The inventories are valued at cost and contain $2 million worth of old bottled water (Quencher) that can be sold, but will have to be relabelled at a cost of $250,000. However, as the expected selling price of these bottles will be $3 million ($2 million × 150%), their net realisable value is $2,750,000. Thus it is correct to carry them at cost i.e. they are not impaired. The future expenditure on the plant is a matter for the following year's financial statements.

Applying this, the revised carrying amount of the net assets of Mossel's cash-generating unit (CGU) would be $25 million ($32 million − $7 million re the brand). The CGU has a recoverable amount of $20 million, thus there is an impairment loss of $5 million. This would be applied first to goodwill (of which there is none) then to the remaining assets pro rata. However the inventories should not be reduced as their fair value less cost to sell is in excess of their carrying amount. This would give revised carrying amounts at 30 September 20X5 of:

	$000
Brand	nil
Land containing spa (12,000 − (12,000/20,000 × 5,000))	9,000
Purifying and bottling plant (8,000 − (8,000/20,000 × 5,000))	6,000
Inventories	5,000
	_____
	20,000
	_____

16 LINNET

Key answer tips

Part (a) is a routine question on long-term construction contracts which should not present you with too many problems.

Your answer to part (b) should do more than calculate the inventory write down and state that the company should recognize a provision or a contingent liability. It is not clear how much of the loss in value of the inventory is due to the water leak or whether Myriad is liable to pay compensation to Securiprint and you should cover all the possibilities (meeting the requirement to discuss).

(a) (i) Long-term construction contracts span more than one accounting year-end. This leads to the problem of determining how the uncompleted transactions should be dealt with over the life of the contract. Normal sales are not recognized until the production and sales cycle is complete. Prudence is the most obvious concept that is being applied in these circumstances, and this is the principle that underlies the completed contract basis. Where the outcome of a long-term contract cannot be reasonably foreseen due to inherent uncertainty, the completed contracts basis should be applied. The effect of this is that revenue earned to date is matched to the cost of sales and no profit is taken.

The problem with the above is that for say a three-year contract it can lead to a situation where no profits are recognized, possibly for two years, and in the year of completion the whole of the profit is recognized (assuming the contract is profitable). This seems consistent with the principle that only realized profits should be recognized in profit or loss. The problem is that the overriding requirement is for financial statements to faithfully represent economic reality. In the above case it can be argued that the company has been involved in a profitable contract for a three-year period, but its financial statements over the three years show a profit in only one period. This also leads to volatility of profits which many companies feel is undesirable and not favoured by analysts.

An alternative approach is to apply the matching/accruals concept which underlies the percentage of completion method. This approach requires the percentage of completion of a contract to be assessed (there are several methods of doing this) and then recognising in profit or loss that percentage of the total estimated profit on the contract. This method has the advantage of more stable profit recognition and can be argued gives a fairer presentation than the completed contract method. A contrary view is that this method can be criticized as being a form of profit smoothing which, in other circumstances, is considered to be an (undesirable) example of creative accounting.

Accounting standards require the use of the percentage of completion method where the outcome of the contract is reasonably foreseeable. It should also be noted that where a contract is expected to produce a loss, the whole of the loss must be recognized as soon as it is anticipated.

(ii) **Linnet – statement of comprehensive income extract – year to 31 March 20X4** (see working below):

	$ million
Revenue	70
Cost of sales (64 +17)	(81)
	———
Loss for period	(11)
	———

Linnet – statement of financial position extracts – as at 31 March 20X4
Current assets
Gross amounts due from customers for contract work (w(iii))   59

Workings

	Cumulative 1 April 20X3 $ million	Cumulative 31 March 20X4 $ million	Amounts for year $ million
Revenue	150	(see below) 220	70
Cost of sales	(112)	(176)	(64)
Rectification costs	nil	(17)	(17)
Profit (loss)	38	(see below) 27	(11)

Progress payments received are $180 million. This is 90% of the work certified (at 29 February 20X4), therefore the work certified at that date was $200 million. The value of the further work completed in March 20X4 is given as $20 million, giving a total value of contract revenue at 31 March 20X4 of $220 million.

The total estimated profit (excluding rectification costs) is $60 million:

	$ million
Contract price	300
Cost to date	(195)
Estimated cost to complete	(45)
Estimated total profit	60

The degree of completion (by the method given in the question) is 220/300.

Therefore the profit to date (before rectification costs) is $44 million ($60 million × 220/300). Rectification costs must be charged to the period they were incurred and not spread over the remainder of the contract life. Therefore after rectification costs of $17 million the total reported contract profit to 31 March 20X4 would be $27 million.

With contract revenue of $220 million and profit to date of $44 million, this means contract costs (excluding rectification costs) would be $176 million. The difference between this figure and total cost incurred of $195 million is part of the $59 million of the gross amounts due from customers shown in the statement of financial position.

The gross amounts due from customers is cost to date ($195 million + $17 million) plus cumulative profit ($27 million) less progress billings ($180 million) = $59 million.

(b)   This is a complex situation. The selling prices of some items of inventory after the reporting period end appear to be below their cost and this indicates that part of the closing inventory (at 31 March 20X4) may require writing down to net realisable value with the resultant loss recognized in the current year. This is an adjusting event after the end of the reporting period if the losses are due to circumstances that occurred before the year-end. However, if the losses are due to circumstances that developed in the period after the reporting period end they should be included in the following year's financial statements (to 31 March 20X5). If these losses (in 20X5) are material they should be brought to the attention of shareholders in the notes to the financial statements for the year to 31 March 20X4 as a non-adjusting event. Appling the above to the circumstances of the question would give the following analysis:

	$
Cost	48
Net realisable value (NRV)	41
Apparent loss	7 per pack

The NRV of $41 is the reduced selling price of A4 paper of $45 less the cost of getting the goods into a saleable condition of $4.

From the question it would appear that this loss is partly attributable to the remedial cost of the water leak. This is an adjusting event requiring a write down of $2 per pack of the relevant items. The net realisable value at the year-end would have been $46 (original selling price of $50 less $4 remedial costs), which is $2 below the cost of $48. The remainder of the loss, $5 ($50 – $45), is caused by the price reduction in response to competitive pressure in the period after the reporting period end. This is a non-adjusting event requiring appropriate disclosure if material.

The above ignores the effect of the information concerning the sale to Securiprint. If the 'marks' are due to the water leak or other flaw in manufacture, Linnet will probably be liable to pay compensation to Securiprint. This would be an actual liability requiring a provision to be made in the current year unless the amount cannot be determined reliably (the IASB says this should be rare). The provision would be for a refund of the cost of the goods sold and compensation for consequential losses caused by the faulty goods. If the marks were not due to the actions of Linnet then there would be no liability. It may be that at this early stage there is insufficient information to come to a conclusion as to who is at fault, but this represents at least a contingent liability on the part of Linnet and should be disclosed appropriately in the notes to the financial statements. The information may also indicate that other customers could have similar claims against Linnet.

A final point to consider is that if the above fault is not due to Securiprint, it may mean that all of the inventory affected by the water leak is still damaged (despite the remedial work). If so, this would be evidence that the value of the inventory is impaired and a further provision would be required to write down the inventory (probably to nil) in the current year. Clearly no more of this inventory should be sold until the problem is resolved.

17 BOWTOCK

> 🔑
>
> **Key answer tips**
>
> This is a friendly question covering three separate topics: deferred tax, leasing and events after the reporting period end. You must ensure that you have a broad knowledge of the whole syllabus, rather than a specialised knowledge of just a few topics.
>
> The lease in part (b) is clearly a finance lease since the lease term is five years, which is also the useful life of the asset.

(a) (i) Accounting profit (as reported in a company's financial statements) differs from the profit figure used by the tax authorities to calculate a company's income tax liability for a given period. If deferred tax were ignored (flow through system), then a company's tax charge for a particular period may bear very little resemblance to the reported profit. For example if a company makes a large profit in a particular period, but, perhaps because of high levels of capital expenditure, it is entitled to claim large tax allowances for that period, this would reduce the amount of tax it had to pay. The result of this would be that the company reported a large profit, but very little, if any, tax charge. This situation is usually 'reversed' in subsequent periods such that tax charges appear to be much higher than the reported profit would suggest that they should be.

Many commentators feel that such a reporting system is misleading in that the profit after tax, which is used for calculating the company's earnings per share, may bear very little resemblance to the pre tax profit. This can mean that a government's fiscal policy may distort a company's profit trends. Providing for deferred tax goes some way towards relieving this anomaly, but it can never be entirely corrected due to items that may be included in the statement of comprehensive income, but will never be allowed for tax purposes (referred to as permanent differences in some jurisdictions). Where tax depreciation is different from the related accounting depreciation charges this leads to the tax base of an asset being different to its carrying value on the statement of financial position (these differences are called temporary differences) and a provision for deferred tax is made. This 'statement of financial position liability' approach is the general principle on which IAS 12 bases the calculation of deferred tax. The effect of this is that it usually brings the total tax charge (i.e. the provision for the current year's income tax plus the deferred tax) in proportion to the profit reported to shareholders.

The main area of debate when providing for deferred tax is whether the provision meets the definition of a liability. If the provision is likely to crystallize, then it is a liability, however if it will not crystallize in the foreseeable future, then arguably, it is not a liability and should not be provided for. The IASB takes a prudent approach and IAS 12 does not accept the latter argument.

UK SYLLABUS FOCUS ONLY

Revaluations

Under FRS 19 a revaluation of a fixed asset is not considered to create an unavoidable tax liability and so does not affect the deferred tax provision. The exception to this rule is where a binding agreement has been entered into to dispose of the asset at the revalued amount and any gains or losses expected to arise on disposal have been recognised at the balance sheet date. In this situation deferred tax is to be recognised on the timing difference and recorded directly in the revaluation reserve.

Long-term deferred tax balances

Under FRS 19 entities are permitted to discount long-term deferred tax balances to take into account the time value of money. This is not mandatory however and is a choice allowed per the standard. IAS 12 does not permit the discounting of deferred tax balances due to the complexities and difficulties involved.

(ii) IAS 12 requires deferred tax to be calculated using the 'statement of financial position liability method'. This method requires the temporary difference to be calculated and the rate of income tax applied to this difference to give the deferred tax asset or liability. Temporary differences are the differences between the carrying amount of an asset and its tax base.

Carrying value at 30 September 20X3	$000	$000
Cost of plant		2,000
Accumulated depreciation at 30 September 20X3		
(2,000 – 400)/8 years for 3 years		(600)
		——
Carrying value		1,400
		——
Tax base at 30 September 20X3		
Initial tax base (original cost)		2,000
Tax depreciation		
Year to 30 September 20X1 (2,000 × 40%)	800	
Year to 30 September 20X2 (1,200 × 20%)	240	
Year to 30 September 20X3 (960 × 20%)	192	(1,232)
	——	
Tax base 30 September 20X3		768
		——
Temporary differences at 30 September 20X3 (1,400 – 768)		632
Deferred tax liability at 30 September 20X3 (632 × 25% tax rate)		158
Statement of comprehensive income credit – year to 30 September 20X3 ((200 accounts depn – 192 tax depn) × 25%)		2

(b)

	$
Statement of comprehensive income extracts year to 30 September 20X3	
Depreciation of leased asset (W1)	10,400
Lease interest expense (W2)	2,672
Statement of financial position extracts as at 30 September 20X3	
Leased asset at cost	52,000
Accumulated depreciation (7,800 + 10,400 (W1))	18,200
	———
Carrying value	33,800
	———
Non-current liabilities	
Obligations under finance leases (W2)	21,696
Current liabilities	
Accrued lease interest (W2)	1,872
Obligations under finance leases (W2)	9,504

Workings

(W1) Depreciation for the year ended 30 September 20X2 would be $7,800 ($52,000 × 20% × 9/12). Depreciation for the year ended 30 September 20X3 would be $10,400 ($52,000 × 20%)

(W2) The lease obligations are calculated as follows:

Cash price/fair value	52,000
Rental 1 January 20X2	(12,000)
	———
	40,000
Interest to 30 September 20X2 (40,000 × 8% × 9/12)	2,400
Interest to 1 January 20X3 (40,000 × 8% × 3/12)	800
	———
	43,200
Rental 1 January 20X3	(12,000)
	———
Capital outstanding 1 January 20X3	31,200
Interest to 30 September 20X3 (31,200 × 8% × 9/12)	1,872
Interest to 1 January 20X4 (31,200 × 8% × 3/12)	624
	———
	33,696
	———

The lease interest expense for the year to 30 September 20X3 is $2,672 (800 + 1,872 from above), of which $1,872 is a current liability. The total capital amount outstanding at 30 September 20X3 is $31,200 (the same as at 1 January 20X3 as no further payments have been made). This must be split between current and non-current liabilities. Next year's payment will be $12,000 of which $2,496 (1,872 + 624) is interest. Therefore capital repaid in the next year will be $9,504 (12,000 – 2,496). This leaves capital of $21,696 (31,200 – 9,504) as a non-current liability.

(c)   (i)   Most events occurring after the reporting period end should be properly reflected in the following year's financial statements. There are two circumstances where events occurring after the reporting period end are relevant to the current year's financial statements. The first category, known as adjusting events, provides additional evidence of conditions that existed at the reporting period end. This usually means they help to determine the value of an item that may have been uncertain at the year-end. Common examples of this are post statement of financial position receipts from accounts receivable and sales of inventory. These receipts help to confirm the bad debt and inventory write down allowances.

The second category is non-adjusting events. As the name suggests these do not affect the amounts contained in the financial statements, but are considered of such importance that unless they are disclosed, users of financial statements would not properly be able to assess the financial position of the company. Common examples of these would be the loss of a major asset (say due to a fire) after the reporting period end or the sale of an investment (often a subsidiary) after the reporting period end.

(ii)   **Inventory**

Sales of goods after the reporting period end are normally a reflection of circumstances that existed prior to the year end. They are usually interpreted as a confirmation of the value of inventory as it existed at the year end, and are thus adjusting events. In this case the sale of the goods after the year-end confirmed that the value of the inventory was correctly stated as it was sold at a profit. Goods remaining unsold at the date the new legislation was enacted are worthless. Whilst this may imply that they should be written off in preparing the financial statements to 30 September 20X3, this is not the case. What it is important to realize is that the event that caused the inventory to become worthless did not exist at the year end and its consequent losses should be reflected in the following accounting period. Thus there should be no adjustment to the value of inventory in the draft financial statements, but given that it is material, it should be disclosed as a non-adjusting event.

Construction contract

On first appearance this new legislation appears similar to the previous example, but there is a major difference. Profits on an uncompleted long term construction contract are based on assessment of the overall eventual profit that the contract is expected to make. This new legislation will mean the overall profit is $500,000 less than originally thought. This information must be taken into account when calculating the profit at 30 September 20X3. This is an adjusting event.

18   MULTIPLEX

(a)   **Statement of comprehensive income extracts**:

	$000	$000
Loan stock interest paid ($80 million × 8%)		6,400
Required accrual of finance cost		1,844
		─────
Total finance cost for loan stock ($68,704,000 × 12%)		8,244
		─────

Statement of financial position extracts:

Non-current liabilities		
8% loan stock 20X4	68,704	
Accrual of finance costs	1,844	70,548
	─────	─────
Equity and liabilities		
Share options		11,296

Workings

IAS 32 and IFRS 9, dealing with financial instruments, require compound or hybrid financial instruments such as convertible loan stock to be treated under the substance of the contractual agreement. For this type of instrument this means that its equity element and liability (debt) element must be separately identified and presented as such on the statement of financial position. There are several methods of calculating the split between the two elements. For example there are several option pricing models. However, given the limited information in the question, the split can only be calculated by a 'residual value of equity' approach. This involves calculating the present value of the cash flows attributable to a 'pure' debt instrument and treating the difference between this and the issue proceeds (the residue) as the equity component.

	Cash flow	Factor	Discounted cash flow
	$m	12%	$000
Year 1 interest	6.4	× 0.89	5,696
Year 2 interest	6.4	× 0.80	5,120
Year 3 interest	6.4	× 0.71	4,544
Year 4 interest	6.4	× 0.64	4,096
Year 5 interest and capital	86.4	× 0.57	49,248
			─────
			68,704
Residual equity element (share options)			11,296
			─────
Proceeds of issue			80,000
			─────

(b)

	Assets: 1 Jan 20X0 $000	First impair- ment $000	Revised assets: 1 Feb 20X0 $000	Second impair- ment $000	Revised assets: 31 Mar 20X0 $000
Goodwill	200	(200)	nil		nil
Operating licence	1,200	(200)	1,000	(100)	900
Property – train stations/land	300	(50)	250	(50)	200
Rail track and coaches	300	(50)	250	(50)	200
Steam engines	500		500		500
	2,500	(500)	2,000	(200)	1,800

Notes

The first impairment loss amounts to $1 million in total:

- of this $500,000 must first be written off one of the engines as one of them no longer exists and is no longer part of the cash-generating unit
- the remaining impairment loss of $500,000 can then be written off against the cash generating unit
- the goodwill of $200,000 must be eliminated first; and
- the balance of $300,000 is allocated pro rata to the remaining net assets (other than the engine which must not be reduced below its net selling price of $500,000), so (1,200/1,200 + 300 + 300) to the operating licence and so on.

The second impairment loss of $200,000:

- the first $100,000 is applied to the licence to write it down to its net selling price
- the balance is applied pro rata to assets other than those carried at their net selling prices i.e. $50,000 to both the property and the rail track and coaches.

Tutorial note

As Multiplex owns 100% of Steamdays, there is no grossing up of notional goodwill for the amount attributable to a non-controlling interest.

(c) Under IFRS 5 *Non-current Assets Held for Sale and Discontinued Operations* the engineering division meets the definition of a disposal group which must be treated in the financial statements in the same way as an asset 'held for sale'. As the division was not sold until after the year end then the directors must include it in the statement of financial position at the lower of the carrying amount and the fair value less costs to sell.

The current carrying value of the division is $46m ($66m – $20m) and the fair value less costs to sell is the agreed value of $30m. Therefore the division should be presented in the statement of financial position at 31 March 20X0 at a value of $30m below current assets. The impairment of $16m ($46m – $30m) must be recognized in the statement of comprehensive income.

As the division is classified as 'held for sale', represents a separate major line of business and is part of a single co-ordinated plant to dispose of this separate major line, then it meets the IFRS 5 definition of discontinued operations. Therefore in the statement of comprehensive income there should be a single amount comprising the total post-tax profit or loss of the division and the $16m impairment required to measure the division at fair value less costs to sell.

As the company is committed to the closure it should also recognize a provision for the cost of the closure (as required by IAS 37).

The total provision should be made up of the following amounts:

	$m
Redundancies	2.0
Professional costs	1.5
Penalty costs	3.0
	6.5

The operating losses of $4.5 million in the period from 1 April 20X0 until the date of closure cannot be provided for at the date the closure is announced. IAS 37 *Provisions, Contingent Liabilities and Contingent Assets* prohibits this type of provision unless it relates to losses on 'onerous contracts'. There is no indication in the question that these future losses relate to onerous contracts.

(d)   **Statement of comprehensive income year to 31 March 20X0**

	$m
Contract revenue (W2)	18.0
Contract costs recognized (balancing figure)	(14.1)
Contract profit (W3)	3.9

Statement of financial position extracts as at 31 March 20X0	$m
Current assets	
Gross amounts due from customers (W5)	11.0

Note to the financial statements

Contingent asset

The company is in the process of attempting to recover $2.5 million from a firm of civil engineers. The engineers were contracted to design the structure of a road bridge to be built by Multiplex. The engineers incorrectly specified certain materials to be used on the contract, which had to be replaced at a later date. The company's lawyers have advised that there is a good prospect of a successful recovery of these costs.

Workings

(W1) **The percentage of completion is calculated as:**

	at 31 March 19W9		at 31 March 20X0	
$\dfrac{\text{Work certified}}{\text{Contract price}}$	$\dfrac{\$12\,\text{million}}{\$40\,\text{million}}$	= 30%	$\dfrac{\$30\,\text{million}}{\$45\,\text{million}}$	= 66.7% (or $^2/_3$)

The figure for 20X0 includes the variation to the contract.

(W2) The accumulated contract revenues at 31 March 20X0 would be $30 million (2/3 × $45 million). The contract revenue to be recognized in 20X0 would be $18 million i.e. accumulated revenue of $30 million less the contract revenue of $12 million reported in the previous year.

(W3) The accumulated profit at 31 March 20X0 would have been 2/3 of the revised estimated total profit of $15 million ($45 million contract price less $30 million costs) = $10 million. However the cost of the rectification work of $2.5 million must be charged to the year in which it occurs (i.e. the year to 31 March 20X0).

This gives a profit for the year of $3.9 million ($10 million − $3.6 million in 19W9 − $2.5 million rectification work).

(W4) The statement of comprehensive income for the year to 31 March 19W9 would be:

	$m
Contract revenue	12.0
Contract costs incurred (balancing figure)	(8.4)
Profit ((40 − 28) × 30%)	3.6

(W5) The gross amount due from customers is made up of:

Costs incurred to date	28.5
Plus recognized profits (3.6 + 3.9)	7.5
less Progress billings	(25.0)
	11.0

19 TORRENT

Key answer tips

The best way is to deal with the accounting for construction contracts is to work through one contract at a time, establishing whether over its life the contract is expected to generate profits (recognize only by the stage of completion method) or incur losses (recognize in full immediately). The requirement that unplanned rectification costs should be recognized in full in the year in which they are incurred (rather than being a normal cost which is spread over the life of the contract) is quite tricky.

(a) **Statement of comprehensive income for the year ended 31 March 20X6**

	Alpha $m	Beta $m	Ceta $m	Total $m
Revenue (W1 – W3)	8	2.0	4.8	14.8
Cost of sales (W1 – W3)	(7)	(3.5)	(4.0)	(14.5)
Profit/(loss)	1	(1.5)	0.8	0.3

Statement of financial position at 31 March 20X6

Current assets

Gross amounts due from customers for contract

work (W4)	1.0		4.8	5.8

Receivables – amounts recoverable on contracts

((14 – 12.6) and (2 – 1.8))	1.4	0.2		1.6

Current liabilities

Gross amounts due to customers for contract work (W4)	(1.5)		(1.5)

Workings ($m)

(W1) **Alpha**

	At 31.3.05	At 31.3.06	Year to 31.3.06
Work invoiced	6.0 (5.4/90%)	14.0 (12.6/90%)	8
Cost of sales (β)	(4.5)	(11.5)	(7)
Profit	1.5	2.5	1

Profit is calculated as:

% complete	30% (6/20 × 100)	70% (14/20 × 100)
Attributable profit	1.5 ((20 – 15) × 30%)	2.5 ((20 – 15) × 70%) – 1 rectification)

Rectification costs must be charged in the year in which they are incurred.

(W2) **Beta**

Due to the increase in the estimated cost, Beta is a loss-making contract and the whole of the loss must be provided for as soon as it is can be anticipated. The loss is expected to be $1.5 million ($7.5m – $6m). The revenue of the contract at 31 March 20X6 is $2 million ($1.8/90%), thus the cost of sales must be recorded as $3.5 million. As costs to date are $2 million, this means a provision of $1.5 million is required.

(W3) **Ceta**

Based on the costs to date at 31 March 20X6 of $4 million and the total estimated costs of $10 million, this contract is 40% complete. The estimated profit is $2 million ($12m – $10m); therefore the profit at 31 March 20X6 is $0.8 million ($2m × 40%). This gives an imputed revenue (and receivable) value of $4.8 million.

(W4) **Gross amount due to/from customers**

	Alpha $m	Beta $m	Ceta $m	Total $m
Contract cost incurred	12.5	2.0	4.0	18.5
Recognized profits/(losses)	2.5	(1.5)	0.8	1.8
Progress billings	(14.0)	(2.0)	(nil)	(16.0)
Due from customers	1.0		4.8	5.8
Due to customers		(1.5)		(1.5)

(b) (i) Savoir – EPS year ended 31 March 20X4:

The issue on 1 July 20X3 at full market value needs to be weighted:

Old shares (10/25c)	40m	3/12 =	10m
New shares	8m		
	48m	× 9/12 =	36m
			46m

Without the bonus issue this would give an EPS of 30c ($13.8m/46m × 100).

The bonus issue of one for four would result in 12 million new shares giving a total number of ordinary shares of 60 million. The dilutive effect of the bonus issue would reduce the EPS to 24c (30c × 48m/60m).

The comparative EPS (for 20X3) would be restated at 20c (25c × 48m/60m).

EPS year ended 31 March 20X5:

The rights issue of two for five on 1 October 20X4 is half way through the year. The theoretical ex rights value can be calculated as:

Holder of	100 shares worth $2.40 =	$240	
Subscribes for	40 shares at $1 each =	$40	
Now holds	140 worth (in theory)	$280	i.e. $2 each.

Weighting:

	60m × 6/12 × 2.40/2.00 =	36 million
Rights issue (2 for 5)	24m	
New total	84m × 6/12 –	42 million
Weighted average		78 million

EPS is therefore 25c ($19.5m/78m × 100).

The comparative (for 20X4) would be restated at 20c (24c × 2.00/2.40).

(ii) The basic EPS for the year ended 31 March 20X6 is 30c ($25.2m/84m × 100).

Dilution

Convertible loan stock

On conversion loan interest of $1.2 million after tax would be saved ($20 million × 8% × (100% − 25%)) and a further 10 million shares would be issued ($20m/$100 × 50).

Directors' options

Options for 12 million shares at $1.50 each would yield proceeds of $18 million. At the average market price of $2.50 per share this would purchase 7.2 million shares ($18m/$2.50). Therefore the 'bonus' element of the options is 4.8 million shares (12m − 7.2m).

Using the above figures the diluted EPS for the year ended 31 March 20X6 is 26.7c ($25.2m + $1.2m)/(84m + 10m + 4.8m)).

20 PINGWAY *Walk in the footsteps of a top tutor*

Key answer tips

This question requires you to demonstrate your knowledge of IAS 32/ IFRS 9 relating to a convertible loan and how it should be accounted for in the financial statements. Ensure you do not simply calculate the effect of the convertible loan as you must discuss the accounting implication to be eligible for all the marks available in the question. The highlighted words are key phrases that markers are looking for.

Accounting correctly for the convertible loan note in accordance with IAS 32 *Financial Instruments: Presentation* and IFRS 9 *Financial Instruments* mean that virtually all the financial assistant's observations are incorrect. The convertible loan note is a compound financial instrument containing a (largely) debt component and an equity component – the value of the option to receive equity shares. These components must be calculated using the residual equity method and appropriately classified (as debt and equity) on the statement of financial position. As some of the proceeds of the instrument will be equity, the gearing will not be quite as high as if a non-convertible loan was issued, but gearing will be increased. However, if the loan note is converted to equity in March 2010, gearing will be reduced. The interest rate that would be applicable to a non-convertible loan (8%) is representative of the true finance cost and should be applied to the carrying amount of the debt to calculate the finance cost to be charged to the statement of comprehensive income thus giving a much higher charge than the assistant believes.

Accounting treatment: financial statements year ended 31 March 2008

Statement of comprehensive income:
Finance costs (see working)	$693,920

Statement of financial position:
Non-current liabilities
3% convertible loan note (8,674 + 393.92)	$9,067,920

Equity
Option to convert	$1,326,000

Working (figures in brackets in $000)

	Cash flows	Factor at 8%	Present value $000
Year 1 interest	300	0.93	279
Year 2 interest	300	0.86	258
Year 3 interest and capital	10,300	0.79	8,137
Total value of debt component			8,674
Proceeds of the issue			10,000
Equity component (residual amount)			1,326

The interest cost in the statement of comprehensive income should be $693,920 (8,674 × 8%), requiring an accrual of $393,920 (693.92 – 300 i.e. 10,000 × 3%). This accrual should be added to the carrying value of the debt.

Examiner's comments

This question proved to be the most difficult question for the majority of candidates with a significant percentage not even attempting it. A few answers were very good, although the majority were very poor.

The question required candidates to account for the issue of a $10 million convertible loan and comment on some misguided views expressed by a financial assistant in relation to its issue.

The convertible loan note had a coupon (nominal) interest rate of 3%, but an effective rate of 8%. The proceeds of the loan had to be split between debt and equity by discounting the future cash flows at 8% to give the debt element with the balance being the value of the equity option. Common mistakes were to project the cash flows with an interest rate of 8% (rather than 3%), to discount them at 3% (rather than 8%) and to calculate the interest charge to the statement of comprehensive income as 3% of $10 million (rather than 8% of the debt element).

The financial assistant suggested that the profit would be higher (implying he/she assumed the interest cost would be only 3%) and the loan note could be included as equity because most loan note holders would be expected to choose the equity option. Both of these comments are wrong, but many weaker candidates found themselves agreeing with them, thus showing a complete lack of understanding of this type of financial instrument.

Taken as a whole this was by far the worst answered question, which is surprising as this topic has been asked on many occasions, often as part of a larger question.

ACCA marking scheme	
	Marks
1 mark per valid comment up to	4
Use of 8%	1
Initial carrying amount of debt and equity	2
Finance cost	2
Carrying amount of debt at 31 March 2008	1
	___
Total	10
	___

21   ERRSEA

(a)   **Errsea – statement of comprehensive income extracts year ended 31 March 2007**

	$
Loss on disposal of plant – see note below ((90,000 – 60,000) – 12,000)	18,000
Depreciation for year (wkg (i))	75,000
Government grants (a credit item) – see note below and (wkg (iv))	(19,000)

Note: The repayment of government grant of $3,000 may instead have been included as an increase of the loss on disposal of the plant.

Errsea – statement of financial position extracts as at 31 March 2007

	Cost $	Accumulated depreciation $	Carrying amount $
Property, plant and equipment (wkg (v))	360,000	195,000	165,000

Non-current liabilities	$
Government grants (wkg (iv))	39,000
Current liabilities	
Government grants (wkg (iv))	27,000

Workings

(i)   **Depreciation for year ended 31 March 2007**

	$
On acquired plant (wkg (ii))	52,500
Other plant (wkg (iii))	22,500
	75,000

(ii)   The cost of the acquired plant is recorded at $210,000 being its base cost plus the costs of modification and transport and installation. Annual depreciation over three years will be $70,000. Time apportioned for year ended 31 March 2007 by 9/12 = $52,500.

(iii)   The other remaining plant is depreciated at 15% on cost

	$
(b/f 240,000 – 90,000 (disposed of) × 15%)	22,500

(iv)   **Government grants**

Transferred to income for the year ended 31 March 2007:

	$
From current liability in 2006 (10,000 – 3,000 (repaid))	7,000
From acquired plant (see below):	12,000
	19,000

Non-current liability

	$
B/f	30,000
Transferred to current	(11,000)
On acquired plant (see below)	20,000
	39,000

Grant on acquired plant is 25% of base cost only = $48,000

This will be treated as:

	$
To income in year ended 31 March 2007 (48,000/3 × 9/12)	12,000
Classified as current liability (48,000/3)	16,000
Classified as a non-current liability (balance)	20,000
	48,000

Note: Government grants are accounted for from the date they are receivable (i.e. when the qualifying conditions for the grant have been met).

Current liability

	$
Transferred from non-current (per question)	11,000
On acquired plant (see above)	16,000
	27,000

(v)

	Cost	Accumulated depreciation	Carrying amount
	$	$	$
Property, plant and equipment			
Balances b/f	240,000	180,000	60,000
Disposal	(90,000)	(60,000)	(30,000)
Addition (w (ii))	210,000	52,500	157,500
Other plant depreciation for year (wkg (iii))		22,500	(22,500)
Balances at 31 March 2007	360,000	195,000	165,000

(b) (i) This is an example of an adjusting event within IAS 10 *Events after the reporting date*. This means that an impairment of trade receivables of $23,000 must be recognised (and charged to income). The increase in the receivable after the year end should be written off in the following year's financial statements.

(ii)   Sales of the year-end inventory in the following accounting period may provide evidence that the inventory's net realisable value has fallen below its cost. This appears to be the case for product W32 and is another example of an adjusting event. With a selling price of $5.40 and after paying a 15% commission, the net realisable value of W32 is $4.59 each. Assuming that the fall in selling price is not due to circumstances that occurred after the year end and that the selling price is typical of what the remainder of the product will sell for, inventory should be written down (via a charge to the statement of comprehensive income) by $16,920 ((6.00 – 4.59) × 12,000 units).

(iii)   Tentacle has correctly treated the outstanding litigation as a contingent liability. The settlement of a court case after the reporting date may confirm (or otherwise) the existence of an obligation at the year end and would be an example of an adjusting event. This would then require that either the disclosure note of the contingency is removed or the obligation should be provided for dependent on the outcome of the litigation. However, this is not quite the case in Tentacle's example. The circumstances of the claim against Tentacle are different from those of the recently settled case. So this settlement does not appear to have any effect on the likelihood of Tentacle losing the case. What it does (potentially) affect is the estimated amount of the liability. IAS 10 refers to this situation as an updating disclosure. The only required change to the financial statements would be to update the disclosure note on the contingent liability to reflect that the potential liability has increased from $500,000 to $750,000.

(iv)   Normally the effect of price increases of materials after the reporting date would be a matter for the following year's financial statements as such increases do not affect the costs as they existed at the reporting date (i.e. they would not be an adjusting event). However, Tentacle's method of recognising profit (using a cost basis to determine the percentage of completion) requires an estimate (at 31 March 2007) of the future costs of the contract. This estimate directly determines the amount of profit recognised at 31 March 2007. Therefore the information indicating that the total estimated costs of the contract have increased should be taken as providing additional evidence of conditions that existed at the year end. Thus this is an adjusting event which requires the recognised profit to be recalculated. The original estimate of the recognised profit at 31 March 2007 of $1.2 million would be half of the estimated total profit of $2.4 million (percentage of completion is 50% i.e. $3 million/$6 million). The increase in the costs of $1.5 million means the revised estimated total profit is only $900,000 (2.4m – 1.5m). The revised total costs are $7.5 million (6m + 1.5m). Thus the recognised profit on the contract should be recalculated as $360,000 (900,000 × 3m/7.5m) with appropriate amendments to the statement of comprehensive income and statement of financial position figures.

22   TUNSHILL

(a)   Management's choices of which accounting policies they may adopt are not as wide as generally thought. Where an International Accounting Standard, IAS or IFRS (or an Interpretation) specifically applies to a transaction or event the accounting policy used must be as prescribed in that Standard (taking in to account any Implementation Guidance within the Standard). In the absence of a Standard, or where a Standard contains a choice of policies, management must use its judgement in applying accounting policies that result in information that is relevant and reliable given the circumstances of the transactions and events. In making such judgements, management should refer to guidance in the Standards related to similar issues and the definitions, recognition criteria and measurement concepts for assets, liabilities, income and expenses in the IASB's Conceptual Framework for Financial Reporting. Management may also consider pronouncements of other standard-setting bodies that use a similar conceptual framework to the IASB.

A change in an accounting policy usually relates to a change of principle, basis or rule being applied by an entity. Accounting estimates are used to measure the carrying amounts of assets and liabilities, or related expenses and income. A change in an accounting estimate is a reassessment of the expected future benefits and obligations associated with an asset or a liability. Thus, for example, a change from non-depreciation of a building to depreciating it over its estimated useful life would be a change of accounting policy. To change the estimate of its useful life would be a change in an accounting estimate.

(b)   (i)   The main issue here is the estimate of the useful life of a non-current asset. Such estimates form an important part of the accounting estimate of the depreciation charge. Like most estimates, an annual review of their appropriateness is required and it is not unusual, as in this case, to revise the estimate of the remaining useful life of plant. It appears, from the information in the question, that the increase in the estimated remaining useful life of the plant is based on a genuine reassessment by the production manager. This appears to be an acceptable reason for a revision of the plant's life, whereas it would be unacceptable to increase the estimate simply to improve the company's reported profit. That said, the assistant accountant's calculation of the financial effect of the revised life is incorrect. Where there is an increase (or decrease) in the estimated remaining life of a non-current asset, its carrying amount (at the time of the revision) is allocated over the new remaining life (after allowing for any estimated residual value). The carrying amount at 1 October 2009 is $12 million ($20 million − $8 million accumulated depreciation) and this should be written off over the estimated remaining life of six years (eight years in total less two already elapsed). Thus a charge for depreciation of $2 million would be required in the year ended 30 September 2010 leaving a carrying amount of $10 million ($12 million – $2 million) in the statement of financial position at that date. A depreciation charge for the current year cannot be avoided and there will be no credit to the statement of profit or loss as suggested by the assistant accountant. It should be noted that the incremental effect of the revision to the estimated life of the plant would be to improve the reported profit by $2 million being the difference between the depreciation based on the old life ($4 million) and the new life ($2 million).

(ii)   The appropriateness of the proposed change to the method of valuing inventory is more dubious than the previous example. Whilst both methods (FIFO and AVCO) are acceptable methods of valuing inventory under IAS 2 Inventories, changing an accounting policy to be consistent with that of competitors is not a convincing reason. Generally changes in accounting policies should be avoided unless a change is required by a new or revised accounting standard or the new policy provides more reliable and relevant information regarding the entity's position. In any event the assistant accountant's calculations are again incorrect and would not meet the intention of improving reported profit. The most obvious error is that changing from FIFO to AVCO will cause a reduction in the value of the closing inventory at 30 September 2010 effectively reducing, rather than increasing, both the valuation of inventory and reported profit. A change in accounting policy must be accounted for as if the new policy had always been in place (retrospective application). In this case, for the year ended 30 September 2010, both the opening and closing inventories would need to be measured at AVCO which would reduce reported profit by $400,000 (($20 million – $18 million) – ($15 million – $13.4 million) – i.e. the movement in the values of the opening and closing inventories). The other effect of the change will be on the retained earnings brought forward at 1 October 2009. These will be restated (reduced) by the effect of the reduced inventory value at 30 September 2009 i.e. $1.6 million ($15 million – $13.4 million). This adjustment would be shown in the statement of changes in equity.

ACCA marking scheme			
			Marks
(a)		1 mark per valid point	5
(b)	(i)	recognise as a change in accounting estimate	1
		appears an acceptable basis for change	1
		correct method is to allocate carrying amount over new remaining life	1
		depreciation for current year should be $2 million	1
		carrying amount at 30 September 2010 is $10 million	1
			—
			5
	(ii)	proposed change is probably not for a valid reason	1
		change would cause a decrease (not an increase) in profit	1
		changes in policy should be applied retrospectively	1
		decrease in year to 30 September 2010 is $400,000	1
		retained earnings restated by $1.6 million	1
			—
			5
			—
Total			15
			—

23   MANCO

Key answer tips

Be careful as the question asks you to explain how the closure impacts the financial statements and calculations alone will not earn full marks.

From the information in the question, the closure of the furniture making operation is a restructuring as defined in IAS *37 Provisions, contingent liabilities and contingent assets* and, due to the timing of the decision, a provision for the closure costs will be required in the year ended 30 September 2010. Although the Standard says that a Board of directors' decision to close an operation is alone not sufficient to trigger a provision the other actions of the management, informing employees, customers and a press announcement indicate that this is an irreversible decision and that therefore there is an obligating event.

Commenting on each element in turn for both years:

(i)   **Factory and plant**

At 30 September 2010 – these assets cannot be classed as 'held-for-sale' as they are still in use (i.e. generating revenue) and therefore are not available for sale. Both assets will therefore continue to be depreciated.

Despite this, it does appear that the plant is impaired. Based on its carrying amount of $2.8 million an impairment charge of $2.3 million ($2.8 million – $0.5 million) would be required (subject to any further depreciation for the three months from July to September 2010). The expected gain on the sale of the factory cannot be recognised or used to offset the impairment charge on the plant. The impairment charge is not part of the restructuring provision, but should be reported with the depreciation charge for the year.

At 30 September 2011 – the realised profit on the disposal of the factory and any further loss on the disposal of the plant will both be reported in the income statement.

(ii)   **Redundancy and retraining costs**

At 30 September 2010 – a provision for the redundancy costs of $750,000 should be made, but the retraining costs relate to the ongoing actives of Manco and cannot be provided for.

At 30 September 2011 – the redundancy costs incurred during the year will be offset against the provision created last year. Any under- or over-provision will be reported in the income statement. The retraining costs will be written off as they are incurred.

(iii)   **Trading losses**

The losses to 30 September 2010 will be reported as part of the results for the year ended 30 September 2010. The expected losses from 1 October 2010 to the closure on 31 January 2011 cannot be provided in the year ended 30 September 2010 as they relate to ongoing activities and will therefore be reported as part of the results for the year ended 30 September 2011 as they are incurred.

It should also be considered whether the closure fulfils the definition of a discontinued operation in accordance with IFRS 5 *Non-current assets held for sale and discontinued operations*. As there is a co-ordinated plan to dispose of a separate major line of business (the furniture making operation is treated as an operating segment) this probably is a discontinued operation. However, the timing of the closure means that it is not a discontinued operation in the year ended 30 September 2010; rather it is likely that it will be such in the year ended 30 September 2011. Some commentators believe that this creates an anomalous situation in that most of the closure costs are reported in the year ended 30 September 2010 (as described above), but the closure itself is only identified and reported as a discontinued operation in the year ended 30 September 2011 (although the comparative figures for 2010 would then restate this as a discontinued operation).

ACCA marking scheme	
	Marks
closure is a restructuring under IAS 37	1
it is an obligating event in year ended 30 September 2010	1
provide for impairment of plant	1
cannot recognise gain on property until sold	1
provide for redundancy in year ended 30 September 2010	1
cannot provided for retraining costs in current year	1
inclusion of trading losses in correct periods	2
consider if and when closure should be treated as a discontinued operation	2
Total	10

24   SITUATIONS

(a)   (i)   This is an example of a contingent liability. As it was only considered possible that AB would have to pay damages there has been no provision made for this liability. However under IFRS 3 XY must recognize the fair value of this contingent liability within net assets acquired for the purpose of the goodwill calculation.

(ii)   At the acquisition date there was no obligation to incur the integration costs and no liability should be recognized within net assets acquired (IFRS 3 and IAS 37).

(b)   Finance cost   =   Total payments payable in respect of an instrument *minus* Net proceeds on issue of the instrument

			$m
Total payments	=	Interest (5 × 4% × $50m)	10
		+ Repayment amount	60
			70

Assuming that the borrowings were issued at par:

			$m
Net proceeds on issue	=	Gross proceeds	50.0
		minus Direct costs of the issue	(0.5)
			49.5

∴ Total finance cost   =   70 − 49.5 = $20.5m

(c) Under IFRS 9 an investment in equity instruments will be initially measured at fair value (with the price paid to acquire the financial asset initially regarded as fair value) and thereafter will have the designation of fair value through profit or loss.

Therefore at the time of the initial acquisition the investment would have been included in the statement of financial position as such at a value of $51,000 (60,000 × 85c).

At 31 March 20X5 the investment would be remeasured to fair value of $52,500 (60,000 × 87.5c) and would appear in the statement of financial position at this value. The gain on the remeasurement of $1,500 would be recognized in profit or loss.

The investment cannot be categorised as fair value through other comprehensive income as it is considered to be held for trading.

(d) The results of a subsidiary that is held exclusively with a view to resale are not consolidated line by line in the normal way, provided that the subsidiary qualifies as 'held for sale' under IFRS 5 *Non-current Assets Held for Sale and Discontinued Operations*. To be classified as 'held for sale' management must be committed to the sale, the disposal must be highly probable and the sale must be expected to take place within 12 months of the date of acquisition (i.e. before December 20X6). In these circumstances the subsidiary is treated as a discontinued operation and its result is presented as a one-line adjustment to profit for the year from continuing activities.

Tutorial note

Such a subsidiary is consolidated in the statement of financial position, but with all its assets and all its liabilities presented as two line items. They are not consolidated line by line.

(e) As this is a hybrid financial instrument it should be recognized in the statement of financial position as partly debt and partly capital. The measurement of the equity element is the residual value once the present value of the liability element has been computed using the 6% interest rate for such debt without conversion terms.

	$
Present value of principal (10,000 × 50 × 0.747)	373,500
Present value of interest payments (500,000 × 5% × 4.212)	105,300
Debt element	478,800
Equity element (balance)	21,200
	500,000

25   PROMOIL   *Walk in the footsteps of a top tutor*

> **Key answer tips**
>
> This question covers IAS 37 provisions, contingent assets and contingent liabilities. Part (a) requires the definition of liabilities and provisions and how the definitions enhance the faithful representation of financial statements. Part (b) requires both the discussion and accounting for a long-term environmental provision – don't miss the discussion element as you will be restricted on the marks that can be achieved.

(a)   A liability is a present obligation of an entity arising from past events, the settlement of which is expected to result in an outflow of economic benefits (normally cash). Provisions are defined as liabilities of uncertain timing or amount, i.e. they are normally estimates. In essence provisions should be recognised if they meet the definition of a liability. Equally they should not be recognised if they do not meet the definition. A statement of financial position would not give a 'fair representation' if it did not include all of an entity's liabilities (or if it did include, as liabilities, items that were not liabilities). These definitions ensure financial statements are presented fairly by preventing profits from being 'smoothed' by making a provision to reduce profit in years when they are high and releasing those provisions to increase profit in years when they are low. It also means that the statement of financial position cannot avoid the immediate recognition of long-term liabilities (such as environmental provisions) on the basis that those liabilities have not matured.

(b)   (i)   Future costs associated with the acquisition/construction and use of non-current assets, such as the environmental costs in this case, should be treated as a liability as soon as they become unavoidable. For Promoil this would be at the same time as the platform is acquired and brought into use. The provision is for the present value of the expected costs and this same amount is treated as part of the cost of the asset. The provision is 'unwound' by charging a finance cost to the statement of comprehensive income each year and increasing the provision by the finance cost. Annual depreciation of the asset effectively allocates the (discounted) environmental costs over the life of the asset.

Statement of comprehensive income for the year ended 30 September 2008

	$000
Depreciation (see below)	3,690
Finance costs ($6.9 million × 8%)	552

Statement of financial position as at 30 September 2008
Non-current assets

Cost ($30 million + $6.9 million ($15 million × 0.46))	36,900
Depreciation (over 10 years)	(3,690)
	33,210

Non-current liabilities

Environmental provision ($6.9 million × 1.08)	7,452

(ii)   If there was no legal requirement to incur the environmental costs, then Promoil should not provide for them as they do not meet the definition of a liability. Thus the oil platform would be recorded at $30 million with $3 million depreciation and there would be no finance costs.

However, if Promoil has a published policy that it will voluntarily incur environmental cleanup costs of this type (or if this may be implied by its past practice), then this would be evidence of a 'constructive' obligation under IAS 37 and the required treatment of the costs would be the same as in part (i) above.

Examiner's comments

Part (a) asked candidates to define liabilities and provisions and describe when and when they should not be recognised, along with giving two examples of how the definitions have enhanced the faithful representation of financial statements. In general this was well answered with most candidates scoring well on the definitions, but many of the examples given were rather trivial such as accrued audit fees or trade creditors. These types of liability have never been at issue in terms of the reliability of financial statements, whereas when and if environmental provisions should be recognised and the use of 'big bath' and 'profit smoothing' provisions do need robust definitions in order to ensure their correct treatment.

Part (b)(i) asked candidates how the construction of an oil platform and the related environmental 'clean up 'costs should be treated. It required candidates to discount the future clean up costs and provide for them immediately with the same amount being added to the cost of the oil platform.

On the whole most candidates that attempted this question had the right idea, if not a perfect understanding. Common errors were not to include the cleanup costs in non-current assets (some even deducted them), failure to discount the cleanup costs and it was very common not to 'unwind' the liability to arrive at a finance cost.

Weaker candidates thought this was a construction contract question.

In **part (ii)** of this section, the question asked how the answer would differ if there was no requirement to undertake the environmental costs. Most candidates did say that the company would not have to provide for the costs, but stopped at that. An important aspect of this subject area is whether, in the absence of a legal requirement, there may be a constructive obligation. Only a few candidates discussed this aspect.

---

26   DEARING *Walk in the footsteps of a top tutor*

Key answer tips

To achieve the marks in this question you must have a knowledge of the difference between capital and revenue expenditure. Once the cost of the asset has been determined you are required to apply your knowledge of IAS 16 property, plant and equipment. The question complications include calculating depreciation and the treatment of subsequent expenditure.

Year ended/as at:	30 September 2006 $	30 September 2007 $	30 September 2008 $
Statement of comprehensive income			
Depreciation (see workings)	180,000	270,000	119,000
Maintenance (60,000/3 years)	20,000	20,000	20,000
Discount received (840,000 × 5%)	(42,000)		
Staff training	40,000		
	198,000	290,000	139,000

Statement of financial position (see below)			
Property, plant and equipment			
Cost	920,000	920,000	670,000
Accumulated depreciation	(180,000)	(450,000)	(119,000)
Carrying amount	740,000	470,000	551,000

Workings

	$
Manufacturer's base price	1,050,000
Less trade discount (20%)	(210,000)
Base cost	840,000
Freight charges	30,000
Electrical installation cost	28,000
Pre-production testing	22,000
Initial capitalised cost	920,000

> **Tutorial note**
>
> *This question requires depreciation to be calculated on a machine hours basis rather than the standard straight-line or reducing balance basis. Make sure you read the information in the question carefully.*

The depreciable amount is $900,000 (920,000 – 20,000 residual value) and, based on an estimated machine life of 6,000 hours, this gives depreciation of $150 per machine hour. Therefore depreciation for the year ended 30 September 2006 is $180,000 ($150 × 1,200 hours) and for the year ended 30 September 2007 is $270,000 ($150 × 1,800 hours).

Note: Early settlement discount, staff training in use of machine and maintenance are all revenue items and cannot be part of capitalised costs.

Carrying amount at 1 October 2007	470,000
Subsequent expenditure	200,000
	———
Revised 'cost'	670,000
	———

The revised depreciable amount is $630,000 (670,000 − 40,000 residual value) and with a revised remaining life of 4,500 hours, this gives a depreciation charge of $140 per machine hour. Therefore depreciation for the year ended 30 September 2008 is $119,000 ($140 × 850 hours).

Examiner's comments

This question was rather better answered than the equivalent question of recent diets, although a significant number did not attempt it. This was possibly a timing issue, it being the last question.

The question gave details of the purchase of a machine with related expenditures and its estimated life expressed in machine hours. Candidates had to identify which related expenses should be capitalised and which should be expensed. Most candidates did reasonably well on this question, but common errors were;

– treating an early settlement discount as a reduction of cost rather than discounts received

– failing to deduct the residual value before calculating the machine hour depreciation

– even when items where correctly excluded from the cost of the asset, candidates often forgot to include them in the statement of comprehensive income thus missing out on some easy marks

During year three there was additional expenditure on the machine and revisions to its estimated residual value and life. Most candidates that got this far correctly identified the expenditure as an improvement (and capitalised it) and also correctly accounted for the revisions.

---

27 WAXWORK

(a) Events after the reporting period are defined by IAS 10 Events after the Reporting Period as those events, both favourable and unfavourable, that occur between the end of the reporting period and the date that the financial statements are authorised for issue (normally by the Board of directors).

An adjusting event is one that provides further evidence of conditions that existed at the end of the reporting period, including an event that indicates that the going concern assumption in relation to the whole or part of the entity is not appropriate. Normally trading results occurring after the end of the reporting period are a matter for the next reporting period, however, if there is an event which would normally be treated as non-adjusting that causes a dramatic downturn in trading (and profitability) such that it is likely that the entity will no longer be a going concern, this should be treated as an adjusting event.

A non-adjusting event is an event after the end of the reporting period that is indicative of a condition that arose after the end of the reporting period and, subject to the exception noted above, the financial statements would not be adjusted to reflect such events.

The outcome (and values) of many items in the financial statements have a degree of uncertainty at the end of the reporting period. IAS 10 effectively says that where events occurring after the end of the reporting period help to determine what those values were at the end of the reporting period, they should be taken in account (i.e. adjusted for) in preparing the financial statements.

If non-adjusting events, whilst not affecting the financial statements of the current year, are of such importance (i.e. material) that without disclosure of their nature and estimated financial effect, users' ability to make proper evaluations and decisions about the future of the entity would be affected, then they should be disclosed in the notes to the financial statements.

(b) (i) This is normally classified as a non-adjusting event as there was no reason to doubt that the value of warehouse and the inventory it contained was worth less than its carrying amount at 31 March 2009 (the last day of the reporting period). The total loss suffered as a result of the fire is $16 million. The company expects that $9 million of this loss will be recovered from an insurance policy. Recoveries from third parties should be assessed separately from the related loss. As this event has caused serious disruption to trading, IAS 10 would require the details of this non-adjusting event to be disclosed as a note to the financial statements for the year ended 31 March 2009 as a total loss of $16 million and the effect of the insurance recovery to be disclosed separately.

The severe disruption in Waxwork's trading operations since the fire, together with the expectation of large trading losses for some time to come, may call in to question the going concern status of the company. If it is judged that Waxwork is no longer a going concern, then the fire and its consequences become an adjusting event requiring the financial statements for the year ended 31 March 2009 to be redrafted on the basis that the company is no longer a going concern (i.e. they would be prepared on a liquidation basis).

(ii) 70% of the inventory amounts to $322,000 (460,000 × 70%) and this was sold for a net amount of $238,000 (280,000 × 85%). Thus a large proportion of a class of inventory was sold at a loss after the reporting period. This would appear to give evidence of conditions that existed at 31 March 2009 i.e. that the net realisable value of that class of inventory was below its cost. Inventory is required to be valued at the lower of cost and net realisable value, thus this is an adjusting event. If it is assumed that the remaining inventory will be sold at similar prices and terms as that already sold, the net realisable value of the whole of the class of inventory would be calculated as:

$280,000/70% = $400,000, less commission of 15% = $340,000.

Thus the carrying amount of the inventory of $460,000 should be written down by $120,000 to its net realisable value of $340,000.

In the unlikely event that the fall in the value of the inventory could be attributed to a specific event that occurred after the date of the statement of financial position then this would be a non-adjusting event.

(iii) The date of the government announcement of the tax change is beyond the period of consideration in IAS 10. Thus this would be neither an adjusting nor a non-adjusting event. The increase in the deferred tax liability will be provided for in the year to 31 March 2010. Had the announcement been before 6 May 2009, it would have been treated as a non-adjusting event requiring disclosure of the nature of the event and an estimate of its financial effect in the notes to the financial statements.

ACCA marking scheme			
			Marks
(a)	Definition		1
	discussion of adjusting events		2
	reference to going concern		1
	discussion of non-adjusting events		1
	Maximum		5
(b)	(i) to (iii) 1 mark per valid point as indicated	Maximum	10
Total			15

Examiner's comments

I was particularly disappointed with candidates' performance on this question. Part (a) was straightforward for anyone who had read IAS 10 Events after the Reporting Period (or variant equivalents) and the three illustrative examples are well documented in the Standard and text books. In part (a) many candidates attempted to distinguish between adjusting and non-adjusting events through the use of examples rather than by description. Examples were not asked for in Part (a) and therefore did not earn marks.

In **part (a)** there was a lot of confusion over the period covered by the Standard, many candidates thought there is a set time (e.g. 3 or 6 months) or that the period extends to the AGM. To state that an adjusting event requires adjustment – and a non-adjusting event doesn't – did not earn any marks as it says nothing and certainly does not relate to the issues raised by IAS 10. Many candidates also thought that the determining factor regarding whether to adjust or not lies with whether the item is material or not. Several candidates suggested that examples (ii) and (iii) were not material, despite the note to the question providing clear guidance on this point. Weaker candidates confused the topic with prior period adjustments and the use of provisions and contingent items.

Unsurprisingly, if candidates were not able to correctly answer part (a), they did not gain many marks in the examples in part (b), however many candidates who did know the definitions in (a) still could not apply the circumstances to the part (b) scenarios. There were a lot of comments in (b) that contradicted definitions given in part (a).

(b)(i) This example dealt with the consequences a fire after the reporting period. The common errors were to say this was an adjusting event (it was non-adjusting), most candidates netted off potential insurance proceeds from the losses and did not appreciate that the losses and the related insurance claim required different considerations. Hardly anyone realised that the subsequent disruption of trading may have brought into question the going concern of the company (which would then make it an adjusting event). Even those candidates who correctly stated this was a non-adjusting event proceeded, often at great length, to itemise the journal entries needed as if it was an adjusting event (without any mention of the going concern aspects). **(ii)** This was an example of sale of inventory at a loss after the reporting period. Most candidates focused on the sale itself and said it should be dealt with in the following year therefore no adjustment was required. Some correctly appreciated that the relevant issue was that the inventory's value should be adjusted because its net realisable value was below cost. However two further errors were common; either they did not extend the lower of NRV or cost principle to the whole of the inventory (instead just the 70% that had been sold) or they wanted to put the sale through the current year's accounts rather than just write the inventory down. Weaker candidates stated the transaction was a non-adjusting event, as it took place after the reporting date, but, in contradiction, then proceeded to explain at great length the adjustments that the sale and commission would create. **(iii)** This concerned a change in taxation legislation after the financial statements had been authorised. The main point of this example was the timing of the event, specifically after the financial statements had been authorised by the board and was thus neither an adjusting nor non-adjusting event (it was outside the scope of the Standard). Most candidates did not appreciate the timing of the event and even those that did still wanted to adjust for it and proceeded to explain the nature and purpose of deferred tax.

I would also point out that there were many candidates that were on the right lines with this question, but simply did not discuss all the elements of the scenarios which inevitably limited the marks gained.

28 FLIGHTLINE

Flightline – Statement of comprehensive income for the year ended 31 March 2009

	$000
Depreciation (w (i))	13,800
Loss on write off of engine (w (iii))	6,000
Repairs – engine	3,000
– Exterior painting	2,000

Statement of financial position as at 31 March 2009

Non-current asset – Aircraft

	Cost	Accumulated depreciation	Carrying amount
	$000	$000	$000
Exterior (w (i))	120,000	84,000	36,000
Cabin fittings (w (ii))	29,500	21,500	8,000
Engines (w (iii))	19,800	3,700	16,100
	169,300	109,200	60,100

Workings (figures in brackets in $000)

(i)   The exterior of the aircraft is depreciated at $6 million per annum (120,000/ 20 years). The cabin is depreciated at $5 million per annum (25,000/5 years). The engines would be depreciated by $500 ($18 million/36,000 hours) i.e. $250 each, per flying hour.

The carrying amount of the aircraft at 1 April 2008 is:

	Cost	Accumulated depreciation	Carrying amount
	$000	$000	$000
Exterior (13 years old)	120,000	78,000	42,000
Cabin (3 years old)	25,000	15,000	10,000
Engines (used 10,800 hours)	18,000	5,400	12600
	163,000	98,400	64,600

Depreciation for year to 31 March 2009:		$000
Exterior (no change)		6,000
Cabin fittings – six months to 30 September 2008 (5,000 × 6/12)		2,500
– six months to 31 March 2009 (w (ii))		4,000
Engines – six months to 30 September 2008 (500 × 1,200 hours)		600
– six months to 31 March 2009 ((400 + 300) w (iii))		700
		13,800

(ii)   Cabin fittings – at 1 October 2008 the carrying amount of the cabin fittings is $7.5 million (10,000 – 2,500). The cost of improving the cabin facilities of $4.5 million should be capitalised as it led to enhanced future economic benefits in the form of substantially higher fares. The cabin fittings would then have a carrying amount of $12 million (7,500 + 4,500) and an unchanged remaining life of 18 months. Thus depreciation for the six months to 31 March 2009 is $4 million (12,000 × 6/18).

(iii)   Engines – before the accident the engines (in combination) were being depreciated at a rate of $500 per flying hour. At the date of the accident each engine had a carrying amount of $6 million ((12,600 – 600)/2). This represents the loss on disposal of the written off engine. The repaired engine's remaining life was reduced to 15,000 hours. Thus future depreciation on the repaired engine will be $400 per flying hour, resulting in a depreciation charge of $400,000 for the six months to 31 March 2009. The new engine with a cost of $10.8 million and a life of 36,000 hours will be depreciated by $300 per flying hour, resulting in a depreciation charge of $300,000 for the six months to 31 March 2009. Summarising both engines:

	Cost	Accumulated depreciation	Carrying amount
	$000	$000	$000
Old engine	9,000	3,400	5,600
New engine	10,800	300	10,500
	19,800	3,700	16,100

Note: Marks are awarded for clear calculations rather than for detailed explanations. Full explanations are given for tutorial purposes

ACCA marking scheme	
	Marks
Statement of comprehensive income	
depreciation – exterior	1
– cabin fittings	2
– engines	2
loss on write off of engine repairs	1
Repairs	1
Statement of financial position	
carrying amount at 31 March 2009	3
Total	10

Examiner's comments

This question required candidates to depreciate the separate components of a 'complex' asset (an aircraft) dealing with different methods of depreciation and distinguishing between capital and revenue expenditures.

A significant number of candidates did not start this question and many more that did appeared to run out of time. There were no general issues here with candidates not understanding what they were meant to do or not reading the requirements properly, however many answers lacked a methodical approach meaning they got hopelessly lost in the detail. Generally the exterior structure of the aircraft was dealt with correctly although many capitalised the repainting costs (which is revenue expenditure). For the cabin fittings, the upgrade was often correctly capitalised but then the depreciation was calculated on (total) cost, not the new carrying amount and also over the wrong period. The engines caused the most problems. Candidates often tried to perform the calculations of them together, instead of separating them, and then became confused in what they were doing.

Conclusion

As reported in the introduction, the overall performance of candidates was rather disappointing with too many candidates pinning their hopes on passing by just learning the main topics or relying on numerical skills alone. There was evidence of poor examination technique, including poor planning, time management and question spotting. Markers reported that the scripts of poorly prepared candidates did not seem to have mastered the understanding and techniques examinable at F3. Basic depreciation, accruals and an inability to correctly classify items in the financial statements (e.g. receivables included in the statement of comprehensive income) were notable weaknesses of some of these candidates.

In fairness, many of the above comments on the individual questions have concentrated candidates' weak areas. This has been done for reasons of directing future study and highlighting poor techniques such that candidates can improve future performance. This does give a pessimistic view of performance, but I would like draw attention to a good number of excellent papers where it was apparent that candidates had done a great deal of studying and were rewarded appropriately.

29 DARBY

(a) There are four elements to the assistant's definition of a non-current asset and he is substantially incorrect in respect of all of them.

The term non-current assets will normally include intangible assets and certain investments; the use of the term 'physical asset' would be specific to tangible assets only.

Whilst it is usually the case that non-current assets are of relatively high value this is not a defining aspect. A waste paper bin may exhibit the characteristics of a non-current asset, but on the grounds of materiality it is unlikely to be treated as such. Furthermore the past cost of an asset may be irrelevant; no matter how much an asset has cost, it is the expectation of future economic benefits flowing from a resource (normally in the form of future cash inflows) that defines an asset according to the IASB's *Conceptual Framework for Financial Reporting*.

The concept of ownership is no longer a critical aspect of the definition of an asset. It is probably the case that most noncurrent assets in an entity's statement of financial position are owned by the entity; however, it is the ability to 'control' assets (including preventing others from having access to them) that is now a defining feature. For example: this is an important characteristic in treating a finance lease as an asset of the lessee rather than the lessor.

It is also true that most non-current assets will be used by an entity for more than one year and a part of the definition of property, plant and equipment in IAS 16 *Property, plant and equipment* refers to an expectation of use in more than one period, but this is not necessarily always the case. It may be that a non-current asset is acquired which proves unsuitable for the entity's intended use or is damaged in an accident. In these circumstances assets may not have been used for longer than a year, but nevertheless they were reported as non-currents during the time they were in use. A non-current asset may be within a year of the end of its useful life but (unless a sale agreement has been reached under IFRS 5 *Non-current assets held for sale and discontinued operations*) would still be reported as a non-current asset if it was still giving economic benefits. Another defining aspect of non-current assets is their intended use i.e. held for continuing use in the production, supply of goods or services, for rental to others or for administrative purposes.

(b) (i) The expenditure on the training courses may exhibit the characteristics of an asset in that they have and will continue to bring future economic benefits by way of increased efficiency and cost savings to Darby. However, the expenditure cannot be recognised as an asset on the statement of financial position and must be charged as an expense as the cost is incurred. The main reason for this lies with the issue of 'control'; it is Darby's employees that have the 'skills' provided by the courses, but the employees can leave the company and take their skills with them or, through accident or injury, may be deprived of those skills. Also the capitalisation of staff training costs is specifically prohibited under International Financial Reporting Standards (specifically IAS 38 *Intangible assets*).

(ii)   The question specifically states that the costs incurred to date on the development of the new processor chip are research costs. IAS 38 states that research costs must be expensed. This is mainly because research is the relatively early stage of a new project and any future benefits are so far in the future that they cannot be considered to meet the definition of an asset (probable future economic benefits), despite the good record of success in the past with similar projects.

Although the work on the automatic vehicle braking system is still at the research stage, this is different in nature from the previous example as the work has been commissioned by a customer, As such, from the perspective of Darby, it is work in progress (a current asset) and should not be written off as an expense. A note of caution should be added here in that the question says that the success of the project is uncertain which presumably means it may not be completed. This does not mean that Darby will not receive payment for the work it has carried out, but it should be checked to the contract to ensure that the amount it has spent to date ($2.4 million) will be recoverable. In the event that say, for example, the contract stated that only $2 million would be allowed for research costs, this would place a limit on how much Darby could treat as work in progress. If this were the case then, for this example, Darby would have to expense $400,000 and treat only $2 million as work in progress.

(iii)   The question suggests the correct treatment for this kind of contract is to treat the costs of the installation as a non-current asset and (presumably) depreciate it over its expected life of (at least) three years from when it becomes available for use. In this case the asset will not come into use until the next financial year/reporting period and no depreciation needs to be provided at 30 September 2009.

The capitalised costs to date of $58,000 should only be written down if there is evidence that the asset has become impaired. Impairment occurs where the recoverable amount of an asset is less than its carrying amount. The assistant appears to believe that the recoverable amount is the future profit, whereas (in this case) it is the future (net) cash inflows. Thus any impairment test at 30 September 2009 should compare the carrying amount of $58,000 with the expected net cash flow from the system of $98,000 ($50,000 per annum for three years less future cash outflows to completion the installation of $52,000 (see note below)). As the future net cash flows are in excess of the carrying amount, the asset is not impaired and it should not be written down but shown as a non-current asset (under construction) at cost of $58,000.

Note: As the contract is expected to make a profit of $40,000 on income of $150,000, the total costs must be $110,000, with costs to date at $58,000 this leaves completion costs of $52,000.

ACCA marking scheme			
			Marks
(a)	1 mark per valid point		4
			___
		Maximum	4.0
			___
(b)	(i) to (iii)– 1 mark per valid point as indicated		11.0
			___
		Maximum	11.0
			___
Total			15
			___

Examiner's comments

Part (a) asked candidates to criticise the definition included in the question of non-current assets that had been given by an assistant. Many candidates did not directly criticise the points in the assistant's definition, instead they gave the definition of non-current assets as per the IASB Framework without comparing it to the given definition. This is a classic example of not answering the question that was asked. Good answers did focus on issues of control (rather than ownership) and reference to intangible assets as well, as 'physical' assets. Some answers 'rambled on' giving examples of every type of non-current assets the candidate could think of (again nothing to do with the question asked).

Part (b) gave three examples of how the assistant had treated items in the financial statements and asked candidates to comment (and advise) on their treatment. **Item (i)** was expenditure on staff training costs that the assistant wanted to treat as an intangible assets. Most candidates realised that such costs could not be treated as an asset and should be expensed, but very few said why.

Item (ii) gave two examples of research expenditure. Again most candidates correctly said that (in most cases) research cannot be treated as an asset. Despite saying this some candidates thought that as the company had a successful history of bringing projects similar to the first example to profitable conclusions, it was acceptable to treat these research costs as an asset. The second example was research commissioned by a customer and as such was in fact work-in-progress and therefore should not have been written off (as suggested by the assistant). Even where candidates did advocate the correct treatment, they rarely explained why.

The last **item (iii)** caused most difficulty. It was about whether expenditure on a partially completed non-current asset (a satellite dish system) was impaired. The assistant thought it was because the expected profit from the asset was less than the amount already spent on it. What most candidates failed to realise was that the asset would only be impaired where the recoverable amount, being the value in use (based on future cash flows, not profit), was less than the carrying amount (ignoring the possibility of selling the asset).

Many candidates thought this was a (long-term) construction contract, presumably because the asset would be used to earn revenue for at least three years. In fact the period of construction of the asset was only two months and the contract was for the rental (not the construction) of the asset (the question specifically said that it was not a finance lease). This showed a fundamental lack of understanding of what construction contracts are.

30 BARSTEAD 🔑 *Walk in the footsteps of a top tutor*

> 🔑
>
> **Key answer tips**
>
> This question not only required the calculation of EPS but also how the three different measures of profit can give the users of the financial statements differing impressions. To score well in this question you need to have a firm grasp of accounting for basic and diluted EPS. The highlighted words are key phrases that markers are looking for.

(a)   Whilst profit after tax (and its growth) is a useful measure, it may not give a fair representation of the true underlying earnings performance. In this example, users could interpret the large annual increase in profit after tax of 80% as being indicative of an underlying improvement in profitability (rather than what it really is: an increase in absolute profit). It is possible, even probable, that (some of) the profit growth has been achieved through the acquisition of other companies (acquisitive growth). Where companies are acquired from the proceeds of a new issue of shares, or where they have been acquired through share exchanges, this will result in a greater number of equity shares of the acquiring company being in issue. This is what appears to have happened in the case of Barstead as the improvement indicated by its earnings per share (EPS) is only 5% per annum. This explains why the EPS (and the trend of EPS) is considered a more reliable indicator of performance because the additional profits which could be expected from the greater resources (proceeds from the shares issued) is matched with the increase in the number of shares. Simply looking at the growth in a company's profit after tax does not take into account any increases in the resources used to earn them. Any increase in growth financed by borrowings (debt) would not have the same impact on profit (as being financed by equity shares) because the finance costs of the debt would act to reduce profit.

The calculation of a diluted EPS takes into account any potential equity shares in issue. Potential ordinary shares arise from financial instruments (e.g. convertible loan notes and options) that may entitle their holders to equity shares in the future. The diluted EPS is useful as it alerts existing shareholders to the fact that future EPS may be reduced as a result of share capital changes; in a sense it is a warning sign. In this case the lower increase in the diluted EPS is evidence that the (higher) increase in the basic EPS has, in part, been achieved through the increased use of diluting financial instruments. The finance cost of these instruments is less than the earnings their proceeds have generated leading to an increase in current profits (and basic EPS); however, in the future they will cause more shares to be issued. This causes a dilution where the finance cost per potential new share is less than the basic EPS.

(b) (Basic) EPS for the year ended 30 September 2009
($15 million/43.25 million × 100)   34.7   cents

Comparative (basic) EPS (35 × 3.60/3.80)   33.2   cents

Effect of rights issue (at below market price)

100 shares at $3.80   380

25 shares at $2.80   70
                                                                          ____   ____

125 shares at $3.60 (calculated theoretical ex-rights value)   450
                                                                          ____   ____

Weighted average number of shares

36 million × 3/12 × $3.80/$3.60   9.50   million

45 million × 9/12   33.75   million
                                                                                      _____

                                                                          43.25   million
                                                                                      _____

Diluted EPS for the year ended 30 September 2009
($15.6 million/45.75 million × 100)   34.1   cents

Adjusted earnings

15 million + (10 million × 8% × 75%) $15.6   million

Adjusted number of shares

43.25 million + (10 million × 25/100)   45.75   million

ACCA marking scheme		
		Marks
(a)	1 mark per valid point	4
		___
	Maximum	4.0
		___
(b)	Basic EPS for 2009	3.0
	Restated EPS for 2008	1.0
	Diluted EPS for 2009	2.0
		___
	Maximum	6.0
		___
Total		10
		___

Examiner's comments

Part (a) of this question asked candidates to explain why three different measures of performance for the same company (profit after tax, basic EPS and diluted EPS) gave different impressions of increased performance. This seemed to baffle most candidates. Where candidates did try to explain this, they gave examples of improvements in profit performance that would apply to the other measures of performance. An increase in profit of 80% (as per the question) would also give an increase of 80% in the EPS if there was no change in the capital structure. Few candidates could relate the given differentials to new shares being issued. A number of candidates did realise that the diluted EPS was something to do with convertible shares or share options.

Part (b) of the question was a calculation of basic and diluted EPS. Encouragingly this was answered much better and redeemed the question for many. There were some poor answers showing basic errors, commonly thinking that the rights issue caused the dilution rather than the existence of the convertible loan stock. Less worrying errors were incorrect weighting of the rights issue and getting the dilution factor the wrong way round (the inverse). Weaker candidates calculated many meaningless figures that were scattered, seemingly randomly, all over the page and expected the marker to make sense of them.

31   APEX   *Walk in the footsteps of a top tutor*

Key answer tips

This question focuses on IAS 23 Borrowing costs, being a specific element of accounting for tangible assets and should be a relatively straightforward question to answer and score well on if borrowing costs have been revised. The highlighted words are key phrases that markers are looking for.

(a)   Where borrowing costs are directly incurred on a 'qualifying asset', they must be capitalised as part of the cost of that asset. A qualifying asset may be a tangible or an intangible asset that takes a substantial period of time to get ready for its intended use or eventual sale. Property construction would be a typical example, but it can also be applied to intangible assets during their development period. Borrowing costs include interest based on its effective rate (which incorporates the amortisation of discounts, premiums and certain expenses) on overdrafts, loans and (some) other financial instruments and finance charges on finance leased assets. They may be based on specifically borrowed funds or on the weighted average cost of a pool of funds. Any income earned from the temporary investment of specifically borrowed funds would normally be deducted from the amount to be capitalised.

Capitalisation should commence when expenditure is being incurred on the asset, which is not necessarily from the date funds are borrowed. Capitalisation should cease when the asset is ready for its intended use, even though the funds may still be incurring borrowing costs. Also capitalisation should be suspended if there is a suspension of active development of the asset.

Any borrowing costs that are not eligible for capitalisation must be expensed. Borrowing costs cannot be capitalised for assets measured at fair value.

(b)   The finance cost of the loan must be calculated using the effective rate of 7.5%, so the total finance cost for the year ended 31 March 2010 is $750,000 ($10 million × 7.5%). As the loan relates to a qualifying asset, the finance cost (or part of it in this case) can be capitalised under IAS 23.

The Standard says that capitalisation commences from when expenditure is being incurred (1 May 2009) and must cease when the asset is ready for its intended use (28 February 2010); in this case a 10-month period. However, interest cannot be capitalised during a period where development activity is suspended; in this case the two months of July and August 2009. Thus only eight months of the year's finance cost can be capitalised = $500,000 ($750,000 × 8/12). The remaining four-months finance costs of $250,000 must be expensed. IAS 23 also says that interest earned from the temporary investment of specific loans should be deducted from the amount of finance costs that can be capitalised. However, in this case, the interest was earned during a period in which the finance costs were NOT being capitalised, thus the interest received of $40,000 would be credited to the statement of comprehensive income and not to the capitalised finance costs.

In summary:

	$
Statement of comprehensive income for the year ended 31 March 2010:	
Finance cost (debit)	(250,000)
Investment income (credit)	40,000
Statement of financial position as at 31 March 2010:	
Property, plant and equipment (finance cost element only)	500,000

UK SYLLABUS FOCUS ONLY

Under UK GAAP a choice is allowed of whether to capitalise borrowing costs or to recognise them as an expense in profit or loss when recognition criteria met. This choice is not allowed internationally. Under IFRS if the recognition criteria from IAS 23 are met then borrowing costs MUST be capitalised.

Under UK GAAP the amount to be capitalised is limited to the finance costs on the expenditure incurred whereas internationally the amount capitalised is limited to the borrowing costs on the total related funds less the investment income from any temporary investment of those funds.

ACCA marking scheme		
		Marks
(a)	1 mark per valid point	5
(b)	use of effective rate of 7.5%	1
	capitalise for eight months	2
	charge to statement of comprehensive income	1
	interest received to statement of comprehensive income	1
		–––
	Maximum	5
		–––
Total		10
		–––

32   WELLMAY

Statement of comprehensive income year ended 31 March 2007

	$000	$000
Revenue (4,200 – 500 (w (i)))		3,700
Cost of sales (w (ii))		(2,417)
Gross profit		1,283
Operating expenses (470 + 8 depreciation)		(478)
Investment property – rental income	20	
– fair value loss (400 – 375)	(25)	(5)
Finance costs (w (iii))		(113)
Profit before tax		687
Income tax (360 + 30 (w (v)))		(390)
Profit for the period		297

Statement of changes in equity – year ended 31 March 2007

	Equity shares	Equity option	Revaluation reserve	Retained earnings	Total
	$000	$000	$000	$000	$000
Balances at 1 April 2006	1,200		350	2,615	4,165
Equity conversion option (w (iv))		40			40
Bonus issue (1 for 4)	300			(300)	
Revaluation of factory (w (vi))			190		190
Profit for the period				297	297
Dividends				(400)	(400)
Balances at 31 March 2007	1,500	40	540	2,212	4,292

Statement of financial position as at 31 March 2007

	$000	$000
Non-current assets		
Property, plant and equipment (w (vi))		4,390
Investment property (w (vi))		375
		4,765
Current assets (1,400 + 200 inventory (w (i)))		1,600
Total assets		6,365
Equity and liabilities (see statement of changes in equity above)		
Equity shares of 50 cents each		1,500
Equity option (w (iv))		40
		1,540
Reserves:		
Revaluation reserve	540	
Retained earnings	2,212	2,752
		4,292
Non-current liabilities		
Deferred tax (w (v))	210	
8% Convertible loan note ((560 + 8) (w (iv)))	568	778
Current liabilities (820 – 75 (w (ii)))	745	
Loan from Westwood (500 + 50 accrued interest (w (i)))	550	1,295
Total equity and liabilities		6,365

Workings (Note: All figures in $000)

(i)   The 'sale' to Westwood is, in substance, a secured loan. The repurchase price is the cost of sale plus compound interest at 10% for two years. The correct accounting treatment is to reverse the sale with the goods going back into inventory and the 'proceeds' treated as a loan with accrued interest of 10% ($50,000) for the current year.

(ii)   **Cost of sales**

From draft financial statements	c	2,700
Sale of goods added back to inventory (see above)		(200)
Reversal of contingency provision (see below)		(75)
Depreciation transferred to operating costs (40 × 20%)		(8)
		2,417

General or non-specific provisions do not meet the definition of a liability in IAS 37 *Provisions, contingent liabilities and contingent assets* and must therefore be reversed.

(iii)   **Finance costs**

From draft financial statements	55
Additional accrued interest on convertible loan (w (iv))	8
Finance cost on in-substance loan (500 × 10%)	50
	113

(iv)   **Convertible loan**

This is a compound financial instrument that contains an element of debt and an element of equity (the option to convert). IAS 32 *Financial instruments: disclosure and presentation* requires that the substance of such instruments should be applied to the reporting of them. The value of the debt element is calculated by discounting the future cash flows (at 10%). The residue of the issue proceeds is recorded as the value of the equity option.

	Cash flows	Factor at 10%	Present value $000
Year 1 interest	48	0.91	43.6
Year 2 interest	48	0.83	39.8
Year 3 interest	48	0.75	36.0
Year 4 interest, redemption premium and capital	648	0.68	440.6
Total value of debt component			560.0
Proceeds of the issue			600.0
Equity component (residual amount)			40.0

For the year ended 31 March 2007, the interest cost for the convertible loan in the statement of comprehensive income should be increased from $48,000 to $56,000 (10% × 560) by accruing $8,000, which should be added to the carrying value of the debt.

(v)   **Taxation**

The required deferred tax balance is $210,000 (600 × 35%), the current balance is $180,000, and thus a further transfer of $30,000 (via the statement of comprehensive income) is required.

(vi)   **Properties**

The fair value model in IAS 40 Investment property requires the loss of $25,000 on the fair value of investment properties to be reported in the statement of comprehensive income. This differs from revaluations of other properties. IAS 16 Property, plant and equipment requires surpluses and deficits to be recorded as movements in equity (a revaluation reserve). After depreciation of $40,000 for the year ended 31 March 2007, the factory (used by Wellmay) would have a carrying amount of $1,160,000 (1,200 − 40). The valuation of $1,350,000 at 31 March 2007 would give a further revaluation surplus of $190,000 (1,350 − 1,160) and a carrying amount of property, plant and equipment of $4,390,000 (4,200 + 190) at that date.

33   LLAMA

Key answer tips

This published accounts question has a heavy IAS 16 focus so there are many easy marks available. For parts (a) and (b) you need to ensure that you set your answer up in advance outlining the proformas. Once these have been set up, keep moving through the question building up the answer as you go. Part (c) required the calculation of EPS following a rights issue of shares. Ensure that you use the profit figure calculated in part (a) to do this.

(a)   **Llama – Statement of comprehensive income – Year ended 30 September 2007**

	$000	$000
Revenue		180,400
Cost of sales (w (i))		(81,700)
Gross profit		98,700
Distribution costs (11,000 + 1,000 depreciation)	(12,000)	
Administrative expenses (12,500 + 1,000 depreciation)	(13,500)	(25,500)
Investment income	2,200	
Gain on fair value of investments (27,100 − 26,500)	600	2,800
Finance costs (w (ii))		(2,400)
Profit before tax		73,600
Income tax expense		
(18,700 − 400 − (11,200 − 10,000) deferred tax)		(17,100)
Profit for the period		56,500

(b)   **Llama – Statement of financial position as at 30 September 2007**

	$000	$000
Assets		
Non-current assets		
Property, plant and equipment (w (iv))		228,500
Investments at fair value through profit and loss		27,100
		255,600
Current assets		
Inventory	37,900	
Trade receivables	35,100	73,000
Total assets		328,600
Equity and liabilities		
Equity		
Equity shares of 50 cents each ((60,000 + 15,000) w (iii))		75,000
Share premium (w (iii))	9,000	
Revaluation reserve (14,000 – 3,000 (w (iv)))	11,000	
Retained earnings (56,500 + 25,500)	82,000	102,000
		177,000
Non-current liabilities		
2% loan note (80,000 + 1,600 (w (ii)))	81,600	
Deferred tax (40,000 × 25%)	10,000	91,600
Current liabilities		
Trade payables	34,700	
Bank overdraft	6,600	
Current tax payable	18,700	60,000
Total equity and liabilities		328,600

Workings (monetary figures in brackets are in 000)

(i)   Cost of sales:

	$000
Per question	89,200
Plant capitalised (w (iv))	(24,000)
Depreciation (w (iv)) – buildings	3,000
– plant	13,500
	81,700

(ii)   The loan has been in issue for six months. The total finance charge should be based on the effective interest rate of 6%. This gives a charge of $2.4 million (80,000 × 6% × 6/12). As the actual interest paid is $800,000 an accrual (added to the carrying amount of the loan) of $1.6 million is required.

(iii)   The rights issue was 30 million shares (60 million/50 cents is 120 million shares at 1 for 4) at a price of 80 cents this would increase share capital by $15 million (30 million × 50 cents) and share premium by $9 million (30 million × 30 cents).

(iv)   Non-current assets/depreciation: Land and buildings: On 1 October 2006 the value of the buildings was $100 million (130,000 – 30,000 land). The remaining life at this date was 20 years, thus the annual depreciation charge will be $ million (3,000 to cost of sales and 1,000 each to distribution and administration). Prior to the revaluation at 30 September 2007 the carrying amount of the building was $95 million (100,000 – 5,000). With a revalued amount of $92 million, this gives a revaluation deficit of $3 million which should be debited to the revaluation reserve. The carrying amount of land and buildings at 30 September 2007 will be $122 million (92,000 buildings + 30,000 land (unchanged)).

Plant

The existing plant will be depreciated by $12 million ((128,000 – 32,000) × 12½%) and have a carrying amount of $84 million at 30 September 2007.

The plant manufactured for internal use should be capitalised at $24 million (6,000 + 4,000 + 8,000 + 6,000). Depreciation on this will be $1.5 million (24,000 × 12½% × 6/12). This will give a carrying amount of $22.5 million at 30 September 2007. Thus total depreciation for plant is $13.5 million with a carrying amount of $106.5 million (84,000 + 22,500)

	$000
Summarising the carrying amounts:	
Land and buildings	122,000
Plant	106,500
Property, plant and equipment	228,500

(c)   **Earnings per share (eps) for the year ended 30 September 2007**

Theoretical ex rights value			$
Holding (say)	100	at $1	100
Issue (1 for 4)	25	at 80 cents	20
New holding	125	ex rights price is 96 cents	120

Weighted average number of shares		
120,000,000	× 9/12 × 100/96	93,750,000
150,000,000 (120 × 5/4)	× 3/12	37,500,000
		131,250,000

Earnings per share ($56,500,000/131,250,000) 43 cents

UK SYLLABUS FOCUS ONLY

Limited liability companies are required by law to prepare and publish financial statements annually. The form and content may be regulated primarily by national legislation, and in most cases must also comply with Financial Reporting Standards (FRS). In the UK, all companies must comply with the provisions of the Companies Act 2006 (CA 2006).

Every UK registered company is required to prepare financial statements for each financial year which give a true and fair view (i.e. balance sheet and profit and loss account). The annual financial statements must be approved and signed on behalf of the board of directors and a copy filed with the registrar.

Examiner's comments

This question asked candidates to prepare an statement of comprehensive income and statement of financial position from a trial balance after dealing with several notes. A calculation of earnings per share (eps) was also required.

Most candidates did well on this question scoring good marks even if they did not fully understand all the issues or were not able to complete all the parts. The main adjustments contained in the question were generally well understood and correctly accounted for. Again, in order to assist future studies, the common errors were:

– Confusion over the timing of the revaluation of the land and buildings. The question clearly stated that the revaluation was at the end of the year. This meant that the annual deprecation charge for the buildings should be based on the value at the beginning of the year (i.e. the value included in the trial balance) and the revaluation (giving a impairment/deficit in this example) should be based on the carrying amount of the asset after the year's depreciation had been deducted.

  It was common to see candidates performing the revaluation at the beginning of the year. Another surprisingly common error was calculating depreciation of the plant based on cost rather than the reducing balance. Most candidates did correctly identify the capitalisation of the internally manufactured plant, although many did not realise that this occurred half way through the year necessitating time-apportioned depreciation.

– Another common error was to reduce cost of sales by the closing inventory; by definition cost of sales has already been adjusted for closing inventory.

– A number of candidates did not appreciate that the loan interest paid was for only six months and that the year's finance costs should be based on the effective interest rate of 6% rather than the nominal rate of 2%. Those that did correctly account for the accrued finance costs in the statement of comprehensive income often forgot to add it to the carrying amount of the loan in the statement of financial position.

– The tax calculation was often confused. The opening credit balance of $400,000 was often treated as charge (debit) and the adjustment for deferred tax was often taken as $40 million rather than 25% of $40 million.

- Similar to question 1, many candidates could not correctly account for the share capital and share premium of a rights issue, often showing a combined figure or showing it as a suspense account in the statement of financial position.

- The revaluation reserve was often left at its opening balance without taking account of the revaluation of the land and buildings.

- A very common and basic error was to include the bank overdraft in current assets.

- Answers to the calculation of the eps were very mixed. A significant number of candidates did not attempt it and those that did often struggled with effect of the rights issue on the ex-rights price and the weighting exercise.

	ACCA marking scheme	Marks
(a)	Statement of comprehensive income	
	Revenue	½
	Cost of sales	3½
	Distribution costs and administrative expenses	1
	Investment income and gain on investment	1½
	Finance costs	1
	Tax	1½
		——
		9
		——
(b)	Statement of financial position	
	Property, plant and equipment	3
	Investments	1
	Current assets	1
	Equity shares	1
	Share premium	1
	Revaluation reserve	1
	Retained earnings	1
	2% loan notes	1½
	Deferred tax	1
	Trade payables and overdraft	1
	Income tax provision	½
		——
		13
		——
(c)	Earnings per share	
	Calculation of theoretical ex rights value	1
	Weighted average number of shares	1
	Earnings and calculation of eps	1
		——
		3
		——
Total		25
		——

34 DEXON

> **Key answer tips**
>
> Part (a) required a recalculation of profit – you were expected to consider how the further information would therefore affect profit. Remember a credit entry to the statement of comprehensive income will increase profit whereas a debit entry will reduce profit. Part (b) required you to prepare a SOCIE, many easy marks could be gained here – you need to recognise that the share issue had already been recorded so you are required to work backwards to find the opening balances. Part (c) required you to restate the statement of financial position. An added complication in this question exists with deferred tax. You are required to calculate the deferred tax relating to the revaluation reserve as well the statement of comprehensive income movement.

(a)

		$000	$000
Retained profit for period per question			96,700
Dividends paid (w (i))			15,500
Draft profit for year ended 31 March 2008			112,200
Discovery of fraud (w (ii))			(2,500)
Goods on sale or return (w (iii))			(600)
Depreciation (w (iv))	– buildings (165,000/15 years)	11,000	
	– plant (180,500 × 20%)	36,100	(47,100)
Increase in investments ((12,500 × 1,296/1,200) – 12,500)			1,000
Provision for income tax			(11,400)
Increase in deferred tax (w (v))			(800)
Recalculated profit for year ended 31 March 2008			50,800

(b) **Dexon – Statement of Changes in Equity – Year ended 31 March 2008**

	Ordinary shares $000	Share premium $000	Revaluation reserve $000	Retained earnings $000	Total $000
At 1 April 2007	200,000	30,000	18,000	12,300	260,300
Prior period adjustment (w (ii))				(1,500)	(1,500)
Restated earnings at 1 April 2007				10,800	
Rights issue (see below)	50,000	10,000			60,000
Total comprehensive income (from (a) and (w (iv)))			4,800	50,800	55,600
Dividends paid (w (i))				(15,500)	(15,500)
At 31 March 2008	250,000	40,000	22,800	46,100	358,900

Rights issue: 250 million shares in issue after a rights issue of one for four would mean that 50 million shares were issued (250,000 × 1/5). As the issue price was $1.20, this would create $50 million of share capital and $10 million of share premium.

(c)   **Dexon – Statement of financial position as at 31 March 2008:**

	$000	$000
Non-current assets		
Property (w (iv))		180,000
Plant (180,500 – 36,100 depreciation see (a))		144,400
Investments at fair value through profit and loss (12,500 + 1,000 see (a))		13,500
		337,900
Current assets		
Inventory (84,000 + 2,000 (w (iii)))	86,000	
Trade receivables (52,200 – 4,000 – 2,600 (w (ii) and (iii)))	45,600	
Bank	3,800	135,400
Total assets		473,300
Equity and liabilities		
Equity (from (b))		
Ordinary shares of $1 each		250,000
Share premium	40,000	
Revaluation reserve	22,800	
Retained earnings	46,100	108,900
		358,900
Non-current liabilities		
Deferred tax (19,200 + 2,000 (w (v)))		21,200
Current liabilities (81,800 + 11,400 income tax)		93,200
Total equity and liabilities		473,300

Workings (figures in brackets in $000)

(i)   **Dividends paid**

The dividend in May 2007 would be $8 million (200 million shares at 4 cents) and in November 2007 would be $7.5 million (250 million shares × 3 cents). Total dividends would therefore have been $15.5 million.

(ii)   The discovery of the fraud means that $4 million should be written off trade receivables. $1.5 million debited to retained earnings as a prior period adjustment (in the statement of changes in equity) and $2.5 written off in the statement of comprehensive income for the year ended 31 March 2008.

(iii) **Goods on sale or return**

The sales over which customers still have the right of return should not be included in Dexon's recognised revenue. The reversing effect is to reduce the relevant trade receivables by $2.6 million, increase inventory by $2 million (the cost of the goods (2,600 × 100/130)) and reduce the profit for the year by $600,000.

(iv) **Property**

The carrying amount of the property (after the year's depreciation) is $174 million (185,000 − 11,000). A valuation of $180 million would create a revaluation surplus of $6 million of which $1.2 million (6,000 × 20%) would be transferred to deferred tax.

(v) **Deferred tax**

An increase in the taxable temporary differences of $10 million would create a transfer (credit) to deferred tax of $2 million (10,000 × 20%). Of this $1.2 million relates to the revaluation of the property and is debited to the revaluation reserve. The balance, $800,000, is charged to the statement of comprehensive income.

Examiner's comments

This question asked candidates to recalculate the annual profit, prepare a statement of changes in equity (SOCIE) and redraft a given statement of financial position after accounting for a series of adjustments. The adjustments required were for: reversing a sale or return transaction, depreciation (after a revaluation), an increase in the value of investments, correcting for a discovered fraud, tax and deferred tax and dealing with the effects of a share issue and dividend payments.

For those that knew how to tackle this type of question, the recalculation/restatement of the annual profit was done quite well with many candidates gaining 5 or 6 out of the 8 marks available. The most common errors were:

– failing to add back the dividends to the retained earnings for the year to give a starting point for the profit for the year

– adjusting for the sales revenue rather than the profit made on goods subject to an outstanding sale and return agreement (some adjusted for both the sales revenue and the cost of sales which was marked as correct)

– taking the revaluation of the land and buildings as if it were at the beginning of the year (the question clearly stated it was at the end of the year)

– deducting the whole of the cost of a fraud from the current year's profit (part of it related to the previous year and should have been treated as a prior period adjustment in the SOCIE)

– taking the whole of the increase in deferred tax to the statement of comprehensive income (part of it related to the property revaluation and should also have been included in the SOCIE)

Many of the errors made in the recalculation of the profit for the year were carried on to the SOCIE or/and the statement of financial position. Additionally in the SOCIE many candidates did not realise that the share issue had already been accounted for (the question made this quite clear) thus they treated the figures in the statement of financial position as if they were at the beginning of the year rather than at the end of the year and consequently calculated the wrong share capital and share premium movements. Very few included the deferred tax effect of the revaluation and an incorrect calculation of the dividends was also common (or omitted completely).

The statement of financial position was generally well done and most of the errors that were made generally related to the following through of earlier (previously mentioned) errors. For example it was common not to eliminate the sale and return receivable and not to include the related inventory in current assets. Strangely a few candidates spent time trying to calculate an ex-rights price for the share issue. This was not asked for.

ACCA marking scheme		Marks
(a)	Adjustments:	
	add back dividends	1
	balance of fraud loss	1
	goods on sale or return	1
	depreciation charges	2
	investment gain	1
	taxation provision	1
	deferred tax	1
	Maximum	8
(b)	Statement of changes in equity	
	balances b/f	1
	restated earnings b/f	1
	rights issue	2
	total comprehensive income	3
	dividends paid	1
	Maximum	8
(c)	Statement of financial position	
	Property	1
	Plant	1
	Investment	1
	Inventory	1
	trade receivables	2
	equity from (b)	1
	deferred tax	1
	current liabilities	1
	Maximum	9
Total		25

35   TOURMALET

Key answer tips

IFRS 5 requires that the post tax results of the discontinued operations are shown as a single amount on the face of the statement of comprehensive income. In this question we have no information about the tax effects of the closure, therefore only the figures given can be shown.

(a)   The sale of the plant has been incorrectly treated on two counts. Firstly even if it were a genuine sale it should not have been included in sales and cost of sales, rather it should have been treated as the disposal of a non-current asset. Only the profit or loss on the disposal would be included in profit or loss (requiring separate disclosure if material).   However even this treatment would be incorrect.   Under   IFRS   the transaction is considered to be a sale and finance leaseback arrangement as Tourmalet continues to use the asset for the rest of its useful economic life and therefore generating benefit from it.   As such the asset should be derecognised and the profit or loss recognised (deferred) over the lease term.   The asset should then be reinstated in accordance with the rules of IAS 17 and the liability under the finance lease recognised.   Subsequent measurement will include depreciation of the asset and the use of the actuarial method for the finance lease itself.

(b)   **Tourmalet – Statement of comprehensive income for the year ending 30 September 20X3**

	$000
Continuing operations	
Revenue (313,000 – 50,000 – 15,200 (discontinued)	247,800
Cost of sales (W1 – 16,000 discontinued**)**	(128,800)
Gross profit	119,000
Distribution expenses	(26,400)
Administrative expenses (W2)	(20,000)
Finance costs (W3)	(7,800)
Loss on investment properties (10,000 – 9,800)	(200)
Investment income	1,200
Profit before tax	65,800
Income tax expense (9,200 – 2,100)	(7,100)
Profit for the period from continuing operations	58,700
Discontinued operations	
Loss for the period from discontinued operations (15,200 – 16,000 – 3,200 – 1,500) (W4)	(5,500)
Profit for the period	53,200

(c) **Tourmalet Statement of changes in equity – Year to 30 September 20X3**

	Ordinary shares	Revaluation reserve	Retained earnings	Total
	$000	$000	$000	$000
At 1 October 20X2	50,000	18,500	61,800	130,300
Profit for period			53,200	53,200
Transfer to realized profit		(500)	500	
Ordinary dividends paid			(2,500)	(2,500)
At 30 September 20X3	50,000	18,000	113,000	181,000

Note: IAS 32 *Financial Instruments: Presentation* says redeemable preference shares have the substance of debt and should be treated as non-current liabilities and not as equity. This also means that preference dividends are treated as a finance cost in the statement of comprehensive income.

Workings

(W1) **Cost of sales:**

	$000
Opening inventory	26,550
Purchases	158,450
Sale and leaseback	(40,000)
Profit on disposal (W5)	(2,000)
Depreciation (W2)	27,800
Closing inventory (28,500 – (4,500 – 2,000) see below)	(26,000)
	144,800

The slow moving inventory should be written down to its estimated realisable value. Despite the optimism of the Directors, it would seem prudent to base the realisable value on the best offer so far received (i.e. $2 million).

(W2) **Non-current assets depreciation**

	$000
Buildings $120/40 years	3,000
Plant – per trial balance ((98,600 – 24,600) × 20%)	14,800
Finance lease plant (W5)	10,000
	27,800

Note: Investment properties do not require depreciating under the fair value model in IAS 40. Instead they are revalued each year with the surplus or deficit being recognized in profit or loss.

For information only:

In the statement of financial position	Cost/ valuation	Accumulated depreciation	Net book value
	$000	$000	$000
Land and buildings	150,000	12,000	138,000
Plant – per trial balance	98,600	39,400	59,200
Finance leased plant (W5)	50,000	10,000	40,000
			237,200

(W3) **Finance costs: statement of comprehensive income**

	$000
Finance lease interest (W5)	6,000
Preference dividends (30,000 × 6% – half accrued)	1,800
	7,800

(W4) The penalty on the early termination of the lease has been accrued for as it would appear to be unlikely that the permission for change of use will be granted. The $1.5m has therefore been included in the loss from discontinuing operations.

(W5) **Step 1:** Correct incorrect treatment of disposal proceeds

Note: Asset already removed from trial balance figures so need to remove the incorrect entries from revenue/cost of sales and calculate the profit on disposal (to be spread over the five year lease term).

	$000	$000
Dr Revenue	50,000	
Cr Cost of sales		40,000
Cr Profit on disposal (1 year)		2,000
Cr Deferred income (4 years)		8,000

Step 2: Recognise asset/lease liability under rules from IAS 17

	$000	$000
Dr Non-current asset	50,000	
Cr Finance lease		50,000
Dr Depreciation expense	10,000	
Cr Accumulated depreciation		10,000
(50,000 / 5 years)		

Amortised cost:

Year	B/f	Int – 12%	o/s	Rental	C/f
	$000	$000	$000	$000	$000
1	50,000	6,000	56,000	(14,000)	42,000
2	42,000	5,040	47,040	(14,000)	33,040

Note: This statement of financial position is provided for information only. It does not form part of the answer or marking scheme.

Tourmalet – Statement of financial position as at 30 September 20X3

	$000	$000
Non-current assets		
Property, plant and equipment (W2)		237,200
Investment properties		9,800
		247,000
Current assets		
Inventory (W1)	26,000	
Trade receivables	31,200	
Bank	3,700	60,900
Total assets		307,900
Equity and liabilities		
Equity:		
Ordinary shares of 20c each		50,000
Retained earnings	113,000	
Revaluation reserve (see (c))	18,000	131,000
		181,000
Non-current liabilities		
6% Redeemable preference shares	30,000	
Finance lease (W5)	33,040	
Deferred income (W5)	6,000	
Current liabilities		69,040
Trade payables	35,300	
Accrued penalty cost (W4)	1,500	
Finance lease (W5)	8,960	
Deferred income (W5)	2,000	
Preference dividend accrual	900	
((30,000 × 6% payable) – 900 paid)		
Taxation	9,200	
		57,860
Total equity and liabilities		307,900

36   HARRINGTON

Key answer tips

In the statement of comprehensive income most of the adjustments are reflected in cost of sales but there are other adjustments for investment income, loan interest and taxation as well. In part (b) take care with the share capital and share premium as the rights issue has already been recorded, therefore you will need to work backwards to find the opening balances.

(a)   **Harrington:**

Restated statement of comprehensive income – Year to 31 March 20X5

	$000
Revenue (13,700 – 300 plant sale proceeds)	13,400
Cost of sales (W1)	(8,910)
Gross profit	4,490
Operating expenses	(2,400)
Investment income (1,320 – 1,200 increase in market value)	120
Loan interest (25 + 25 per (c))	(50)
Profit before tax	2,160
Income tax expense (55 + 260 + (350 – 280 deferred tax))	(385)
Profit for the period	1,775
Other comprehensive income	
Gain on property revaluation (W2)	1,800
Total comprehensive income for the period	3,575

(b)   **Statement of changes in equity – Year to 31 March 20X5**

	Ordinary shares	Share premium	Revaluation reserve	Retained profits	Total
	$000	$000	$000	$000	$000
At 1 April 20X4	1,600	40	Nil	2,990	4,630
Rights issue (see below)	400	560			960
Total comprehensive income for the period			1,800	1,775	3,575
Transfer to realized profit (W2)			(80)	80	nil
Ordinary dividends paid				(500)	(500)
At 31 March 20X5	2,000	600	1,720	4,345	8,665

The number of 25c ordinary shares at the year end is 8 million ($2 million × 4). This is after a rights issue of 1 for 4. Thus the number of shares prior to the issue would be 6.4 million (8 million × 4/5) and the rights issue would have been for 1.6 million shares. The rights issue price is 60c each which would be recorded as an increase in share capital of $400,000 (1.6 million × 25c) and an increase in share premium of $560,000 (1.6 million × 35c).

(c)   **Statement of financial position as at 31 March 20X5**

	$000	$000
Non-current assets		
Property, plant and equipment (6,710 + 1,350 (W2)		8,060
Investments (1,200 × 110%)		1,320
		–––––
		9,380
Current assets		
Inventory	1,750	
Trade receivables	2,450	
Bank	350	4,550
	–––––	–––––
Total assets		13,930
		–––––
Equity and liabilities:		
Ordinary shares of 25c each		2,000
Reserves (see (b)):		
Share premium	600	
Revaluation reserve	1,720	
Retained earnings	4,345	6,665
	–––––	–––––
		8,665
Non-current liabilities		
10% loan note (issued 20X2)	500	
Deferred tax (1,400 × 25%)	350	850
	–––––	
Current liabilities		
Trade payables	4,130	
Accrued loan interest ((500 × 10%) – 25 paid)	25	
Current tax payable	260	4,415
	–––––	–––––
Total equity and liabilities		13,930
		–––––

Workings (all figures in $000):

(W1) **Cost of sales:**

Per question	9,200
Profit on sale of plant ((900 – 630 (W3)) – 300 proceeds)	(30)
Depreciation – plant (W3)	450
– buildings (W2)	290
Capitalized expenses net of error (W2)	(1,000)
	–––––
	8,910
	–––––

(W2) Land and buildings: cost/revaluation depreciation

	Cost/revaluation	Depreciation
Self constructed (see below)	1,000	50 (20-year life)
Revalued	6,000	240 (see below)
	─────	─────
	7,000	290
	─────	─────

The carrying value of the land and buildings at 31 March 20X5 is $6,710,000 (7,000 – 290).

Depreciation on the building element will be $240 (4,800/20 years). The revaluation of the land and buildings will create a revaluation reserve initially of $1,800 (6,000 – (1,000 + 3,200)), however a transfer of $80 ((4,800 – 3,200)/20 building element of the revaluation) to retained earnings is required.

Self constructed asset:

Purchased materials	150
Direct labour	800
Supervision	65
Design and planning costs	20
Error in construction (10 + 25)	(35)
	─────
	1,000
	─────

Note: The cost of the error cannot be capitalized; it must therefore be written off.

(W3) Plant

	Cost	Depreciation 31 March 20X4	Carrying value
Per statement of financial position	5,200	3,130	
Disposal	(900)	(630)	
	─────	─────	
	4,300	2,500	1,800
	─────	─────	─────

Depreciation for the current year will be $450,000 (25% reducing balance), giving a carrying value at 31 March 20X5 of $1,350,000.

37 TINTAGEL 🖪 *Online question assistance*

🔑

Key answer tips

The question is very clear in saying what you have to do. In part (a), start with the draft figures provided, then go through each of points (i) to (vi) in turn to state the adjustments necessary. In part (b), we take the statement of financial position provided in the question as the proforma into which to slot in your corrected figures.

(a)

	$000	$000
Retained earnings at 1 April 20X3		52,500
Reversal of provision plant overhaul (W4)		6,000
		———
		58,500
Profit for the year to 31 March 20X4	47,500	
Lease rental charge added back (W1)	3,200	
Lease interest (W1)	(800)	
Depreciation (W2) – building	2,600	
– owned plant	22,000	
– leased plant	2,800	
	———	
	(27,400)	
Loss on investment property (15,000 – 12,400)	(2,600)	
Write down of inventory (W3)	(2,400)	
Unrecorded trade payable	(500)	
Reversal of provision for plant overhaul (W4)	6,000	
Increase in deferred tax (22.5 – 18.7)	(3,000)	
Loan note interest (W5)	(846)	18,354
	———	———
Retained earnings at 31 March 20X4		76,854
		———

(b) **Tintagel – Statement of financial position as at 31 March 20X4**

Non-current assets	$000	$000
Freehold property (126,000 – 2,600 (W2))		123,400
Plant – owned (110,000 – 22,000 (W2))		88,000
– leased (11,200 – 2,800 (W2))		8,400
Investment property		12,400
		———
		232,200
Current assets		
Inventory (60,400 – 2,400 (W3))	58,000	
Trade receivables and prepayments	31,200	
Bank	13,800	103,000
	———	———
Total assets		335,200
		———

	$000	$000
Equity and liabilities		
Capital and Reserves:		
Ordinary shares of 25c each		150,000
Reserves:		
Share premium	10,000	
Retained earnings – 31 March 20X4 (part (a))	76,854	86,854
		236,854
Non-current liabilities		
Deferred tax	22,500	
Finance lease obligations (W1)	5,600	
8% Loan note (W5)	14,346	
		42,446
Current liabilities		
Trade payables (47,400 + 500 (W3))	47,900	
Accrued loan note interest (W5)	600	
Finance lease obligation (W1)	3,200	
Taxation	4,200	55,900
Total equity and liabilities		335,200

Workings

(W1) **Finance lease:**

The lease has been incorrectly treated as an operating lease. Treating it as a finance lease gives the following figures:

	$000
Cash price/recorded cost	11,200
First instalment (reversed in statement of comprehensive income)	(3,200)
Capital outstanding at 1 April 20X3	8,000
Interest at 10% p.a. to 31 March 20X4 (current liability)	800

The capital outstanding of $8 million must be split between current and non-current liabilities. The second instalment payable on 1 April 20X4 will contain $800,000 of interest (8,000 × 10%), therefore the capital element in this payment will be $2.4 million and this is a current liability. This leaves $5˙6 million (8,000 – 2,400) as a non-current liability.

(W2) **Non-current assets depreciation:**

	$000
Buildings (130,000 × 2%)	2,600
Non-leased plant (110,000 × 20%)	22,000
Leased plant (11,200 × 25%)	2,800

(W3) The damaged and slow moving inventory should be written down to its estimated realisable value. This is $3˙6 million ($4 million less sales commission at 10%). Therefore the required write down is $2.4 million ($6 million – $3.6 million).

The unrecorded invoice would be an addition to purchases therefore a deduction from profit.

(W4) A provision for a future major overhaul does not meet the definition of a liability in IAS 37 *Provisions, Contingent Liabilities and Contingent Assets* and must be reversed; this will increase the current year's profit and the previous year's profit by $6 million each.

(W5) International accounting standards require issue costs, discounts on issue and premiums on redemptions of loan instruments to be included as part of the finance costs: The net proceeds are $14.1 million (($15 million × 95%) less $0.15 million issue costs) per the suspense account. The finance cost and liability amounts are computed as:

Amortised cost:

Year	b/fwd	Int – 6% (6 months)	Int accrued (6 months)	C/fwd
1	14,100	846	(600)	14,346

Of this $600,000 is represented by the cash payment to be made on 1 April 20X4 (current liability) and the $14.346 million remainder is a long-term liability.

38 CAVERN

Key answer tips

This is a typical style question requiring the preparation of financial statements from a trial balance. This is a time consuming question so ensure you get the straightforward marks for tax and non-current assets. Be wary of the share issue that has already been recorded – you will need to work backwards to determine the value of the share issued and the opening balance.

(a) **Cavern – Statement of comprehensive income for the year ended 30 September 2010**

	$000
Revenue	182,500
Cost of sales (w (i))	(137,400)
Gross profit	45,100
Distribution costs	(8,500)
Administrative expenses (25,000 – 18,500 dividends (w (iii)))	(6,500)
Loss on investments (700 – (15,800 – 13,500))	(1,600)
Finance costs (300 + 400 (w (ii)) + 3,060 (w (iv)))	(3,760)
Profit before tax	24,740
Income tax expense (5,600 + 900 – 250 (w (v)))	(6,250)
Profit for the year	18,490
Other comprehensive income	
Gain on revaluation of land and buildings (w (ii))	800
Total comprehensive income	19,290

(b)   **Cavern – Statement of changes in equity for the year ended 30 September 2010**

	Share capital	Share premium	Revaluation reserve	Retained earnings	Total equity
	$000	$000	$000	$000	$000
Balance at 1 October 2009	40,000	nil	7,000	15,100	62,100
Rights issue (w (iii))	10,000	11,000			21,000
Dividends (w (iii))				(18,500)	(18,500)
Comprehensive income			800	18,490	19,290
Balance at 30 September 2010	50,000	11,000	7,800	15,090	83,890

(c)   **Cavern – Statement of financial position as at 30 September 2010**

	$000	$000
Assets		
Non-current assets		
Property, plant and equipment (41,800 + 51,100 (w (ii)))		92,900
Financial asset investments		13,500
		106,400
Current assets		
Inventory	19,800	
Trade receivables	29,000	
		48,800
Total assets		155,200
Equity and liabilities		
Equity (see (b) above)		
Equity shares of 20 cents each		50,000
Share premium	11,000	
Revaluation reserve	7,800	
Retained earnings	15,090	
		33,890
		83,890
Non-current liabilities		
Provision for decontamination costs (4,000 + 400 (w (ii)))	4,400	
8% loan note (w (iv))	31,260	
Deferred tax (w (v))	3,750	
		39,410
Current liabilities		
Trade payables	21,700	
Bank overdraft	4,600	
Current tax payable	5,600	
		31,900
Total equity and liabilities		155,200

Workings (monetary figures in brackets in $'000)

(i)   **Cost of sales**

Per trial balance	128,500
Depreciation of building (36,000/18 years)	2,000
Depreciation of new plant (14,000/10 years)	1,400
Depreciation of existing plant and equipment	5,500
((67,400 – 10,000 – 13,400) × 12.5%)	
	137,400

(ii)   **Property, plant and equipment**

The new plant of $10 million should be grossed up by the provision for the present value of the estimated future decontamination costs of $4 million to give a gross cost of $14 million. The 'unwinding' of the provision will give rise to a finance cost in the current year of $400,000 (4,000 × 10%) to give a closing provision of $4.4 million.

The gain on revaluation and carrying amount of the land and building will be:

Valuation – 30 September 2009	43,000
Building depreciation (w (i))	(2,000)
Carrying amount before revaluation	41,000
Revaluation – 30 September 2010	41,800
Gain on revaluation	800

The carrying amount of the plant and equipment will be:	
New plant (14,000 – 1,400)	12,600
Existing plant and equipment (67,400 – 10,000 – 13,400 – 5,500)	38,500
	51,100

(iii) **Rights issue/dividends paid**

Based on 250 million (50 million × 5 – as shares are 20 cents each) shares in issue at 30 September 2010, a rights issue of 1 for 4 on 1 April 2010 would have resulted in the issue of 50 million new shares (250 million – (250 million × 4/5)). This would be recorded as share capital of $10 million (50,000 × 20 cents) and share premium of $11 million (50,000 × (42 cents – 20 cents)).

The dividend of 3 cents per share paid on 30 November 2009 would have been based on 200 million shares and been $6 million. The dividend of 5 cents per share paid on 31 May 2010 would have been based on 250 million shares and been $12.5 million. Therefore the total dividends paid, incorrectly included in administrative expenses, were $18.5 million.

(iv) **Loan note**

The finance cost of the loan note, at the effective rate of 10% applied to the carrying amount of the loan note of $30.6 million, is $3.06 million. The interest actually paid is $2.4 million. The difference between these amounts of $660,000 (3,060 – 2,400) is added to the carrying amount of the loan note to give $31.26 million (30,600 + 660) for inclusion as a non-current liability in the statement of financial position.

(v) Deferred tax

Provision required at 30 September 2010 (15,000 × 25%)	3,750
Provision at 1 October 2009	(4,000)
Credit (reduction in provision) to income statement	250

ACCA marking scheme			Marks
(a)	statement of comprehensive income:		
	Revenue		1½
	cost of sales		3
	distribution costs		½
	administrative expenses		1
	investment income loss		1
	finance costs		2½
	income tax expense		2
	gain on revaluation of land and buildings		½
		Maximum	11
(b)	Statement of changes in equity		
	balances b/f		½
	rights issue		1
	dividends		1
	revaluation gain		½
	profit for year		1
		Maximum	4
(c)	statement of financial position		
	property, plant and equipment		2½
	financial asset investments		½
	inventory		½
	trade receivables		½
	contamination provision		1
	8% loan note		1
	deferred tax		1
	trade payables		½
	bank overdraft		½
	current tax payable		1
		Maximum	9
Total			25

39   CANDEL *Walk in the footsteps of a top tutor*

Key answer tips

Make sure you remember to complete all parts of the question – a statement of changes in equity is required as well as a statement of comprehensive income and statement of financial position. Be wary of the revaluation. The revaluation takes place at the end of the year, therefore a full year depreciation should be applied before you undertake the revaluation.

(a)   **Candel – Statement of comprehensive income for the year ended 30 September 2008**

	$000
Revenue (300,000 – 2,500)	297,500
Cost of sales (w (i))	(225,400)
	———
Gross profit	72,100
Distribution costs	(14,500)
Administrative expenses (22,200 – 400 + 100 see note below)	(21,900)
Finance costs (200 + 1,200 (w (ii)))	(1,400)
	———
Profit before tax	34,300
(Income tax expense (11,400 + (6,000 – 5,800 deferred tax))	(11,600)
	———
Profit for the year	22,700
Other comprehensive income	
Loss on leasehold property revaluation (w (iii))	(4,500)
	———
Total comprehensive income for the year	18,200
	———

Note: As it is considered that the outcome of the legal action against Candel is unlikely to succeed (only a 20% chance) it is inappropriate to provide for any damages. The potential damages are an example of a contingent liability which should be disclosed (at $2 million) as a note to the financial statements. The unrecoverable legal costs are a liability (the start of the legal action is a past event) and should be provided for in full.

(b) **Candel – Statement of changes in equity for the year ended 30 September 2008**

	Equity shares	Revaluation reserve	Retained earnings	Total equity
	$000	$000	$000	$000
Balances at 1 October 2007	50,000	10,000	24,500	84,500
Dividend			(6,000)	(6,000)
Comprehensive income		(4,500)	22,700	18,200
Balances at 30 September 2008	50,000	5,500	41,200	96,700

(c) **Candel – Statement of financial position as at 30 September 2008**

	$000	$000
Assets		
Non-current assets (w (iii))		
Property, plant and equipment (43,000 + 38,400)		81,400
Development costs		14,800
		96,200
Current assets		
Inventory	20,000	
Trade receivables	43,100	63,100
Total assets		159,300
Equity and liabilities:		
Equity (from (b))		
Equity shares of 25 cents each		50,000
Revaluation reserve	5,500	
Retained earnings	41,200	46,700
		96,700
Non-current liabilities		
Deferred tax	6,000	
8% redeemable preference shares (20,000 + 400 (w (ii)))	20,400	26,400
Current liabilities		
Trade payables (23,800 – 400 + 100 – re legal action)	23,500	
Bank overdraft	1,300	
Current tax payable	11,400	36,200
Total equity and liabilities		159,300

Workings **(figures in brackets in $000)**

(i) **Cost of sales:**

	$000
Per trial balance	204,000
Depreciation (w (iii)) – leasehold property	2,500
– plant and equipment	9,600
Loss on disposal of plant (4,000 – 2,500)	1,500
Amortisation of development costs (w (iii))	4,000
Research and development expenses (1,400 + 2,400 (w (iii)))	3,800
	225,400

(ii)

Tutorial note

This requires knowledge of accounting for financial instruments under IAS 32 &IFRS 9.

The finance cost of $1.2 million for the preference shares is based on the effective rate of 12% applied to $20 million issue proceeds of the shares for the six months they have been in issue (20m × 12% × 6/12). The dividend paid of $800,000 is based on the nominal rate of 8%. The additional $400,000 (accrual) is added to the carrying amount of the preference shares in the statement of financial position. As these shares are redeemable they are treated as debt and their dividend is treated as a finance cost.

(iii) **Non-current assets:**

Leasehold property

Valuation at 1 October 2007	50,000
Depreciation for year (20 year life)	(2,500)
Carrying amount at date of revaluation	47,500
Valuation at 30 September 2008	(43,000)
Revaluation deficit	4,500

Tutorial note

Remember to write off the disposed asset, both cost and b/fwd accumulated depreciation before calculating the current year depreciation charge.

	$000
Plant and equipment per trial balance (76,600 – 24,600)	52,000
Disposal (8,000 – 4,000)	(4,000)
	48,000
Depreciation for year (20%)	(9,600)
Carrying amount at 30 September 2008	38,400

Tutorial note

Remember research costs are to be expensed and development costs are to be capitalised only when the recognition criteria in IAS38 are met. In this question- the directors do not become confident that the project will be successful until 1 April – therefore development costs on the new project in January – March must be expensed.

Capitalised/deferred development costs	
Carrying amount at 1 October 2007 (20,000 – 6,000)	14,000
Amortised for year (20,000 × 20%)	(4,000)
Capitalised during year (800 × 6 months)	4,800
Carrying amount at 30 September 2008	14,800

Note: Development costs can only be treated as an asset from the point where they meet the recognition criteria in IAS 38 *Intangible assets*. Thus development costs from 1 April to 30 September 2008 of $4.8 million (800 × 6 months) can be capitalised. These will not be amortised as the project is still in development. The research costs of $1.4 million plus three months' development costs of $2.4 million (800 × 3 months) (i.e. those incurred before 1 April 2008) are treated as an expense.

UK SYLLABUS FOCUS ONLY

Revaluation losses

Under UK GAAP revaluation losses are dealt with as follows:

A loss clearly due to consumption of economic benefit is taken in its entirety to the profit and loss account whether previously revalued or not. Whereas, losses due to other causes than consumption of economic benefit on assets previously revalued upwards should be allocated first to the STRGL until the carrying amount reaches depreciated historical cost and then to the profit and loss account. Finally, losses due to other causes than consumption of economic benefit on assets not previously revalued upwards should be allocated in the profit and loss account.

Development costs

Under UK GAAP the capitalisation of development expenditure that meets the recognition criteria is optional whereas it is compulsory under IFRS if the recognition criteria are met. In addition to this, development costs previously written off can be reinstated if the uncertainties which led to it being written off no longer apply whereas they cannot be reinstated under IFRS. That would mean in Candel the development costs written off for Jan – Mar could in actual fact be capitalised.

Examiner's comments

This was a fairly standard question requiring candidates to prepare an statement of comprehensive income, a statement of financial position and a statement of changes in equity (SOCIE) after accounting for a series of adjustments.

The adjustments required were for depreciation (after a revaluation), correcting a sale of plant included as a revenue sale, capitalisation of development costs, dealing with a contingent liability, using the effective interest rate on preference shares and current and deferred tax.

As with question 1 this was a popular question and many candidates scored well. The ability to produce financial statements from a trial balance seems well understood, but some of the adjustments created difficulties:

– careless mistake was to add back the sale proceeds of the plant to revenues (it should have been deducted)

– timing of the revaluation of a leasehold property was at the end of the period, but many candidates answered as if it was at the beginning of the period

– research and development caused many problems. Development costs can only be capitalised from the point at which management become confident of the success of the project. Up to this point they must be written off along with research expenditure. Very few candidates could put this into practice.

– reversal of a provision for a contingent liability (they should not be provide for); however the associated unrecoverable legal costs should have been provided for. Candidates often only got one of these two adjustments correct. A similar error occurred with the related current liability.

– most candidates did realise that the effective interest rate should be used for the preference shares, but made common errors of adding the nominal rate as well (thus double counting it) and/or not realising the shares were issued half way through the year thus only 6 moths interest was required.

– deferred tax caused problems; ether the movement was credited to income (it should have been debited) or the whole of the provision was charged to income (rather than the movement).

The statement of financial position was generally well answered when allowing for 'knock on' errors from the statement of comprehensive income calculations.

The SOCIE was more mixed; it was often completely ignored and errors such as including in the SOCIE the issue of the redeemable preference shares and their dividend (they are debt) and not including the equity dividend.

40 PRICEWELL

(a) **Pricewell – Statement of comprehensive income for the year ended 31 March 2009:**

	$000
Revenue (310,000 + 22,000 (w (i)) – 6,400 (w (ii)))	325,600
Cost of sales (w (iii))	(255,100)
Gross profit	70,500
Distribution costs	(19,500)
Administrative expenses	(27,500)
Finance costs (4,160 (w (v)) + 1,248 (w (vi)))	(5,408)
Profit before tax	18,092
Income tax expense (4,500 +700 – (8,400 – 5,600 deferred tax)	(2,400)
Profit for the year	15,692

(b) **Pricewell – Statement of financial position as at 31 March 2009:**

	$000	$000
Assets		
Non-current assets		
Property, plant and equipment (24,900 + 41,500 w (iv))		66,400
Current assets		
Inventory	28,200	
Amount due from customer (w (i))	17,100	
Trade receivables	33,100	
Bank	5,500	83,900
Total assets		150,300
Equity and liabilities:		
Equity shares of 50 cents each		40,000
Retained earnings (w (vii))		12,592
		52,592
Non-current liabilities		
Deferred tax	5,600	
Finance lease obligation (w (vi))	5,716	
6% Redeemable preference shares (41,600 + 1,760 (w (v)))	43,360	54,676
Current liabilities		
Trade payables	33,400	
Finance lease obligation (10,848 – 5,716) (w (vi)))	5,132	
Current tax payable	4,500	43,032
Total equity and liabilities		150,300

Workings (figures in brackets in $000)

		$000
(i)	**Construction contract:**	
	Selling price	50,000
	Estimated cost	
	To date	(12,000)
	To complete	(10,000)
	Plant	(8,000)
		———
	Estimated profit	20,000
		———

Work done is agreed at $22 million so the contract is 44% complete (22,000/50,000).

Revenue	22,000
Cost of sales (= balance)	(13,200)
	———
Profit to date (44% × 20,000)	8,800
	———
Cost incurred to date materials and labour	12,000
Plant depreciation (8,000 × 6/24 months)	2,000
Profit to date	8,800
	———
	22,800
Cash received	(5,700)
	———
Amount due from customer	17,100
	———

(ii) Pricewell is acting as an agent (not the principal) for the sales on behalf of Trilby. Therefore the statement of comprehensive income should only include $1.6 million (20% of the sales of $8 million). Therefore $6.4 million (8,000 – 1,600) should be deducted from revenue and cost of sales. It would also be acceptable to show agency sales (of $1.6 million) separately as other income.

Cost of sales

Per question	234,500
Contract (w (i))	13,200
Agency cost of sales (w (ii))	(6,400)
Depreciation (w (iv))– leasehold property	1,800
– owned plant ((46,800 – 12,800) × 25%)	8,500
– leased plant (20,000 × 25%)	5,000
Surplus on revaluation of leasehold property (w (iv))	(1,500)
	———
	255,100
	———

$000

(iv) **Non-current assets**

Leasehold property

valuation at 31 March 2008	25,200
depreciation for year (14 year life remaining)	(1,800)
carrying amount at date of revaluation valuation at 31 March 2009	23,400
valuation at 31 March 2008	(24,900)
revaluation surplus (to statement of comprehensive income – see below)	1,500

The $1.5 million revaluation surplus is credited to the statement of comprehensive income as this is the partial reversal of the $2.8 million impairment loss recognised in the statement of comprehensive income in the previous period (i.e. year ended 31 March 2008).

Plant and equipment

– owned (46,800 – 12,800 – 8,500)	25,500
– leased (20,000 – 5,000 – 5,000)	10,000
– contract (8,000 – 2,000 (w (i)))	6,000
Carrying amount at 31 March 2009	41,500

(v) The finance cost of $4,160,000 for the preference shares is based on the effective rate of 10% applied to $41.6 million balance at 1 April 2008. The accrual of $1,760,000 (4,160 – 2,400 dividend paid) is added to the carrying amount of the preference shares in the statement of financial position. As these shares are redeemable they are treated as debt and their dividend is treated as a finance cost.

(vi) **Finance lease liability**

balance at 31 March 2008	15,600
interest for year at 8%	1,248
lease rental paid 31 March 2009	(6,000)
total liability at 31 March 2009	10,848
interest next year at 8%	868
lease rental due 31 March 2010	(6,000)
total liability at 31 March 2010	5,716

(vii) **Retained earnings**

balance at 1 April 2008	4,900
profit for year	15,692
equity dividend paid	(8,000)
balance at 31 March 2009	12,592

UK SYLLABUS FOCUS ONLY

The amounts to be disclosed as current assets under SSAP 9 amount to the same as under IAS 11, but they are calculated differently and disclosed as two separate long-term contract figures. The first is an inventory-based figure; the second is a receivables-based figure. Under IAS 11 the latter is not identified as relating to construction contracts.

Included under stock/inventory

Total costs to date (12,000 + 2,000 dep'n)	14,000
Transferred to cost of sales	(13,200)
Long term contact balance	**800**

Included under debtors/receivables

Cumulative turnover	22,000
Progress billings	(5,700)
Amounts recoverable on contracts	**16,300**

ACCA marking scheme		
		Marks
(a)	Statement of comprehensive income	
	Revenue	2
	Cost of sales	5
	Distribution costs	½
	Administrative expenses	½
	Finance costs	2
	Income tax expense	2
		———
	Maximum	12
(b)	Statement of financial position	
	Property, plant and equipment	2½
	Inventory	½
	Due on construction contract	2
	Trade receivables	½
	Bank	½
	Equity shares	½
	Retained earnings (1 for dividend)	1½
	Deferred tax	1
	Finance lease – non-current liability	½
	Preference shares	1
	Trade payables	½
	Finance lease – current liability	1
	Current tax payable	1
		———
	Maximum	13
		———
Total		25
		———

Examiner's comments

This was a familiar question of preparing financial statements from a trial balance with various adjustments. These involved a revaluation of a non-current asset, dealing with a finance lease agreement, accounting for a construction contract, a revenue recognition issue, an effective rate finance cost for a financial instrument and taxation.

This question was the second best answered question, but it was not as well answered as I have come to expect. The most common errors were:

- deducting from revenue the agency sales, without recognising the commission earned

- rather worryingly, a number of candidates deducted the closing inventory from the cost of sales (by definition it has already been deducted)

- basing calculations of the depreciation and impairment reversal of the leasehold property on the revaluation as if it had been at the beginning of the year (the question clearly stated it was at the end of the year)

- taking the reversal of the impairment to reserves rather than through the statement of comprehensive income as, on this occasion, this reversed a previous impairment loss recognised in the statement of comprehensive income

- also worryingly, a number of candidates depreciated the owned plant and equipment using cost rather than carrying value; the distinction between straight line and reducing balance depreciation should be very familiar to candidates at this stage

- a number of candidates decided that the leasehold property and the leased plant (and hence the finance lease payment) were the same asset; this produced some very unhelpful workings and balances

- many complex (and unnecessary) lease calculations were provided – if future payments are to be discounted, the appropriate factors will be provided as part of the question – the finance cost of the redeemable preference shares was incorrectly calculated at the nominal rate of its dividend rather than at the effective rate based on the carrying amount at the start of the period. Also the dividends are part of the finance cost in the statement of comprehensive income and the shares themselves are classified as debt on the statement of financial position; redeemable preference shares do not have the characteristics of an equity instrument

- there were errors in the treatment of the taxation in both the statement of comprehensive income and the statement of financial position, these included: crediting the under provision of tax from the previous year to the statement of comprehensive income (as a debit balance it should have been charged); treating the closing provision for deferred tax as the charge in the statement of comprehensive income (it should be the movement on the provision that appears in the statement of comprehensive income); showing the current tax net of the under-provision as a current liability (only the current year's tax is a current liability).

- many candidates made a fair attempt at the construction contract figures in the workings (credit was given for this), but often did not follow them through to the financial statements

> - the treatment of the finance lease caused problems, many candidates based the finance cost and current/noncurrent liability on the carrying amount of the leased asset rather than on the opening liability for the lease obligation
>
> - a number of candidates are still showing equity dividends in the statement of comprehensive income rather than as part of the retained earnings (or statement of changes in equity if it had been required).
>
> The statement of financial position was generally well done and most of the errors that were made generally related to the following through of errors from the statement of comprehensive income.

41   SANDOWN

> **Key answer tips**
>
> This question required the preparation of a statement of comprehensive income and a statement of financial position and had the usual published accounts adjustments such as tax and non-current asset accounting. Be wary when dealing with the convertible loan this has already been accounted for in 2008 and you are now required to account for the second year of the convertible loan.

(a)   **Sandown – Statement of comprehensive income for the year ended 30 September 2009**

	$000
Revenue (380,000 – 4,000 (w (i)))	376,000
Cost of sales (w (ii))	(265,300)
	———
Gross profit	110,700
Distribution costs	(17,400)
Administrative expenses (50,500 – 12,000 (w (iii)))	(38,500)
Investment income (1,300 + 2,500 (w (iv))	3,800
Finance costs (w (v))	(1,475)
	———
Profit before tax	57,125
Income tax expense (16,200 + 2,100 – 1,500 (w (vi)))	(16,800)
	———
Profit for the year	40,325
	———

(b)   **Sandown – Statement of financial position as at 30 September 2009**

	$000	$000
Assets		
Non-current assets		
Property, plant and equipment (w (vii))		67,500
Intangible – brand (15,000 – 2,500 (w (ii)))		12,500
Investment property (w (iv))		29,000
		109,000
Current assets		
Inventory	38,000	
Trade receivables	44,500	
Bank	8,000	90,500
Total assets		199,500
Equity and liabilities		
Equity		
Equity shares of 20 cents each		50,000
Equity option		2,000
Retained earnings (33,260 + 40,325 – 12,000 dividend (w (iii)))		61,585
		113,585
Non-current liabilities		
Deferred tax (w (vi))	3,900	
Deferred income (w (i))	2,000	
5% convertible loan note (w (v))	18,915	24,815
Current liabilities		
Trade payables	42,900	
Deferred income (w (i))	2,000	
Current tax payable	16,200	61,100
Total equity and liabilities		199,500

Workings (figures in brackets in $000)

(i)   IAS 18 Revenue requires that where sales revenue includes an amount for after sales servicing and support costs then a proportion of the revenue should be deferred. The amount deferred should cover the cost and a reasonable profit (in this case a gross profit of 40%) on the services. As the servicing and support is for three years and the date of the sale was 1 October 2008, revenue relating to two years' servicing and support provision must be deferred: ($1.2 million × 2/0.6) = $4 million. This is shown as $2 million in both current and non-current liabilities.

(ii)　**Cost of sales**

Per question		246,800
Depreciation	– building (50,000/50 years – see below)	1,000
	– plant and equipment (42,200 – 19,700) × 40%))	9,000
Amortisation	– brand (1,500 + 2,500 – see below)	4,000
Impairment of brand (see below)		4,500
		265,300

The cost of the building of $50 million (63,000 – 13,000 land) has accumulated depreciation of $8 million at 30 September 2008 which is eight years after its acquisition. Thus the life of the building must be 50 years. The brand is being amortised at $3 million per annum (30,000/10 years). The impairment occurred half way through the year, thus amortisation of $1.5 million should be charged prior to calculation of the impairment loss. At the date of the impairment review the brand had a carrying amount of $19.5 million (30,000 – (9,000 + 1,500)). The recoverable amount of the brand is its fair value of $15 million (as this is higher than its value in use of $12 million) giving an impairment loss of $4.5 million (19,500 – 15,000). Amortisation of $2.5 million (15,000/3 years × 6/12) is required for the second-half of the year giving total amortisation of $4 million for the full year.

(iii)　A dividend of 4.8 cents per share would amount to $12 million (50 million × 5 (i.e. shares are 20 cents each) × 4.8 cents). This is not an administrative expense but a distribution of profits that should be accounted for through equity.

(iv)　The gain on the investment property is shown below

Fair value at 1 October 2008	26,500
Fair value at 30 September 2009	29,000
Gain on investment property	2,500

The investment property is to be reported in the statement of financial position at fair value of $29 million at 30 September 2009 which gives a fair value increase (credited to the statement of comprehensive income) of $2.5 million.

(v)　The finance cost of the convertible loan note is based on its effective rate of 8% applied to $18,440,000 carrying amount at 1 October 2008 = $1,475,000 (rounded). The accrual of $475,000 (1,475 – 1,000 interest paid) is added to the carrying amount of the loan note giving a figure of $18,915,000 (18,440 + 475) in the statement of financial position at 30 September 2009.

(vi)　**Deferred tax**

Credit balance required at 30 September 2009 (13,000 × 30%)	3,900
Balance at 1 October 2008	(5,400)
Credit (reduction in balance) to statement of comprehensive income	1,500

(vii) **Non-current assets**

Freehold property (63,000 – (8,000 + 1,000)) (w (ii))	54,000
Plant and equipment (42,200 – (19,700 + 9,000)) (w (ii))	13,500
	———
Property, plant and equipment	67,500
	———

Examiner's comments

A 'familiar' question requiring candidates to prepare a statement of comprehensive income and a statement of financial position. A series of adjustments were required: for deferred revenue, a dividend paid, an effective interest rate calculation, basic depreciation, taxation and the impairment and amortisation of a brand.

As with question 1 this was a popular question and many candidates scored well. The ability to produce financial statements from a trial balance seems well understood, but some of the adjustments created difficulties:

- few candidates correctly calculated the amount of revenue to be deferred in relation to a sale (of $16 million) with ongoing service support. Most candidates deferred the whole of the revenue rather than the amount of the support costs (plus appropriate profit) relating to the remaining two years of service support. Some candidates increased revenue rather than defer it and some thought it was an in-substance loan

- many candidates applied the effective rate of interest (8%) to the nominal amount ($20 million) of a convertible loan rather than its carrying amount of $18.44 million. A few candidates made complicated calculations of the split between debt and equity for the loan not realising that it was the second year after its issue and the split had been made a year before

- most candidates got the taxation aspects correct, but there were still some basic errors such as charging the whole of the deferred tax provision to income (rather than the movement) and treating the underpayment of tax in the previous period as a credit.

- it was worrying that a number of candidates made basic errors on straight forward depreciation calculations. Some used the straight line method for the plant (not reading the question properly which stated the use of the reducing balance method) and some charged the accumulated depreciation to cost of sales rather than the charge for the period. Amortisation and impairment of the brand caused many problems; not calculating two 6 month charges (before and after the impairment) and not using the (higher) realisable value of the brand as the basis for the impairment charge.

The statement of financial position was generally well answered; most problems were follow-on errors from mistakes made in the statement of comprehensive income. A number of candidates are still incorrectly treating dividends as part of the statement of comprehensive income. Overall, a well-answered question.

---

42 DUNE

Key answer tips

This question contained many of the usual adjustments that you would expect with a published accounts question such as depreciation and tax adjustments. You were also expected to demonstrate your knowledge of accounting for held for sale assets, financial assets and liabilities and construction contracts which therefore makes this a time consuming question. Ensure that when you look at these adjustments you remember to update both the statement of comprehensive income and statement of financial position accordingly.

(a) **Dune – Statement of comprehensive income for the year ended 31 March 2010**

	$000
Revenue (400,000 – 8,000 + 12,000 (w (i) and (ii)))	404,000
Cost of sales (w (iii))	(315,700)
Gross profit	88,300
Distribution costs	(26,400)
Administrative expenses (34,200 – 500 loan note issue costs)	(33,700)
Investment income	1,200
Profit (gain) on investments at fair value through profit or loss (28,000 – 26,500)	1,500
Finance costs (200 + 1,950 (w (iv)))	(2,150)
Profit before tax	28,750
Income tax expense (12,000 – 1,400 – 1,800 (w (v)))	(8,800)
Profit for the year	19,950

(b) **Dune – Statement of financial position as at 31 March 2010**

	$000	$000
Assets		
Non-current assets		
Property, plant and equipment (w (vi))		46,400
Investments at fair value through profit or loss		28,000
		74,400
Current assets		
Inventory	48,000	
Construction contract – amounts due from customer (w (ii))	13,400	
Trade receivables (40,700 – 8,000 (w (i)))	32,700	94,100
Non-current assets held for sale (w (iii))		33,500
Total assets		202,000

Equity and liabilities

Equity

Equity shares of $1 each	60,000
Retained earnings (38,400 + 19,950 – 10,000 dividend paid)	48,350
	108,350

Non-current liabilities

Deferred tax (w (v))	4,200	
5% loan notes (2012) (w (iv))	20,450	24,650

Current liabilities

Trade payables	52,000	
Bank overdraft	4,500	
Accrued loan note interest (w (iv))	500	
Current tax payable	12,000	69,000
Total equity and liabilities		202,000

Workings (figures in brackets in $000)

(i) This appears to be a 'cut off' error in that Dune has invoiced goods that are still in inventory. The required adjustment is to remove the sale of $8 million (6,000 × 100/75) from revenue and trade receivables. No adjustment is required to cost of sales or closing inventory.

(ii) **Construction contract:**

	$000	$000
Agreed selling price		40,000
Costs to date	8,000	
Costs to complete	15,000	
Plant (12,000 – 3,000)	9,000	(32,000)
Total estimated profit		8,000

Amounts for inclusion in the statement of comprehensive income for the year ended 31 March 2010

Revenue (40,000 × 30%)	12,000
Cost of sales (balance)	(9,600)
Gross profit (8,000 × 30%)	2,400

Amounts for inclusion in the statement of financial position as at 31 March 2010

Cost to date – materials, labour and other direct costs	8,000
Plant depreciation ((12,000 – 3,000) × 6/18)	3,000
	11,000
Profit to date	2,400
	13,400
Payments received	(nil)
Amounts due from customer	13,400

(iii) **Cost of sales**

	$000
Per question	294,000
Construction contract (w (ii))	9,600
Depreciation of leasehold property (see below)	1,500
Impairment of leasehold property (see below)	4,000
Depreciation of plant and equipment ((67,500 – 23,500) × 15%)	6,600
	315,700

The leasehold property must be classed as a non-current asset held for sale from 1 October 2009 at its fair value less costs to sell. It must be depreciated for six months up to this date (after which depreciation ceases). This is calculated at $1.5 million (45,000/15 years × 6/12). Its carrying amount at 1 October 2009 is therefore $37.5 million (45,000 – (6,000 + 1,500)).

Its fair value less cost to sell at this date is $33.5 million ((40,000 × 85%) – 500). It is therefore impaired by $4 million (37,500 – 33,500).

(iv) The finance cost of the loan note, at the effective rate of 10% applied to the correct carrying amount of the loan note of $19.5 million is, $1.95 million (the issue costs must be deducted from the proceeds of the loan note; they are not an administrative expense). The interest actually paid is $500,000 (20,000 × 5% × 6/12); however, a further $500,000 needs to be accrued as a current liability (as it will be paid soon). The difference between the total finance cost of $1.95 million and the $1 million interest payable is added to the carrying amount of the loan note to give $20.45 million (19,500 + 950) for inclusion as a non-current liability in the statement of financial position.

(v) **Deferred tax**

Provision required at 31 March 2010 (14,000 × 30%)	4,200
Provision at 1 April 2009	(6,000)
	———
Credit (reduction in provision) to statement of comprehensive income	1,800
	———

(vi) **Property, plant and equipment**

Property, plant and equipment (67,500 – 23,500 – 6,600)	37,400
Construction plant (12,000 – 3,000)	9,000
	———
	46,400
	———

UK SYLLABUS FOCUS ONLY

Held for sale asset

There is no equivalent standard in UK GAAP for assets held for sale. Under UK accounting when the decision to sell an asset is made no reclassification is required. A gain or loss is only reported when the asset is actually disposed of.

Construction contract

The amounts to be disclosed as current assets under SSAP 9 amount to the same as under IAS 11, but they are calculated differently and disclosed as two separate long-term contract figures. The first is an inventory-based figure; the second is a receivables-based figure. Under IAS 11 the latter is not identified as relating to construction contracts. For example:

Included under stock/inventory

Total costs to date (12,000 + 2,000 dep'n)	11,000	
Transferred to cost of sales	(9,600)	
Long term contact balance		**1,400**

Included under debtors/receivables

Cumulative turnover	12,000	
Progress billings	nil	
Amounts recoverable on contracts		**12,000**

ACCA marking scheme		
		Marks
(a)	**Statement of comprehensive income**	
	revenue	2½
	cost of sales	4½
	distribution costs	½
	administrative expenses	1
	investment income	½
	gain on investments	½
	finance costs	1½
	income tax expense	2
		———
	Maximum	13
(b)	**Statement of financial position**	
	property, plant and equipment	1½
	investments	½
	inventory	½
	construction contract	1
	trade receivables	1
	non-current asset held for sale	1
	equity shares	½
	retained earnings (1 for dividend)	2
	deferred tax	1
	5% loan note	1
	trade payables	½
	accrued loan note interest	½
	bank overdraft	½
	current tax payable	½
		———
	Maximum	12
		———
Total		25
		———

Examiner's comments

This was a familiar question of preparing financial statements from a trial balance with various adjustments required. These involved the dealing with a sales 'cut off' error, the use of the effective interest rate for a loan, a fair valued investment, an impairment of a leasehold property (including presenting it as 'held for sale'), a construction contract and accounting for taxation.

As with question 1, this question was competently answered by the majority of candidates showing good knowledge of the format and presentation of the two financial statements.

To help with future preparation, the most common errors were:

- 'cut off error': generally dealt with quite well, but there were errors in grossing up the cost (or only adjusting by the profit element) to give the correct revenue/turnover figure

- loan: the issue costs were often ignored (they should have been deducted from the proceeds and also deducted from administrative expenses) and calculating the finance charge at the nominal rate of 5% instead of the effective rate of 10%. Omission of accrued interest from current liabilities or including it at the incorrect amount

- despite the investment being described as 'fair value through profit and loss', many candidates credited the gain directly to equity

- leasehold property: a failure to depreciate it up to the date it became 'held for sale'; not calculating the subsequent impairment loss and most candidates continuing to show it as a non-current (rather than a current) asset [the latter point not applicable to UK based papers]

- construction contract: often completely ignored, incorrect calculation of cost (usually omitting the plant depreciation), incorrect (or non-existent) presentation in current assets (amount due from customers) or non-current assets (carrying amount of the plant). A lot of candidates who prepared workings for the contract then made no attempt to include the relevant figures in their financial statements.

- there were many errors in the treatment of the taxation in both the statement of comprehensive income and the statement of financial position, these included: debiting (should be credited) the over provision of the previous year's tax; treating the closing provision (rather than the movement) of deferred tax as the charge in the statement of comprehensive income; and confusion over which amounts of tax should appear as non-current and current liabilities.

- a number of candidates are still showing equity dividends in the statement of comprehensive income (as an expense) rather than as part of the calculation of retained earnings.

43 JKL

(a) **Basic and diluted earnings per share**

Basic earnings per share: $\dfrac{2,763,000}{6,945,922\,(W3)} = 39.8c$

Diluted EPS: $\dfrac{2,858,200\,(W4)}{9,045,922\,(W5)} = 31.6c$

(W1) **Calculate the theoretical ex-rights price after the rights issue**

	¢
4 shares × 145¢	580
1 share ×125¢	125
Theoretical value of holding of 5 shares	705
Theoretical ex-rights price of 1 share after rights issue: 705/5	141

(W2) **Calculate bonus fraction**

$\dfrac{\text{Fair value of one share before rights issue}}{\text{Theoretical ex-rights price of one share (W1)}} = \dfrac{145}{141}$

(W3) **Weighted average number of shares in issue in the year to 31 August 20X4**

	Number of shares
1 September 20X3 – 1 February 20X4	
6,000,000 × 145/141×5/12	2,570,922
1 February 20X4 – 31 August 20X4	
7,500,000×7/12	4,375,000
	6,945,922

(W4) Adjustment to profits for calculation of diluted EPS

	$
Profits	2,763,000
Add: Interest after tax	
(2,000,000 × 7%)×(1−0.32)	95,200
Adjusted profits	2,858,200

(W5) Adjustment to number of shares for calculation of diluted EPS

Note: Use the most advantageous (for loan stockholders) conversion rate.

	Number of shares
Weighted average shares in issue in year to 31 August 20X4 (W3)	6,945,922
Add: Dilutive effect 2,000,000/100 × 105	2,100,000
Diluted shares	9,045,922

(b)   Much of the information contained in financial statements refers to events that have occurred in the past, and so it is of relatively restricted usefulness in making decisions. Diluted earnings per share, however, can be quite useful to investors and potential investors in that it incorporates some information about likely future events. Where potentially dilutive financial instruments have been issued, it is helpful to investors to be able to appreciate the impact full dilution would have upon the earnings of the business. However, it should be appreciated that only some elements of the calculation relate to the future. One of the key elements of the calculation, the basic earnings for the period, relates to events that have already taken place and that may not be replicated in the future.

BUSINESS COMBINATIONS

44   HIGHMOOR   *Walk in the footsteps of a top tutor*

Key answer tips

This question has some unusual complications. The goodwill is negative and should therefore be taken to profit or loss per IFRS 3. On the intra-group loan there is a payment in transit that is part interest and part capital repayment that needs to be accounted for before the reconciled loan can be eliminated.

(a)   **Consolidated Statement of financial position of Highmoor as at 30 September 20X3**

	$ million	$ million
Assets		
Non-current assets		
Property, plant and equipment (585 + 172)		757
Intangible:		
Software (W7)		24
Investments (225 – 120 cash to buy sub shares – 5		68
Capital repayment receivable from Slowmoor – 45		
inter-co loan (W6) + 13)		
		———
		849
Current assets		
Inventory (85 + 42)	127	
Accounts receivable (95 – 4 in transit (W6) + 36)	127	
Tax asset	80	
Bank (20 + 9 in transit (W6))	29	363
	———	———
Total assets		1,212
		———
Equity and liabilities		
Equity attributable to owners of the parent		
Ordinary shares $1 each		400
Retained earnings (W5)		322
		———
		722
Non-controlling interest (W4)		43
		———
		765
Non-current liabilities		
12% loan notes		35
Current liabilities		
Accounts payable (210 + 71)	281	
Overdraft	17	
Taxation	70	
Contingent consideration (W3)	44	412
	———	———
Total equity and liabilities		1,212
		———

Workings (**Note:** All figures in $ million)

(W1) **Group structure**

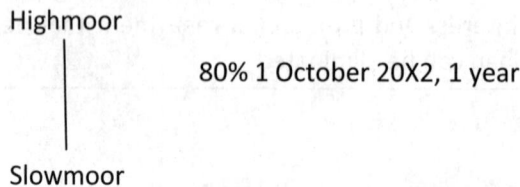

Highmoor

| 80% 1 October 20X2, 1 year

Slowmoor

(W2) **Net assets in subsidiary**

> **Tutorial note**
>
> *A net asset working really helps.*

	At acquisition	At reporting period end
	$m	$m
Share capital	100	100
Retained earnings	150	115
	250	215

(W3) **Goodwill**

	$m
Parent holding (investment) at fair value:	
Cash (80% × 100 × $1.50)	120
Contingent consideration (80% × 100 × $0.60) × $1/1.1^2$	40
	160
NCI value at acquisition	50
(20% × $250 (W2))	
	210
Less:	
Fair value of net assets at acquisition (W2)	(250)
Excess of net assets acquired over consideration given (Bargain purchase)	(40)

> **Tutorial note**
>
> *Per IFRS 3 (revised 2008) contingent consideration should be recognised by the acquirer at its fair value at the acquisition date. The question states that the fair value is to be measured at the present value of the future cash flow i.e. there is a potential future cash flow of $48 million (i.e. 100 × 80% × $0.60). Discounted at a rate of 10% per annum gives a present value of $40 million (i.e. $48 million × $1 / 1.1^2$). $40 million has therefore been included within the cost of the investment.*
>
> *Since Highmoor have not recorded the contingent consideration, a liability equal to $40 million should have been recorded as at 1 October 20X2 (the date of acquisition). This liability should be unwound at a rate of 10% per annum such that at 30 September 20X3 it is recorded at $44 million (i.e. $40 million × 110%). The increase of $4 million will be charged as a finance cost against Highmoor's profits in W5.*

> **Tutorial note**
>
> *The excess of net assets acquired over consideration given (negative goodwill/bargain purchase) of $40 million will be recognised immediately in profit or loss.*

(W4) **Non-controlling interest**

	$m
NCI value at acquisition (W3)	50
NCI share of post-acquisition reserves	(7)
(20% × ($215 – 250))	
	43

(W5) **Retained earnings**

	$m
Highmoor	330
Excess of net assets acquired over consideration given	40
Unwinding of contingent consideration (W3)	(4)
Unrealised profit (W7)	(16)
Slowmoor – group share post acquisition losses 80% × 35	(28)
	322

(W6) **Elimination of loan and accrued interest**

After removing the purchase consideration of $120 million (W3) for Slowmoor, the balance of Highmoor's investments will include an unadjusted amount of $50 million as a loan to Slowmoor. The cash in transit of $9 million from Slowmoor should be applied $4 million to cancel the accrued interest receivable and the balance of $5 million to the investment (loan). When this adjustment is made the remaining investment in Slowmoor and the loan will cancel each other out.

(W7) **Software**

The carrying value of the software in Slowmoor's books is $40 million (50 less 20%). If the software had been depreciated on its original cost of $30 million it would have a book value of $24 million ($30 less $6 million depreciation at 20% per annum). Thus there is an unrealized profit on the sale of the software by Highmoor of $16 million ($40 million – $24 million).

(b) The consideration given for a business may be less than the fair value of the net assets acquired. Intuitively it does not make sense for a vendor to sell net assets for less than they are worth. This view is reflected by the IASB which is rather sceptical about the existence of what is often described as negative goodwill (bargain purchase). They say where an acquisition appears to create negative goodwill, a careful check of the value of the assets acquired and whether any liabilities have been omitted is required.

The consideration may be less than the net assets acquired for several reasons; the most obvious is that there has been a bargain purchase. This may occur through the vendor being in a poor financial position and needing to realize assets quickly, or it may be due to good negotiating skills on the part of the acquirer, or the vendor may not realize how much the assets are really worth.

A more controversial situation is where a company, in determining the amount of consideration it is willing to pay for a business, will take into account the cost of anticipated future losses and post acquisition reorganization expenditure that it believes will be required. The effect of this is that it would reduce the consideration offered/paid. As these costs cannot generally be recognized as a liability at the date of purchase, this can lead to the consideration being lower than the recognisable net assets.

In relation to the acquisition of Slowmoor the following are questionable issues:

– Highmoor may be trying to deliberately create losses at Slowmoor to avoid paying the further consideration. An example of this may be the transfer price of the software.

– The tax asset of Slowmoor may be questionable. Accounting standards are quite restrictive over the recognition of tax assets.

UK SYLLABUS FOCUS ONLY

Under FRS 10 *Goodwill and Intangible Assets*, negative goodwill is recognised as a separate item within goodwill. Negative goodwill is therefore capitalised and amortised over the life of assets to which they relate.

---

45 HIGHVELDT   *Walk in the footsteps of a top tutor*

Key answer tips

Part (a) of this question requires the three standard workings for the consolidated statement of financial position – goodwill, non-controlling interest and consolidated reserves. These should be well known to students but as the rest of the consolidated statement of financial position is not required there are more complications than in a normal statement of financial position question. Read carefully through each of the notes (i) to (vi) and think about how they will affect your figures. There are not only fair value adjustments to make but also an accounting policy adjustment with regards to the development expenditure. Note the deferred element of the consideration which should be discounted and the unwinding of the discount shown as a reduction of consolidated profits.

Leave enough time for part (b) which is 5 easy marks on the advantages to users of consolidated financial statements.

(a) (i) **Goodwill**

	$m
Parent holding (investment) at fair value:	
Cash (75% × 80m × $3.50)	210
Deferred consideration (108 × 1/1.08)	100
	310
NCI value at acquisition	83
	393
less:	
Fair value of net assets at acquisition (W2)	(296)
Goodwill	97
Impairment	(20)
Goodwill after impairment	77

(ii) **Non-controlling interest**

	$m
NCI value at acquisition (W3)	83
NCI share of post-acquisition reserves	
(25% × (348 – 296)) (W2)	13
Impairment – NCI share	(5)
($20 × 25%)	
	91

(iii) **Consolidated share premium**

	$m
Parent only	80

Consolidated revaluation reserve

	$m
Parent	45
Subsidiary – post-acquisition (75% × 4m)	3
	48

Consolidated retained earnings

	$m
Parent	350
Add: interest receivable (60m × 10%)	6
Less: unwinding of discount on deferred consideration 100 × 8%	(8)
	―――
	348
Subsidiary – group share post acquisition (ex 4 re land and buildings taken to revaluation reserve)	
75% × ((348 – 296) – 4) (W2)	36
Less: impairment of goodwill (part i) (75% × $20)	(15)
	―――
	369
	―――

Workings

(W1) **Group structure**

Highveldt

| 1 April 20X4   75%

Samson

(W2) **Net assets**

Tutorial note

A net asset working really helps.

	At acquisition $m	At reporting period end $m
Share capital	80	80
Share premium	40	40
Retained earnings	134	210
	―――	―――
	254	330
Fair value adjustments:		
Land and buildings	20	20
Brand	40	40
Revaluation	–	4
Amortisation of Brand	–	(4)
Research and development	(18)	(40)
PUP (W3)		(2)
	―――	―――
	296	348
	―――	―――

Tutorial note

The brand should be recognized in the consolidated statement of financial position even though it is not included in Samson's own statement of financial position. As the brand has been professionally valued then it can be 'reliably measured' and should be included in the consolidated statement of financial position as effectively 'purchased' by the group.

(W3) **Unrealized profit in inventory**

Profit = $6m

Still in inventory = 1/3 × $6m = $2m

(b) The objective of consolidated financial statements is to show the financial performance and position of the group as if it was a single economic entity. There is a view that, as the entity financial statements of the parent company contain the investments in subsidiaries as non-current assets, they reflect the assets of the group as a whole. The more traditional view is that entity financial statements do not provide users with sufficient information about subsidiaries for them to make a reliable assessment of the performance of the group as a whole. The following illustrates benefits of consolidated financial statements:

- they identify the nature and classification of the subsidiary's assets. For example, the investment in a subsidiary may be almost entirely in intangible assets or conversely they may be substantially land and buildings. Such a distinction is of obvious importance to users.

- the amount of the subsidiary's debt could not be assessed from the parent's entity financial statements. In effect the subsidiary's assets and liabilities are netted off when it is shown as an investment. This means group liquidity and gearing cannot be properly assessed.

- the cost of the investment does not reflect the size of a company. For example a parent company may show an investment in a subsidiary at a cost of $10 million. This may represent the purchase of a subsidiary that has $10 million of assets and no liabilities. Alternatively this could be a subsidiary that has $100 million in assets and $90 million of liabilities. Clearly the latter subsidiary would be a much larger company than the former.

- the cost of the investment may be a fair representation of its value at the date of purchase, but with the passage of time (assuming the subsidiary is profitable), its value will increase. This increase would not be reflected in the original cost, but it would be reflected in the consolidated net assets of the subsidiary (and the increase in group reserves).

- the cost of the investment might represent all of the ownership of the subsidiary or only just over half of it i.e. there would be no indication of the non-controlling interest.

To summarize, in the absence of a consolidated statement of financial position, users would have no information on the current value of a subsidiary, its size, the composition of its net assets and how much of it was owned by the group.

46   PREMIER *Walk in the footsteps of a top tutor*

Key answer tips

This question requires the preparation of both a consolidated statement of profit or loss and other comprehensive income and a statement of financial position which makes it particularly time consuming. Ensure you get the easy, basic consolidation marks by combining the parent and subsidiary results first. Remember the statement of profit or loss is for a period, so the results of the subsidiary must be time apportioned to reflect the post acquisition period but the statement of financial position is at a point in time and the subsidiary results must not be time apportioned.

Consolidated statement of profit or loss and other comprehensive income for the year ended 30 September 2010

	$000
Revenue (92,500 + (45,000 × 4/12) − 4,000 intra-group sales)	103,500
Cost of sales (W6)	(78,850)
Gross profit	24,650
Distribution costs (2,500 + (1,200 × 4/12))	(2,900)
Administrative expenses (5,500 + (2,400 × 4/12))	(6,300)
Finance costs	(100)
Profit before tax	15,350
Income tax expense (3,900 + (1,500 × 4/12))	(4,400)
Profit for the year	10,950
Other comprehensive income:	
Gain on FVTOCI investments	300
Gain on revaluation of property	500
Total other comprehensive income for the year	800
Total comprehensive income	11,750

Profit for year attributable to:	
Equity holders of the parent	10,760
Non-controlling interest ((1,300 (below) − 400 PURP + 50 reduced depreciation) × 20%)	190
	——
	10,950
	——

Total comprehensive income attributable to:	
Equity holders of the parent (10,760 + 300 + 500)	11,560
Non-controlling interest (from above)	190
	——
	11,750
	——

Sanford's profits for the year ended 30 September 2010 of $3.9 million are $2.6 million (3,900 × 8/12) pre-acquisition and $1.3 million (3,900 × 4/12) post-acquisition.

(b) **Consolidated statement of financial position as at 30 September 2010.**

	$000
Non-current assets	
Property, plant and equipment	38,250
(25,500 + 13,900 − 1,200 (FV adj) + 50 (FV adj))	
Goodwill (W3)	9,300
Investments (1,800 − 800 (consideration) + 300 (gain on FVTOCI))	1,300
	——
	48,850
Current assets (12,500 + 2,400 − 350 (intra-group) − 400 (W2)(a))	14,150
	——
	63,000
	——
Equity	
Equity shares of $1 each ((12,000 + 2,400 (W3))	14,400
Share premium (W3)	9,600
Land revaluation reserve	2,000
Other equity reserve (500 + 300 (gain on FVTOCI))	800
Retained earnings (W5)	13,060
	——
	39,860
Non-controlling interest (W4)	3,690
	——
	43,550
Non-current liabilities	
6% loan notes	3,000
Current liabilities (10,000 + 6,800 − 350 intra group balance)	16,450
	——
	63,000
	——

> **Tutorial note**
>
> *Per IFRS 9 Financial Instruments, investments classified at fair value through other comprehensive income (FVTOCI) should be taken to the statement of financial position at their fair value at the year end and the gain or loss reported in other equity. The gain or loss, must also be disclosed as other comprehensive income at the foot of the profit or loss account.*

Workings in $000

(W1) **Group structure**

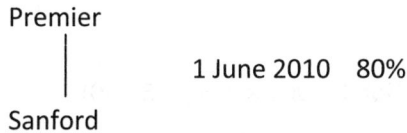

Premier

| 1 June 2010   80%

Sanford

(W2) **Net assets**

> **Tutorial note**
>
> *A net asset working really helps.*

	At acquisition	At reporting date
Share capital	5,000	5,000
Retained earnings (4,500 − (3900 × 4/12))	3,200	4,500
	8,200	9,500
Property fair value	(1,200)	(1,200)
Depreciation reduction		50
PURP (below)		(400)
	7,000	7,950

The unrealised profit (PURP) in inventory is calculated as $2 million × 25/125 = $400,000.

> **Tutorial note**
>
> *The fair value adjustment for property is a downwards fair value adjustment and therefore should be deducted from W2 and non-current assets. The reduction in depreciation should be added back in W2 and added back to non-current assets.*

(W3) Goodwill

Parent holding (investment) at fair value:	
Shares ((5,000 × 80%) × 3/5 × $5)	12,000
Loan note issue ((5,000 × 80%) / 500 × 100)	800
	———
	12,800
NCI value at acquisition ((5,000 × 20%) × $3.50)	3,500
	———
	16,300
Less:	
Fair value of net assets at acquisition (W2)	(7,000)
	———
Goodwill on acquisition	9,300
	———

> **Tutorial note**
>
> The 2.4 million shares (5,000 × 80% × 3/5) issued by Premier at $5 each would be recorded as share capital of $2.4 million and share premium of $9.6 million.

(W4) Non-controlling interest

NCI value at acquisition	3,500
NCI share of post acquisition reserves	190
(7,950 – 7,000 (W2)) × 20%	———
	3,690
	———

(W5) Consolidated retained earnings

Premier	12,300
Post acquisition in Sanford post acquisition reserves	
(7,950 – 7,000 (W2)) × 80%	760
	———
	13,060
	———

(W6) **Cost of sales**

Premier	70,500
Sanford (36,000 × 4/12)	12,000
Intra-group purchases	(4,000)
PURP in inventory	400
Reduction of depreciation charge	(50)
	78,850

	ACCA marking scheme		
			Marks
(a)	statement of comprehensive income:		
	Revenue		1½
	cost of sales		3
	distribution costs		½
	administrative expenses		½
	finance costs		½
	income tax		½
	other comprehensive income – gain on investments		½
	other comprehensive income – gain on property		½
	non-controlling interest – profit for year		1
	split of total comprehensive income		½
		Maximum	9
(b)	statement of financial position:		
	property, plant and equipment		2
	Goodwill		3½
	Investments		1
	current assets		1½
	equity shares		1
	share premium		1
	revaluation reserve		½
	other equity reserve		1
	retained earnings		1½
	non-controlling interest		1½
	6% loan notes		½
	current liabilities		1
		Maximum	16
Total			25

47   HAPSBURG   *Walk in the footsteps of a top tutor*

Key answer tips

One of the main complications in part (a) is the deferred consideration. As you are given a discount factor for three years' time this is a big hint that you must discount the deferred consideration element when calculating the goodwill. There are further added complications with the unwinding of the discount on this deferred consideration and the fair value of the plant but otherwise the adjustments required are fairly straightforward.

Note that although the question requires full goodwill to be calculated in respect of the subsidiary (Sundial), when it comes to the associate (Aspen) only the parent's share of goodwill is included in the Investment in Associate in the same way that only the parent's share of the associate's net assets are included.

Make sure that you write enough in part (b) to deserve the 5 marks available. A quick 10-line note will not be enough.

(a)   **Consolidated Statement of financial position of Hapsburg as at 31 March 20X4**

	$000	$000
Non-current assets		
Goodwill (W3)		13,000
Property, plant and equipment (41,000 + 34,800 + 5,000 – 1,250 (W2))		79,550
Investments:		
– in associate (W6)	15,000	
– ordinary (3,000 + 1,500 (fair value increase))	4,500	19,500
		112,050
Current assets		
Inventory (9,900 + 4,800 – 300 (W4))	14,400	
Trade receivables (13,600 + 8,600)	22,200	
Cash (1,200 + 3,800)	5,000	41,600
Total assets		153,650
Equity and liabilities		
Ordinary share capital (20,000 + 16,000)		36,000
Reserves:		
Share premium (8,000 + 16,000)	24,000	
Retained earnings (W5)	8,300	32,300
		68,300
Non-controlling interests (W4)		8,950

Non-current liabilities

10% Loan note (16,000 + 4,200)	20,200	
Deferred consideration (18,000 + 1,800 (W3)	19,800	
		40,000

Current liabilities:

Trade payables (16,500 + 6,900)	23,400	
Taxation (9,600 + 3,400)	13,000	36,400
Total equity and liabilities		153,650

Workings – Note: All working figures in $000.

(W1) The 80% (24m/30m shares) holding in Sundial gives Hapsburg control and means it is a subsidiary and should be consolidated. The 80% holding was acquired on 1 April 20X3 and so has been held for one year. The 30% (6m/20m shares) holding in Aspen is likely to give Hapsburg significant influence rather than control and thus it should be equity accounted. The 30% holding was acquired on 1 October 20X3 and so has been held for 6 months.

(W2) **Net assets**

> **Tutorial note**
>
> *A net asset working really helps.*

	At acquisition $000	At reporting period end $000
Share capital	30,000	30,000
Share premium	2,000	2,000
Retained earnings (8,500 – 4,500)	4,000	8,500
	36,000	40,500
Fair value – Plant (15,000 – 10,000)	5,000	5,000
– Investment (4,500 – 3,000)	1,500	1,500
Dep'n on Plant (1/4 × 5,000)		(1,250)
	42,500	45,750

(W3) Goodwill on acquisition

	$000	$000
Parent holding (investment) at fair value:		
Shares ((24m × 2/3) × $2)		32,000
Cash ((24m × $1) × 0.75)		18,000
		50,000
NCI value at acquisition		9,000
		59,000
Less:		
Fair value of net assets at acquisition		(42,500)
Goodwill on acquisition		16,500
Impairment		(3,500)
Carrying goodwill		13,000

(W4) Non-controlling interest

	$000
NCI value at acquisition	9,000
NCI share of post acquisition reserves	650
(45,750 − 42,500 × 20%)	
NCI share of impairment (20% × 3,500)	(700)
	8,950

(W5) Consolidated retained earnings

	$000
Hapsburg	10,600
Post acquisition in Sundial	
(45,750 − 42,500 (W2)) × 80%	2,600
Post acquisition in Aspen	
(6,000 × 6/12) × 30%	900
Less impairment of subsidiary (80% × 3,500)	(2,800)
Less impairment of associate	(900)
Less: unwinding of discount (W8)	(1,800)
Less: unrealised profit in inventory (W7)	(300)
	8,300

(W6) **Investment in associate**

		$000
Cost		15,000
Post acquisition profits (6,000 × 6/12) × 30%		900
		15,900
Impairment (balance)		(900)
Carrying value per question		15,000

(W7) **Unrealised profit in inventory**

	$000
Aspen (associate) selling to Hapsburg (parent)	
(2.5m × 4m -2.4m/4m) × 30% =	300
Debit Consolidated retained earnings	300
Credit Consolidated inventory	300

(W8) **Unwinding of deferred consideration**

Debit Consolidated retained earnings (W5) (18,000 × 10%)	1,800
Credit Deferred consideration	1,800

(b) In recent years many companies have increasingly conducted large parts of their business by acquiring substantial non-controlling interests in other companies. There are broadly three levels of investment. Below 20% of the equity shares of an investee would normally be classed as an ordinary financial asset investment, measured according to the IFRS 9 *Financial Instruments* rules for the particular category of asset.

A holding of above 50% normally gives control and would create subsidiary company status and consolidation is required. Between these two, in the range of over 20% up to 50%, the investment would normally be deemed to be an associate. (*Note:* The level of shareholding is not the only determining criterion.) The relevance of this level of shareholding is that it is presumed to give significant influence over the operating and financial policies of the investee (but this presumption can be rebutted). If such an investment were treated as an ordinary investment, the investing company would have the opportunity to manipulate its profit. The most obvious example of this would be by exercising influence over the size of the dividend the associated company paid. This would directly affect the reported profit of the investing company. Also, as companies tend not to distribute all of their profits as dividends, over time the cost of the investment in the statement of financial position may give very little indication of its underlying value.

Equity accounting for associated companies is an attempt to remedy these problems. In the statement of comprehensive income any dividends received from an associate are replaced by the investor's share of the associate's results. In the statement of financial position the investment is initially recorded at cost and subsequently increased by the investor's share of the retained earnings of the associate (any other gains such as the revaluation of the associate's assets would also be included in this process). This treatment means that the investor would show the same profit irrespective of the size of the dividend paid by the associate and the statement of financial position more closely reflects the worth of the investment.

The problem of off balance sheet finance relates to the fact that it is the net assets that are shown in the investor's statement of financial position. Any share of the associate's liabilities is effectively hidden because they have been offset against the associate's assets. As a simple example, say a holding company owned 100% of another company that had assets of $100 million and debt of $80 million; both the assets and the debt would appear on the consolidated statement of financial position. Whereas if this single investment was replaced by owning 50% each of two companies that had the same statements of financial position (i.e. $100 million assets and $80 million debt), then under equity accounting only $20 million ((100 – 80) × 50% × 2) of net assets would appear on the statement of financial position thus hiding the $80 million of debt. Because of this problem, it has been suggested that proportionate consolidation is a better method of accounting for associated companies, as both assets and debts would be included in the investor's statement of financial position.

IAS 28 *Investments in Associates and Joint Ventures* does not permit the use of proportionate consolidation of associates.

48 HOSTERLING *Walk in the footsteps of a top tutor*

> **Key answer tips**
>
> Parts (a) and (b) are relatively easy marks. Note that in part (a) you are asked to calculate the goodwill at acquisition so before any impairment. When preparing the statement of comprehensive income remember that you are dealing with losses in the associate.

(a) **Goodwill arising on acquisition of Sunlee – at 1 October 20X5:**

	$000
Parent holding (investment) at fair value:	
Shares ((20,000 × 80% × 3/5) × $5)	48,000
NCI value at acquisition (20% × 50,000) (W2)	10,000
Less:	
Fair value of net assets at acquisition (W2)	(50,000)
Goodwill	8,000

(b) **Carrying amount of Amber 30 September 20X6 (prior to impairment loss):**

	$000
Cost of investment:	
Cash (6,000 × $3)	18,000
6% loan notes (6,000 × $100/100)	6,000
	24,000
Less	
Post acquisition losses (20,000 × 40% × 3/12)	(2,000)
	22,000

(c)   **Hosterling Group**

Consolidated statement of comprehensive income for the year ended 30 September 20X6

	$000
Revenue (105,000 + 62,000 – 18,000 intra group)	149,000
Cost of sales (see working)	(89,000)
Gross profit	60,000
Distribution costs (4,000 + 2,000)	(6,000)
Administrative expenses (7,500 + 7,000 + 2,000 impairment)	(16,500)
Finance costs (1,200 + 900)	(2,100)
Income from associate (40% × (-20,000 × 3/12) – 500 imp	(2,500)
Profit before tax	32,900
Income tax expense (8,700 + 2,600)	(11,300)
Profit for the period	21,600
Attributable to:	
Owners of the parent	19,200
Non-controlling Interest ((13,000 – 1,000 depreciation adjustment) × 20%)	2,400
	21,600

Note: The dividend from Sunlee is eliminated on consolidation.

Working

	$000
Cost of sales	
Hosterling	68,000
Sunlee	36,500
Intra group purchases	(18,000)
Additional depreciation of plant ((35,000 – 30,000)/5 years)	1,000
Unrealized profit in inventories (7,500 × 25%/125%)	1,500
	89,000

(W2) Net assets in Sunlee

Tutorial note

A net asset working really helps.   Only the acquisition date net assets are required so that you are able to calculate goodwill for part (a).

	At acquisition $000
Share capital	20,000
Retained earnings	18,000
Fair value adjustments:	
Intellectual property (22,000 – 18,000)	4,000
Land (20,000 – 17,000)	3,000
Plant (35,000 – 30,000)	5,000
Dep'n (5,000 × 1/5)	
	50,000

49 PARENTIS *Walk in the footsteps of a top tutor*

Key answer tip

This question requires the preparation of a statement of financial position for a parent and subsidiary. The cost of investment includes the more technical aspects of fair value adjustments. A complication in this question involves the intellectual property write off and the government compensation. This adjustment is not essential to securing a pass in the question.

Consolidated statement of financial position of Parentis as at 31 March 2007

	$ million	$ million
Non-current assets		
Property, plant and equipment (640 + 340 + 40 – 2)		1,018
Intellectual property (30 – 30)		
Goodwill (W3)		130
		1,148
Current assets		
Inventory (76 + 22 – 2 PURP)	96	
Trade receivables (84 + 44 – 4 CIT – 7 intra-group)	117	
Receivable re intellectual property	10	
Bank (4 + 4 CIT)	8	231
Total assets		1,379

Equity and liabilities

Equity shares 25c each (W3)		375
Reserves:		
Share Premium (W3)	150	
Retained earnings (W5)	261	411
		786
Non-controlling interest (W4)		114
Total equity		
		900
Non-current liabilities		
10% loan notes (120 + 20)		140
Current liabilities		
Trade payables (130 + 57 − 7 intra-group)	180	
Cash consideration due 1 April 2007 (60 + 6 interest)	66	
Overdraft	25	
Taxation (45 + 23)	68	339
Total equity and liabilities		1,379

Workings (*Note:* All figures in $ million)

(W1) **Group structure**

Parentis

| 1 April 20X6   75%

Offspring

(W2) **Net assets**

> **Tutorial note**
>
> *A net asset working really helps.*

	At acquisition $000	At reporting date $000
Share capital	200	200
Retained earnings	120	140
Fair value adjustment	40	40
Fair value depreciation		(2)
Intellectual property w/off		(30)
Compensation receivable		10
PURP		(2)
	360	356

(W3) Goodwill

Parent holding (investment) at fair value:	
Share exchange ((600 × 1 / 2) × $0.75)	225
10% loan notes (see below)	120
Cash (600 × $0.11/1.1 i.e. discounted at 10%)	60
	———
	405
NCI value at acquisition (given)	125
	———
	530
Less:	
Fair value of net assets at acquisition (W2)	(360)
	———
Goodwill on acquisition	170
Impairment	(40)
	———
	130
	———

(W4) Non-controlling interest

NCI value at acquisition	125
NCI share of post acquisition reserves (25% × ($356 − 360) (W2))	(1)
NCI share of impairment (25% × $40)	(10)
	———
	114
	———

(W5) Retained earnings

Parentis	300
Unwinding of the discount (60 × 10%)	(6)
Goodwill impairment (40 × 75%)	(30)
75% Offspring post acquisition reserves (75% × ($356 − 360) (W2))	(3)
	———
	261
	———

Tutorial note

The unrealised profit in inventory (PURP) is $5m/$15m of the profit of $6 million made by Offspring. Offspring's retained earnings should be updated to reflect the unreal profit at (W2).

UK SYLLABUS FOCUS ONLY

Goodwill is to be amortised over its useful economic life. There is a rebuttable presumption that this is not more than 20 years (FRS 10). The amortisation charge would have the effect of reducing both the carrying value of the goodwill and the group retained earnings. Parentis purchased the shares in Offspring one year ago and therefore only one year's amortisation charge would be required.

50 PLATEAU *Walk in the footsteps of a top tutor*

Key answer tip

Part (a) required the preparation of a statement of financial position that is relatively straightforward. Ensure that you do not include the associate on a line-by-line basis and equity account instead. One of the complications in this question is a negative fair value adjustment. The highlighted words are key phrases that markers are looking for.

(a) **Consolidated statement of financial position of Plateau as at 30 September 2007**

	$000	$000
Assets		
Non-current assets:		
Property, plant and equipment (18,400 + 10,400 – 400) (W8)		28,400
Goodwill (W3)		6,000
Investments – associate (W6)		10,500
– other (fair value through profit or loss)		9,000
		53,900
Current assets		
Inventory (6,900 + 6,200 – 300 PURP) (W7)	12,800	
Trade receivables (3,200 + 1,500)	4,700	17,500
Total assets		71,400

Equity		
Equity shares of $1 each (10,000 + 1,500) (W3)		11,500
Reserves:		
Share premium (W3)	7,500	
Retained earnings (W5)	30,300	37,800
		49,300
Non-controlling interest (W4)		3,900
		3,900
Total equity		53,200
Non-current liabilities		
7% Loan notes (5,000 + 1,000)		6,000
Current liabilities (8,000 + 4,200)		12,200
Total equity and liabilities		71,400

Workings

(W1) Group structure

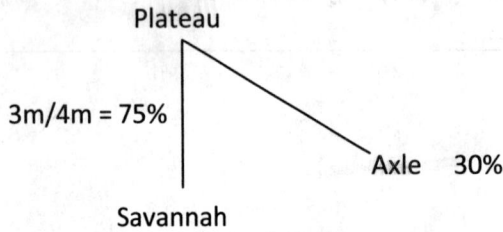

Plateau

3m/4m = 75%

Axle 30%

Savannah

Both investments occurred on 1 October 2006 and so have been held for 1 year.

(W2) Net assets of Savannah

> **Tutorial note**
>
> *A net asset working really helps.*

	At acquisition	At reporting date
	$000	$000
Share capital	4,000	4,000
Retained earnings	6,500	8,900
Fair value adjustment	(500)	–
PURP on inventory (W7)		(300)
	10,000	12,600

> **Tutorial note**
>
> The fair value adjustment does not need recording at the reporting date since Savannah had written the asset down in their books after acquisition. It should have been written down at acquisition and hence the adjustment is required at this date.

(W3) **Goodwill**

	$000
Parent holding (investment) at fair value:	
Share exchange((3,000 × ½) × $6)	9,000
Cash (3,000 × $1.25)	3,750
	———
	12,750
NCI value at acquisition (25% × 4000) × $3.25	3,250
	———
	16,000
Less:	
Fair value of net assets at acquisition (W2)	(10,000)
	———
	6,000
	———

> **Tutorial note**
>
> The share consideration given on the acquisition of Savannah has not been recorded. Therefore share capital should be increased by (3,000 × ½ × $1) $1,500 and share premium should be increased by (3,000 × ½ × $5) $7,500.

(W4) **Non-controlling interest**

NCI value at acquisition (25% × 4000) × $3.25	3,250
NCI share of post acquisition reserves ((12,600 – 10,000) × 25% (W2))	650
	———
	3,900
	———

(W5) **Consolidated reserves**

	$000
Plateau (16,000 + 9,250)	25,250
Acquisition costs to be expensed	(500)
PURP on non-current asset (W8)	(400)
Fair value through profit or loss investments (9,000 – 6,500)	2,500
Savannah (75% × (12,600 – 10,000))	1,950
Axle (W6)	1,500
	30,300

(W6) **Investment in Associate**

Cost of investment (30% × 4,000 × $7.50)	9,000
Post acquisition profits (30% × 5,000)	1,500
	10,500

(W7) **Provision for unrealised profit on inventory**

Profit on sale = 50/150 × 2,700 = 900

Profit in inventory = 1/3 × 900 = 300

(W8) **Provision for unrealised profit on non-current asset**

Book value in Savannah's books (2,500 – (2,500 × 1/5))	2,000
Book value required in group books (2,000 – (2,000 × 1/5))	1,600
Adjustment required	400

(b) IFRS 3 *Business Combinations* requires the purchase consideration for an acquired entity to be allocated to the fair value of the assets, liabilities and contingent liabilities acquired (henceforth referred to as net assets and ignoring contingent liabilities) with any residue being allocated to goodwill. This also means that those net assets will be recorded at fair value in the consolidated statement of financial position. This is entirely consistent with the way other net assets are recorded when first transacted (i.e. the initial cost of an asset is normally its fair value). The purpose of this process is that it ensures that individual assets and liabilities are correctly classified (and valued) in the consolidated statement of financial position. Whilst this may sound obvious, consider what would happen if say a property had a carrying amount of $5 million, but a fair value of $7 million at the date it was acquired. If the carrying amount rather than the fair value was used in the consolidation it would mean that tangible assets (property, plant and equipment) would be understated by $2 million and intangible assets (goodwill) would be overstated by the same amount.

(*Note:* In the consolidated statement of financial position of Plateau the opposite effect would occur as the fair value of Savannah's land is below its carrying amount at the date of acquisition.) There could also be a 'knock on' effect with incorrect depreciation charges in the years following an acquisition and incorrect calculation of any goodwill impairment. Thus the use of carrying amounts rather than fair values would not give a 'faithful representation' as required by the Framework.

The assistant's comment regarding the inconsistency of value models in the consolidated statement of financial position is a fair point, but it is really a deficiency of the historical cost concept rather than a flawed consolidation technique. Indeed the fair values of the subsidiary's net assets are the historical costs to the parent. To overcome much of the inconsistency, there would be nothing to prevent the parent company from applying the revaluation model to its property, plant and equipment.

UK SYLLABUS FOCUS ONLY

Minority interest is always measured at its share of net assets (FRS 6) similar to the proportion of net assets method allowed under IFRS rather than the fair value method that Plateau has adopted above. Minority interests should be presented separately from shareholders' funds (FRS 2).

Under UK GAAP acquisition related costs are to be added to the cost of investment in the subsidiary and therefore affect goodwill (FRS 7) whereas internationally acquisition costs are expensed immediately.

Examiner's comments

Required the preparation of a consolidated statement of financial position for a parent, subsidiary and an associate (equity accounted) followed by a short 5 mark section requiring an explanation of why fair values are used for the subsidiary's assets on its acquisition. The consolidated statement of financial position was well answered, but few candidates got to grips with the written section and many did not attempt it at all.

The main areas where candidates went wrong were:

In **part (a)**

–   most candidates incorrectly deducted a $500,000 reduction in the fair value of the land from the property, plant and equipment. This effectively double counted the fall in value as the question clearly stated that the land had already been written down in the post acquisition period. The point of the information is that the fall in the value of the land should have been treated as an adjustment between pre and post acquisition profits (affecting goodwill). Also many candidates failed to adjust for the $100,000 additional deprecation on the plant.

–   some confusion existed over the value of the associate with many simply showing it in the statement of financial position at cost rather than using equity accounting. A very small minority proportionally consolidated the associate (some even proportionately consolidated the subsidiary).

–   many candidates did correctly calculate the unrealised profit on inventory but did not always eliminate it from retained earnings.

–   surprisingly, many candidates failed to adjust share capital and premium for the share issue relating to the acquisition.

–   generally candidates scored well in the calculation of retained earnings, but the most common errors were not adjusting the subsidiary's post acquisition profit for the revaluation of land (mentioned earlier), failing to adjust for the unrealised profit in the plant and not including the gain on investments (often incorrectly shown as a revaluation reserve).

In **part (b)** the answers were quite disappointing. Generally candidates stated that the use of fair values was simply a requirement of accounting standards or discussed, sometimes at length, the definition of fair values. Most answers did not even try to address the inconsistency between the value of the subsidiary's assets and those of the parent. Better answers did refer to fair presentation of the statement of financial position and the effect that the use of fair values had on consolidated goodwill.

51   PATRONIC   *Walk in the footsteps of a top tutor*

Key answer tip

Part (a) requires the calculation of goodwill considering fair value adjustment s to both the purchase consideration and the subsidiaries net assets. Part (b) requires the preparation of a consolidated statement of comprehensive income – be careful to ensure that you pro-rate the subsidiaries results to take into account that they have only been a subsidiary for eight months. Part (c) requires you to discuss the criteria of an associate company and to identify that Acerbic is no longer an associate. The highlighted words are key phrases that markers are looking for.

(a)   **Cost of control in Sardonic:**

	$000	$000
Parent holding (investment) at fair value:		
Share exchange (18,000 × 2/3 × $5.75)		69,000
Deferred payment ((18,000 × 2.42) × $1/1.1^2$)		36,000
		———
		105,000
NCI value at acquisition		30,500
		———
		135,500
Less:		
Equity shares	24,000	
Pre-acquisition reserves:		
At 1 April 2007	69,000	
To date of acquisition (13,500 × 4/12)	4,500	
Fair value adjustments (4,100 + 2,400)	6,500	
	———	
		(104,000)
		———
		31,500
		———

Tutorial note

The acquisition of 18 million out of a total of 24 million equity shares is a 75% interest.

(b) **Patronic Group**

Consolidated statement of comprehensive income for the year ended 31 March 2008

	$000
Revenue (150,000 + (78,000 × 8/12) – (1,250 × 8 months intra group))	192,000
Cost of sales (W1)	(119,100)
Gross profit	72,900
Distribution costs (7,400 + (3,000 × 8/12))	(9,400)
Administrative expenses (12,500 + (6,000 × 8/12))	(16,500)
Finance costs (W2)	(5,000)
Impairment of goodwill	(2,000)
Share of profit from associate (6,000 × 30%)	1,800
Profit before tax	41,800
Income tax expense (10,400 + (3,600 × 8/12))	(12,800)
Profit for the year	29,000
Attributable to:	
Equity holders of the parent	27,400
Non-controlling interest (W3)	1,600
	29,000

(c) An associate is defined by IAS 28 *Investments in Associates and Joint Ventures* as an investment over which an investor has significant influence. There are several indicators of significant influence, but the most important are usually considered to be a holding of 20% or more of the voting shares and board representation. Therefore it was reasonable to assume that the investment in Acerbic (at 31 March 2008) represented an associate and was correctly accounted for under the equity accounting method.

The current position (from May 2008) is that although Patronic still owns 30% of Acerbic's shares, Acerbic has become a subsidiary of Spekulate as it has acquired 60% of Acerbic's shares. Acerbic is now under the control of Spekulate (part of the definition of being a subsidiary), therefore it is difficult to see how Patronic can now exert significant influence over Acerbic. The fact that Patronic has lost its seat on Acerbic's board seems to reinforce this point. In these circumstances the investment in Acerbic falls to be treated under IFRS 9 *Financial Instruments*. It will cease to be equity accounted from the date of loss of significant influence. Its carrying amount at that date will be its initial recognition value under IFRS 9 (stated and fair value) and thereafter it will be accounted for in accordance with IFRS 9.

Workings

(W1) **Cost of sales**

	$000	$000
Patronic		94,000
Sardonic (51,000 × 8/12)		34,000
Intra group purchases (1,250 × 8 months)		(10,000)
Additional depreciation: plant (2,400/ 4 years × 8/12)	400	
Property (per question)	200	600
Unrealised profit in inventories (3,000 × 20/120)		500
		119,100

Tutorial note:

For both sales revenues and cost of sales, only the post acquisition intra group trading should be eliminated.

(W2) **Finance costs**

	$000
Patronic per question	2,000
Unwinding interest – deferred consideration (36,000 × 10% × 8/12)	2,400
Sardonic (900 × 8/12)	600
	5,000

(W3) **Non-controlling interest**

Sardonic's post acquisition profit (13,500 × 8/12)	9,000
Less post acquisition additional depreciation (W1)	(600)
Less NCI share of impairment	(2,000)
	6,400
	× 25% = 1,600

Examiner's comments

Required the calculation of goodwill and the preparation of a consolidated statement of comprehensive income for a parent, subsidiary and an associate (equity accounted) followed by a short 4 mark section requiring an explanation of how an investment in an associate should be treated after it became a subsidiary of another company. The consolidation was generally well answered, but answers to the written section were more 'patchy'.

The main areas where candidates went wrong were:

In **part (a)** – goodwill calculation

– most candidates correctly calculated the share exchange consideration, but failed to discount (for two years) the deferred cash consideration correctly. The calculation of the pre-acquisition equity was also done quite well, but the most common mistakes were not including an apportionment (4 months) of the current year's profit as part of the pre-acquisition figure and incorrectly including post acquisition adjustments for additional depreciation and unrealised profits as pre-acquisition items. It was also common for candidates to forget to include the subsidiary's share capital in the calculation of equity.

Part (b) – consolidated statement of comprehensive income

– a surprisingly common error was not time apportioning (for 8 months) the subsidiary's results, instead a full year's results were often included. This is a fundamental error showing a lack of understanding of the principle that a subsidiary's results are only included the consolidated accounts from date it becomes a member of the group. A small minority of candidates proportionally consolidated, rather than equity accounted, the associate (some even proportionately consolidated the subsidiary), however this error is now becoming much less common.

– many candidates did not correctly eliminate the intra-group trading; either no adjustment at all or eliminating pre-acquisition trading as well.

– the unrealised profit in inventory was often calculated as a gross profit percentage, whereas the question stated it was a mark up was on cost. It was also common for this adjustment to be deducted from cost of sales rather than added.

– impairment/amortisation of goodwill was often omitted.

– the finance cost relating to the unwinding of the deferred consideration was omitted by most candidates.

– the calculation of the non-controlling interest (now called non-controlling interest) was sometimes ignored or did not take account the post acquisition additional depreciation adjustment or time apportionment.

In **part (c)** the answers were very disappointing; many not attempting it all. The question was based on how an associate, that had previously been equity accounted, would be treated in the following year when it had lost its 'significant influence' due to the associate becoming a subsidiary of another entity. Of those that did attempt this section many wasted time by reproducing (as an answer) the scenario given in the question rather than actually answering the question. Others did not think the investment should be treated any differently in the following year saying that the percentage of share ownership is all that matters (despite the loss of a seat on the board). Some candidates thought the question asked for an explanation of how the investment should be treated in the current year. The correct answer is that it should be treated as an 'ordinary investment' (no longer an associate) under IFRS 9.

ACCA marking scheme		
		Marks
(a)	Goodwill of Sardonic:	
	consideration	2
	net assets acquired calculated as:	
	equity shares	1
	pre acquisition reserves	2
	fair value adjustments	1
	Maximum	6
(b)	Statement of comprehensive income:	
	revenue	2
	cost of sales	5
	distribution costs and administrative expenses	1
	finance costs	2
	impairment of goodwill	1
	share of associate's profit	1
	income tax	1
	Non-controlling interest	2
	Maximum	15
(c)	1 mark per relevant point to	4
Total		25

52   PEDANTIC   *Walk in the footsteps of a top tutor*

Key answer tips

This question requires the preparation of a fairly straightforward consolidated statement of comprehensive income and a consolidated statement of financial position. The biggest problem for candidates is to complete the tasks in the exam time available. Ensure you pro-rate the subsidiary's results in part (a) to gain the easy marks available.

(a)   **Consolidated statement of comprehensive income for the year ended 30 September 2008**

	$000
Revenue (85,000 + (42,000 × 6/12) – 8,000 intra-group sales)	98,000
Cost of sales (w (i))	(72,000)
Gross profit	26,000
Distribution costs (2,000 + (2,000 × 6/12))	(3,000)
Administrative expenses (6,000 + (3,200 × 6/12))	(7,600)
Finance costs (300 + (400 × 6/12))	(500)
Profit before tax	14,900
Income tax expense (4,700 + (1,400 × 6/12))	(5,400)
Profit for the year	9,500

Attributable to:

Equity holders of the parent	9,300
Non-controlling interest	
(((3,000 × 6/12) – (800 URP + 200 depreciation)) × 40%)	200
	9,500

(b) **Consolidated statement of financial position as at 30 September 2008**

Assets

Non-current assets

Property, plant and equipment

(40,600 + 12,600 + 2,000 – 200 depreciation adjustment (W2))	55,000
Goodwill (W3)	4,500
	59,500
Current assets (W8)	21,400
Total assets	80,900

Equity and liabilities

Equity attributable to owners of the parent

Equity shares of $1 each (10, 000 + 1,600 (W3))	11,600
Share premium (W3)	8,000
Retained earnings (W5)	35,700
	55,300
Non-controlling interest (W4)	6,100
Total equity	61,400
Non-current liabilities	
10% loan notes (4,000 + 3,000)	7,000
Current liabilities (8,200 + 4,700 – 400 intra-group balance)	12,500
Total equity and liabilities	80,900

***Workings* (figures in brackets in $000)**

(W1) **Group structure**

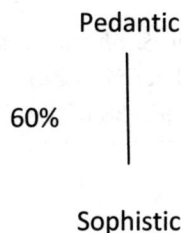

Pedantic

60%

Sophistic

Investments occurred on 1 April 2008 so has been held for 6 months.

(W2) **Net assets of Sophistic**

> **Tutorial note**
>
> A net asset working really helps.

	At acquisition	At reporting date
	$000	$000
Share capital	4,000	4,000
Retained earnings	5,000	6,500
Fair value adjustment:		
Plant	2,000	2,000
Depreciation (2,000 / 5 years) × 6 months		(200)
PURP on inventory (W6)		(800)
	11,000	11,500

(W3) **Goodwill**

	$000
Parent holding (investment) at fair value:	
Share exchange ((4,000 × 60%) × 2/3 × $6)	9,600
NCI value at acquisition (given)	5,900
	15,500
Less:	
Fair value of net assets at acquisition (W2)	(11,000)
	4,500

> **Tutorial note**
>
> The share consideration given on the acquisition of Sophistic has not been recorded. Therefore share capital should be increased by ((4,000 x60%) × 2/3 × $1) $1,600 and share premium should be increased by ((4,000 × 60%) × 2/3 × $5) $8,000.

(W4) Non-controlling interest

	$000
NCI value at acquisition	5,900
NCI share of post acquisition reserves ((11,500 – 11,000) × 40%)	200
	6,100

(W5) Consolidated reserves

	$000
Pedantic	35,400
Sophistic (60% × (11,500 – 11,000))	300
	35,700

(W6) Provision for unrealised profit on inventory

The unrealised profit (PURP) in inventory is calculated as ($8 million – $5.2 million) × 40/140 = $800,000.

(W7) Cost of sales

	$000
Pedantic	63,000
Sophistic (32,000 × 6/12)	16,000
Intra-group sales	(8,000)
PURP in inventory	800
Additional depreciation (2,000/5 years × 6/12)	200
	72,000

(W8) Current assets

	$000
Pedantic	16,000
Sophistic	6,600
PURP in inventory	(800)
Cash in transit	200
Intra-group balance	(600)
	21,400

Examiner's comments

This question required the preparation of a consolidated statement of comprehensive income and statement of financial position for a parent and a single subsidiary that had been acquired half way through the accounting period.

The question involved a share exchange, fair value adjustments and the elimination of intra-group trading and current accounts. This was generally well answered by most candidates with a number achieving full marks. There was evidence of a rote learned/mechanical approach to parts of the question which is not necessarily a bad thing, as it can increase speed and accuracy, but several candidates clearly did not understand the principle of such an approach and came unstuck with some of the more challenging adjustments. There were two areas of particularly serious errors which demonstrated a poor understanding of the principles of consolidation:

1   Failure to time apportion the results of the subsidiary to include only its post-acquisition results (many candidates included a full year's results in the consolidated statement of comprehensive income)

2   Incorrectly consolidated 60% of the subsidiary' figures (proportional consolidation). This perhaps is the most worrying of the errors.

The above are fundamental errors that display a lack of understanding of consolidation procedure and principles.

The main areas where candidates made more routine errors:

In **part (a)**, statement of comprehensive income

–   eliminating the cost of the intra-group sales from the cost of sales (the selling (transfer) price of the goods should be deducted from both sales and cost of sales)

–   incorrect calculation of the PURP in inventories

–   charging a full year's additional depreciation, when it should have been only for the post-acquisition period of six months

–   non-controlling interest in the statement of comprehensive income was often confused with the figure for the statement of financial position

–   unrealised profit on inventory and the additional depreciation as an adjustment to the parent's profit (it should have been to the subsidiaries).

Part (b), statement of financial position

–   goodwill calculation: many candidates had difficulty determining the pre-acquisition reserves; often taking 6/12 of the entire subsidiary's retained earnings (the 6/12 adjustment should been applied to the profit of the year of acquisition to obtain its pre and post acquisition split).

–   recording the new share capital and share premium created by the share exchange

–   difficulties with eliminating cash in transit and intra- group payables/receivables

–   group retained earnings were often not adjusted for the PURP in inventory and additional deprecation

53 PACEMAKER *Walk in the footsteps of a top tutor*

Key answer tips

This question requires the preparation of a three company consolidated statement of financial position and is a reasonably time pressured question. There is a strong focus on fair value adjustments to both the cost of investment and the net assets of the subsidiary company and is therefore a good practice question. Remember not to consolidate the associate company results – Vardine must be equity accounted for instead. It is worth noting the date of acquisition of the shares – Syclop's share capital was purchased 2 years ago, thus affecting the fair value depreciation and Vardine's share capital was purchased 6 months ago, thus affecting the post-acquisition profit required for the equity accounting.

Consolidated statement of financial position of Pacemaker as at 31 March 2009:

	$ million	$ million
Non-current assets		
Property, plant and equipment (520 + 280 +20 – 2)		818
Intangible		
Goodwill (W3)		23
Brand (25 – 5 (25/10 × 2 years' post acq amortisation))		20
Investments		
Investment in associate (W6)		144
Other: fair value through profit or loss (82 + 37)		119
		1,124
Current assets		
Inventory (142 + 160 – 16 PURP (W5))	286	
Trade receivables (95 + 88)	183	
Cash and bank (8 + 22)	30	499
Total assets		1,623
Equity and liabilities		
Equity attributable to the parent		
Equity shares (500 + 75 (W6))		575
Share premium (100 + 45 (W6))	145	
Retained earnings (W5)	247	392
		967
Non-controlling interest (W4)		91
Total equity		1,058
Non-current liabilities		
10% loan notes (180 + 20)		200
Current liabilities (200 + 165)		365
Total equity and liabilities		1,623

Workings (all figures in $ million)

(W1) Group structure

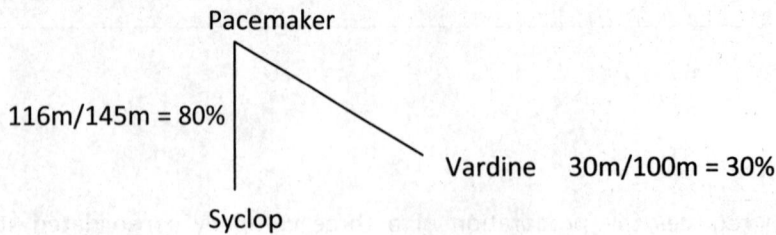

Pacemaker

116m/145m = 80%

Vardine   30m/100m = 30%

Syclop

(W2) Net assets

> **Tutorial note**
>
> *A net asset working really helps.*

	At acquisition	At reporting date
	$000	$000
Share capital	145	145
Retained earnings	120	260
Fair value adjustment:		
Property	20	20
Fair value depreciation		(2)
(20 / 20 yrs × 2 yrs)		
Brand	25	25
Fair value amortisation		(5)
FVTPL investment loss (40 – 37)		(3)
	310	440

(W3) Goodwill

Parent holding (investment) at fair value	
– Cash	210
– loan note (116/200 × $100)	58
	268
NCI value at acquisition	65
Less:	
Fair value of net assets at acquisition (W2)	(310)
Goodwill	23

(W4) **Non-controlling interest**

NCI value at acquisition	65
NCI share of post-acquisition reserves ((440 – 310) × 20% (W2))	26
	91

(W5) **Group retained earnings**

Pacemaker's retained earnings	130
Gain on investments – Pacemaker (see below)	5
Syclop's post-acquisition profits ((440 – 310) × 80% (W2))	104
Vardine's post-acquisition profits (100 – 20) × 30%	24
PURP in Inventories (56 × 40/140)	(16)
	247

Gain on the value of Pacemaker's fair value through profit or loss investments:	
Carrying amount at 31 March 2008 (345 – 210 cash – 58 loan note)	77
Carrying amount at 31 March 2009	82
Gain to profit or loss	5

(W6) **Investment in associate**

	$million
Investment at cost (75 × $1.60)	120
Share of post-acquisition profit (100 – 20) × 30%	24
	144

Tutorial note

The purchase consideration by way of a share exchange (75 million shares in Pacemaker for 30 million shares in Vardine) would be recorded as an increase in share capital of $75 million ($1 nominal value) and an increase in share premium of $45 million (75 million × $0.60).

ACCA marking scheme	
	Marks
Property, plant and equipment	2
Brand	1
Goodwill	4.5
Investment in associate	2
Other investments	1
Inventories	2
Trade receivables, cash and bank	1
Equity shares	1
Share premium	1
Retained earnings	6.5
Non-controlling interest	2
Loan notes	0.5
Current liabilities	0.5
Total	25

Examiner's comments

This question required the preparation of a consolidated statement of financial position (balance sheet) for a parent, a subsidiary (line-by-line consolidation) and an associate (equity accounted). The question required the calculation of goodwill with the consideration based on a cash payment and loan note issue (that had already been accounted for) and included some fair value adjustments. This was the best answered question demonstrating that most candidates have a sound knowledge of consolidation techniques. The main areas where candidates went wrong were:

- goodwill calculation: a failure to account for loan note element of the consideration and/or the non-controlling interest element of the goodwill (not applicable to UK stream) and incorrectly accounting for the new property by using its fair value rather than the excess of fair value over cost

- not realising the post-acquisition period was two years, many candidates only accounted for one year's additional depreciation on the new property and amortisation of the brand

- the detailed components of the consolidated retained earnings were often missed; depreciation adjustments, unrealised profit (PURP) in inventory (often calculated wrongly as well – see below), gain/loss on available-for-sale investments

- many candidates did not calculate the non-controlling interest under the revised Standard by taking the fair value at acquisition (as given) and then adjusting for post-acquisition profits/losses (not applicable to UK stream)

- the PURP was often calculated as a gross profit percentage, whereas the question stated it was a mark up was on cost. Some candidates eliminated the cost of the inventory rather than the PURP in the inventory and many incorrectly split the PURP between the parent and the subsidiary even though the parent had made the sale

- a small minority of candidates are still proportionally consolidating the associate (some even proportionally consolidated the subsidiary); others fully consolidated the associate and computed a non-controlling interest of 70%

- many candidates did not account for the effect of the share exchange on acquisition of the interest in the associate on the share capital and share premium.

54   PANDAR   *Walk in the footsteps of a top tutor*

(a)   (i)   **Goodwill in Salva at 1 April 2009:**

	$000	$000
Parent holding (investment) at fair value:		
Share exchange		
((120 million × 80%) × 3/5 × $6)		345,600
NCI value at acquisition		
(120 million × 20% × $3.20)		76,800
		———
		422,400
Equity shares	120,000	
Pre-acquisition reserves:		
At 1 October 2008	152,000	
To date of acquisition (see below)	11,500	
Fair value adjustments (5,000 + 20,000)	25,000	308,500
	———	———
Goodwill arising on acquisition		113,900
		———

Tutorial note

The interest on the 8% loan note is $2 million ($50 million × 8% × 6/12). This is included in Salva's statement of comprehensive income in the post-acquisition period. Thus Salva's profit for the year of $21 million has a split of $11.5 million pre-acquisition ((21 million + 2 million interest) × 6/12) and $9.5 million post-acquisition.

(ii)   **Carrying amount of investment in Ambra at 30 September 2009**

	$000
Cost (40 million × 40% × $2)	32,000
Share of post-acquisition losses (5,000 × 40% × 6/12)	(1,000)
Impairment charge	(3,000)
	———
	28,000
	———

(b)   **Pandar Group**

Consolidated statement of comprehensive income for the year ended 30 September 2009

	$000	$000
Revenue (210,000 + (150,000 × 6/12) – 15,000 intra-group sales)		270,000
Cost of sales (w (W1))		(162,500)
		————
Gross profit		107,500
Distribution costs (11,200 + (7,000 × 6/12))		(14,700)
Administrative expenses (18,300 + (9,000 × 6/12))		(22,800)
Investment income (W2)		1,100
Finance costs (W3)		(2,300)
Share of loss from associate (5,000 × 40% × 6/12)	(1,000)	
Impairment of investment in associate	(3,000)	(4,000)
	————	————
Profit before tax		64,800
Income tax expense (15,000 + (10,000 × 6/12))		(20,000)
		————
Profit for the year		44,800
		————
Attributable to:		
Owners of the parent		43,000
Non-controlling interest (W4)		1,800
		————
		44,800
		————

Workings (figures in brackets in $000)

(W1) **Cost of sales**

	$000
Pandar	126,000
Salva (100,000 × 6/12)	50,000
Intra-group purchases	(15,000)
Additional depreciation: plant (5,000/5 years × 6/12)	500
Unrealised profit in inventories (15,000/3 × 20%)	1,000
	————
	162,500
	————

Tutorial note

As the registration of the domain name is renewable indefinitely (at only a nominal cost) it will not be amortised.

(W2) Investment income

	$000
Per statement of comprehensive income	9,500
Intra-group interest (50,000 × 8% × 6/12)	(2,000)
Intra-group dividend (8,000 × 80%)	(6,400)
	1,100

(W3) Finance costs

	$000
Pandar	1,800
Salva post-acquisition ((3,000 – 2,000) × 6/12 + 2,000)	2,500
Intra-group interest (W2)	(2,000)
	2,300

(W4) Non-controlling interest

Salva's post-acquisition profit (see part (i) above)	9,500	
Less: post-acquisition additional depreciation (W1)	(500)	
	9,000	
	× 20%	= 1,800

ACCA marking scheme				Marks
(a)	(i)	Goodwill of Salva:		
		Consideration		2.0
		net assets acquired calculated as:		
		equity shares		1.0
		pre acquisition reserves		2.0
		fair value adjustments		1.0
			Maximum	6.0
	(ii)	Carrying value of Ambra		
		Cost		1.0
		share of post-acquisition losses		1.0
		impairment charge		1.0
			Maximum	3.0
(b)		Statement of comprehensive income:		
		Revenue		2.0
		cost of sales		4.0
		distribution costs and administrative expenses		1.0
		investment income		2.5
		finance costs		1.5
		share of associate's losses and impairment charge		1.0
		income tax		1.0
		non-controlling interests		2.0
		domain name not amortised		1.0
			Maximum	16.0
Total				25

Examiner's comments

Question 1 required calculation of consolidated goodwill (a)(i), the carrying amount of an associate (a)(ii) and the preparation of a consolidated statement of comprehensive income (b) of a parent and a single subsidiary and an associate that had been acquired half way through the accounting period. The question involved a share exchange, fair value adjustments and the elimination of intra-group trading and unrealised profits on inventory. This was generally well answered; most candidates have grasped the main principles of consolidation with only the more complex aspects posing problems. There were a very small minority of candidates that used proportional consolidation (for the associate and some even for the subsidiary) and a similar number failed to time apportion the consolidation. This gave the impression that such candidates have never practised any past questions.

The main areas where candidates made errors were:

In **part (a)** calculation of goodwill and associate:

- generally well answered (gaining 4 or 5 from 6 marks), but very few candidates correctly allowed for the interest on an 8% loan being entirely charged to the post-acquisition period (it was treated as accruing evenly throughout the period) when calculating the retained earnings at the date of acquisition. A significant number of candidates sitting International Standards based papers did not calculate the non-controlling interest at its (full) fair value (the 'new' method under IFRS 3), instead calculating it at the proportionate share of the fair value of the subsidiary's net assets.

- the calculation of the carrying amount of the associate was also very good, often gaining full marks. The main problems were not apportioning (by 6/12) the losses in the year of acquisition and not applying the 40% group holding percentage. Some treated the losses as profits.

The consolidated statement of comprehensive income (b). Again well-prepared candidates gained good marks with most understanding the general principles. The main errors were with the more complex adjustments:

- a full year's additional depreciation of the plant was charged, but it should have been only for the post-acquisition period of six months

- many candidates incorrectly amortised the domain name; its registration was renewable indefinitely at negligible cost so it should not have been amortised

- surprisingly a number of candidates incorrectly calculated the PURP on inventory by treating the gross profit of 25% as if it were a mark up on cost of 25%

- the elimination of intra-group dividend was often ignored or the full $8 million was eliminated instead

- often the trading and impairment losses of the associate were ignored in preparing the statement of comprehensive income

- the non-controlling interest was frequently ignored and where it was calculated, many forgot to adjust for the additional depreciation on the fair value of the plant.

Despite the above, this was the best answered question and many candidates gained good marks.

55 PICANT *Walk in the footsteps of a top tutor*

> **Key answer tips**
>
> Part (a) required the preparation of a statement of financial position that is relatively straightforward. Ensure that you do not include the associate on a line-by-line basis and equity account instead. One of the complications in this question is the contingent consideration. The contingent consideration should be accounted for at the acquisition date regardless of its probability providing it can be reliably measured. The fair value of the consideration has then changed at the year end. Under IFRS the change in the consideration is taken via group retained earnings and the goodwill calculation is not adjusted for. Part (b) required you to have knowledge of the reliance that may be placed on consolidated financial statements when granting credit. The highlighted words are key phrases that markers are looking for.

(a) **Consolidated statement of financial position of Picant as at 31 March 2010**

	$000	$000
Non-current assets:		
Property, plant and equipment (37,500 + 24,500 + 2,000 – 100)		63,900
Goodwill (16,000 – 3,800 (W3))		12,200
Investment in associate (W6))		13,200
		89,300
Current assets		
Inventory (10,000 + 9,000 + 1,800 GIT – 600 PURP (W7))	20,200	
Trade receivables (6,500 + 1,500 – 3,400 intra-group (W7))	4,600	24,800
Total assets		114,100
Equity and liabilities		
Equity attributable to owners of the parent		
Equity shares of $1 each		25,000
Share premium	19,800	
Retained earnings (W5))	27,500	47,300
		72,300
Non-controlling interest (W4))		8,400
Total equity		80,700
Non-current liabilities		
7% loan notes (14,500 + 2,000)		16,500
Current liabilities		
Contingent consideration	2,700	
Other current liabilities (8,300 + 7,500 – 1,600 intra-group (W7))	14,200	16,900
Total equity and liabilities		114,100

Workings (all figures in $ million)

(W1) Group structure

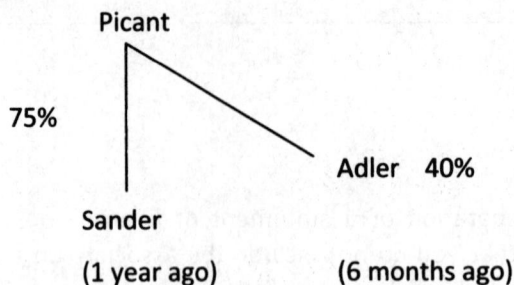

Picant

75%

Adler   40%

Sander

(1 year ago)   (6 months ago)

(W2) Net assets

> **Tutorial note**
>
> *A net asset working really helps.*

	At acquisition	At reporting date
	$000	$000
Share capital	8,000	8,000
Retained earnings	16,500	17,500
Fair value adjustment:		
Factory	2,000	2,000
Fair value depreciation		(100)
Software w/off	(500)	
	26,000	27,400

> **Tutorial note**
>
> *The effect of the software having no recoverable amount is that its write-off in the post-acquisition period should be treated as a fair value adjustment at the date of acquisition for consolidation purposes. The consequent effect is that this will increase the post-acquisition profit for consolidation purposes by $500,000.*

(W3) **Goodwill**

Parent holding (investment) at fair value	
– Share exchange (8,000 × 75% × 3/2 × $3.20)	28,800
– Contingent consideration	4,200
	———
	33,000
NCI value at acquisition (8,000 × 25% × $4.50)	9,000
	———
	42,000
Less:	
Fair value of net assets at acquisition (W2)	(26,000)
	———
Goodwill on acquisition	16,000
Impairment	(3,800)
	———
	12,200
	———

(W4) **Non-controlling interest**

NCI value at acquisition (W3)	9,000
NCI share of post-acquisition reserves	
((27,400 – 26,000) × 25% (W2))	350
NCI share of impairment (3,800 × 25%)	(950)
	———
	8,400
	———

(W5) **Group retained earnings**

Picant's retained earnings	27,200
Sanders post-acquisition profits ((27,400 – 26,000) × 75% (W2))	1,050
Group share of impairment (3,800 × 25%)	(2,850)
Adler's post-acquisition profits (6,000 × 6/12 × 40%)	1,200
PURP in inventories (1,800 × 50/150)	(600)
Gain from reduction of contingent consideration	
(4,200 – 2,700 see below)	1,500
	———
	27,500
	———

Tutorial note

The adjustment to the provision for contingent consideration due to events occurring after the acquisition is reported in income (goodwill is not recalculated).

(W6) Investment in associate

Investment at cost:

Cash consideration (5,000 × 40% × $4)	8,000
7% loan notes (5,000 × 40% × $100/50)	4,000
	12,000
Adler's post-acquisition profits (6,000 × 6/12 × 40%)	1,200
	13,200

(W7) Goods in transit and unrealised profit (PURP)

The intra-group current accounts differ by the goods-in-transit sales of $1.8 million on which Picant made a profit of $600,000 (1,800 × 50/150). Thus inventory must be increased by $1.2 million (its cost), $600,000 is eliminated from Picant's profit, $3.4 million is deducted from trade receivables and $1.6 million (3,400 − 1,800) is deducted from trade payables (other current liabilities).

(b) Although the concept behind the preparation of consolidated financial statements is to treat all the members of the group as if they were a single economic entity, it must be understood that the legal position is that each member is a separate legal entity and therefore the group itself does not exist as a separate legal entity. This focuses on a criticism of group financial statements in that they aggregate the assets and liabilities of all the members of the group. This can give the impression that all of the group's assets would be available to discharge all of the group's liabilities. This is not the case.

Applying this to the situation in the question, it would mean that any liability of Trilby to Picant would not be a liability of any other member of the Tradhat group. Thus the fact that the consolidated statement of financial position of Tradhat shows a strong position with healthy liquidity is not necessarily of any reassurance to Picant. Any decision on granting credit to Trilby must be based on Trilby's own (entity) financial statements (which Picant should obtain), not the group financial statements. The other possibility, which would take advantage of the strength of the group's statement of financial position, is that Picant could ask Tradhat if it would act as a guarantor to Trilby's (potential) liability to Picant. In this case Tradhat would be liable for the debt to Picant in the event of a default by Trilby.

UK SYLLABUS FOCUS ONLY

Under UK GAAP the contingent consideration is added to the cost of investment if, at the acquisition date, it is probable that it will become payable. Subsequent adjustments to the amount of contingent consideration are related back to the acquisition date, increasing or decreasing goodwill accordingly (FRS 7). This is different to the international treatment seen in part (a) where the contingent consideration is accounted for regardless of probability and any subsequent adjustments are not made to goodwill but to profit or loss instead.

	ACCA marking scheme		
			Marks
(a)	**Statement of financial position:**		
	property, plant and equipment		2
	goodwill		5
	investment in associate		1½
	inventory		1½
	receivables		1
	equity shares		½
	share premium		½
	retained earnings		4½
	non-controlling interest		2
	7% loan notes		½
	contingent consideration		1
	other current liabilities		1
			———
		Maximum	21
(b)	1 mark per relevant point		4
			———
Total			25
			———

Examiner's comments

This question required (in part (a)) the preparation of a consolidated statement of financial position (balance sheet) for a parent, a subsidiary and an equity accounted associate. The question specifically required the calculation of consolidated goodwill (involving contingent consideration and two fair value adjustments), intra- group adjustments and an impairment of goodwill. Part (b) was a 4 mark written section.

The **preparation of the consolidated statement of financial position** was generally well answered, but answers to the written section were very mixed.

The main errors by candidates in the consolidation were:

- goodwill calculation: using an incorrect share price for the share issue and incorrectly revising the value of the contingent consideration as a goodwill adjustment (it should be to retained earnings. Incorrectly or not adjusting for software that had no recoverable value. Also a number of candidates failed to include the non-controlling interest at its fair value with the consequential effect on goodwill [not applicable to UK-based papers].

- the adjustment to the value of the software was also often written off the value of non-currents (even though the question said it had already been written off) and rarely was it accounted for as part of the subsidiary's post acquisition profit calculation.

- the intra-group adjustments for goods-in-transit, PURP (often calculated incorrectly) and current account balances were often wrong with no clear pattern of mistakes; just about every combination of error was reported

- the profit of the associate was often not time apportioned

- the impairment of goodwill was not apportioned between the parent and non-controlling interest [not applicable to UK-based papers]

- a lot of errors/omissions made in earlier calculations were carried through to the calculation of consolidated retained earnings

- some candidates accounted for the share exchange issue (effectively double counting it) even though the question said it had already been accounted for

- some answers used proportional consolidation for the associate (some even proportionally consolidated the subsidiary); others consolidated the associate (rather than using equity accounting) – thankfully this is now only a tiny minority of candidates.

Part (b) was a short (4 marks) written section testing candidate knowledge of the legal position of a subsidiary within the context of group financial statements. The subsidiary provided a copy of the group's consolidated financial statements to support an application for credit. Answers to this were generally poor and even alarming.

The majority of candidates thought that a parent (or other subsidiaries) was responsible for the debts of its subsidiary. This is not the case. Without a guarantee from the parent, a strong group statement of financial position does not give any assurance to a potential creditor of a subsidiary. It is essential to base any extension of credit on the individual (entity) financial statements of the subsidiary itself. Another misinterpretation of this section was that some candidates thought it was a question on ratio analysis and described the ratios they would calculate to determine the liquidity position of the group.

ANALYSING AND INTERPRETING FINANCIAL STATEMENTS

56   HARDY   *Walk in the footsteps of a top tutor*

Key answer tips

This question requires an appraisal of a company that is experiencing problems as a result of a global recession, so do not be surprised when some profitability ratios produce negative results. A weak answer will simply refer to ratio movements as having increased or decreased, whereas a strong answer will refer to improvements or deteriorations in the ratios and will aim to relate it to the scenario provided by the examiner.

Note: references to 2009 and 2010 should be taken as being to the years ended 30 September 2009 and 2010 respectively.

Profitability:

Statement of profit or loss performance:

Hardy's statement of profit or loss results dramatically show the effects of the downturn in the global economy; revenues are down by 18% (6,500/36,000 × 100), gross profit has fallen by 60% and a healthy after tax profit of $3.5 million has reversed to a loss of $2.1 million. These are reflected in the profit (loss) margin ratios shown in the appendix (the 'as reported' figures for 2010). This in turn has led to a 15.2% return on equity being reversed to a negative return of 11.9%. However, a closer analysis shows that the results are not quite as bad as they seem. The downturn has directly caused several additional costs in 2010: employee severance, property impairments and losses on investments (as quantified in the appendix). These are probably all non-recurring costs and could therefore justifiably be excluded from the 2010 results to assess the company's 'underlying' performance. If this is done the results of Hardy for 2010 appear to be much better than on first sight, although still not as good as those reported for 2009. A gross margin of 27.8% in 2009 has fallen to only 23.1% (rather than the reported margin of 13.6%) and the profit for period has fallen from $3.5 million (9.7%) to only $2.3 million (7.8%). It should also be noted that as well as the fall in the value of the investments, the related investment income has also shown a sharp decline which has contributed to lower profits in 2010.

Given the economic climate in 2010 these are probably reasonably good results and may justify the Chairman's comments. It should be noted that the cost saving measures which have helped to mitigate the impact of the downturn could have some unwelcome effects should trading conditions improve; it may not be easy to re-hire employees and a lack of advertising may cause a loss of market share.

Statement of financial position:

Perhaps the most obvious aspect of the statement of financial position is the fall in value ($8.5 million) of the non-current assets, most of which is accounted for by losses of $6 million and $1.6 million respectively on the properties and investments. Ironically, because these falls are reflected in equity, this has mitigated the fall in the return of the equity (from 15.2% to 13.1% underlying) and contributed to a perhaps unexpected improvement in asset turnover from 1.6 times to 1.7 times.

Liquidity:

Despite the downturn, Hardy's liquidity ratios now seem at acceptable levels (though they should be compared to manufacturing industry norms) compared to the low ratios in 2009. The bank balance has improved by $1.1 million. This has been helped by a successful rights issue (this is in itself a sign of shareholder support and confidence in the future) raising $2 million and keeping customer's credit period under control. Some of the proceeds of the rights issue appear to have been used to reduce the bank loan which is sensible as its financing costs have increased considerably in 2010. Looking at the movement on retained earnings (6,500 − 2,100 − 3,600) it can be seen that the company paid a dividend of $800,000 during 2010. Although this is only half the dividend per share paid in 2009, it may seem unwise given the losses and the need for the rights issue. A counter view is that the payment of the dividend may be seen as a sign of confidence of a future recovery. It should also be mentioned that the worst of the costs caused by the downturn (specifically the property and investments losses) are not cash costs and have therefore not affected liquidity.

The increase in the inventory and work-in-progress holding period and the trade receivables collection period being almost unchanged appear to contradict the declining sales activity and should be investigated. Although there is insufficient information to calculate the trade payables credit period as there is no analysis of the cost of sales figures, it appears that Hardy has received extended credit which, unless it had been agreed with the suppliers, has the potential to lead to problems obtaining future supplies of goods on credit.

Gearing:

On the reported figures debt to equity shows a modest increase due to statement of profit or loss losses and the reduction of the revaluation reserve, but this has been mitigated by the repayment of part of the loan and the rights issue.

Conclusion:

Although Hardy's results have been adversely affected by the global economic situation, its underlying performance is not as bad as first impressions might suggest and supports the Chairman's comments. The company still retains a relatively strong statement of financial position and liquidity position which will help significantly should market conditions improve. Indeed the impairment of property and investments may well reverse in future. It would be a useful exercise to compare Hardy's performance during this difficult time to that of its competitors – it may well be that its 2010 results were relatively very good by comparison.

Appendix:

An important aspect of assessing the performance of Hardy for 2010 (especially in comparison with 2009) is to identify the impact that several 'one off' charges have had on the results of 2010. These charges are $1.3 million redundancy costs and a $1.5 million (6,000 – 4,500 previous surplus) property impairment, both included in cost of sales and a $1.6 million loss on the market value of investments, included in administrative expenses. Thus in calculating the 'underlying' figures for 2010 (below) the adjusted cost of sales is $22.7 million (25,500 – 1,300 – 1,500) and the administrative expenses are $3.3 million (4,900 – 1,600). These adjustments feed through to give an underlying gross profit of $6.8 million (4,000 + 1,300 + 1,500) and an underlying profit for the year of $2.3 million (– 2,100 + 1,300 + 1,500 + 1,600).

Note: it is not appropriate to revise Hardy's equity (upwards) for the one-off losses when calculating equity based underlying figures, as the losses will be a continuing part of equity (unless they reverse) even if/when future earnings recover.

	2010 underlying	as reported	2009
Gross profit % (6,800/29,500 × 100)	23.1%	13.6%	27.8%
Profit (loss) for period % (2,300/29,500 × 100)	7.8%	(7.1)%	9.7%
Return on equity (2,300/17,600 × 100)	13.1%	(11.9)%	15.2%
Net asset (taken as equity) turnover (29,500/17,600)	1.7 times	same	1.6 times
Debt to equity (4,000/17,600)	22.7%	same	21.7%
Current ratio (6,200:3,400)	1.8:1	same	1.0:1
Quick ratio (4,000:3,400)	1.2:1	same	0.6:1
Receivables collection (in days) (2,200/29,500 × 365)	27 days	same	28 days
Inventory and work-in-progress holding period (2,200/25,500 × 365)	31 days	same	27 days

Note: the figures for the calculation of the 2010 'underlying' ratios have been given; those of 2010 'as reported' and 2009 are based on equivalent figures from the summarised financial statements provided.

Alternative ratios/calculations are acceptable, for example net asset turnover could be calculated using total assets less current liabilities.

ACCA marking scheme		Marks
(a)	Comments – 1 mark per valid point, up to	15
	A good answer must consider the effects of 'one off' cost ratios – up to	10
Total		25

57   **RYTETREND**

Key answer tips

Although you are specifically asked for ratios in part (b), most of the marks can be gained through observation and analysis. As well as the statement of comprehensive income and statement of financial position, you should refer to the statement of cash flows that you prepared in part (a). This highlights a central issue: the heavy expenditure on non-current assets during the year.

(a)   **Rytetrend – Statement of cash flows for the year to 31 March 20X3**

	$000	$000
Cash flows from operating activities		
[*Note:* Figures in brackets are in $000]		
Operating profit per question		3,860
Capitalization of installation costs		
less depreciation (300 – 20%) (W1)		240
Adjustments for:		
Depreciation of non-current assets (W1)	7,410	
Loss on disposal of plant (W1)	700	
	–––––	8,110
Increase in warranty provision (500 – 150)		350
Decrease in inventory (3,270 – 2,650)		620
Decrease in receivables (1,950 – 1,100)		850
Increase in payables (3,300 – 2,260)		1,040
		–––––
Cash generated from operations		15,070
Interest paid		(400)
Income taxes paid (W2)		(910)
		–––––
Net cash from operating activities		13,700
Net cash used in investing activities		
Purchase of non-current assets (W1)		(15,550)
Cash flows from financing activities:		
Issue of ordinary shares (1,500 + 1,500)	3,000	
Issue of 6% loan note	2,000	
Repayment of 10% loan notes	(4,000)	
Ordinary dividends paid	(600)	
	–––––	
Net cash from financing activities		400
		–––––
Net decrease in cash and cash equivalents		(1,450)
Cash and cash equivalents at beginning of period		400
		–––––
Cash and cash equivalents at end of period		(1,050)
		–––––

Workings

(W1) **Non-current assets – cost**

	$000
Balance b/f	27,500
Disposal	(6,000)
Balance c/f (37,250 + 300 re installation)	(37,550)
Cost of assets acquired	(16,050)
Trade in allowance	500
Cash flow for acquisitions	(15,550)

Depreciation

Balance b/f	(10,200)
Disposal (6,000 × 20% × 4 years)	4,800
Balance c/f (12,750 + (300 × 20%))	12,810
Difference – charge for year	7,410

Disposal

Cost	6,000
Depreciation	(4,800)
Carrying value	1,200
Trade in allowance	(500)
Loss on sale	700

(W2) **Tax paid:**

Tax provision b/f	(630)
Statement of comprehensive income tax charge	(1,000)
Tax provision c/f	720
Difference – cash paid	(910)

(b) **REPORT**

Subject: The financial performance of Rytetrend for the year ended 31 March 20X3

Operating performance

(i)   Revenue up $8.3 million representing an increase of 35.3% on 20X2 figure of $23.5 million.

(ii) Costs of sales up by $6.5 million (40.6% increase on 20X2 figure of $16 million).

Overall the increase in activity has led to an increase in gross profit of $1.8 million, however the gross profit margin has eased slightly from 31.9% in 20X2 to 29.2% in 20X3. Perhaps the slight reduction in margins gave a boost to sales.

(iii) Operating expenses have increased by $840,000, an increase of 18.3% on 20X2 figure of $4.6 million but this is considerably lower than the increase in revenue.

(iv) Interest costs reduced by $40,000. It is worth noting that the composition of them has changed. It appears that Rytetrend has taken advantage of a cyclic reduction in borrowing cost and redeemed its 10% loan notes and (partly) replaced these with lower cost 6% loan notes. From the interest cost figure, this appears to have taken place half way through the year. Although borrowing costs on long-term finance have decreased, other factors have led to a substantial overdraft which has led to further interest of $200,000.

(v) The accumulated effect is an increase in profit before tax of $1 million (up 41.7% on 20X2) which is reflected by an increase in dividends of $200,000.

(vi) The company has invested heavily in acquiring new non-current assets (over $15 million – see statement of cash flows). The refurbishment of the equipment may be responsible for the increase in the company's sales and operating performance.

Analysis of financial position

(vii) Inventory and receivables have both decreased markedly. Inventory is now at 43 days (2,650/22,500 × 365) from 75 days (3,270/16,000 × 365), this may be due to new arrangements with suppliers or that the different range of equipment that Rytetrend now sells may offer less choice requiring lower inventory. Receivables are only 13 days (1,100/31,800 × 365) (from 30 days (1,950/23,500 × 365)). This low figure is probably a reflection of a retailing business.

(viii) Although payables have increased significantly, they still represent only 54 days ((3,300/22,500 × 365) based on cost of sales) which is almost the same as in 20X2 (2,260/16,000 × 365).

(ix) A very worrying factor is that the company has gone from net current assets of $2,580,000 to net current liabilities of $1,820,000. This is mainly due to a combination of the above mentioned item: decreased inventory and receivables and increased trade payables leading to a fall in cash balances of $1,450,000. That said, traditionally acceptable norms for liquidity ratios are not really appropriate to a mainly retailing business.

(x) Long-term borrowing has fallen by $2 million; this has lowered gearing from 20% (4,000/(4,000 + 15,880)) to only 9% (2,000/(2,000 + 20,680)).This is a very modest level of gearing.

The statement of cash flows

This indicates very healthy cash flows generated from operations of $15,070,000, more than sufficient to pay interest costs, taxation and dividends. The main reason why the overall cash balance has fallen is that new non-current assets (costing over $15 million) have largely been financed from operating cash flows (only $1 million net of new capital has been raised). If Rytetrend continues to generate operating cash flows in the order of the current year, its liquidity will soon get back to healthy levels.

58   BIGWOOD

> **Key answer tips**
>
> Be sure that you know the IAS 7 format for the statement of cash flows before the exam, so that you can quickly slot in the required figures to earn full marks. Part (b) tells you exactly what is required. Make sure that you refer to your statement of cash flows from part (a) as instructed.

(a)   **Bigwood – Statement of cash flows for the year to 30 September 20X4:**

Cash flows from operating activities

	$000	$000
Note: Figures in brackets are in $000		
Net profit before tax		700
Adjustments for:		
depreciation – non-current assets (W1)	3,800	
loss on disposal of fixtures (W1)	1,250	
interest expense	300	5,350
Operating profit before working capital changes		6,050
Increase in inventory (2,900 – 1,500)		(1,400)
Increase in trade receivables (100 – 50)		(50)
Increase in trade payables (3,100 – 2,150)		950
Cash generated from operations		5,550
Interest paid		(300)
Income tax paid (W2)		(480)
Net cash from operating activities		4,770
Cash flow from investing activities		
Purchase of Property, plant and equipment (W1)	(10,500)	
Disposal costs of fixtures (W1)	(50)	
Net cash used in investing activities		(10,550)
Cash flows from financing activities		
Issue of ordinary shares (2,000 + 1,000)	3,000	
Long term loans (3,000 – 1,000)	2,000	
Equity dividend paid	(600)	
Net cash from financing activities		4,400
Net decrease in cash and cash equivalents		(1,380)
Cash and cash equivalents at beginning of period		450
Cash and cash equivalents at end of period		(930)

Workings (all figures in $000)

(W1)   **Property, plant and equipment – cost**

Balance b/f	9,500
Disposal	(3,000)
Balance c/f	(17,000)
	————
Difference cash purchase	(10,500)
	————
Depreciation	
Balance b/f	(3,000)
Disposal (3,000 – 1,200)	1,800
Balance c/f	5,000
	————
Difference charge for year	3,800
	————
Disposal	
Cost	3,000
Depreciation	(1,800)
	————
Carrying value	1,200
Cost of disposal	50
	————
Total loss on disposal	(1,250)
	————

(W2)   **Income tax paid:**

Provision b/f	(450)
Statement of comprehensive income tax charge	(250)
Provision c/f	220
	————
Difference cash paid	(480)
	————

(b)   **REPORT**

Subject: The financial performance of Bigwood for the two years ended 30 September 20X4

Operating performance

Bigwood's overall performance as measured by the return on capital employed has deteriorated markedly. This ratio is effectively a composite of the company's profit margins and its asset utilization. The expansion represented by the acquisition of the five new stores has considerably increased investment in net assets. The asset turnover (a measure of asset utilization) has fallen from 3.3 times to just 2.1 times. This is a relatively large fall and is partly responsible for the deteriorating performance. However, it should be borne in mind that it often takes some time before new investment generates the same level of sales as existing capacity so it may be that the situation will improve in future years.

Of more concern in the current year is the deteriorating gross profit margin of the company's clothing sales. This has fallen from 18.6% to 9.4%. The effect of this is all the more marked because sales of clothing (in the current year) represents nearly 70% (16,000 as % of 23,000) of revenue. It should also be noted that the inventory holding period of clothing has also increased significantly from 39 days in 20X3 to 68 days in the current year. This may be a reflection of a company policy to increase inventory levels in order to attract more sales, but it may also be an indication that there is some slow-moving or obsolete inventory. The clothing industry is notoriously susceptible to fashion changes; the new designs may not have gone down well with the buying public. By contrast the profit margin on food sales has increased substantially (from 25% to 32.1%) as indeed have the sales themselves (up 75% on last year). These improvements have helped to offset the weaker performance of clothing sales.

A more detailed analysis shown by the ratios in the appendix confirms the position. The expansion has created a 35% increase in the sales floor area, but the proportionate increase in revenue is only 17.3%. Breaking this down between the two sectors shows that the clothing sector is responsible for this deterioration; an increase in capacity of 37% has led to an increase in sales of only 2.6%, whereas a more modest increase of 20% in the food floor area has led to a remarkable increase of 75% in food sales. In the current year food retailing has generated sales of $1,167,000 per square metre, whereas clothing sales per square metre has fallen from $446,000 to $333,000. When the relative profit margins of clothing and food are considered it can be seen that food retailing has been far more profitable than clothing retailing and this gap in margins has increased during the current year.

This deterioration in trading margins has continued through to net profit margins (falling from 7.1% to only 2.0%). It can be observed that operating expenses have increased considerably, but this is to be expected and is probably in line with the increase in the number of stores.

In summary, the increase in capacity has focused on clothing rather than food retailing. On reflection this seems misguided as the performance of food retailing was superior to that of clothing (in 20X3) and this has continued (even more so) during the current year.

Liquidity/solvency

The increase in the investment in new stores and the refurbishment of existing stores has been largely financed by increasing long term loans by $2 million and issuing $3 million of equity. The effect of this is an increase in gearing from 17% to 28%. Although the level of gearing is still modest, the interest cover has fallen from a very healthy 25 times to a worrying low 3.3 times. The investment has also taken its toll on the bank balance falling from $450,000 in hand to an overdraft of $930,000. This probably explains why the company has stretched its payment of accounts payable to 59 days in 20X4 from 50 days in 20X3.

The company's current liquidity position has deteriorated slightly from 0.77 : 1 to 0.71 : 1. No quick ratios have been given, nor would they be useful. Liquidity ratios are difficult to assess for retailing companies. Most of the sales generated by such companies are for cash (thus there will be few trade receivables) and normal liquidity benchmarks are not appropriate. The statement of cash flows reveals cash flows generated from operations of $5,550,000. This is a far more reliable indicator of the company's liquidity position. The $5,550,000 is more than adequate to service the tax and the dividend payments. Indeed the operating cash flows have contributed significantly to the financing of the expansion programme.

Share price and dividends

Bigwood's share price has halved from $6.00 to $3.00 during the current year. The dilution effect of the share issue at $1.50 per share (2 million shares for $3 million) would account for some of this fall (to approximately $4.20), but the further fall probably represents the market's expectations of the company's performance. It is worth noting that the company has maintained its dividends at $600,000 despite an after tax profit of only $450,000. Whilst this dividend policy cannot be maintained indefinitely (at the current level of profits), the directors may be trying to convey to the market a feeling of confidence in the future profitability of the company. It may also be a reaction designed to support the share price. It should also be noted that although the total dividend has been maintained, the dividend per share will have decreased due to the share issue during the year.

Summary

The above analysis of performance seems to give mixed messages, the company has invested heavily in new and upgraded stores, but operating performance has deteriorated and the expansion may have been miss-focused. This appears to have affected the share price adversely. Alternatively, it may be that the expansion will take a little time to bear fruit and the deterioration may be a reflection of the current state of the economy. Cash generation remains sound and if this continues, the poor current liquidity position will soon be reversed.

Appendix

The following additional ratios can be calculated:

	Clothing		Food		Overall	
Increase in sales area	(13,000/35,000)	37%	(1,000/5,000)	20%	(14,000/40,000)	35%
Increase in revenue	(400/15,600)	2.6%	(3,000/4,000)	75%	(3,400/19,600)	17.3%

	Sales per sq mtr 20X4		Sales per sq mtr 20X3	
		$000		$000
Overall	(23,000/54)	426	(19,600/40)	490
Clothing	(16,000/48)	333	(15,600/35)	446
Food	(7,000/6)	1,167	(4,000/5)	800

59   MINSTER 🔲 *Online question assistance*

🔑

Key answer tips

The question asks you to analyse the performance of the company from the statement of cash flows you have prepared and the financial statements given. There is therefore no need to calculate any ratios.

(a)   **Statement of cash flows of Minster for the Year ended 30 September 20X6:**

	$000	$000
Cash flows from operating activities		
Profit before tax		142
Adjustments for:		
Depreciation of property, plant and equipment	255	
Amortization of software (180 – 135)	45	300
		────
Investment income		(20)
Finance costs		40
		────
		462
Working capital adjustments		
Decrease in trade receivables (380 – 270)	110	
Increase in amounts due from construction contracts (80 – 55)	(25)	
Decrease in inventories (510 – 480)	30	
Decrease in trade payables (555 – 350)	(205)	(90)
	────	────
Cash generated from operations		372
Interest paid (40 – (150 × 8%) re unwinding of environmental provision)		(28)
Income taxes paid (w (ii))		(54)
		────
Net cash from operating activities		290
Cash flows from investing activities		
Purchase of – property, plant and equipment (w (i))	(410)	
– software	(180)	
– investments (150 – (15 + 125))	(10)	
Investment income received (20 – 15 gain on investments)	5	
	────	
Net cash used in investing activities		(595)

Cash flows from financing activities		
Proceeds from issue of equity shares (w (iii))	265	
Proceeds from issue of 9% loan note	120	
Dividends paid (500 × 4 × 5 cents)	(100)	
	———	
Net cash from financing activities		285
		———
Net decrease in cash and cash equivalents		(20)
Cash and cash equivalents at beginning of period (40 – 35)		(5)
		———
Cash and cash equivalents at end of period		(25)
		———

Note: Interest paid may be presented under financing activities and dividends paid may be presented under operating activities.

Workings (in $000)

(i)   Property, plant and equipment:

Carrying amount b/f	940
Non-cash environmental provision	150
Revaluation	35
Depreciation for period	(255)
Carrying amount c/f	(1,280)
	———
Difference is cash acquisitions	(410)
	———

(ii)   Taxation:

Tax provision b/f	(50)
Deferred tax b/f	(25)
Statement of comprehensive income charge	(57)
Tax provision c/f	60
Deferred tax c/f	18
	———
Difference is cash paid	(54)
	———

(iii)   Equity shares

Balance b/f	(300)
Bonus issue (1 for 4)	(75)
Balance c/f	500
	———
Difference is cash issue	125
	———
Share premium	
Balance b/f	(85)
Bonus issue (1 for 4)	75
Balance c/f	150
	———
Difference is cash issue	140
	———

Therefore the total proceeds of cash issue of shares are $265,000 (125 + 140).

(b)   **REPORT**

Subject: The financial position of Minster for the year ended 30 September 20X6

Minster shows healthy operating cash inflows of $372,000 (prior to finance costs and taxation). This is considered by many commentators as a very important figure as it is often used as the basis for estimating the company's future maintainable cash flows. Subject to (inevitable) annual expected variations and allowing for any changes in the company's structure this figure is more likely to be repeated in the future than most other figures in the statements of cash flows which are often 'one-off' cash flows such as raising loans or purchasing non-current assets. The operating cash inflow compares well with the underlying profit before tax $142,000. This is mainly due to depreciation charges of $300,000 being added back to the profit as they are a non-cash expense. The cash inflow generated from operations of $372,000 after the reduction in net working capital of $90,000 is more than sufficient to cover the company's taxation payments of $54,000, interest payments of $28,000 and the dividend of $100,000 and leaves an amount to contribute to the funding of the increase in non-current assets. It is important that these short term costs are funded from operating cash flows; it would be of serious concern if, for example, interest or income tax payments were having to be funded by loan capital or the sale of non-current assets.

There are a number of points of concern. The dividend of $100,000 gives a dividend cover of less than one (85/100 = 0.85) which means the company has distributed previous year's profits. This is not a tenable situation in the long-term. The size of the dividend has also contributed to the lower cash balances (see below). There is less investment in both inventory levels and trade receivables. This may be the result of more efficient inventory control and better collection of receivables, but it may also indicate that trading volumes may be falling. Also of note is a large reduction in trade payable balances of $205,000. This too may be indicative of lower trading (i.e. less inventory purchased on credit) or pressure from suppliers to pay earlier. Without more detailed information it is difficult to come to a conclusion in this matter.

Investing activities:

The statement of cash flows shows considerable investment in non-current assets, in particular $410,000 in property, plant and equipment. These acquisitions represent an increase of 44% of the carrying amount of the property, plant and equipment as at the beginning of the year. As there are no disposals, the increase in investment must represent an increase in capacity rather than the replacement of old assets. Assuming that this investment has been made wisely, this should bode well for the future (most analysts would prefer to see increased investment rather than contraction in operating assets). An unusual feature of the required treatment of environmental provisions is that the investment in non-current assets as portrayed by the statement of cash flows appears less than if statement of financial position figures are used. The statement of financial position at 30 September 20X6 includes $150,000 of non-current assets (the discounted cost of the environmental provision), which does not appear in the cash flow figures as it is not a cash 'cost'. A further consequence is that the 'unwinding' of the discounting of the provision causes a financing expense in the statement of comprehensive income which is not matched in the statement of cash flows as the unwinding is not a cash flow. Many commentators have criticized the required treatment of environmental provisions because they cause financing expenses which are not (immediate) cash costs and no 'loans' have been taken out. Viewed in this light, it may be that the information in the statement of cash flows is more useful than that in the statement of comprehensive income and statement of financial position.

Financing activities:

The increase in investing activities (before investment income) of $600,000 has been largely funded by an issue of shares at $265,000 and raising a 9% $120,000 loan note. This indicates that the company's shareholders appear reasonably pleased with the company's past performance (or they would not be very willing to purchase further shares). The interest rate of the loan at 9% seems quite high, and virtually equal to the company's overall return on capital employed of 9.1% (162/(1,660 + 120)). Provided current profit levels are maintained, it should not reduce overall returns to shareholders.

Cash position:

The overall effect of the year's cash flows has worsened the company's cash position by an increased net cash liability of $20,000. Although the company's short term borrowings have reduced by $15,000, the cash at bank of $35,000 at the beginning of the year has now gone. In comparison to the cash generation ability of the company and considering its large investment in non-current assets, this $20,000 is a relatively small amount and should be relieved by operating cash inflows in the near future.

Summary

The above analysis shows that Minster has invested substantially in new non-current assets suggesting expansion. To finance this, the company appears to have no difficulty in attracting further long-term funding. At the same time there are indications of reduced inventories, trade receivables and payables which may suggest the opposite i.e. contraction. It may be that the new investment is a change in the nature of the company's activities (e.g. mining) which has different working capital characteristics. The company has good operating cash flow generation and the slight deterioration in short term net cash balance should only be temporary.

Yours ………………….

60 PENDANT

Key answer tips

(a) You are given two statements of financial position but no statement of comprehensive income. You must therefore reconstruct the statement of comprehensive income from the information you are given, in order to derive the first figure in the statement of cash flows, the profit for the year.

(b) Don't calculate any ratios, as told. Just identify the important features of the statement of cash flows you have produced in part (a)

(a) **Statement of cash flows of Pendant for the year to 31 March 20X1**

	$000	$000
Cash flows from operating activities		
Operating profit (profit before interest and tax (W1))		176
Adjustments for:		
Depreciation – leasehold buildings	20	
– 'purchased' plant (W3)	193	
– leased plant (140 – 30)	110	323
Profit of disposal of – freehold (800 – 580)	(220)	
– plant (from question)	(18)	(238)
Operating profit before working capital changes		261
Decrease in inventory (540 – 490)		50
Increase in trade receivables (787 – 584)		(203)
Increase in trade payables (663 – 602)		61
Cash generated from operations		169
Interest paid (35 + 10) (W1)		(45)
Income taxes paid (W2)		(321)
Net cash used in operating activities		(197)
Cash flows from investing activities		
Purchase of property, plant and equipment (W4)	(630)	
Proceeds from the sale of property, plant and equipment (W4)	875	
Software development (300 – 100)	(200)	
Interest received (from question)	15	
Net cash from investing activities		60
Cash flows from financing activities		
Proceeds from issue of equity shares (100 + 70)	170	
Payments of finance lease liabilities (W5)	(230)	
Sale of government securities (180 – 30 + 27 profit)	177	
Dividends paid	(150)	
Net cash used in financing		(33)
Net decrease in cash and cash equivalents		(170)
Cash and cash equivalents b/f		125
Cash and cash equivalents c/f		(45)

Workings

(W1) In the absence of a statement of comprehensive income the figure for the operating profit before interest and tax has to be derived from the statements of financial position plus the information given in the notes. The basic technique is to start with the change in the retained earnings, which would equal the retained profit or loss for the year, and work back to the profit before interest and tax. In this case there is a decrease in retained earnings indicating a small retained loss for the period.

	$000
Decrease in retained earnings (1,084 – 1,092)	(8)
Dividends paid	150
Income taxes (from question)	31
Interest – payable on finance lease (from question)	35
– bank overdraft (from question)	10
– receivable (from question)	(15)
Profit on sale of Government securities (from question)	(27)
Profit before interest and income tax	176

(W2) **Income tax**

Tax provision b/f	(213)
Deferred tax b/f	(172)
Statement of comprehensive income charge (from question)	(31)
Tax provision c/f	83
Deferred tax c/f	12
Difference is cash paid	(321)

(W3) **'Purchased' plant**

	$000	$000
Cost b/f		620
Disposals		(200)
Balance c/f		(550)
Difference is cash purchases		(130)
Cost of disposal		200
Proceeds		(75)
Profit on disposal		18
Difference is accumulated depreciation on disposal		143
Depreciation b/f		200
Less – disposal (above)		(143)
Depreciation c/f		(250)
Depreciation charge for year		(193)

(W4) **Capital expenditure**

Purchase of	– leasehold		(500)
	– plant (W3)		(130)
			(630)
Sale of	– freehold	800	
	– plant	75	875

(W5) **Lease obligation**

Balances b/f (30 + 60)	(90)
Additions (650 – 150)	(500)
Balances c/f (70 + 290)	360
Difference – capital repayment for $265,000 – $35,000 interest)	(230)

(b) From the information in the question and the above statement of cash flows, the following observations can be made:

(i) The (derived) operating profit of $176,000 is much the same as the cash generated from operations of $169,000. A closer inspection of the figures reveals a more worrying picture. The operating profit has been boosted by some non-recurring items: a large profit of $220,000 on the sale of the company's freehold and a profit of $18,000 on the sale of some plant. Without these items the operating profit of $176,000 would have been an operating loss of $62,000.

Overall the company's profitability should cause concern over the future prospects of the company.

(ii) Despite there being positive cash flows from operations of $169,000, this figure is inadequate for the continued liquidity of the company. It is woefully insufficient to pay net interest costs of $30,000, a tax bill of $321,000 and the dividends to shareholders of $150,000. If the company had not sold its freehold for $800,000 and some investments for $177,000 its liquidity and solvency position would be very serious. Even with these sales the company's bank account has gone from a healthy balance of $125,000 to an overdraft of $45,000.

(iii) Other factors that may also be an indication of cash flow difficulties are a move towards leasing rather than purchasing plant, a sizeable reduction in inventory levels (this may be welcomed provided it does not jeopardize future sales) and an increase in the level of trade payables.

In summary Pendant seems to have undertaken a number of measures that have improved both the current year's profit and cash flows, but most of these are unsustainable and do not bode well for the future.

61   CHARMER

> **Key answer tips**
>
> Read the question carefully. You may find it helpful to tick off items of information as you deal with them. Set out your workings clearly and cross reference them to your main answer.

Charmer statement of cash flows for the year to 30 September 20X1

Note: Figures in brackets are in $000

	$000	$000
Cash flows from operating activities		
Net profit before interest and tax (3,198 – 1,479)		1,719
Adjustments for:		
Depreciation – buildings (W1)	80	
– plant (W1)	276	
Loss on disposal of plant (W1)	86	442
Amortization of government grants (W2)		(125)
Negligence claim previously provided		(120)
Operating profit before working capital changes		1,916
Increase in inventories (1,046 – 785)		(261)
Increase in accounts receivable (935 – 824)		(111)
Decrease in accounts payable (760 – 644)		(116)
Cash generated from operations		1,428
Interest paid (260 + 25 – 10)		(245)
Income tax paid (W4)		(368)
Dividends paid		(180)
Net cash from operating activities		635
Cash flows from investing activities		
Purchase of land and buildings (W1)	(50)	
Purchase of plant (W1)	(848)	
Purchase of non-current investments	(690)	
Purchase of treasury bills (120 – 50)	(70)	
Proceeds of sale of plant (W1)	170	
Receipt of government grant (W2)	175	
Investment income	120	
Net cash used in investing activities		(1,193)
Cash flows from financing activities		
Issue of ordinary shares (W3)		300
Net decrease in cash and cash equivalents		(258)
Cash and cash equivalents b/f		122
Cash and cash equivalents at the end of the period		(136)

Workings

(W1) **Non-current assets**

	$000
Land and buildings – cost/valuation	
Balance b/f	1,800
Revaluation surplus	150
Balance c/f	(2,000)
Difference cash purchase	(50)

Plant – cost	
Balance b/f	1,220
Disposal	(500)
Balance c/f	(1,568)
Difference cash purchase	(848)

Depreciation of non-current assets:	
Building (760 – 680)	80
Plant (464 – (432 – 244))	276

The plant had a carrying value of $256,000 at the date of its disposal (500 cost – 244 depreciation). As there was a loss on sale of $86,000 (given in question), the sale proceeds must have been $170,000 (i.e. 256 – 86).

(W2) **Government grant**

	$000
Balances b/f – current	(125)
– non-current	(200)
Amortization credited to cost of sales	125
Balances c/f – current	100
– non-current	275
Difference cash receipt	175

(W3) **Share capital and convertible loan stock**

A reconciliation of share capital, share premium and the revaluation reserve shows the shares issued for cash:

	Share capital $000	Share premium $000	Revaluation reserve $000
Opening balance	(1,000)	(160)	(40)
Revaluation of land	Nil	Nil	(150)
Bonus issue 1 for 10	(100)	100	Nil
Conversion of loan stock (see below)	(100)	(300)	Nil
Closing balance	1,400	460	190
Difference issued for cash	200	100	Nil

The 10% convertible loan stock had a carrying value of $400,000 at the date of conversion to equity shares. This would be taken as the consideration for the shares issued which would be 100,000 $1 shares (i.e. 400,000/100 × 25). This would increase issued share capital by $100,000 and share premium by $300,000.

(W4) **Income tax**

	$000
Tax provision b/f	(367)
Deferred tax b/f	(400)
Statement of comprehensive income tax charge	(520)
Tax provision c/f	480
Deferred tax c/f	439
Difference cash paid	(368)

62 CASINO

Key answer tips

Part (a) is a standard, although quite long, statement of cash flows question. Note that the starting point is an operating loss which then becomes a net cash outflow from operating activities. Take care when calculating the tax cash flow as you will need to include the opening and closing deferred tax balances as well as the balances for current tax.

(a) Statement of cash flows of Casino for the Year to 31 March 20X5:

	$m	$m
Cash flows from operating activities		
Operating loss		(32)
Adjustments for:		
Depreciation – buildings (W1)	12	
– plant (W2)	81	
– intangibles (510 – 400)	110	
Loss on disposal of plant (from question)	12	215
Operating profit before working capital changes		183
Decrease in inventory (420 – 350)		70
Increase in trade receivables (808 – 372)		(436)
Increase in trade payables (530 – 515)		15
Cash generated from operations		(168)
Interest paid		(18)
Income tax paid (W3)		(81)
Net cash used in operating activities		(267)
Cash flows from investing activities		
Purchase of – land and buildings (W1)	(110)	
– plant (W2)	(60)	
Sale of plant (W2)	15	
Interest received (12 – 5 + 3)	10	
Net cash used in investing activities		(145)

Cash flows from financing activities

Issue of ordinary shares (100 + 60)	160	
Issue of 8% variable rate loan	160	
Repayments of 12% loan (150 + 6 penalty)	(156)	
Dividends paid	(25)	
	———	
Net cash from financing activities		139
		———
Net decrease in cash and cash equivalents		(273)
Cash and cash equivalents at beginning of period (120 + 75)		195
		———
Cash and cash equivalents at end of period (125 – (32 + 15))		(78)
		———

Interest and dividends received and paid may be shown as operating cash flows or as investing or financing activities as appropriate.

Workings (in $ million)

(W1) **Land and buildings**

Carrying value b/f	420
Revaluation gains	70
Depreciation for year (balance after revaluation)	(12)
Carrying value c/f	(588)
	———
Difference is cash purchases	(110)
	———

(W2) **Plant:**

Cost b/f	445
Additions from question	60
Balance c/f	(440)
	———
Difference is cost of disposal	65
Loss on disposal	(12)
Proceeds	(15)
	———
Difference accumulated depreciation of plant disposed of	38
	———
Depreciation b/f	105
Less – disposal (above)	(38)
Depreciation c/f	(148)
	———
Charge for year	(81)
	———

(W3) **Taxation:**

Tax provision b/f	(110)
Deferred tax b/f	(75)
Statement of comprehensive income net charge	(1)
Tax provision c/f	15
Deferred tax c/f	90
	———
Difference is cash paid	(81)
	———

(W4) **Revaluation reserve:**

Balance b/f	45
Revaluation gains	70
Transfer to retained earnings	(3)
Balance c/f	112

(W5) **Retained earnings:**

Balance b/f	1,165
Loss for period	(45)
Dividends paid	(25)
Transfer from revaluation reserve	3
Balance c/f	1,098

(b) The accruals/matching concept applied in preparing a statement of comprehensive income has the effect of smoothing cash flows for reporting purposes. This practice arose because interpreting 'raw' cash flows can be very difficult and the accruals process has the advantage of helping users to understand the underlying performance of a company. For example if an item of plant with an estimated life of five years is purchased for $100,000, then in the statement of cash flows for the five year period there would be an outflow in year 1 of the full $100,000 and no further outflows for the next four years. Contrast this with the statement of comprehensive income where by applying the accruals principle, depreciation of the plant would give a charge of $20,000 per annum (assuming straight-line depreciation). Many would see this example as an advantage of a statement of comprehensive income, but it is important to realize that profit is affected by many items requiring judgements. This has led to accusations of profit manipulation or creative accounting, hence the disillusionment of the usefulness of the statement of comprehensive income.

Another example of the difficulty in interpreting cash flows is that counter-intuitively a decrease in overall cash flows is not always a bad thing (it may represent an investment in increasing capacity which would bode well for the future), nor is an increase in cash flows necessarily a good thing (this may be from the sale of non-current assets because of the need to raise cash urgently).

The advantages of cash flows are:

–   it is difficult to manipulate cash flows, they are real and possess the characteristic of objectivity (as opposed to profits affected by judgements).

–   cash flows are an easy concept for users to understand, indeed many users misinterpret statement of comprehensive income items as being cash flows.

–   cash flows help to assess a company's liquidity, solvency and financial adaptability. Healthy liquidity is vital to a company's going concern.

–   many business investment decisions and company valuations are based on projected cash flows.

–   the 'quality' of a company's operating profit is said to be confirmed by closely correlated cash flows. Some analysts take the view that if a company shows a healthy operating profit, but has low or negative operating cash flows, there is a suspicion of profit manipulation or creative accounting.

63 **TABBA** *Walk in the footsteps of a top tutor*

> **Key answer tips**
>
> The statement of cash flows has the usual standard calculations but take care with the government grant and finance leases which both have balances in both current and non-current liabilities. Part (b) requires an analysis of the company based on the information revealed in the statement of cash flows rather than by standard ratio analysis. The highlighted words are key phrases that markers are looking for.

(a) **Statement of cash flows of Tabba for the year ended 30 September 20X5:**

Cash flows from operating activities	$000	$000
Profit before tax	50	
Adjustments for:		
Depreciation (W1)	2,200	
Amortization of government grant (W3)	(250)	
Profit on sale of factory (W1)	(4,600)	
Increase in insurance claim provision (1,500 – 1,200)	(300)	
Interest receivable	(40)	
Interest expense	260	
	(2,680)	
Working capital adjustments:		
Increase in inventories (2,550 – 1,850)	(700)	
Increase in trade receivables (3,100 – 2,600)	(500)	
Increase in trade payables (4,050 – 2,950)	1,100	
Cash outflow from operations	(2,780)	
Interest paid	(260)	
Income taxes paid (W4)	(1,350)	
Net cash outflow used in operating activities		(4,390)
Cash flows from investing activities		
Sale of factory	12,000	
Purchase of non-current assets (W1)	(2,900)	
Receipt of government grant (from question)	950	
Interest received	40	

Net cash from investing activities		10,090
Cash flows from financing activities		
Issue of 6% loan notes	800	
Redemption of 10% loan notes	(4,000)	
Repayment of finance leases (W2)	(1,100)	
	———	
Net cash used in financing activities		(4,300)
		———
Net increase in cash and cash equivalents		1,400
Cash and cash equivalents at beginning of period		(550)
		———
Cash and cash equivalents at end of period		850
		———

Note: Interest paid may also be presented as a financing activity and interest received as an operating cash flow.

Workings ($000)

(W1) **Non-current assets:**

Cost/valuation b/f	20,200
New finance leases (from question)	1,500
Disposals	(8,600)
Acquisitions – balancing figure	2,900
	———
Cost/valuation c/f	16,000
	———
Depreciation b/f	4,400
Disposal	(1,200)
Depreciation c/f	(5,400)
	———
Charge for year – balancing figure	(2,200)
	———
Sale of factory:	
Carrying value	7,400
Proceeds (from question)	(12,000)
	———
Profit on sale	(4,600)
	———

(W2) **Finance lease obligations:**

Balance b/f	– current	800
	– over 1 year	1,700
New leases (from question)		1,500
Balance c/f	– current	(900)
	– over 1 year	(2,000)
		———
Cash repayments – balancing figure		1,100
		———

(W3) Government grant:

Balance b/f	– current	400
	– over 1 year	900
Grants received in year (from question)		950
Balance c/f	– current	(600)
	– over 1 year	(1,400)
Difference – amortization credited to statement of comprehensive income		250

(W4) Taxation:

Current provision b/f	1,200
Deferred tax b/f	500
Tax credit in statement of comprehensive income	(50)
Current provision c/f	(100)
Deferred tax c/f	(200)
Tax paid – balancing figure	1,350

(W5) Reconciliation of retained earnings

Balance b/f	850
Transfer from revaluation reserve	1,600
Profit for period	100
Balance c/f	2,550

(b) Consideration of the statement of cash flows reveals some important information in assessing the change in the financial position of Tabba in the year ended 30 September 20X5. There is a huge net cash outflow from operating activities of $4,390,000 despite Tabba reporting a modest operating profit of $270,000. More detailed analysis of this difference reveals some worrying concerns for the future. Many companies experience higher operating cash flows than the underlying operating profit mainly due to depreciation charges being added back to profits to arrive at the cash flows. This is certainly true in Tabba's case, where operating profits have been 'improved' by $2.2 million during the year in terms of the underlying cash flows.

However, the major reconciling difference is the profit on the sale of Tabba's factory of $4.6 million. This amount has been credited in the statement of comprehensive income and has dramatically distorted the operating profit. If the sale and leaseback of the factory had not taken place, Tabba's operating profits would be in a sorry state showing losses of $4.33 million (4,600 – 270 ignoring any possible tax effects). When Tabba publishes its financial statements this profit will almost certainly require separate disclosure which should make the effects of the transaction more transparent to the users of the financial statements. A further indication of poor operating profits is that they have been boosted by $300,000 due to an increase in the insurance claim provision (again this is not a cash flow) and $250,000 amortization of government grants.

Many commentators believe that the net cash flow from operating activities is the most important figure in the statement of cash flows. This is because it is a measure of expected or maintainable future cash flows. In Tabba's case this highlights a very important point; although Tabba has increased its cash position during the year by $1.4 million, $12 million has come from the sale of its factory. Clearly this is a one off transaction that cannot be repeated in future years. If the drain on the operating cash flows continues at the current rates, the company will not survive for very long.

The tax position is worthy of comment. There is a small tax credit in the statement of comprehensive income, whereas the statement of cash flows shows that tax of $1.35 million has been paid during the year. This payment of tax is on what must have been a substantial profit for the previous year. This seems to confirm the deteriorating position of the company.

Another relevant point is that there has been a very small increase in working capital of $100,000 (700 + 500 − 1,100). However, underlying this is the fact that both inventories and trade receivables are showing substantial increases (despite the profit deterioration), which may indicate the presence of bad debts or obsolete inventories, and trade payables have also increased substantially (by $1.1 million) which may be a symptom of liquidity problems prior to the sale of the factory.

On the positive side there has been substantial investment in non-current assets (after stripping out the sale of the factory), but even this is partly due to leasing assets of $1.5 million (companies often lease assets when they do not have the resources to purchase them outright) and finance from a government grant of $950,000.

The company appears to have taken advantage of the proceeds from the sale of the factory to redeem the expensive 10% $4 million loan note (this has partly been replaced by a less expensive 6% $800,000 loan note).

In conclusion the statement of cash flows reveals some interesting and worrying issues that may indicate a bleak future for Tabba and serves as an illustration of the importance of a statement of cash flows to the users of financial statements.

64   PINTO *Walk in the footsteps of a top tutor*

Key answer tip

Part (a) – Many easy marks to gain from the statement of cash flow. Set up the proforma and build up the cash flow ticking off from the face of the question every time a figure is used.   Get the easy marks first such as movement in working capital, share capital and loans. The loan penalty is an additional cost incurred in repaying the loan notes early. Part (b) specifically asks for the statement of cash flow to be analysed. The examiner specifically stated that ratio calculations will not be awarded any marks so do not waste time preparing such calculations. Ensure that you comment on the overall movement in cash and the sources and uses of cash during the year. The highlighted words are key phrases that markers are looking for.

(a) **Statement of cash flows of Pinto for the Year to 31 March 2008:**

	$000	$000
Cash flows from operating activities		
Profit before tax		440
Adjustments for:		
Depreciation of property, plant and equipment	280	
Loss on sale of property, plant and equipment	90	370
Increase in warranty provision (200 – 100)		100
Investment income		(60)
Finance costs		50
Redemption penalty costs included in administrative expenses		20
		920
Working capital adjustments		
Increase in inventories (1,210 – 810)	(400)	
Decrease in trade receivables (540 – 480)	60	
Increase in trade payables (1,410 – 1,050)	360	20
Cash generated from operations		940
Finance costs paid		(50)
Income tax refund (w (ii))		60
Net cash from operating activities		950
Cash flows from investing activities		
Purchase of property, plant and equipment (w (i))	(1,440)	
Sale of property, plant and equipment (240 – 90)	150	
Investment income received (60 – 20 gain on investment property)	40	
Net cash used in investing activities		(1,250)
Cash flows from financing activities		
Proceeds from issue of equity shares (400 + 600)	1,000	
Redemption of loan notes (400 plus 20 penalty)	(420)	
Dividends paid (1,000 × 5 × 3 cents)	(150)	
Net cash from financing activities		430
Net increase in cash and cash equivalents		130
Cash and cash equivalents at beginning of period		(120)
Cash and cash equivalents at end of period		10

Note: Investment income received and dividends paid may alternatively be shown in operating activities.

Workings **(in $000)**

(i)   Property, plant and equipment:

carrying amount b/f	1,860
revaluation	100
depreciation for period	(280)
disposal	(240)
carrying amount c/f	(2,880)
difference is cash acquisitions	(1,440)

(ii)   Income tax:

tax asset b/f	50
deferred tax b/f	(30)
statement of comprehensive income charge	(160)
tax provision c/f	150
deferred tax c/f	50
difference is cash received	60

(b)   Comments on the cash management of Pinto

Operating cash flows:

Pinto's operating cash inflows at $940,000 (prior to investment income, finance costs and taxation) are considerably higher than the equivalent profit before investment income, finance costs and tax of $120,000. This shows a satisfactory cash generating ability and is more than sufficient to cover finance costs, taxation (see later) and dividends. The major reasons for the cash flows being higher than the operating profit are due to the (non-cash) increases in the depreciation and warranty provisions. Working capital changes are relatively neutral; a large increase in inventory appears to be being financed by a substantial increase in trade payables and a modest reduction in trade receivables. The reduction in trade receivables is perhaps surprising as other indicators point to an increase in operating capacity which has not been matched with an increase in trade receivables. This could be indicative of good control over the cash management of the trade receivables (or a disappointing sales performance).

An unusual feature of the cash flow is that Pinto has received a tax refund of $60,000 during the current year. This would indicate that in the previous year Pinto was making losses (hence obtaining tax relief). Whilst the current year's profit performance is an obvious improvement, it should be noted that next year's cash flows are likely to suffer a tax payment (estimated at $150,000 in current liabilities at 31 March 2008) as a consequence. In any forward planning, Pinto should be aware that the tax reversal position will create an estimated total incremental outflow of $210,000 in the next period.

Investing activities:

There has been a dramatic investment/increase in property, plant and equipment. The carrying value at 31 March 2008 is substantially higher than a year earlier (admittedly $100,000 is due to revaluation rather than a purchase). It is difficult to be sure whether this represents an increase in operating capacity or is the replacement of the plant disposed of. (The voluntary disclosure encouraged by IAS 7 *Statement of cash flows* would help to assess this issue more accurately). However, judging by the level of the increase and the (apparent) overall improvement in profit position, it seems likely that there has been a successful increase in capacity. It is not unusual for there to be a time lag before increased investment reaches its full beneficial effect and in this context it could be speculated that the investment occurred early in the accounting year (because its effect is already making an impact) and that future periods may show even greater improvements.

The investment property is showing a good return which is composed of rental income (presumably) of $40,000 and a valuation gain of $20,000.

Financing activities:

It would appear that Pinto's financial structure has changed during the year. Debt of $400,000 has been redeemed (for $420,000) and there has been a share issue raising $1 million. The company is now nil geared compared to modest gearing at the end of the previous year. The share issue has covered the cost of redemption and contributed to the investment in property, plant and equipment. The remainder of the finance for the property, plant and equipment has come from the very healthy operating cash flows. If ROCE is higher than the finance cost of the loan note at 6% (nominal) it may call into question the wisdom of the early redemption especially given the penalty cost (which has been classified within financing activities) of the redemption.

Cash position:

The overall effect of the year's cash flows is that they have improved the company's cash position dramatically. A sizeable overdraft of $120,000, which may have been a consequence of the (likely) losses in the previous year, has been reversed to a modest bank balance of $10,000 even after the payment of a $150,000 dividend.

Summary

The above analysis indicates that Pinto has invested substantially in renewing and/or increasing its property, plant and equipment. This has been financed largely by operating cash flows, and appears to have brought a dramatic turnaround in the company's fortunes. All the indications are that the future financial position and performance will continue to improve.

Examiner's comments

Part (a) required the preparation of a statement of cash flow followed by an interpretation of the company's cash flow management. Cash flows are generally a popular question and this one proved no exception with many candidates scoring well. A significant number of candidates had very little idea of which item should be included in which section of the statement (poor format knowledge).

A number of candidates had difficulty with the fact that the tax cash flow was a refund rather than the usual payment and the revaluation of a property was often not taken into account when calculating the cash outflow on non-current assets.

Weaker answers did not seem to know the difference between cash and non-cashflows, for example reserve movements, provisions (for a warranties) and the loss on the disposal of plant were treated as cash flows. Other common errors included getting the cash movements the wrong way round and incorrectly calculating the dividend as $30,000 instead of $150,000 by not realising the shares were 20 cents each.

Part (b), the interpretive part of the question, often lacked depth by failing to draw valid conclusions from correctly calculated figures and not really making any attempt to analyse/interpret the statement of cash flow. Many candidates calculated and commented on ratios, even though the question specifically gave instructions not to calculate ratios and that no marks would be awarded for them. This led to discussion of many aspects of performance such as return on capital employed, asset utilisation and profit margins that are not part of cash management which was the topic of the question that was asked, thus illustrating the dangers of 'question spotting'. Many important issues were not mentioned at all such as the good operating cash flow generating capacity of the company, the effects of a huge investment in non-current assets, the changes in the capital structure due to issuing new shares and redeeming a loan. Hardly anyone mentioned that the company had benefited from a tax refund of $60,000 (implying losses in the previous year) and that a tax payment estimated at $160,000 would be expected next year.

Very weak answers simply described the figures in the statement of cash flow such as inventories have increased by $400,000 or finance cost incurred were $50,000 – this is not interpretation.

ACCA marking scheme		
		Marks
(a)	operating activities	
	profit before tax	½
	depreciation/loss on sale	1
	warranty adjustment	¼
	adjustments for investment income/finance costs	½
	adjustment for redemption penalty	1
	working capital items	1½
	finance costs	1
	income tax received	2
	investing activities (including 1 for investment income)	3
	financing activities	
	issue of equity shares	1
	redemption of 6% loan note	1
	dividend paid	1
	cash and cash equivalents b/f and c/f	1
	Maximum	15
(b)	1 mark per relevant point	10
Total		25

65 HARBIN — *Walk in the footsteps of a top tutor*

(a) **Note:** Figures in the calculations of the ratios are in $million

	2007	Workings	2006	2007 re Fatima (b)
Return on year end capital employed	11.2%	24/(114 + 100) × 100	7.1%	18.9%
Net asset turnover	1.2 times	250/214	1.6	0.6
Gross profit margin (given in question)	20%		16.7%	42.9%
Net profit (before tax) margin	6.4%	16/250	4.4%	31.4%
Current ratio	0.9:1	38/44	2.5	
Closing inventory holding period	46 days	25/200 × 365	37	
Trade receivables' collection period	19 days	13/250 × 365	16	
Trade payables' payment period	42 days	23/200 × 365	32	
Gearing	46.7%	100/214 × 100	Nil	

The gross profit margins and relevant ratios for 2006 are given in the question, and some additional ratios for Fatima are included above to enable a clearer analysis in answering part (b) (references to Fatima should be taken to mean Fatima's net assets).

(b) Analysis of the comparative financial performance and position of Harbin for the year ended 30 September 2007. **Note:** References to 2007 and 2006 should be taken as the years ended 30 September 2007 and 2006.

Introduction

The figures relating to the comparative performance of Harbin 'highlighted' in the Chief Executive's report may be factually correct, but they take a rather biased and one dimensional view. They focus entirely on the performance as reflected in the statement of comprehensive income without reference to other measures of performance (notably the ROCE); nor is there any reference to the purchase of Fatima at the beginning of the year which has had a favourable effect on profit for 2007. Due to this purchase, it is not consistent to compare Harbin's statement of comprehensive income results in 2007 directly with those of 2006 because it does not match like with like. Immediately before the $100 million purchase of Fatima, the carrying amount of the net assets of Harbin was $112 million. Thus the investment represented an increase of nearly 90% of Harbin's existing capital employed. The following analysis of performance will consider the position as shown in the reported financial statements (based on the ratios required by part (a) of the question) and then go on to consider the impact the purchase has had on this analysis.

Profitability

The ROCE is often considered to be the primary measure of operating performance, because it relates the profit made by an entity (return) to the capital (or net assets) invested in generating those profits. On this basis the ROCE in 2007 of 11.2% represents a 58% improvement (i.e. 4.1% on 7.1%) on the ROCE of 7.1% in 2006. Given there were no disposals of non-current assets, the ROCE on Fatima's net assets is 18.9% (22m/100m + 16.5m). *Note:* The net assets of Fatima at the year end would have increased by profit after tax of $16.5 million (i.e. 22m × 75% (at a tax rate of 25%)). Put another way, without the contribution of $22 million to profit before tax, Harbin's 'underlying' profit would have been a loss of $6 million which would give a negative ROCE. The principal reasons for the beneficial impact of Fatima's purchase is that its profit margins at 42.9% gross and 31.4% net (before tax) are far superior to the profit margins of the combined business at 20% and 6.4% respectively. It should be observed that the other contributing factor to the ROCE is the net asset turnover and in this respect Fatima's is actually inferior at 0.6 times (70m/116.5m) to that of the combined business of 1.2 times.

It could be argued that the finance costs should be allocated against Fatima's results as the proceeds of the loan note appear to be the funding for the purchase of Fatima. Even if this is accepted, Fatima's results still far exceed those of the existing business.

Thus the Chief Executive's report, already criticised for focussing on the statement of comprehensive income alone, is still highly misleading. Without the purchase of Fatima, underlying sales revenue would be flat at $180 million and the gross margin would be down to 11.1% (20m/180m) from 16.7% resulting in a loss before tax of $6 million. This sales performance is particularly poor given it is likely that there must have been an increase in spending on property plant and equipment beyond that related to the purchase of Fatima's net assets as the increase in property, plant and equipment is $120 million (after depreciation).

Liquidity

The company's liquidity position as measured by the current ratio has deteriorated dramatically during the period. A relatively healthy 2.5:1 is now only 0.9:1 which is rather less than what one would expect from the quick ratio (which excludes inventory) and is a matter of serious concern. A consideration of the component elements of the current ratio suggests that increases in the inventory holding period and trade payables payment period have largely offset each other. There is a small increase in the collection period for trade receivables (up from 16 days to 19 days) which would actually improve the current ratio. This ratio appears unrealistically low, it is very difficult to collect credit sales so quickly and may be indicative of factoring some of the receivables, or a proportion of the sales being cash sales. Factoring is sometimes seen as a consequence of declining liquidity, although if this assumption is correct it does also appear to have been present in the previous year. The changes in the above three ratios do not explain the dramatic deterioration in the current ratio, the real culprit is the cash position, Harbin has gone from having a bank balance of $14 million in 2006 to showing short-term bank borrowings of $17 million in 2007.

A statement of cash flow would give a better appreciation of the movement in the bank/short term borrowing position.

It is not possible to assess, in isolation, the impact of the purchase of Fatima on the liquidity of the company.

Dividends

A dividend of 10 cents per share in 2007 amounts to $10 million (100m × 10 cents), thus the dividend in 2006 would have been $8 million (the dividend in 2007 is 25% up on 2006). It may be that the increase in the reported profits led the Board to pay a 25% increased dividend, but the dividend cover is only 1.2 times (12m/10m) in 2007 which is very low. In 2006 the cover was only 0.75 times (6m/8m) meaning previous years' reserves were used to facilitate the dividend. The low retained earnings indicate that Harbin has historically paid a high proportion of its profits as dividends, however in times of declining liquidity, it is difficult to justify such high dividends.

Gearing

The company has gone from a position of nil gearing (i.e. no long-term borrowings) in 2006 to a relatively high gearing of 46.7% in 2007. This has been caused by the issue of the $100 million 8% loan note which would appear to be the source of the funding for the $100 million purchase of Fatima's net assets. At the time the loan note was issued, Harbin's ROCE was 7.1%, slightly less than the finance cost of the loan note. In 2007 the ROCE has increased to 11.2%, thus the manner of the funding has had a beneficial effect on the returns to the equity holders of Harbin. However, it should be noted that high gearing does not come without risk; any future downturn in the results of Harbin would expose the equity holders to much lower proportionate returns and continued poor liquidity may mean payment of the loan interest could present a problem. Harbin's gearing and liquidity position would have looked far better had some of the acquisition been funded by an issue of equity shares.

Conclusion

There is no doubt that the purchase of Fatima has been a great success and appears to have been a wise move on the part of the management of Harbin. However, it has disguised a serious deterioration of the underlying performance and position of Harbin's existing activities which the Chief Executive's report may be trying to hide. It may be that the acquisition was part of an overall plan to diversify out of what has become existing loss making activities. If such a transition can continue, then the worrying aspects of poor liquidity and high gearing may be overcome.

Examiner's comments

Part (a) required the calculation of eight ratios for 2007 equivalent to given ratios for 2006 and **part (b)** required candidates to assess the performance of the company in light of the given financial statements and calculated ratios.

In general candidates did well in the calculation of the ratios typically gaining six to eight marks (the maximum). The ROCE and gearing calculations were the most troublesome for candidates. Unfortunately the performance assessment report that followed was usually quite poor. Many candidates did not take sufficient notice of the question's requirement which specifically asked candidates to refer to the Chief Executive's comments and the effect of the acquisition of the net assets of a separate business (Fatima). Weaker answers did not even point out the rather obvious issues below:

- whilst the Chief Executive's comments may have been factually correct, they were very selective (biased) and potentially misleading. Few candidates recognised the fact that the focus of the Chief Executive's report hid the underlying poor performance; some candidates even said the company was doing well

- without the favourable purchase of Fatima, the underlying business would have made a loss

- the payment of the high (cover only 1.2 times) and increased dividend (calculated as $10 million) exacerbated the poor liquidity position

- the purchase of Fatima has left the company with high gearing (46.7%) and its subsequent risks including much increased finance costs

As with similar questions in the past, many candidates' attempt at interpretation was simply to reiterate in words what the movement in the ratios had been, without any attempt to suggest what may have caused the change in the ratio or what it may indicate for the company's future prospects.

Interpretation is an area where the majority of candidates need to improve their understanding and technique.

ACCA marking scheme		
		Marks
(a)	One mark per required ratio	8
(b)	For consideration of Chief Executive's report	
		3
	Impact of purchase	6
	Remaining issues 1 mark per valid point	8
		——
		17
		——
Total		25
		——

66 GREENWOOD

(a) **Note:** IFRS 5 uses the term discontinued operation. The answer below also uses this term, but it should be realised that the assets of the discontinued operation are classed as held for sale and not yet sold. In some literature this may be described as a *discontinuing* operation.

Profitability/utilisation of assets

An important feature of the company's performance in the year to 31 March 2007 is to evaluate the effect of the discontinued operation. When using an entity's recent results as a basis for assessing how the entity may perform in the future, emphasis should be placed on the results from continuing operations as it is these that will form the basis of future results. For this reason most of the ratios calculated in the appendix are based on the results from continuing operations and ratio calculations involving net assets/capital employed generally exclude the value of the assets held for sale.

On this basis, it can be seen that the overall efficiency of Greenwood (measured by its ROCE) has declined considerably from 33.5% to 29.7% (a fall of 11.3%). The fall in the asset turnover (from 1.89 to 1.67 times) appears to be mostly responsible for the overall decline in efficiency. In effect the company's assets are generating less sales per $ invested in them. The other contributing factors to overall profitability are the company's profit margins. Greenwood has achieved an impressive increase in headline sales revenues of nearly 30% (6.3m on 21.2m) whilst being able to maintain its gross profit margin at around 29% (no significant change from 2006). This has led to a substantial increase in gross profit, but this has been eroded by an increase in operating expenses. As a percentage of sales, operating expenses were 10.5% in 2007 compared to 11.6% in 2006 (they appear to be more of a variable than a fixed cost). This has led to a modest improvement in the profit before interest and tax margin which has partially offset the deteriorating asset utilisation.

The decision to sell the activities which are classified as a discontinued operation is likely to improve the overall profitability of the company. In the year ended 31 March 2006 the discontinued operation made a modest pre tax profit of $450,000 (this would represent a return of around 7% on the activity's assets of $6.3 million).This poor return acted to reduce the company's overall profitability (the continuing operations yielded a return of 33.5%). The performance of the discontinued operation continued to deteriorate in the year ended 31 March 2007 making a pre tax operating loss of $1.4 million which creates a negative return on the relevant assets. Despite incurring losses on the measurement to fair value of the discontinued operation's assets, it seems the decision will benefit the company in the future as the discontinued operation showed no sign of recovery.

Liquidity and solvency

Superficially the current ratio of 2.11 in 2007 seems reasonable, but the improvement from the alarming current ratio in 2006 of 0.97 is more illusory than real. The ratio in the year ended 31 March 2007 has been distorted (improved) by the inclusion of assets of the discontinued operation under the heading of 'held for sale'. These have been included at fair value less cost to sell (being lower than their cost – a requirement of IFRS 5). Thus the carrying amount should be a realistic expectation of the net sale proceeds, but it is not clear whether the sale will be cash (they may be exchanged for shares or other assets) or how Greenwood intends to use the disposal proceeds. What can be deduced is that without the assets held for sale being classified as current, the company's liquidity ratio would be much worse than at present (at below 1 for both years). Against an expected norm of 1, quick ratios (acid test) calculated on the normal basis of excluding inventory (and in this case the assets held for sale) show an alarming position; a poor figure of 0.62 in 2006 has further deteriorated in 2007 to 0.44. Without the proceeds from the sale of the discontinued operation (assuming they will be for cash) it is difficult to see how Greenwood would pay its payables (and tax liability), given a year end overdraft of $1,150,000.

Further analysis of the current ratios shows some interesting changes during the year. Despite its large overdraft Greenwood appears to be settling its trade payables quicker than in 2006. At 68 days in 2006 this was rather a long time and the reduction in credit period may be at the insistence of suppliers – not a good sign. Perhaps to relieve liquidity pressure, the company appears to be pushing its customers to settle early. It may be that this has been achieved by the offer of early settlement discounts, if so the cost of this would have impacted on profit. Despite holding a higher amount of inventory at 31 March 2007 (than in 2006), the company has increased its inventory turnover; given that margins have been held, this reflects an improved performance.

Gearing

The additional borrowing of $3 million in loan notes (perhaps due to liquidity pressure) has resulted in an increase in gearing from 28.6% to 35.6% and a consequent increase in finance costs. Despite the increase in finance costs the borrowing is acting in the shareholders' favour as the overall return on capital employed (at 29.7%) is well in excess of the 5% interest cost.

Summary

Overall the company's performance has deteriorated in the year ended 31 March 2007. Management's action in respect of the discontinued operation is a welcome measure to try to halt the decline, but more needs to be done. The company's liquidity position is giving cause for serious concern and without the prospect of realising $6 million from the assets held for sale it would be difficult to envisage any easing of the company's liquidity pressures.

Appendix

ROCE: continuing operations	2007		2006
$(4,500 + 400)/(14,500 + 8,000 - 6,000))$	29.7%	$(3,500 + 250)/(12,500 + 5,000 - 6,300)$	33.5%

The return has been taken as the profit before interest (on loan notes only) and tax from continuing operations. The capital employed is the normal equity plus loan capital (as at the year end), but less the value of the assets held for sale. This is because the assets held for sale have not contributed to the return from continuing operations.

Gross profit percentage (8,000/27,500)	29.1%	(6,200/21,200)	29.2%
Operating expense percentage of sales revenue (2,900/27,500)	10.5%	(2,450/21,200)	11.6%
Profit before interest and tax margin (5,100/27,500)	18.5%	(3,750/21,200)	17.7%
Asset turnover (27,500/16,500)	1.67	(21,200/11,200)	1.89
Current ratio (9,500:4,500)	2.11	(3,700:3,800)	0.97
Current ratio (excluding held for sale) (3,500:4,500)	0.77	Not applicable	
Quick ratio (excluding held for sale) (2,000:4,500)	0.44	(2,350:3,800)	0.62
Inventory (closing) turnover (19,500/1,500)	13.0	(15,000/1,350)	11.1
Receivables (in days) (2,000/27,500) × 365	26.5	(2,300/21,200) × 365	39.6
Payables/cost of sales (in days) (2,400/19,500) × 365	44.9	(2,800/15,000) × 365	68.1
Gearing (8,000/8,000 + 14,500)	35.6%	(5,000/5,000 + 12,500)	28.6%

(b)   Financial statements represent the past performance of a company and generally are based on historical costs and as such the impact of price level changes is completely ignored. The basic nature of financial statements is historic. Past performance carries no guarantee of future results. However, through the analysis of past data, trends can be established. Financial statements are neither complete nor exact. They reflect only monetary transactions of a business and economic and social factors are left out. As a result, the financial position disclosed by these statements is not correct and accurate. Only quantitative factors are taken into account. But qualitative factors such as reputation and prestige of the business with the public, the efficiency and loyalty of its employees etc. do not appear in the financial statement. The financial statements include many items that have been based on estimation techniques. For example; provision of depreciation, inventory valuation, irrecoverable debts provision etc. depend on the personal judgment of accountant.

67   VICTULAR   *Walk in the footsteps of a top tutor*

Key answer tips

This style of question is naturally time consuming – ensure you answer all parts of the question and do not spend too much time calculating ratios. Part (c) offers easy marks and is independent of the rest of the question – try doing part (c) first to ensure you do not miss out on such easy marks. When interpreting the results in part (b) be wary of making generalisations – you must ensure that you relate it to the information given in the question. Presentation is also crucial in part (b) the marker cannot award you any marks if they cannot read what you have written.

(a)   **Equivalent ratios from the financial statements of Merlot (workings in $000)**

Return on year end capital employed (ROCE)	20.9%	(1,400 + 590)/(2,800 + 3,200 + 500 + 3,000) × 100
Pre tax return on equity (ROE)	50%	1,400/2,800 × 100
Net asset turnover	2.3 times	20,500/(14,800 – 5,700)
Gross profit margin	12.2%	2,500/20,500 × 100
Operating profit margin	9.8%	2,000/20,500 × 100
Current ratio	1.3:1	7,300/5,700
Closing inventory holding period	73 days	3,600/18,000 × 365
Trade receivables' collection period	66 days	3,700/20,500 × 365
Trade payables' payment period	77 days	3,800/18,000 × 365
Gearing	71%	(3,200 + 500 + 3,000)/ 9,500 × 100
Interest cover	3.3 times	2,000/600
Dividend cover	1.4 times	1,000/700

As per the question, Merlot's obligations under finance leases (3,200 + 500) have been treated as debt when calculating the ROCE and gearing ratios.

(b)   **Assessment of the relative performance and financial position of Grappa and Merlot for the year ended 30 September 2008**

Introduction

This report is based on the draft financial statements supplied and the ratios shown in (a) above. Although covering many aspects of performance and financial position, the report has been approached from the point of view of a prospective acquisition of the entire equity of one of the two companies.

Profitability

The ROCE of 20.9% of Merlot is far superior to the 14.8% return achieved by Grappa. ROCE is traditionally seen as a measure of management's overall efficiency in the use of the finance/assets at its disposal. More detailed analysis reveals that Merlot's superior performance is due to its efficiency in the use of its net assets; it achieved a net asset turnover of 2.3 times compared to only 1.2 times for Grappa. Put another way, Merlot makes sales of $2.30 per $1 invested in net assets compared to sales of only $1.20 per $1 invested for Grappa. The other element contributing to the ROCE is profit margins. In this area Merlot's overall performance is slightly inferior to that of Grappa, gross profit margins are almost identical, but Grappa's operating profit margin is 10.5% compared to Merlot's 9.8%. In this situation, where one company's ROCE is superior to another's it is useful to look behind the figures and consider possible reasons for the superiority other than the obvious one of greater efficiency on Merlot's part.

A major component of the ROCE is normally the carrying amount of the non-current assets. Consideration of these in this case reveals some interesting issues. Merlot does not own its premises whereas Grappa does. Such a situation would not necessarily give a ROCE advantage to either company as the increase in capital employed of a company owning its factory would be compensated by a higher return due to not having a rental expense (and *vice versa*). If Merlot's rental cost, as a percentage of the value of the related factory, was less than its overall ROCE, then it would be contributing to its higher ROCE. There is insufficient information to determine this. Another relevant point may be that Merlot's owned plant is nearing the end of its useful life (carrying amount is only 22% of its cost) and the company seems to be replacing owned plant with leased plant. Again this does not necessarily give Merlot an advantage, but the finance cost of the leased assets at only 7.5% is much lower than the overall ROCE (of either company) and therefore this does help to improve Merlot's ROCE. The other important issue within the composition of the ROCE is the valuation basis of the companies' non-current assets. From the question, it appears that Grappa's factory is at current value (there is a property revaluation reserve) and note (ii) of the question indicates the use of historical cost for plant. The use of current value for the factory (as opposed to historical cost) will be adversely impacting on Grappa's ROCE. Merlot does not suffer this deterioration as it does not own its factory.

The ROCE measures the overall efficiency of management; however, as Victular is considering buying the equity of one of the two companies, it would be useful to consider the return on equity (ROE) – as this is what Victular is buying. The ratios calculated are based on pre-tax profits; this takes into account finance costs, but does not cause taxation issues to distort the comparison. Clearly Merlot's ROE at 50% is far superior to Grappa's 19.1%. Again the issue of the revaluation of Grappa's factory is making this ratio appear comparatively worse (than it would be if there had not been a revaluation). In these circumstances it would be more meaningful if the ROE was calculated based on the asking price of each company (which has not been disclosed) as this would effectively be the carrying amount of the relevant equity for Victular.

Gearing

From the gearing ratio it can be seen that 71% of Merlot's assets are financed by borrowings (39% is attributable to Merlot's policy of leasing its plant). This is very high in absolute terms and double Grappa's level of gearing. The effect of gearing means that all of the profit after finance costs is attributable to the equity even though (in Merlot's case) the equity represents only 29% of the financing of the net assets. Whilst this may seem advantageous to the equity shareholders of Merlot, it does not come without risk. The interest cover of Merlot is only 3.3 times whereas that of Grappa is 6 times. Merlot's low interest cover is a direct consequence of its high gearing and it makes profits vulnerable to relatively small changes in operating activity. For example, small reductions in sales, profit margins or small increases in operating expenses could result in losses and mean that interest charges would not be covered.

Another observation is that Grappa has been able to take advantage of the receipt of government grants; Merlot has not. This may be due to Grappa purchasing its plant (which may then be eligible for grants) whereas Merlot leases its plant. It may be that the lessor has received any grants available on the purchase of the plant and passed some of this benefit on to Merlot via lower lease finance costs (at 7.5% per annum, this is considerably lower than Merlot has to pay on its 10% loan notes).

Liquidity

Both companies have relatively low liquid ratios of 1.2 and 1.3 for Grappa and Merlot respectively, although at least Grappa has $600,000 in the bank whereas Merlot has a $1.2 million overdraft. In this respect Merlot's policy of high dividend payouts (leading to a low dividend cover and low retained earnings) is very questionable. Looking in more depth, both companies have similar inventory days; Merlot collects its receivables one week earlier than Grappa (perhaps its credit control procedures are more active due to its large overdraft), and of notable difference is that Grappa receives (or takes) a lot longer credit period from its suppliers (108 days compared to 77 days). This may be a reflection of Grappa being able to negotiate better credit terms because it has a higher credit rating.

Summary

Although both companies may operate in a similar industry and have similar profits after tax, they would represent very different purchases. Merlot's sales revenues are over 70% more than those of Grappa, it is financed by high levels of debt, it rents rather than owns property and it chooses to lease rather than buy its replacement plant. Also its remaining owned plant is nearing the end of its life. Its replacement will either require a cash injection if it is to be purchased (Merlot's overdraft of $1.2 million already requires serious attention) or create even higher levels of gearing if it continues its policy of leasing. In short although Merlot's overall return seems more attractive than that of Grappa, it would represent a much more risky investment. Ultimately the investment decision may be determined by Victular's attitude to risk, possible synergies with its existing business activities, and not least, by the asking price for each investment (which has not been disclosed to us).

(c)   The generally recognised potential problems of using ratios for comparison purposes are:

–   inconsistent definitions of ratios

–   financial statements may have been deliberately manipulated (creative accounting)

–   different companies may adopt different accounting policies (e.g. use of historical costs compared to current values)

–   different managerial policies (e.g. different companies offer customers different payment terms)

–   statement of financial position figures may not be representative of average values throughout the year (this can be caused by seasonal trading or a large acquisition of non-current assets near the year end)

–   the impact of price changes over time/distortion caused by inflation

When deciding whether to purchase a company, Victular should consider the following additional useful information:

–   in this case the analysis has been made on the draft financial statements; these may be unreliable or change when being finalised. Audited financial statements would add credibility and reliance to the analysis (assuming they receive an unmodified Auditors' Report).

–   forward looking information such as profit and financial position forecasts, capital expenditure and cash budgets and the level of orders on the books.

–   the current (fair) values of assets being acquired.

–   the level of risk within a business. Highly profitable companies may also be highly risky, whereas a less profitable company may have more stable 'quality' earnings

–   not least would be the expected price to acquire a company. It may be that a poorer performing business may be a more attractive purchase because it is relatively cheaper and may offer more opportunity for improving efficiencies and profit growth.

Examiner's comments

Part (a) required candidates to calculate ratios (8 marks) for a company equivalent to those given for another company and then do a comparative assessment of the two companies from the prospective of a potential acquisition (12 marks). This was followed by a 5 mark section explaining the limitations of ratios and what further information would be useful. Most candidates scored well when calculating the ratios, but there were some very worrying papers that showed even simple ratio calculations were not understood.

Analysing and interpreting the ratios was a different matter. Weaker scripts simply reiterated what the ratios were or that one company's ratio was higher (or lower) than the other's. Some did not even say which was better; a higher or a lower ratio. There also seemed to be an over emphasis on working capital ratios which was not a fundamental difference between the two companies and therefore not of particular importance.

Much of the information in the scenario, which should be used as 'clues', was often ignored. For example:

- one company revalued its assets the other did not; this could (partly) explain the difference in the ROCEs

- one company owned its premises; the other (presumably) rented its premises

- one company owned its plant (and therefore obtained governments grants); the other company leased its plant

- not many candidates picked up that the plant of one company was old (and would therefore need replacing in the near future) or that its dividend policy was risky given a low the cash balance

All these are very relevant factors affecting the interpretation of the ratios and which company may be the best company to acquire, but very few candidates spent much time, if any, commenting on them.

The **final part** was either ignored, thereby throwing away some relatively easy marks, or answered very well, many gaining the full 5 marks.

68   COALTOWN   *Walk in the footsteps of a top tutor*

Key answer tips

Part (a) proves to be a relatively straightforward statement of cash flow. Watch out for the disposal, unlike the usual disposal proceeds that would be received, Coaltown has an unexpected COST associated with disposal that will represent a cash outflow rather than an inflow. Part (b) requires some ratio calculations and interpretation of such and a slightly unusual trade receivable/payable impact on the bank overdraft.

(a)   **Coaltown – Statement of cash flows for the year ended 31 March 2009:**

Note: Figures in brackets in $000

		$000
Cash flows from operating activities		
Profit before tax		10,200
Adjustments for:		
depreciation of non-current assets (w (i))	6,000	
loss on disposal of displays (w (i))	1,500	
Interest expense		600
Increase in warranty provision (1,000 – 300)		700
increase in inventory (5,200 – 4,400)		(800)
increase in receivables (7,800 – 2,800)		(5,000)
decrease in payables (4,500 – 4,200)		(300)
Cash generated from operations		12,900
Interest paid		(600)
Income tax paid (w (ii))		(5,500)
Net cash from operating activities		6,800
Capital expenditure		
Cash flows from investing activities (w (i))		
Purchase of non-current assets	(20,500)	
Disposal cost of non-current assets	(500)	
Net cash used in investing activities		(21,000)
		(14,200)
Cash flows from financing activities		
Issue of equity shares (8,600 capital + 4,300 premium)	12,900	
Issue of 10% loan notes	1,000	
Equity dividends paid	(4,000)	
Net cash from financing activities		9,900
Net decrease in cash and cash equivalents		(4,300)
Cash and cash equivalents at beginning of period		700
Cash and cash equivalents at end of period		(3,600)

			$000
	Workings		
(i)	Non-current assets		
	Cost		
	Balance b/f		80,000
	Revaluation (5,000 – 2,000 depreciation)		3,000
	Disposal		(10,000)
	Balance c/f		(93,500)
	Cash flow for acquisitions		20,500
	Depreciation		
	Balance b/f		48,000
	Revaluation		(2,000)
	Disposal		(9,000)
	Balance c/f		(43,000)
	Difference – charge for year		6,000
	Disposal of displays		
	Cost		10,000
	Depreciation		(9,000)
	Cost of disposal		500
	Loss on disposal		1,500
(ii)	Income tax paid:		$000
	Provision b/f		(5,300)
	Statement of comprehensive income tax charge		(3,200)
	Provision c/f		3,000
	Difference – cash paid		(5,500)

(b) (i) **Workings** – all monetary figures in $000

(**Note:** References to 2008 and 2009 should be taken as to the years ended 31 March 2008 and 2009)

The effect of a reduction in purchase costs of 10% combined with a reduction in selling prices of 5%, based on the figures from 2008, would be:

Sales (55,000 × 95%)	52,250
Cost of sales (33,000 × 90%)	(29,700)
Expected gross profit	22,550

This represents an expected gross profit margin of 43.2% (22,550/52,250 × 100).

The actual gross profit margin for 2009 is 33.4% (22,000/65,800 × 100).

(ii)   The directors' expression of surprise that the gross profit in 2009 has not increased seems misconceived.

A change in the gross profit margin does not necessarily mean there will be an equivalent change in the absolute gross profit. This is because the gross profit figure is the product of the gross profit margin and the volume of sales and these may vary independently of each other. That said, in this case the expected gross profit margin in 2009 shows an increase over that earned in 2008 (to 43.2% from 40.0% (22,000/55,000 × 100)) and the sales have also increased, so it is understandable that the directors expected a higher gross profit. As the actual gross profit margin in 2009 is only 33.4%, something other than the changes described by the directors must have occurred. Possible reasons for the reduction are:

The opening inventory being at old (higher) cost and the closing inventory is at the new (lower) cost will have caused slight distortion.

Inventory write downs due to damage/obsolescence.

A change in the sales mix (i.e. from higher margin sales to lower margin sales). New (lower margin) products may have been introduced from other new suppliers. Some selling prices may have been discounted because of sales promotions.

Import duties (perhaps not allowed for by the directors) or exchange rate fluctuations may have caused the actual purchase cost to be higher than the trade prices quoted by the new supplier.

Change in cost classification: some costs included as operating expenses in 2008 may have been classified as cost of sales in 2009 (if intentional and material this should be treated as a change in accounting policy) – for example it may be worth checking that depreciation has been properly charged to operating expenses in 2009.

The new supplier may have put his prices up during the year due to market conditions. Coaltown may have felt it could not pass these increases on to its customers.

(iii)   **Note:** All monetary figures in $000

Trade receivables collection period in 2008: 2,800/28,500 × 365 = 35.9 days

Applying the 35.9 days collection period to the credit sales made in 2009:

53,000 × 35.9/365 = 5,213, the actual receivables are 7,800 thus potentially increasing the bank balance by 2,587.

A similar exercise with the trade payables period in 2008: 4,500/33,000 × 365 = 49.8 days

Note the 33,000 above is the cost of sales for 2008. This was the same as the credit purchases as there was no change in the value of inventory. However, in 2009 the credit purchases will be 44,600 (43,800 + 5,200 closing inventory − 4,400 opening inventory).

Applying the 49.8 days payment period to purchases made in 2009 gives:

44,600 × 49.8/365 = 6,085, the actual payables are 4,200 thus potentially increasing the bank balance by 1,885.

Inevitably a shortening of the period of credit offered by suppliers and lengthening the credit offered to customers will put a strain on cash resources. For Coaltown the combination of maintaining the same credit periods for both trade receivables and payables would have led to a reduction in cash outflows of 4,472 (2,587 + 1,885), which would have eliminated the overdraft of 3,600 leaving a balance in hand of 872.

ACCA marking scheme			Marks
(a)	Operating activities		
	Profit before tax		0.5
	Add back interest		0.5
	Depreciation charge		2
	Loss on disposal		1
	Warranty adjustment		0.5
	Working capital items		1.5
	Finance costs		1
	Income tax paid		1
	Purchase of non-current assets		2
	Disposal cost of non-current assets		1
	Issue of equity shares		1
	Issue of 10% loan note		1
	Dividend paid		1
	Cash and cash equivalents b/f and c/f		1
	Maximum		15
(b)	(i) calculation of expected gross profit margin for 2009	Maximum	2
	(ii) comments on directors' surprise and other factors	Maximum	4
	(iii) calculate credit periods (receivables and payables) in	2008	2
	apply to 2009 credit sales/purchases		1
	calculate 'savings' and effect on closing bank balance		1
	Maximum		4
Total			25

Examiner's comments

Part (a) required the preparation of a statement of cash flows for 15 marks followed by some 'targeted' interpretation for 10 marks. Cash flows are generally popular with candidates and many scored well, however, again the overall performance was not as good as I would have expected with surprisingly few candidates earning the maximum marks. Less well-prepared candidates showed poor format knowledge with little idea of which items should appear in which section of the statement nor did they know the difference between cash and noncash flows, for example reserve movements, provisions (for warranties) and the loss on the disposal of the displays were sometimes treated as cash flows. A number of candidates had difficulty with the accumulated depreciation being reset to zero after a revaluation and the cost of the disposal of an asset was often treated as the sale proceeds.

Many candidates could not work out the movement on the accumulated depreciation as they could not follow the impact of the disposal of the displays which gave them a depreciation amount to be credited to the statement of comprehensive income. An area causing many marks to be lost was getting the cash movements the wrong way round (signing errors). For example, the marks for the movement in working capital items are normally for correctly identifying them as inflows or outflows rather than for correct arithmetic. Some candidates split the two finance costs both within the adjustments and the cash outflows (often in different sections of the statement) which was not necessary.

Part (b) gave information about percentage changes in the sales and the cost of sales instigated by the directors actions which was accompanied by information on changes in credit periods. Part (b)(i) required candidates to calculate the gross profit margin that should have resulted from the cost and revenue changes. Many candidates got this correct, but a number did not seem to read the requirement correctly and calculated the actual profit margin (rather than the 'theoretical margin'). A number of candidates made the adjustments to the 2008 revenue and cost of sales figures rather than to the 2009 figures, which may have been caused by not reading the question carefully enough.

Part (ii) was a written section effectively requiring candidates to identify other factors (apart from the cost and revenue changes) that could have caused the change in gross profit margin. This was generally very badly answered; many candidates discussed exclusively the cost changes instigated by the directors as being solely responsible for the overall change in the margin, despite the previous section having already identified the effect of those changes. The same candidates were usually convinced that the changed credit periods were the cause of the changes in the gross margin which shows a lack of understanding between profit and cash. Those candidates that did realise the question required other examples of causes of changes in gross profit margin often gave examples of items that do not affect gross profit such as higher bad debt charges, cash discounts and additional finance costs – these do affect net profit, but not gross profit. A number of candidates did refer to quality issues and returns of goods to suppliers and from customers, with a small number of very perceptive candidates even noting the latter was reinforced by the disproportionate increase in the warranty provision. Part (iii) was again a targeted area of ratio understanding related to the changes in the credit periods (for payables and receivables). The question wanted candidates to quantify the effect it would have had on the bank balance if the previous year's (2008) credit periods been maintained in the current year (2009). This involved calculating 2008's credit periods and then applying those to the credit sales and credit purchases of 2009 to give 'theoretical' receivables and payables balances for 2009. These could then be compared to the actual payables and receivables balances of 2009 to identify the 'theoretical' effect on the bank balance. Many candidates presented a simple comparison of this year's credit periods with those of the previous year; either those candidates did not read the requirement properly or they only have a 'mechanical' understanding of the ratios and cannot adapt to a different scenario. Weaker candidates decided to calculate the inventory turnover figures for both years and then compute the working capital cycle which was of no relevance to the question set.

69 CROSSWIRE *Walk in the footsteps of a top tutor*

(a) (i) Non-current assets

	$000
Property, plant and equipment	
Carrying amount b/f	13,100
Mine (5,000 + 3,000 environmental cost)	8,000
Revaluation (2,000/0.8 allowing for effect of deferred tax transfer)	2,500
Fair value of leased plant	10,000
Plant disposal	(500)
Depreciation	(3,000)
Replacement plant (balance)	2,400
Carrying amount c/f	32,500
Development costs	
Carrying amount b/f	2,500
Additions during year	500
Amortisation and impairment (balance)	(2,000)
Carrying amount c/f	1,000

(ii) Cash flows from investing activities

Purchase of property, plant and equipment (w (i))	(7,400)
Disposal proceeds of plant	1,200
Development costs	(500)
Net cash used in investing activities	(6,700)
Cash flows from financing activities:	
Issue of equity shares (w (ii))	2,000
Redemption of convertible loan notes ((5,000 – 1,000) × 25%)	(1,000)
Lease obligations (w (iii))	(3,200)
Interest paid (400 + 350)	(750)
Net cash used in financing activities	(2,950)

Workings (figures in brackets in $000)

(i)   The cash elements of the increase in property, plant and equipment are $5 million for the mine (the capitalised environmental provision is not a cash flow) and $2.4 million for the replacement plant making a total of $7.4 million.

(ii)   Of the $4 million convertible loan notes (5,000 – 1,000) that were redeemed during the year, 75% ($3 million) of these were exchanged for equity shares on the basis of 20 new shares for each $100 in loan notes. This would create 600,000 (3,000/100 × 20) new shares of $1 each and share premium of $2.4 million (3,000 – 600). As 1 million (5,000 – 4,000) new shares were issued in total, 400,000 must have been for cash. The remaining increase (after the effect of the conversion) in the share premium of $1.6 million (6,000 – 2,000 b/f – 2,400 conversion) must relate to the cash issue of shares, thus cash proceeds from the issue of shares is $2 million (400 nominal value + 1,600 premium).

(iii)   The initial lease obligation is $10 million (the fair value of the plant). At 30 September 2009 total lease obligations are $6.8 million (5,040 + 1,760), thus repayments in the year were $3.2 million (10,000 – 6,800).

(b)   Taking the definition of ROCE from the question:

Year ended 30 September 2009

	$000
Profit before tax and interest on long-term borrowings (4,000 + 1,000 + 400 + 350)	5,750
Equity plus loan notes and finance lease obligations (19,200 + 1,000 + 5,040 + 1,760)	27,000
ROCE	21.3%
Equivalent for year ended 30 September 2008	
(3,000 + 800 + 500)	4,300
(9,700 + 5,000)	14,700
ROCE	29.3%

To help explain the deterioration it is useful to calculate the components of ROCE i.e. operating margin and net asset turnover (utilisation):

	2009		2008
Operating margin (5,750/52,000 × 100)	11.1%	(4,300/42,000)	10.2%
Net asset turnover (52,000/27,000)	1.93 times	(42,000/14,700)	2.86 times

From the above it can be clearly seen that the 2009 operating margin has improved by nearly 1% point, despite the $2 million impairment charge on the write down of the development project. This means the deterioration in the ROCE is due to poorer asset turnover. This implies there has been a decrease in the efficiency in the use of the company's assets this year compared to last year.

Looking at the movement in the non-current assets during the year reveals some mitigating points:

The land revaluation has increased the carrying amount of property, plant and equipment without any physical increase in capacity. This unfavourably distorts the current year's asset turnover and ROCE figures.

The acquisition of the platinum mine appears to be a new area of operation for Crosswire which may have a different (perhaps lower) ROCE to other previous activities or it may be that it will take some time for the mine to come to full production capacity.

The substantial acquisition of the leased plant was half-way through the year and can only have contributed to the year's results for six months at best. In future periods a full year's contribution can be expected from this new investment in plant and this should improve both asset turnover and ROCE.

In summary, the fall in the ROCE may be due largely to the above factors (effectively the replacement and expansion programme), rather than to poor operating performance, and in future periods this may be reversed.

It should also be noted that had the ROCE been calculated on the average capital employed during the year (rather than the year end capital employed), which is arguably more correct, then the deterioration in the ROCE would not have been as pronounced.

		ACCA marking scheme		Marks
(a)	(i)	property, plant and equipment		
		mine		1.5
		land revaluation		1.5
		leased plant		1.0
		plant disposal		1.0
		depreciation		1.0
		replacement plant		1.0
				–––
				7.0
		development expenditure		2.0
				–––
			Maximum	9.0
				–––
	(ii)	Investing activities		
		purchase of property, plant and equipment		2.0
		disposal proceeds of plant		0.5
		development expenditure		1.0
		financing activities		
		issue of equity shares		1.5
		redemption of convertible loan notes		1.0
		lease obligations		1.0
		loan interest		1.0
				–––
			Maximum	8.0
				–––
(b)		Calculation of ROCE		2.0
		supporting components ratios		2.0
		explanatory comments – up to		4.0
				–––
			Maximum	8.0
				–––
Total				25
				–––

Examiner's comments

This question was on the 'usual' topic of cash flows and the calculation and interpretation of ratios, but was somewhat different to many previous questions in that it was more targeted on particular items.

Part (a) required a statement of the movement in the company's non-current assets followed by the (partly) related cash flows of investing and financing activities. Part (b) then required candidates to focus on the calculation and cause of the deterioration in the company's ROCE.

Many candidates gave a good attempt at the movement of non-current assets; most coped with an increase in the 'cost' of an asset due to an environmental provision and recognising (per the question) that the balance of the movement represented the purchase of plant. Weaker candidates showed poor layouts often using ledger accounts with no summary showing the movement on the assets. A number did not include the movement on the development costs.

The required cash flows proved more problematic; common errors were the environmental cost increase being treated as a cash flow and very few accurately accounted for the cash flow aspects of a partial loan to equity conversion.

Again there were a small minority of poor (and sometimes non-existent) answers; some included revaluations, depreciation and reserve movements as cash flows. A number of candidates attempted a full cash flow statement instead of the required extracts.

Part (b) was very poorly answered, though there were some notable exceptions. Very few correct answers were given for the calculation of ROCE (despite the question giving the formula to apply) and even fewer attempted to calculate the components of the ROCE (profit margins and asset turnover) in order to identify the cause of its deterioration. Many candidates mentioned the new lease agreement; changes in capital structure and the asset revaluation without saying what effect these had had on the ROCE. Many candidates showed poor understanding by saying the 'return' had deteriorated due to higher finance cost when the 'return' was, by definition, before finance costs.

70 DELTOID *Walk in the footsteps of a top tutor*

Key answer tips

For part (a) (i) you are required to prepare a statement of cash flow – watch out for the tax calculation as last year there was a tax refund due rather than a tax amount payable. For part (a) (ii) you are required to use your cash flow and information in the question to determine whether or not Deltoid's loan should be renewed. Finally, for part (b) you must consider how a lender would determine whether or not to provide finance to a not-for profit organisation.

(a)   (i)   **Deltoid – Statement of cash flows for the year ended 31 March 2010:**

(*Note:* Figures in brackets are in $000)

	$000	$000
Cash flows from operating activities:		
Loss before tax		(1,800)
Adjustments for:		
depreciation of non-current assets		3,700
loss on sale of leasehold property (8,800 – 200 – 8,500)		100
interest expense		1,000
increase in inventory (12,500 – 4,600)		(7,900)
increase in trade receivables (4,500 – 2,000)		(2,500)
increase in trade payables (4,700 – 4,200)		500
		─────
Cash deficit from operations		(6,900)
Interest paid		(1,000)
Income tax paid (w (i))		(1,900)
		─────
Net cash deficit from operating activities		(9,800)
Cash flows from investing activities:		
Disposal of leasehold property		8,500
Cash flows from financing activities:		
Shares issued (10,000 – 8,000 – 800 bonus issue)	1,200	
Payment of finance lease obligations (w (ii))	(2,100)	
Equity dividends paid (w (iii))	(700)	
	─────	
Net cash from financing activities		(1,600)
		─────
Net decrease in cash and cash equivalents		(2,900)
Cash and cash equivalents at beginning of period		1,500
		─────
Cash and cash equivalents at end of period		(1,400)
		─────

Workings

(i)   **Income tax paid:**

	$000
Provision b/f – current	(2,500)
– deferred	(800)
Statement of comprehensive income tax relief	700
Provision c/f – current	(500)
– deferred	1,200
	─────
Difference – cash paid	(1,900)
	─────

(ii)   **Leased plant:**

Balance b/f	2,500
Depreciation	(1,800)
Leased during year (balance)	5,800
	————
Balance c/f	6,500
	————

Lease obligations:

Balance b/f – current	(800)
– non-current	(2,000)
New leases (from above)	(5,800)
Balance c/f – current	1,700
– non-current	4,800
	————
Difference – repayment during year	(2,100)
	————

(iii)   **Equity dividends paid:**

Retained earnings b/f	6,300
Loss for period	(1,100)
Dividends paid (balance)	(700)
	————
Retained earnings c/f	4,500
	————

(ii)   The main concerns of a loan provider would be whether Deltoid would be able to pay the servicing costs (interest) of the loan and the eventual repayment of the principal amount. Another important aspect of granting the loan would be the availability of any security that Deltoid can offer.

Interest cover is a useful measure of the risk of non-payment of interest. Deltoid's interest cover has fallen from a healthy 15 times (9,000/600) to be negative in 2010. Although interest cover is useful, it is based on profit whereas interest is actually paid in cash. It is usual to expect interest payments to be covered by operating cash flows (it is a bad sign when interest has to be paid from long-term sources of funding such as from the sale of non-current assets or a share issue). Deltoid's position in this light is very worrying; there is a cash deficit from operations of $6.9 million and after interest and tax payments the deficit has risen to $9.8 million.

When looking at the prospect of the ability to repay the loan, Deltoid's position is deteriorating as measured by its gearing (debt including finance lease obligations/equity) which has increased to 65% (5,000 + 6,500/17,700) from 43% (5,000 + 2,800/18,300). What may also be indicative of a deteriorating liquidity position is that Deltoid has sold its leasehold property and rented it back. This has been treated as a disposal, but, depending on the length of the rental agreement and other conditions of the tenancy agreement (which are not specified in the question) it may be that the substance of the sale is a loan/finance leaseback (e.g. if the period of the rental agreement was substantially the same as the remaining life of the property). If this were the case the company's gearing would increase even further. Furthermore, there is less value in terms of ownership of non-current assets which may be used as security (in the form of a charge on assets) for the loan. It is also noteworthy that, in a similar vein, the increase in other non-current assets is due to finance leased plant. Whilst it is correct to include finance leased plant on the statement of financial position (applying substance over form), the legal position is that this plant is not owned by Deltoid and offers no security to any prospective lender to Deltoid.

Therefore, in view of Deltoid's deteriorating operating and cash generation performance, it may be advisable not to renew the loan for a further five years.

(b) Although the sports club is a not-for-profit organisation, the request for a loan is a commercial activity that should be decided on according to similar criteria as would be used for other profit-orientated entities.

The main aspect of granting a loan is how secure the loan would be. To this extent a form of capital gearing ratio should be calculated; say existing long-term borrowings to net assets (i.e. total assets less current liabilities). Clearly if this ratio is high, further borrowing would be at an increased risk. The secondary aspect is to measure the sports club's ability to repay the interest (and ultimately the principal) on the loan. This may be determined from information in the statement of comprehensive income. A form of interest cover should be calculated; say the excess of income over expenditure (broadly the equivalent of profit) compared to (the forecast) interest payments. The higher this ratio the less risk of interest default. The calculations would be made for all four years to ascertain any trends that may indicate a deterioration or improvement in these ratios. As with other profit-oriented entities the nature and trend of the income should be investigated: for example, are the club's sources of income increasing or decreasing, does the reported income contain 'one-off' donations (which may not be recurring) etc? Also matters such as the market value of, and existing prior charges against, any assets intended to be used as security for the loan would be relevant to the lender's decision-making process. It may also be possible that the sports club's governing body (perhaps the trustees) may be willing to give a personal guarantee for the loan.

UK SYLLABUS FOCUS ONLY

Under IAS 7 there are 3 primary headings for a statement of cashflow whereas a UK GAAP cash flow statement per FRS 1, comprises 8 headings in total. These headings include operating activities, returns on investments and servicing of finance, taxation, capital expenditure and financial investment, acquisitions and disposals, equity dividends paid, management of liquid resources and financing. Below for illustration purposes is the cash flow statement of Deltoid presented in accordance with FRS 1.

UK presentation of Deltoid – cash flow statement for the year ended 31 March 2010:

Reconciliation of operating loss to net cash outflow from operating activities

	$000	$000
Operating loss (12,000 – 11,200)		(800)
Adjustments for:		
depreciation charges	3,700	
loss on sale of leasehold property (8,800 – 200 – 8,500)	100	3,800
Working capital adjustments		
increase in stocks (12,500 – 4,600)		(7,900)
increase in debtors (4,500 – 2,000)		(2,500)
increase in creditors (4,700 – 4,200)		500
Net cash outflow from operating activities		(6,900)

Cash flow statement

Net cash outflow from operating activities		(6,900)
Servicing of finance – interest paid		(1,000)
Tax paid (w (i))		(1,900)
Capital expenditure – disposal of leasehold property		8,500
Equity dividends paid (w (ii))		(700)
Cash outflow before financing		(2,000)
Financing (note 1)		(900)
Decrease in cash (1,500 + 1,400)		(2,900)

Note 1
Financing

	$000	$000
Shares issued (10,000 – 8,000 – 800 bonus issue)	1,200	
Capital element of finance lease obligations (w (iii))	(2,100)	(900)

ACCA marking scheme			
			Marks
(a)	(i)	loss before tax	½
		depreciation	1
		loss on sale of leasehold	1
		interest expense adjustment (added back)	½
		working capital items	1½
		interest paid (outflow)	½
		income tax paid	1½
		sale proceeds of leasehold	1
		share issue	1
		repayment of lease obligations	1½
		equity dividends paid	1
		cash b/f	½
		cash c/f	½
		Maximum	12
	(ii)	1 mark per valid point	8
(b)		1 mark per valid point	5
Total			25

Examiner's comments

Although most candidates scored well on the cash flows, a significant number showed a lack of understanding including poor format knowledge.

In **part (a)**(ii) candidates were asked to review the available information (including their statement of cash flows)to advise on the renewal of the loan due three months after the year end. Although there were a few really good answers to this, i.e. those that focussed on the requirement, many candidates answered this as if it were a general interpretation of financial performance giving little regard to addressing the issue of whether they would advise that the loan renewal be granted.

The answer should have concentrated on the expectations of a lender: does the company have good liquidity, interest cover, acceptable gearing and securitisable assets. Good answers referred to the company selling its leasehold property and renting it back as a sign of an inability to generate cash flows from trading activity and that there was a year-end overdraft despite selling the property and issuing shares. Many weaker answers were dominated by profitability issues, such as profit ratios and cost control, and a detailed commentary on inventory and receivables policies, with hardly any reference to the position as portrayed by the statement of cash flows.

Another problem was not understanding that the loan had 'moved' from non-current to current liabilities: many candidates thought that the non-current loan had been paid off and a new loan taken out. This error was also commonly presented in the answer to part (a)(i) although no cash flow(s) had taken place.

For the first time **part (b)** examined an issue relating to a not-for-profit organisation. It was a similar issue to that in part (a)(ii) in that it asked for what ratios could be calculated to decide whether to grant a loan to such an organisation. Many candidates did recognise and state that a not-for-profit organisation doesn't have profits, but despite this then went on to describe many profit-related ratios without even trying to relate them to the types of income, expenses, assets and liabilities of a sports club. The question clearly stated that this was a separate matter to the earlier question. Despite this many candidates calculated (routine) ratios using the figures from the company's financial statements (Deltoid) in part (a) often referring to the sports club as "the company".

What was required in answering this section was a recognition that although the sports club is a not-for-profit organisation, granting it a loan is a commercial activity and should be decided based on similar principles to that of a commercial organisation. Thus the ability to pay interest, capital and the availability of any security is still relevant.

A number of answers completely ignored what the question had asked and instead just gave a rote-learned page of everything they could remember about not-for-profit organisations such as the three E's.

Section 3

PILOT PAPER EXAM QUESTIONS

1 PUMICE

On 1 October 2005 Pumice acquired the following non-current investments:

– 80% of the equity share capital of Silverton at a cost of $13.6 million

– 50% of Silverton's 10% loan notes at par

– 1.6 million equity shares in Amok at a cost of $6.25 each.

The summarized draft statement of financial positions of the three companies at 31 March 2006 are:

	Pumice $000	Silverton $000	Amok $000
Non-current assets			
Property, plant and equipment	20,000	8,500	16,500
Investments	26,000	Nil	1,500
	46,000	8,500	18,000
Current assets	15,000	8,000	11,000
Total assets	61,000	16,500	29,000
Equity and liabilities			
Equity			
Equity shares of $1 each	10,000	3,000	4,000
Retained earnings	37,000	8,000	20,000
	47,000	11,000	24,000
Non-current liabilities			
8% loan note	4,000	Nil	Nil
10% loan note	Nil	2,000	Nil
Current liabilities	10,000	3,500	5,000
Total equity and liabilities	61,000	16,500	29,000

The following information is relevant:

(i) The fair values of Silverton's assets were equal to their carrying amounts with the exception of land and plant. Silverton's land had a fair value of $400,000 in excess of its carrying amount and plant had a fair value of $1.6 million in excess of its carrying amount. The plant had a remaining life of four years (straight-line depreciation) at the date of acquisition.

(ii)   In the post acquisition period Pumice sold goods to Silverton at a price of $6 million. These goods had cost Pumice $4 million. Half of these goods were still in the inventory of Silverton at 31 March 2006. Silverton had a balance of $1.5 million owing to Pumice at 31 March 2006 which agreed with Pumice's records.

(iii) The net profit after tax for the year ended 31 March 2006 was $2 million for Silverton and $8 million for Amok. Assume profits accrued evenly throughout the year.

(iv)   Pumice's policy is to value the non-controlling interest at fair value at the date of acquisition. The fair value of the non-controlling interest at acquisition was determined to be $3 million.

An impairment test at 31 March 2006 concluded that consolidated goodwill was impaired by $500,000 and the investment in Amok was impaired by $200,000.

(v)   No dividends were paid during the year by any of the companies.

Required:

(a)   Discuss how the investments purchased by Pumice on 1 October 2005 should be treated in its consolidated financial statements.   (5 marks)

(b)   Prepare the consolidated statement of financial position for Pumice as at 31 March 2006.   (20 marks)

(Total: 25 marks)

2   KALA

The following trial balance relates to Kala, a publicly listed company, at 31 March 2006:

	$000	$000
Land and buildings at cost (note (i))	270,000	
Plant – at cost (note (i))	156,000	
Investment properties – valuation at 1 April 2005 (note (i))	90,000	
Purchases	78,200	
Operating expenses	15,500	
Loan interest paid	2,000	
Rental of leased plant (note (ii))	22,000	
Dividends paid	15,000	
Inventory at 1 April 2005	37,800	
Trade receivables	53,200	
Revenue		278,400
Income from investment property		4,500
Equity shares of $1 each fully paid		150,000
Retained earnings at 1 April 2005		119,500
8% (actual and effective) loan note (note (iii))		50,000
Accumulated depreciation at 1 April 2005 – buildings		60,000
– plant		26,000
Trade payables		33,400
Deferred tax		12,500
Bank		5,400
	739,700	739,700

The following notes are relevant:

(i)   The land and buildings were purchased on 1 April 1990. The cost of the land was $70 million. No land and buildings have been purchased by Kala since that date. On 1 April 2005 Kala had its land and buildings professionally valued at $80 million and $175 million respectively. The directors wish to incorporate these values into the financial statements. The estimated life of the buildings was originally 50 years and the remaining life has not changed as a result of the valuation.

Later, the valuers informed Kala that investment properties of the type Kala owned had increased in value by 7% in the year to 31 March 2006.

Plant, other than leased plant (see below), is depreciated at 15% per annum using the reducing balance method. Depreciation of buildings and plant is charged to cost of sales.

(ii)   On 1 April 2005 Kala entered into a lease for an item of plant which had an estimated life of five years. The lease period is also five years with annual rentals of $22 million payable in advance from 1 April 2005. The plant is expected to have a nil residual value at the end of its life. If purchased this plant would have a cost of $92 million and be depreciated on a straight-line basis. The lessor includes a finance cost of 10% per annum when calculating annual rentals. (**Note:** You are not required to calculate the present value of the minimum lease payments.)

(iii) The loan note was issued on 1 July 2005 with interest payable six monthly in arrears.

(iv)   The provision for income tax for the year to 31 March 2006 has been estimated at $28.3 million. The deferred tax provision at 31 March 2006 is to be adjusted to a credit balance of $14.1 million.

(v)   The inventory at 31 March 2006 was valued at $43.2 million.

Required:

Prepare for Kala.

(a)   **A statement of profit or loss and other comprehensive income for the year ended 31 March 2006.**   **(10 marks)**

(b)   **A statement of changes in equity for the year ended 31 March 2006.**   **(4 marks)**

(c)   **A statement of financial position as at 31 March 2006.**   **(11 marks)**

                                                                (Total: 25 marks)

3   REACTIVE

Reactive is a publicly listed company that assembles domestic electrical goods which it then sells to both wholesale and retail customers. Reactive's management were disappointed in the company's results for the year ended 31 March 2005. In an attempt to improve performance the following measures were taken early in the year ended 31 March 2006:

–   a national advertising campaign was undertaken,

–   rebates to all wholesale customers purchasing goods above set quantity levels were introduced,

–   the assembly of certain lines ceased and was replaced by bought in completed products. This allowed Reactive to dispose of surplus plant.

Reactive's summarized financial statements for the year ended 31 March 2006 are set out below:

Statement of profit or loss

	$million
Revenue (25% cash sales)	4,000
Cost of sales	(3,450)
	———
Gross profit	550
Operating expenses	(370)
	———
	180
Profit on disposal of plant (note (i))	40
Finance charges	(20)
	———
Profit before tax	200
Income tax expense	(50)
	———
Profit for the period	150
	———

Statement of financial position

	$million	$million
Non-current assets		
Property, plant and equipment (note (i))		550
Current assets		
Inventory	250	
Trade receivables	360	
Bank	Nil	610
Total assets		1,160
Equity and liabilities		
Equity shares of 25 cents each		100
Retained earnings		380
		480
Non-current liabilities		
8% loan notes		200
Current liabilities		
Bank overdraft	10	
Trade payables	430	
Current tax payable	40	480
Total equity and liabilities		1,160

Below are ratios calculated for the year ended 31 March 2005.

Return on year end capital employed (profit before interest and tax over total assets less current liabilities)	28.1%
Net asset (equal to capital employed) turnover	4 times
Gross profit margin	17%
Net profit (before tax) margin	6.3%
Current ratio	1.6:1
Closing inventory holding period	46 days
Trade receivables' collection period	45 days
Trade payables' payment period	55 days
Dividend yield	3.75%
Dividend cover	2 times

Notes

(i)   Reactive received $120 million from the sale of plant that had a carrying amount of $80 million at the date of its sale.

(ii)   The market price of Reactive's shares throughout the year averaged $3.75 each.

(iii) There were no issues or redemption of shares or loans during the year.

(iv)   Dividends paid during the year ended 31 March 2006 amounted to $90 million, maintaining the same dividend paid in the year ended 31 March 2005.

Required:

(a)   Calculate ratios for the year ended 31 March 2006 (showing your workings) for Reactive, equivalent to those provided above.   (10 marks)

(b)   Analyse the financial performance and position of Reactive for the year ended 31 March 2006 compared to the previous year.   (10 marks)

(c)   Explain in what ways your approach to performance appraisal would differ if you were asked to assess the performance of a not-for-profit organization.   (5 marks)

(Total: 25 marks)

4   PORTO

(a)   The fundamental qualitative characteristics of relevance and faithful representation and one of the enhancing qualitative characteristics, comparability identified in the *IASB's Conceptual Framework for Financial Reporting* are some of the attributes that make financial information useful to the various users of financial statements.

Required:

Explain what is meant by relevance, faithful representation and comparability and how they make financial information useful.   (9 marks)

(b)   During the year ended 31 March 2006, Porto experienced the following transactions or events:

(i)   entered into a finance lease to rent an asset for substantially the whole of its useful economic life.

(ii)   a decision was made by the Board to change the company's accounting policy from one of expensing the finance costs on building new retail outlets to one of capitalising such costs.

(iii) the company's income statement prepared using historical costs showed a loss from operating its hotels, but the company is aware that the increase in the value of its properties during the period far outweighed the operating loss.

Required:

Explain how you would treat the items in (i) to (iii) above in Porto's financial statements and indicate on which of the Framework's qualitative characteristics your treatment is based.   (6 marks)

(Total: 15 marks)

5 BEETIE

IAS 11 *Construction contracts* deals with accounting requirements for construction contracts whose durations usually span at least two accounting period.

Required:

(a) **Describe the issues of revenue and profit recognition relating to construction contracts.** **(4 marks)**

(b) Beetie is a construction company that prepares its financial statements to 31 March each year. During the year ended 31 March 2006 the company commenced two construction contracts that are expected to take more than one year to complete. The position of each contract at 31 March 2006 is as follows:

Contract	1	2
	$000	$000
Agreed contract price	5,500	1,200
Estimated total cost of contract at commencement	4,000	900
Estimated total cost at 31 March 2006	4,000	1,250
Agreed value of work completed at 31 March 2006	3,300	840
Progress billings invoiced and received at 31 March 2006	3,000	880
Contract costs incurred to 31 March 2006	3,900	720

The agreed value of the work completed at 31 March 2006 is considered to be equal to the revenue earned in the year ended 31 March 2006. The percentage of completion is calculated as the agreed value of work completed to the agreed contract price.

Required:

Calculate the amounts which should appear in the statement of profit or loss and statement of financial position of Beetie at 31 March 2006 in respect of the above contracts. **(6 marks)**

(Total: 10 marks)

Section 4

ANSWERS TO PILOT PAPER EXAM QUESTIONS

1   PUMICE

(a)   As the investment in shares represents 80% of Silverton's equity, it is likely to give Pumice control of that company. Control is the ability to direct the operating and financial policies of an entity. This would make Silverton a subsidiary of Pumice and require Pumice to prepare group financial statements which would require the consolidation of the results of Silverton from the date of acquisition (1 October 2005). Consolidated financial statements are prepared on the basis that the group is a single economic entity.

The investment of 50% ($1 million) of the 10% loan note in Silverton is effectively a loan from a parent to a subsidiary. On consolidation Pumice's asset of the loan ($1 million) is cancelled out with $1 million of Silverton's total loan note liability of $2 million. This would leave a net liability of $1 million in the consolidated statement of financial position.

The investment in Amok of 1.6 million shares represents 40% of that company's equity shares. This is generally regarded as not being sufficient to give Pumice control of Amok, but is likely to give it significant influence over Amok's policy decisions (e.g. determining the level of dividends paid by Amok). Such investments are generally classified as associates and IAS 28 *Investments in associates* requires the investment to be included in the consolidated financial statements using equity accounting.

(b)   **Consolidated statement of financial position of Pumice at 31 March 2006**

	$000	$000
Non-current assets:		
Plant, property and equipment (20,000+8,500+400+1,600 – 200)		30,300
Goodwill (W3)		4,100
Investments – associate ((W7)		11,400
– other ((26,000 – 13,600 – 10,000 – 1,000 intra-group loan note))		1,400
		———
		47,200
Current assets (15,000 + 8,000 – 1,000 (W6)) – 1,500 current account		20,500
		———
Total assets		67,700
		———

	$000	$000
Equity and liabilities		
Equity attributable to equity holders of the parent		
Equity shares of $1 each		10,000
Reserves:		
Retained earnings (W5)		37,640
		47,640
Non-controlling interest (W6))		3,060
		50,700
Total equity		
Non-current liabilities		
8% Loan note	4,000	
10% Loan note (2,000 – 1,000 intra-group)	1,000	5,000
Current liabilities (10,000 + 3,500 – 1,500 current account)		12,000
		67,700

Workings

(W1) **Group structure**

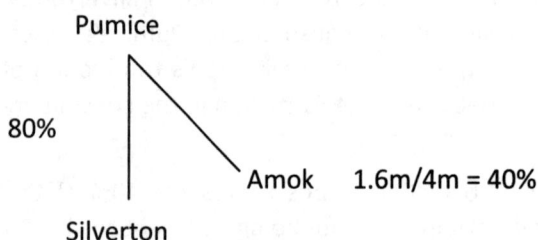

Pumice

80%

Amok   1.6m/4m = 40%

Silverton

Both investments occurred on 1 October 2005 and so have been held for 6 mths.

(W2) **Net Assets of Silverton**

	At acquisition	At reporting date
	$000	$000
Share capital	3,000	3,000
Retained earnings (8,000 – (6/12 × 2,000))	7,000	8,000
Fair value adjustment:		
Land	400	400
Plant	1,600	1,600
Dep'n adj (1,600 × ¼ × 6mths)		(200)
	12,000	12,800

(W3) Goodwill

		Silverton
		$000
Parent holding (investment) at fair value		13,600
NCI value at acquisition		3,000
		16,600
Less:		
Fair value of net assets at acquisition (W2)		(12,000)
Goodwill on acquisition		4,600
Impairment		(500)
Carrying goodwill		4,100

(W4) Non-controlling interest

	$000
NCI value at acquisition	3,000
NCI share post-acquisition reserves	
(20% × (12,800 – 12,000)) (W2)	160
Impairment (20% × 500)	(100)
	3,060

(W5) Consolidated reserves

	$000
Pumice	37,000
PUP (W6)	(1,000)
Silverton (80% × (12,800 – 12,000))	640
Amok (40% × (24,000 – 20,000))	1,600
Impairments – Silverton (80% × 500)	(400)
– Amok	(200)
	37,640

(W6) Provision for unrealised profit

Intra-group sales are $6 million of which Pumice made a profit of $2 million. Half of these are still in inventory, thus there is an unrealized profit of $1 million.

(W7) Investment in Associate

Cost (1,600 × $6.25)	10,000
Share post acquisition profit (8,000 × 6/12 × 40%)	1,600
	11,600
Impairment loss per question	(200)
	11,400

ACCA marking scheme		
		Marks
(a)	1 mark per relevant point	5
(b)	Statement of financial position:	
	Property, plant and equipment	2½
	Goodwill	3½
	Investments — associate	3
	— other	1
	Current assets	2
	Equity shares	1
	Retained earnings	3
	Non-controlling interest	1½
	8% Loan notes	½
	10% Loan notes	1
	Retained earnings	1
	Maximum	20
Total		25

2 KALA

(a) **Kala – statement of profit or loss and other comprehensive income – Year ended 31 March 2006**

	$000	$000
Revenue		278,400
Cost of sales (w (i))		(115,700)
Gross profit		162,700
Operating expenses		(15,500)
		147,200
Investment income – property rental	4,500	
– valuation gain (90,000 × 7%)	6,300	10,800
Finance costs – loan (w (ii))	(3,000)	
– lease (w (iii))	(7,000)	(10,000)
Profit before tax		148,000
Income tax expense (28,300 + (14,100 – 12,500))		(29,900)
Profit for the period		118,100
Other comprehensive income:		
Revaluation gain		45,000
		163,100

(b) **Kala –Statement of changes in equity – Year ended 31 March 2006**

	Equity shares	Revaluation reserve	Retained earnings	Total
	$000	$000	$000	$000
At 1 April 2005	150,000	Nil	119,500	269,500
Profit for period (see (a))			118,100	118,100
Revaluation of property (w (iv))		45,000		45,000
Equity dividends paid			(15,000)	(15,000)
At 31 March 2006	150,000	45,000	222,600	417,600

(c) **Kala – Statement of financial position as at 31 March 2006**

	$000	$000
Non-current assets		
Property, plant and equipment (w (iv))		434,100
Investment property (90,000 + 6,300)		96,300
		530,400
Current assets		
Inventory	43,200	
Trade receivables	53,200	96,400
Total assets		626,800
Equity and liabilities		
Equity (see (b) above)		
Equity shares of $1 each		150,000
Reserves:		
Revaluation	45,000	
Retained earnings	222,600	267,600
		417,600
Non-current liabilities		
8% loan note	50,000	
Deferred tax	14,100	
Lease obligation (w (iii))	55,000	119,100
Current liabilities		
Trade payables	33,400	
Accrued loan interest (w (ii))	1,000	
Bank overdraft	5,400	
Lease obligation (w (iii)) – accrued interest	7,000	
– capital	15,000	
Current tax payable	28,300	90,100
Total equity and liabilities		626,800

Workings in brackets in $000

(i) **Cost of sales:**

	$000
Opening inventory	37,800
Purchases	78,200
Depreciation (w (iv)) – buildings	5,000
– plant: owned	19,500
leased	18,400
Closing inventory	(43,200)
	———
	115,700
	———

(ii) The loan has been in issue for nine months. The total finance cost for this period will be $3 million (50,000 × 8% × 9/12). Kala has paid six months interest of $2 million, thus accrued interest of $1 million should be provided for.

(iii) **Finance lease:**

	$000
Net obligation at inception of lease (92,000 – 22,000)	70,000
Accrued interest 10% (current liability)	7,000
	———
Total outstanding at 31 March 2006	77,000
	———

The second payment in the year to 31 March 2007 (made on 1 April 2006) of $22 million will be $7 million for the accrued interest (at 31 March 2006) and $15 million paid of the capital outstanding. Thus the amount outstanding as an obligation over one year is $55 million (77,000 – 22,000).

(iv) **Non-current assets/depreciation:**

Land and buildings:

At the date of the revaluation the land and buildings have a carrying amount of $210 million (270,000 – 60,000). With a valuation of $255 million this gives a revaluation surplus (to reserves) of $45 million. The accumulated depreciation of $60 million represents 15 years at $4 million per annum (200,000/50 years) and means the remaining life at the date of the revaluation is 35 years. The amount of the revalued building is $175 million, thus depreciation for the year to 31 March 2006 will be $5 million (175,000/35 years). The carrying amount of the land and buildings at 31 March 2006 is $250 million (255,000 – 5,000).

Plant: owned

The carrying amount prior to the current year's depreciation is $130 million (156,000 – 26,000). Depreciation at 15% on the reducing balance basis gives an annual charge of $19.5 million. This gives a carrying amount at 31 March 2006 of $110.5 million (130,000 – 19,500).

Plant: leased

The fair value of the leased plant is $92 million. Depreciation on a straight-line basis over five years would give a depreciation charge of $18.4 million and a carrying amount of $73.6 million.

		$000
Summarising the carrying amounts:		
Land and buildings		250,000
Plant (110,500 + 73,600)		184,100
		————
Property, plant and equipment		434,100
		————

ACCA marking scheme		Marks
(a) Statement of profit or loss and other comprehensive income:		
Revenue		½
Cost of sales		4½
Operating expenses		½
Investment income		1½
Finance costs		1½
Taxation		1½
Maximum		10
(b) Statement of changes in equity		
Brought forward figures		1
Revaluation		1
Profit for period		1
Dividends paid		1
Maximum		4
(c) Statement of financial position		
Land and buildings		2
Plant and equipment		2
Investment property		1
Inventory and trade receivables		1
8 % Loan		½
Deferred tax		½
Lease obligation:		
Interest and capital one year		1
Capital over one year		1
Trade payables and overdraft		1
Accrued interest		½
Income tax provision		½
Maximum		11
		——
Total		25
		——

3   REACTIVE

(a)   *Note:* Figures in the calculations are in $million

Return on year end capital employed	32.3%	220/(1,160 – 480) × 100
Net asset turnover	5.9 times	4,000/680
Gross profit margin	13.8%	(500/4,000) × 100
Net profit (before tax) margin	5.0%	(200/4,000) × 100
Current ratio	1.3:1	610:480
Closing inventory holding period	26 days	250/3,450 × 365
Trade receivables' collection period	44 days	360/4,000 – 1,000) × 365
Trade payables' payment period (based on cost of sales)	45 days	(430/3,450) × 365
Dividend yield	6.0%	(see below)
Dividend cover	1.67 times	150/90

The dividend per share is 22.5 cents (90,000/(100,000 × 4 i.e. 25 cents shares). This is a yield of 6.0% on a share price of $3.75.

(b)   Analysis of the comparative financial performance and position of Reactive for the year ended 31 March 2006

Profitability

The measures taken by management appear to have been successful as the overall ROCE (considered as a primary measure of performance) has improved by 15% (32.3 – 28.1)/28.1). Looking in more detail at the composition of the ROCE, the reason for the improved profitability is due to increased efficiency in the use of the company's assets (asset turnover), increasing from 4 to 5.9 times (an improvement of 48%). The improvement in the asset turnover has been offset by lower profit margins at both the gross and net level. On the surface, this performance appears to be due both to the company's strategy of offering rebates to wholesale customers if they achieve a set level of orders and also the beneficial impact on sales revenue of the advertising campaign. The rebate would explain the lower gross profit margin, and the cost of the advertising has reduced the net profit margin (presumably management expected an increase in sales volume as a compensating factor). The decision to buy complete products rather than assemble them in house has enabled the disposal of some plant which has reduced the asset base. Thus possible increased sales and a lower asset base are the cause of the improvement in the asset turnover which in turn, as stated above, is responsible for the improvement in the ROCE.

The effect of the disposal needs careful consideration. The profit (before tax) includes a profit of $40 million from the disposal. As this is a 'one-off' profit, recalculating the ROCE without its inclusion gives a figure of only 23.7% (180m/(1,160 – 480m + 80m (the 80m is the carrying amount of plant)) and the fall in the net profit percentage (before tax) would be down even more to only 4.0% (160m/4,000m). On this basis the current year performance is worse than that of the previous year and the reported figures tend to flatter the company's underlying performance.

Liquidity

The company's liquidity position has deteriorated during the period. An acceptable current ratio of 1.6 has fallen to a worrying 1.3 (1.5 is usually considered as a safe minimum). With the trade receivables period at virtually a constant (45/44 days), the change in liquidity appears to be due to the levels of inventory and trade payables. These give a contradictory picture. The closing inventory holding period has decreased markedly (from 46 to 26 days) indicating more efficient inventory holding. This is perhaps due to short lead times when ordering bought in products. The change in this ratio has reduced the current ratio, however the trade payables payment period has decreased from 55 to 45 days which has increased the current ratio. This may be due to different terms offered by suppliers of bought in products.

Importantly, the effect of the plant disposal has generated a cash inflow of $120 million, and without this the company's liquidity would look far worse.

Investment ratios

The current year's dividend yield of 6.0% looks impressive when compared with that of the previous year's yield of 3.75%, but as the company has maintained the same dividend (and dividend per share as there is no change in share capital), the 'improvement' in the yield is due to a falling share price. Last year the share price must have been $6.00 to give a yield of 3.75% on a dividend per share of 22.5 cents. It is worth noting that maintaining the dividend at $90 million from profits of $150 million gives a cover of only 1.67 times whereas on the same dividend last year the cover was 2 times (meaning last year's profit (after tax) was $180 million).

Conclusion

Although superficially the company's profitability seems to have improved as a result of the directors' actions at the start of the current year, much, if not all, of the apparent improvement is due to the change in supply policy and the consequent beneficial effects of the disposal of plant. The company's liquidity is now below acceptable levels and would have been even worse had the disposal not occurred. It appears that investors have understood the underlying deterioration in performance as there has been a marked fall in the company's share price.

(c)   It is generally assumed that the objective of stock market listed companies is to maximize the wealth of their shareholders. This in turn places an emphasis on profitability and other factors that influence a company's share price. It is true that some companies have other (secondary) aims such as only engaging in ethical activities (e.g. not producing armaments) or have strong environmental considerations. Clearly by definition not-for-profit organizations are not motivated by the need to produce profits for shareholders, but that does not mean that they should be inefficient. Many areas of assessment of profit oriented companies are perfectly valid for not-for-profit organizations; efficient inventory holdings, tight budgetary constraints, use of key performance indicators, prevention of fraud etc.

There are a great variety of not-for-profit organizations; e.g. public sector health, education, policing and charities. It is difficult to be specific about how to assess the performance of a not-for-profit organization without knowing what type of organization it is. In general terms an assessment of performance must be made in the light of the stated objectives of the organization. Thus for example in a public health service one could look at measures such as treatment waiting times, increasing life expectancy etc, and although such organizations do not have a profit motive requiring efficient operation, they should nonetheless be accountable for the resources they use. Techniques such as 'value for money' and the three Es (economy, efficiency and effectiveness) have been developed and can help to assess the performance of such organizations.

ACCA marking scheme		Marks
(a)	1 mark per ratio	10
(b)	1 mark per valid point	10
(c)	1 mark per valid point	5
Total		25

4   PORTO

(a)   Relevance

Information has the quality of relevance when it can influence, on a timely basis, users' economic decisions. It helps to evaluate past, present and future events by confirming or perhaps correcting past evaluations of economic events. There are many ways of interpreting and applying the concept of relevance, for example, only material information is considered relevant as, by definition, information is material only if its omission or misstatement could influence users. Another common debate regarding relevance is whether current value information is more relevant than that based on historical cost. An interesting emphasis placed on relevance within the Framework is that relevant information assists in the predictive ability of financial statements. That is not to say the financial statements should be predictive in the sense of forecasts, but that (past) information should be presented in a manner that assists users to assess an entity's ability to take advantage of opportunities and react to adverse situations. A good example of this is the separate presentation of discontinued operations in the statement of profit or loss. From this users will be better able to assess the parts of the entity that will produce future profits (continuing operations) and users can judge the merits of the discontinuation i.e. has the entity sold a profitable part of the business (which would lead users to question why), or has the entity acted to curtail the adverse affect of a loss making operation.

Faithful representation

The Framework states that for information to be useful it must faithfully represent that which it purports to portray (i.e. the financial statements are a faithful representation of the entity's underlying transactions). There can be occasions where the legal form of a transaction can be engineered to disguise the economic reality of the transaction. A cornerstone of faithful representation is that transactions must be accounted for according to their substance (i.e. commercial intent or economic reality) rather than their legal or contrived form. In order to faithfully represent transactions, information must be neutral (free from bias). Biased information attempts to influence users (perhaps to come to a predetermined decision) by the manner in which it is presented. It is recognized that financial statements cannot be absolutely accurate due to inevitable uncertainties surrounding their preparation. A typical example would be estimating the useful economic lives of non-current assets. This is addressed by the use of prudence which is the exercise of a degree of caution in matters of uncertainty. However prudence cannot be used to deliberately understate profit or create excessive provisions (this would break the neutrality principle). Further characteristics of faithful representation are such that information must also be complete and free from error. Omitted information (that should be reported) will obviously mislead users.

Comparability

Comparability is fundamental to assessing an entity's performance. Users will compare an entity's results over time and also with other similar entities. This is the principal reason why financial statements contain corresponding amounts for previous period(s). Comparability is enhanced by the use (and disclosure) of consistent accounting policies such that users can confirm that comparative information (for calculating trends) is comparable and the disclosure of accounting policies at least informs users if different entities use different policies. That said, comparability should not stand in the way of improved accounting practices (usually through new Standards); it is recognized that there are occasions where it is necessary to adopt new accounting policies if they would enhance relevance and reliability.

(b) (i) This item involves the characteristic of faithful representation and specifically reporting the substance of transactions. As the lease agreement is for substantially the whole of the asset's useful economic life, Porto will experience the same risks and rewards as if it owned the asset. Although the legal form of this transaction is a rental, its substance is the equivalent to acquiring the asset and raising a loan. Thus, in order for the financial statements to be reliable (and comparable to those where an asset is bought from the proceeds of a loan), the transaction should be shown as an asset on Porto's statement of financial position with a corresponding liability for the future lease rental payments. The statement of profit or loss should be charged with depreciation on the asset and a finance charge on the 'loan'.

(ii) This item involves the characteristic of comparability. Changes in accounting policies should generally be avoided in order to preserve comparability. Presumably the directors have good reason to be believe the new policy presents a reliable and more relevant view. In order to minimize the adverse effect a change in accounting policy has on comparability, the financial statements (including the corresponding amounts) should be prepared on the basis that the new policy had always been in place (retrospective application). Thus the assets (retail outlets) should include the previously expensed finance costs and statement of profit or loss will no longer show a finance cost (in relation to these assets whilst under construction). Any finance costs relating to periods prior to the policy change (i.e. for two or more years ago) should be adjusted for by increasing retained earnings brought forward in the statement of changes in equity.

(iii) This item involves the characteristic of relevance. This situation questions whether historical cost accounting is more relevant to users than current value information. Porto's current method of reporting these events using purely historical cost based information (i.e. showing an operating loss, but not reporting the increases in property values) is perfectly acceptable. However, the company could choose to revalue its hotel properties (which would subject it to other requirements). This option would still report an operating loss (probably an even larger loss than under historical cost if there are increased depreciation charges on the hotels), but the increases in value would also be reported (in equity) arguably giving a more complete picture of performance.

ACCA marking scheme		Marks
(a)	3 marks each for relevance, reliability and comparability	9
(b)	2 marks for each transaction ((i) to (iii)) or event	6
Total		15

5 BEETIE

(a) The correct timing of when revenue (and profit) should be recognized is an important aspect of a statement of profit or loss showing a faithful presentation. It is generally accepted that only realized profits should be included in the statement of profit or loss. For most types of supply and sale of goods it is generally understood that a profit is realized when the goods have been manufactured (or obtained) by the supplier and satisfactorily delivered to the customer. The issue with construction contracts is that the process of completing the project takes a relatively long time and, in particular, will spread across at least one accounting period-end. If such contracts are treated like most sales of goods, it would mean that revenue and profit would not be recognized until the contract is completed (the 'completed contracts' basis). This is often described as following the prudence concept. The problem with this approach is that it may not show a faithful presentation as all the profit on a contract is included in the period of completion, whereas in reality (a faithful representation), it is being earned, but not reported, throughout the duration of the contract. IAS 11 remedies this by recognising profit on uncompleted contracts in proportion to some measure of the percentage of completion applied to the estimated total contract profit. This is sometimes said to reflect the accruals concept, but it should only be applied where the outcome of the contract is reasonably foreseeable. In the event that a loss on a contract is foreseen, the whole of the loss must be recognized immediately, thereby ensuring the continuing application of prudence.

(b)   **Beetie**

Statement of profit or loss

	Contract 1 $000	Contract 2 $000	Total $000
Revenue recognized	3,300	840	4,140
Contract expenses recognized (balancing figure contract 1)	(2,400)	(720)	(3,120)
Expected loss recognized (contract 2)		(170)	(170)
Attributable profit/(loss) (see working)	900	(50)	850

Statement of financial position

Contact costs incurred	3,900	720	4,620
Recognized profit/(losses)	900	(50)	850
	4,800	670	5,470
Progress billings	(3,000)	(880)	(3,880)
Amounts due from customers	1,800		1,800
Amounts due to customers		(210)	(210)

Workings (in $000)

Estimated total profit:

Agreed contract price	5,500	1,200
Estimated contract cost	(4,000)	(1,250)
Estimated total profit/(loss)	1,500	(50)

Percentage complete:

Agreed value of work completed at 31 March 2006	3,300
Contract price	5,500
Percentage complete at 31 March 2006 (3,300/5,500 × 100)	60%
Profit to 31 March 2006 (60% × 1,500)	900

At 31 March 2006 the increase in the expected total costs of contract 2 mean that a loss of $50,000 is expected on this contract. In these circumstances, regardless of the percentage completed, the whole of this loss should be recognized immediately.

ACCA marking scheme		
		Marks
(a)	1 mark per valid point to maximum	4
(b)	Revenue (½ mark for each contract)	1
	Profit/loss (½ mark for each contract)	1
	Amounts due from customers (contract 1)	2
	Amounts due to customers (contract 2)	2
	Maximum	6
Total		10